The Abu-Ghazaleh English-Arabic Dictionary of Accountancy

657

3

THE ABU-GHAZALEH ENGLISH-ARABIC DICTIONARY OF ACCOUNTANCY

Talal Abu-Ghazaleh

M

First published 1978 by
The Macmillan Press Ltd
London and Basingstoke
Associated companies in New York Dublin
Melbourne Johannesburg and Madras

ISBN 0333 21468 4

Phototypeset in Great Britain by
Western Printing Services Ltd, Bristol
and printed in Great Britain by Butler & Tanner Ltd, Frome

DEDICATION

To those great men of my Arab Nation who have honoured me with their confidence and guidance,

To my colleagues in the profession to which I proudly belong and with whom I am privileged to work,

To Diraar Alghanim, to my other partners, and to my colleagues who built this Organisation through professional dedication and competence,

To Nuha, Louai, Qusai, May and Jumanah, my little world that signifies to me all the goodness in this world,

T.A.G.

إهـــــداء

إلى الرجال العظام في أمتي العربية الذين شرفوني بثقتهم وتوجيههم .

إلى الزملاء في المهنة الذين أعتز بأن أكون أحدهم وأن أعمل معهم .

إلى أخي ضرار الغانم وشركائي وزملائي الذين بنوا المؤسسة باخلاصهم للمهنة وكفاءتهم .

إلى نهى ولوءى وقصي ومي وجمانه عالمي الصغير الذى بالنسبة إلى يمثل كل ما في الدنيا من خير .

PREFACE

The purpose of this *Dictionary* is to present, as a first attempt, a unified and comprehensive reference index for the field of my professional specialisation. It is intended to be an accessible tool for the builders of the profession and the makers of its future; and to serve the process of development and creativity. My goal has been to present a nomenclature of terms, to form an integrated language, by which we, the members of the accounting profession, may address the world and each other in one professional language.

This First Edition will allow me to respond to every comment and criticism from you the user in the preparation of subsequent amended editions reflecting the development of our profession. It is a trial endeavour and will not be perfect, but it is God's boon that perfection, although out of immediate reach, should persistently be sought.

My objective has been two-fold. Firstly, to standardise accounting terms, resulting in a language basic to our study and business transactions throughout the Arab World. Secondly, to assist native speakers of English in correctly pronouncing Arabic accounting vocabulary, and to encourage Arabic in professional usage. To those ends, I have placed opposite English words the Arabic equivalent, transliterated in English according to the following generally accepted rules:

ā long 'a' as in English 'stand'
ī long 'e' as in English 'steel'
gh no English equivalent – as Parisians pronounce 'r'
kh no English equivalent – as Germans pronounce 'ch'
ū long 'o' as in English 'stool'
u a throat letter – no English equivalent – as in Arabic 'Amman'
, glottal stop as in 'at', 'ebb' or 'odd'
dh as in English 'this'
aw as in English 'out'
ay as in 'bey' or 'Beirut'.

An English word is given as the main headword and an Arabic translation follows. In certain cases, however, I have added to the main word other words separated by a comma to indicate phrases, for example: Capital (main word); Capital, accumulation of. Words following a main word indicate substitution, for example: Accordance, in – with. The long or short comments in brackets below the main Arabic word denote paraphrase and not a translation.

It is my hope that the basic purposes of this accounting dictionary have been met. The pages contain at least 8,000 current accounting terms and I hope that your work will be a little easier as a result.

Talal Abu-Ghazaleh

إهـــــداء

يهدف هذا القاموس كمحاولة أن يكون أداة موحدة لعملية الاستيعاب في حقل اختصاصي المهني وبعدها أن يصبح أداة موحدة أيضا في أيدي بناة المهنة وصانعي مستقبلها لعملية التطوير والابداع . ان الهدف كان اقتراح تسميات موحدة للاشياء ، مع الاعتراف بأنها ليست حتما الاصح والا الأفضل ، لتشكلّ لغة واحدة نتحدث بها نحن أبناء هذه المهنة الى العالم كما تتحدث كل مهنة في كل لغة من لغات العالم .

وما هذا الا محاولة سأستفيد بعدها من كل توجيه ونقد لأقوم باعداد طبعات مقبلة ومعدلة تتفق والتطور الذى سنستطيع جميعا أن نحققه في مهنتنا . فان جاء هذا النتاج دون الكمال فلأنه المحاولة الأولى أولا ، وبعده لأن نعمة الله علينا ان الكمال لا يمكن إدراكه ولكن يجب السعي دوما إليه .

ولئن كان هدفي الأول توحيد اللفظة المحاسبية ذات المعنى الواحد ، بحيث تصبح لغة دراستنا وعملنا وتعاملنا في الوطن العربي كله وأداة تطويرنا لمهنتنا ، فإن هدفي الثاني هو مساعدة من كانت لغته الأصلية الانجليزية أن ينطق الكلمة العربية المحاسبية نطقا صحيحا محاولة لنشر لغتنا في حقل اختصاصنا . لذلك وضعت أمام كل كلمة انجليزية لفظها المقابل بالعربية مكتوبا باللغة الانجليزية حسب القواعد التالية المتعارف عليها :

ā long 'a' as in English 'stand'

ī long 'e' as in English 'steel'

gh no English equivalent – as Parisians pronounce 'r'

kh no English equivalent – as Germans pronounce 'ch'

ū long 'o' as in English 'stool'

u a throat letter – no English equivalent – as in Arabic 'Amman'

, glottal stop as in 'at', 'ebb' or 'odd'

dh as in English 'this'

aw as in English 'out'

ay as in 'bey' or 'Beirut'.

وتجدون مقابل كل كلمة انجليزية ترجمتها بالعربية وهي الكلمة الرئيسية . الا أنني أضف لها في بعض الحالات كلمات أخرى مفصولة عنها بشارطة (-) وذلك يعني بأن الكلمة الرئيسية تستعمل مع الكلمة التي وردت بعد الشارطة . أما الكلمات التي وضعت ضمن قوسين بعد الكلمة الرئيسية فتستعمل بديلا عن الكلمة الرئيسية . كذلك تجدون تحت الكلمة الرئيسية شرحا إما مطولا أو مختصرا تحته خط لكي يتضح أنه يمثل شرحا وليس الكلمة المترجمة نفسها .

أملي أن أكون حققت الهدفين الاساسيين من وضع هذا القاموس المحاسبي الذى يحتوى على ما لا يقل عن ٨,٠٠٠ كلمة مستعملة في علم المحاسبة .

A.A.R., against all risks	ḍidd jamīʿ al-akhtār	**ضد جميع الأخطار** (تأمين شامل)
A priori	badīhī	**بديـهي** [مسلم به بالاستدلال العقلى]
Abandon	yatruk, yahjor	**يترك ، يهجر** [بسبب القدم أو الاستهلاك]
Abandonment	tark, hijrat eshay'	**ترك ، هجرة الشيء** [الغاء بسبب القدم أو الاستهلاك]
Abandonments	matrūkāt	**متـروكات**
Abatement	1 ingaṣ	**١ - انقاص**
	2 takhfīd	**٢ - تخفيض ـ ضريبة**
	3 takhfīd kulfa	**٣ - تخفيض كلفة** [ايراد طارىء منزل من الكلفة]
Abide by	yataqayyad bi	**يتقيد بـ** (يلتزم بأحكام)
Abnormal cost	taklifa ghayr ʿādiyya	**تكلفة غير عادية**
Abolish	yulghī	**يلغـي**
Abolition	ilghā'	**الغـاء**
Aboriginal cost	taklifa asliyya	**تكلفة أصلية**
Above the line	bawāriz	**البوارز** [البنود التي تظهر عادة في الميزانية وبيان الأرباح والخسائر]
Above par	maʿ ziyāda	**مـع الزيـادة** [فرق السعر الأصلى]
Abrogate	yanqud	**ينقض** (يلغي ، يفسخ)
Abrogation	naqḍ	**نقض** (الغاء ، فسخ)
Absconded debtor	madīn mutawārī	**المدين المتوارى ـ عن دائنيه**
Absence, of consideration	fuqdān	**فقدان ـ في العقود عدم وجود مصلحة**
Absentee	mālik ghā'ib	**المالك الغائب**
Absolute	mutlaq	**مُطـلق**
Absolute majority	aghlabiyya muṭlaqa	**الأغلبية المطلقة** [نصف عدد الأصوات زائدا صوتا]
Absolute nullity	ṣifr muṭlaq	**صفر مطلق** (بطلان مطلق)
Absorb	yastawʿib	**يستوعب** (يتحمل النفقات)
Absorbed cost	taklifa mustawʿaba	**التكلفة المستوعبة** (تقييم البضاعة)
Absorbed overhead	ra'siyyāt mustawʿaba	**الرأسيات المستوعبة** [المصاريف الاستيعابية التي يجري توزيعها على وحدات التكاليف بنسبة معينة]
Absorption	istīʿāb	**استيعاب**
Absorption account	ḥisāb istīʿābī	**حساب استيعابي**
Absorption costing	nižam takālīf istīʿābī	**نظام التكاليف الاستيعابي** [تحميل جميع المصاريف الثابتة والمتغيرة على المواد المنتجة أو الخدمات]
Absorption costing method	ṭarīqat takālīf mustaqilla	**طريقة التكاليف المستقلة** [تحميل الانتاج بجميع بنود التكاليف

		المتغيرة مضافا نصيبه من التكاليف الثابتة بقدر استغلال الطاقة بواسطة معدلات تحميل محددة مقدما]
Absorptive capacity	ṭaqa istīʿābiyya	الطاقة الاستيعابية
Abstain	yamtaniʿ	يمتنع ـ عن التصويب
Abstract number	ʿadad mujarrad	عـدد مجــرد
Abstract of account	khulāṣat al-ḥisāb	خلاصة الحساب (مستخرج حسابي)
Abstract of title	mustakhraj al-milkiyya	مستخرج الملكية (ملخص مستندات الملكية)
Abuse (n.; v.)	sū' istiʿmal	سوء استعمال ـ يسيء الاستعمال
Abuse of confidence	sū' istiʿmāl thiqa	سوء استعمال الثقة
A.C.A. Associate of the Institute of Chartered Accountants in England and Wales	ʿuḍw mushārik fī maʿhad al-muḥāsibīn al-qānūniyyīn fī injiltirā wa wailz	عضو مشارك في معهد المحاسبين القانونيين في انجلترا وويلز
A.C.C.A. Association of Certified and Corporate Accountants	jamʿiyyat al-muḥāsibin al-muʿtamadīn al-qānūniyyīn	جمعية المحاسبين المعتمدين القانونيين
A.A.C.C.A. Associate of the Association of Certified and Corporate Accountants	ʿuḍw mushārīk fī jamʿiyyat al-muḥasibīn al-muʿtamadīn al-qanūniyyīn	عضو مشارك في جمعية المحاسبين المعتمدين القانونيين
Accelerate	yusriʿ	يسـّـرع
Accelerated rate of depreciation	muʿaddal al-istihlāk al-mutazaȳid	معدل الاستهلاك المتزايد
Acceleration clause	shart taʿjīl	شرط التعجيل [شرط يتضمنه العقد ينص على أن الرصيد المستحق المتبقى يصبح مستحقا للسداد فى حالة عدم الوفاء ببعض الشروط الأخرى للعقد]
Accept	yaqbal	يقبل ـ سند أو بضاعة
Acceptability	qabūl	القبــول
Acceptable	maqbūl	مقبــول
Acceptable quality level	mustawa an-nawʿiyya al-maqbūl	مستوى النوعية المقبول
Acceptance	qabūl tijārī	قبـول تجـارى [يعهد بالتسديد في تاريخ الاستحقاق]
Acceptance credit	iʿtimād qabūl	اعتـماد القبـول [يتضمن الدفع المؤجل بموجب سحب على فاتح الاعتماد الذى يقبله ، ويكون الدفع في الموعد المنصوص عنه في الاعتماد]
Acceptance for honour	qabūl ghayrī	قبـول غيـرى [قبول كمبيالة لمصلحة الغير بعد عدم وفائها]
Acceptance houses	buyūt al-qabūl	بيوت القبول ـ للحـوالات
Acceptance liability	iltizām al-qabūl	التـزام القبـول
Acceptance sampling	muʿāyanat awrāq al-qabūl	معاينة أوراق القبول ـ باختبار عينات منها
Acceptance, banker's	waraqat qabūl maṣrafiyya	ورقة قبول مصرفية
Acceptance, clean	waraqat qabūl ghayr mashrūṭ	ورقة قبول غير مشروط

Acceptance, conditional	qabūl kumbiyāla bi-shart	قبول كمبيالة بشرط
Acceptance, local	waraqat qabūl maḥallī	ورقة قبول محلي
Acceptance, partial	waraqat qabūl juz'ī	ورقة قبول جزئي
Acceptance, present for	yuqaddim waraqat lil-qabūl	يقدم ورقة لقبول
Acceptance, qualified	qabūl bi-taḥaffuẓ	قبول بتحفظ
Acceptance, supra-protest	qabūl taḥaffuẓī	قبول تحفظي
Accepted bill	ḥawāla maqbūla	حوالة مقبولة
Acceptor, accepter	al-qābil	القابل ـ للحوالة
Accident insurance	ta'mīn ḍidd al-ḥawādith	تأمين ضد الحوادث
Accommodation	tas-heel	تسهيل ـ تسوية ـ اتفاق
Accommodation bill	kumbiyālat mujāmala	كمبيالة مجاملة (كمبيالة اسعاف ، كمبيالة صورية)
Accommodation endorsement	tajyīr is'āfī	تجيير اسعافي
Accommodation note	waraqat is'āf	ورقة اسعاف
Accommodating party	aṭ-taraf al-mus'if	الطرف المسعف
Accord	ittifāq	اتفـــاق [في أداء الذمم : اتفاق بين المدين والدائن على تسديد الدين بغير ما تم عليه الاتفاق]
Accord of accounts	muṭābaqat al-ḥisābāt	مطابقة الحسابات
Accordance, in – with	ḥasab	حسب (طبقا لـ)
According to	bi-mūjib	بموجب (بناء على)
Account	ḥisāb	حساب
Accounts analysis	taḥlīl al-hisābāt	تحليل الحسابات
Accounts book	daftar ḥisābāt	دفتر حسابات
Accounts card	biṭāqat ḥisābāt	بطاقة حسابات
Account days	ayyām al-ḥisāb	أيام الحساب [أيام تسوية العمليات الآجلة في البورصة]
Accounts department	dā'rat al-ḥisābāt	دائرة الحسابات
Account form	namūdhaj muḥāsabī	نموذج محاسبي
Accounts payable	dhimam dā'ina	ذمم دائنة
Account payee	ḥisāb mustafīd	حساب مستفيد
Accounts receivable	dhimam madīna	ذمم مدينة
Accounts receivable discounted	ḥisāb madīn makhṣūm	حساب مدين مخصوم
Accounts receivable, aging of	ta'mīr dhimam madīna	تعمير الذمم المدينة ـ حسب تواريخ نشوء مفرداتها
Account sales	ḥisāb mabī'āt	حساب مبيعات ـ في بضاعة الأمانة
Account stated	ḥisāb muttafaq 'alayhi	حساب متفق عليه ـ بين الطرفين الدائن والمدين
Account title	ism al-ḥisāb	اسم الحساب
Account(s), annual	ḥisābāt sanawiyya	حسابات سنوية
Account, appropriation	ḥisāb tawzī'	حساب التوزيع
Account(s), audited	ḥisābāt mudaqqaqa	حسابات مدققة

Account(s), balancing of	tarṣīd ḥisābāt	ترصيد الحسابات
Account, blocked	ḥisāb mujammad	حساب مجمد
Account(s), chart of	jadwal bayān al-ḥisābāt	جدول بيان الحسابات
Account, checking (U.S.)	ḥisāb jārī	حساب جاري
Account(s), consolidated	bayānāt mujamma'a	بيانات مجمعة
Account, contra	ḥisāb niẓāmī	حساب نظامي (حساب له مقابل)
Account, control	ḥisāb raqīb	حساب رقيب
Account, current (U.K)	ḥisāb jārī	حساب جاري
Account(s), departmental	ḥisābāt al-aqsām	حسابات الأقسام
Account, direct labour	ḥisāb takalīf al-ujūr al-mubāshira	حساب تكاليف الاجور المباشرة
Account, direct materials	ḥisāb takalīf al-mawādd al-mubashira	حساب تكاليف المواد المباشرة
Account, drawing	ḥisāb al-mas-ḥūbāt	حساب المسحوبات ـ لأحد الشركاء
Account, exploitation	ḥisāb al-istighlāl	حساب الاستغلال
Account, extending balances	naql arṣidāt al-ḥisābāṭ	نقل أرصدة الحسابات
Account(s), final	ḥisābāt khitāmiyya	حسابات ختامية
Account, for the	li-ḥisāb	لحساب
Account(s), group	ḥisābāt al-majmū'a	حسابات المجموعة
Account, income and expenses summary	ḥisāb ijmāli 'l-irādāt wa'l-maṣrūfāt	حساب اجمالي الايرادات والمصروفات
Account(s), interest bearing	ḥisābāt bi-fā'ida	حسابات بفائدة
Account(s), interim	ḥisābāt marḥaliyya	حسابات مرحلية [أى الحسابات التي تتم لفترة معينة ليست كاملة]
Account(s), manufacturing	ḥisābāṭ at-taṣnī'	حسابات التصنيع
Account(s), minus assets	ḥisābat takhfīḍ qīmat al-mawjūdāt	حسابات تخفيض قيمة الموجودات
Account, nominal	ḥisāb ismi	حساب اسمي
Account, on	'ala 'l-ḥisāb	على الحساب
Account, operating	ḥisāb at-tashghīl	حساب التشغيل
Account, overdrawn	ḥisāb makshūf	حساب مكشوف
Account, payment on	daf'a 'ala 'l-ḥisāb	دفعة على الحساب
Account, personal	ḥisāb shakhṣī	حساب شخصي
Account, profit and loss	ḥisāb al-arbāḥ wa'l-khasā'ir	حساب الأرباح والخسائر
Account(s), proprietorship	ḥisābāt ḥuqūq al-mālikīn	حساب حقوق المالكين
Account, provision	ḥisāb al-mukhaṣṣaṣ	حساب المخصص
Account, re-valuation	ḥisāb i'ādat at-taqyīm	حساب اعادة التقييم
Account(s), regular	ḥisābāt muntaẓama	حسابات منتظمة
Account, reserve	ḥisāb al-iḥtiyātī	حساب الاحتياطي
Account, restricted	ḥisāb muqayyad	حساب مقيّد
Account, savings	ḥisāb iddikhār	حساب ادخار
Account, square the	yusawwi 'l-ḥisāb	يسوى الحساب (يرصد الحساب)
Account, statement of	kashf ḥisāb	كشف حساب
Account, suspense	ḥisāb mu'allaq	حساب معلّق

Account, trading	ḥisāb al-mutājara	حساب المتاجرة
Account(s), uncollectable	duyūn ma'dūma	ديون معدومة (غير قابلة للتحصيل)
Account, valuation	ḥisāb taqyīm	حساب تقييم (تثمين)
Accountability unit	waḥda muḥāsabiyya	وحدة محاسبية
Accountable	1 mas'ūl	١ - مسؤول
	2 muṭālab	٢ - مطالب
	3 yastawjib al-qayd	٣ - يستوجب القيد
Accountable condition	'amaliyya tastawjib al-qyd	عملية تستوجب القيد
Accountable person	shakhṣ mas'ūl	شخص مسؤول
Accountancy	muḥāsaba	المحاسبة
Accountant	muḥāsib	محاسب
Accountant general	muḥāsib 'āmm	محاسب عام
Accountant in charge	muḥāsib mas'ūl	محاسب مسؤول
Accountant's responsibility	mas'ūliyyāt al-muḥāsib	مسؤوليات المحاسب
Accountant, certified	muḥāsib qānūnī	محاسب قانوني
Accountant, chartered	muḥāsib qānūnī	محاسب قانوني
Accountantship (U.S.)	muḥāsaba	محاسبة
Accounting	'ilm al-muḥāsaba	علم المحاسبة
Accounting circle	dawra muḥāsabiyya	الدورة المحاسبية
Accounting control	riqāba muḥāsabiyya	الرقابة المحاسبية
Accounting entity (unit)	kiyān muḥāsabī	كيان محاسبي (وحدة محاسبية)
Accounting equation	mu'ādala muhāsabiyya	معادلة محاسبية
Accounting evidence	ithbāt muḥāsibī	اثبات محاسبي
Accounting identity	huwiyya muḥāsabiyya	الهوية المحاسبية
Accounting machine system	niẓām al-muḥāsaba 'l-āliyya	نظام المحاسبة الآلية
Accounting manual	dalīl ḥisābāt	دليل الحسابات
Accounting period	fatra muḥasabiyya	الفترة المحاسبية
Accounting policy	siyāsat muḥāsabiyya	السياسات المحاسبية
Accounting practice	mumārasat mihnat al-muḥāsaba	ممارسة مهنة المحاسبة
Accounting principles	al-uṣūl al-muḥāsabiyya	الاصول المحاسبية
Accounting procedures	aṭ-ṭuruq al-muḥāsabiyya	الطرق المحاسبية
Accounting records	sijel-lāt muḥāsabiyya	السجلات المحاسبية
Accounting reserves	iḥtiyāṭiyyāt muḥāsabiyya	الاحتياطيات المحاسبية
Accounting system	niẓām al-muḥāsaba	نظام المحاسبة
Accounting transaction	'amaliyyat muḥāsaba	عملية محاسبة (قيد محاسبي)
Accounting valuation	taqyīm muḥasabī	تقييم محاسبي (تثمين محاسبي)
Accounting, cash basis of	muḥāsaba wifq al-asās an-naqdī	المحاسبة وفق الأساس النقدى
Accounting, cost	muḥāsabat at-takālīf	محاسبة التكاليف
Accretion	izdiyād	ازدياد (نمو ، تكاثر ، تراكم)
Accrual(s)	mustaḥaqqāt	مستحقات
Accrual basis	asās al-istiḥqāq	أساس الاستحقاق [القيد المحاسبي على أساس الاستحقاق]

Accrual date	tārīkh al-istiḥqāq	تاريخ الاستحقاق
Accrual method	uslūb tajmīʿ al-istiḥqāqāt	اسلوب تجميع الاستحقاقات
Accrue	yazdād	يـزداد (يتجمع ، يتراكم)
Accrued asset	aṣl mustaḥaqq	أصل مستحق
Accrued depreciation	istihlāk mustaḥaqq	استهلاك مستحق
Accrued dividend	ḥissat arbāḥ mustaḥaqqa	حصة أرباح مستحقة [أرباح أسهم معلنة ومستحقة]
Accrued expenses	maṣārīf mustaḥaqqa	مصاريف مستحقة
Accrued expenditures basis	asās istiḥqāq al-maṣārīf	أساس الاستحقاق للمصاريف
Accrued income	irād mustaḥaqq	إيراد مستحق
Accrued interest payable	fā'idat dafʿ mustaḥaqqa	فائدة دفع مستحقة
Accrued interest receivable	fā'idat qabḍ mustaḥaqqa	فائدة قبض مستحقة
Accrued liability	maṭlūb mustaḥaqq	مطلوب مستحق
Accrued revenue	irād mustaḥaqq	إيراد مستحق
Accumulated amount	mablagh mutarākim	مبلغ متراكم
Accumulated dividend	ḥiṣaṣ arbāḥ mutarākima	حصص أرباح متراكمة [أرباح أسهم معلنة متراكمة]
Accumulated depreciation	istihlāk mutarākim	استهلاك متراكم
Accumulated income (or earnings or profits; retained earnings)	irād mutarākim	ايراد متراكم
Accumulation factor	ʿāmil at-tarākum	عامل التراكم
Accumulation of debt	tarākum ad-dayn	تراكم الدين
Accumulation schedule	jadwal at-tarākum	جدول التراكم
Accuracy	ṣiḥḥa	صحـة (دقـة)
Accurate	ṣaḥīḥ	صحيـح (دقيـق)
Acid test	ikhtibār as-suyūla	اختبار السيولة
Acknowledge	yuqirr bi-istilām	يقر (باستلام)
Acknowledge a guarantee	yuqirr bi-ḍamāna	يقـر بضمانة
Acknowledge receipt	yushʿir bi'l-istilām	يشعر بالاستلام (يفيد بالوصول)
Acknowledgement	ishʿār at-taslīm	اشعار التسليم
Acquire	yaḥṣul ʿala	يحصل على (يكتسب ، يقتني)
Acquired right	ḥaqq muktasab	حق مكتسب
Acquired surplus	fā'iḍ muktasab	فائض مكتسب
Acquisition	iqtinā'	اقتناء (كسب ، تملك)
Acquit	yubri' adh-dhimma	يبرىء الذمة
Acquittal	tabri'at adh-dhimma	تبرئة الذمة
Acquittance	ṣakk al-ibrā'	صك الابراء
Acquitted, duly	mu'ashshar ʿalayhi bi's-sadād	مؤشر عليه بالسداد
Acre	faddān injilīzī	فدان انجليزى [يساوى ٤٨٤٠ ياردا مربعا]
Acreage	al-masāḥa bi'l-fadādīn	المساحة بالفدادين
Act of God	qaḍa' wa-qadar	قضاء وقدر (أسباب قاهرة)
Acting	nā'ib	نائب (وكيل)

Action	1 da'wā	١ - دعوى
	2 'amal	٢ - عمل
Action, civil	da'wa madaniyya	دعوى مدنية
Action, concerted	'amal mushtarak	عمل مشترك
Action, criminal	da'wā jinā'iyya	دعوى جنائية
Action, to bring an	yuqīm da'wā	يقيم دعوى
Actionable	qābil li'l-muqāḍāh	قابل للمقاضاة
Active account	ḥisāb nashiṭ	حساب نشط (حساب متحرك)
Active bond	sanad thābit	سند ثابت [سند ذو فائدة محدودة]
Active circulation	awrāq an-naqd al-mutadāwala	أوراق النقد المتداولة
Active member	'udw 'āmil	عضو عامل
Active partner	sharīk 'āmil	شريك عامل
Activity	nashāṭ	نشاط (مجال عمل)
Activity ratio	mu'addal an-nashāṭ	معدل النشاط [عدد الساعات المعيارية المكافئة للعمل التام معبرا عنها بنسبة مئوية من عدد الساعات المعيارية المقدرة بالموازنة التخطيطية]
Actual capacity	aṭ-ṭāqa al-fi'liyya li'l-intāj	الطاقة الفعلية للانتاج
Actual costs	takālīf fi'liyya	التكاليف الفعلية
Actual depreciation	istihlāk fi'lī	استهلاك فعلي
Actual realisations	mutaḥaqqāqat fi'liyya	المتحققات الفعلية
Actuarial	iḥṣā'iyyat ta'mīn	احصائيات التأمين
Actuarial basis	asās iḥṣā'ī	أساس احصائي ـ وفقا لاساليب خبراء التأمين
Actuarial tables	jadāwil ta'mīn iḥṣā'iyya	جداول تأمين احصائية
Actuary	khabīr ḥisābāt at-ta'mīn	خبير حسابات التأمين
Ad hoc, committee	li-gharaḍ muḥaddad	لغرض محدد (لجنة)
Ad valorem	ḥasab at-tathmīn	حسب التثمين [تحديد ضريبة الأملاك أو الاستيراد أو أية ضريبة أخرى كنسبة مئوية من قيمة الاملاك]
Add	yajma'	يجمع
Addenda	mulḥaqāt	ملحقات (ذيول ، اضافات)
Addendum	mulḥaq	ملحق (ذيل ، اضافة)
Addition	jam'	جمع
Additional	iḍāfī	اضافي
Additional markon	iḍāfa ṭāri'a	اضافة طارئة [على السعر المحدد للقطعة لمواجهة مصاريف مستحدثة]
Additional tax	ḍarība iḍāfiyya	ضريبة اضافية
Adequacy	al-ḥadd al-munāsib	الحد المناسب [توفر الحد الادنى من الشروط]

Adequate	munāsib wa kaffi	مناسب وكاف
		[يتوفر فيه الحد الادنى من الشروط]
Adhere to	yataqayyad bi	يتقيد بـ (يرتبط بـ)
Adherence	taqayyud	تقيد (ارتباط)
Adherent member	ʿuḍw murtabit	عضو مرتبط
Adjourn	yu'ajjil	يؤجل (يرجىء ، يعلق)
Adjudicate	yaḥkum	يحكم (حكم المحكمة)
Adjudication	ḥukm qaḍā'ī	حكم قضائي
Adjudication order	ishhār	إشهار - في المحكمة
Adjunct account	ḥisāb mulḥaq	حساب ملحق
Adjust	1 yuʿaddil	١ - يعدل
	2 yuhaddid	٢ - يحدد - المبلغ الواجب دفعه عن خسارة ما
Adjusted actual costs	at-takālif al-fileyah al-muʿaddala	التكاليف الفعلية المعدلة
Adjusted basis	usus muʿaddala	أسس معدلة
		[يجرى بموجبها تحديد الاستهلاك والربح والخسارة الناتجة عن بيع الموجودات الثابتة]
Adjusted gross income	ijmāli ad-dakhl al-muʿaddal	اجمالي الدخل المعدل
Adjusted historical cost	taklifa tārīkhiyya muʿaddala	تكلفة تاريخية معدلة
Adjusting (journal) entry	qayd taʿdīl	قيد تعديل - في دفتر اليومية
Adjustment	taswiya	تسوية (تعديل)
Adjustment account	ḥisāb taswiya	حساب تسوية
Admeasurement	muqāyasa	مقايسة (تحديد الحصة)
Administer	yudīr	يدير (يسير)
Administered price	as-siʿr al-muwajjah	السعر الموجه
		[سعر وحدة من السلع يتحدد فيها الثمن المدفوع أو يتأثر إلى حد كبير بأحد العوامل الموجهة]
Administrative	idārī	اداري
Administration	idāra	ادارة
Administration expenses	maṣārīf idāriyya	مصاريف ادارية
Administration, letter of	amr al-maḥkama bi-taʿyīn waṣī	أمر المحكمة بتعيين وصي
Administrative	idāriyya	ادارية
Administrative accounting	muḥāsaba idāriyya	محاسبة ادارية
Administrative action	ijrā' idārī	اجراء اداري
Administrative audit	tadqīq idārī	تدقيق اداري
Administrative channels	aṭ-ṭuruq al-idāriyya	الطرق الادارية
Administrative cost	takālīf al-khadamāt al-idāriyya	تكاليف الخدمات الادارية
Administrative order	amr idārī	أمر اداري
		[يصدر من المحكمة بادارة أموال المفلس]
Administrative organisation	tanzīm idārī	تنظيم اداري
Administrator	1 mudīr	١ - مدير
	2 waṣī	٢ - وصي
	3 wakīl aʿmāl	٣ - وكيل أعمال

Admissible asset	aṣl maqbūl	أصل مقبول
Admission of a partner	ḍamm sharīk	ضم شريك
Admitted asset	aṣl dhū qīma	أصل ذو قيمة ـ في التصفية
Adopt a resolution	yatabanna qarāran	يتبنى قرارا
Adopt the agenda	yuqirr jadwal al-aʿmāl	يقر جدول الاعمال
Advance (n.; v.)	sulfa	سلفة (يدفع سلفة)
Advance against merchandise	sulfa ʿala biḍāʿa	سلفة على بضاعة
Advance freight	ujrat shaḥn muʿajjala	أجرة شحن معجلة
Advance of (against) securities	sulfa muqābil sanadāt māliyya	سلفة مقابل سندات مالية
Advantage in nature	maziyya muʿayyana	مزية معينة
Adventure	mujāzafa tijāriyya	مجازفة تجارية [ارسال بضاعة للخارج لتباع بأفضل الأسعار]
Adverse balance of trade	mīzān tijārī ʿājiz	ميزان تجارى عاجز
Advertise	yuʿlin	يعلـــن
Advertising campaign	ḥamla iʿlāniyya	حملة اعلانية
Advertising media	wasā'il al-iʿlān	وسائل الاعلان
Advice	ishʿār	اشعار (اخطار)
Advice note	mudhakkirat ishʿār	مذكرة اشعار
Advice of dispatch	ishʿār irsāl	اشعار ارسال
Advice of shipment	ishʿār shaḥn	اشعار شحن
Advice slip	qasīmat ishʿār	قسيمة اشعار
Advise	yushʿir	يشعر (يخطر ، يعلم)
Adviser	mustashār	مستشار
advisory	istishārī	استشارى
Advisory branch	shuʿbat al-fatwa	شعبة الفتوى
Advisory committee (board)	lajna istishāriyya	لجنة استشارية (مجلس استشارى)
Affair	amr	أمـــر (شأن ، عمل)
Affairs, man of	rajul aʿmāl	رجل أعمال
Affidavit	shahāda mashfūʿa bi-qasam	شهادة مشفوعة بقسم
Affiliate; affiliated company	sharika tābiʿa	شركة تابعة
Affiliated	tābiʿ	تابع (مضموم ، مدمج)
Affiliated members	aʿḍā' munḍammūn	أعضاء منضمون
Affiliation	tabaʿiyya	تبعية
Affirm	yuthbit	يثبت (يقرر ، يؤكد)
Affirmative	ithbātī	اثباتي (ايجابي)
Affluence	yusr	يسر (غنى ، وفرة)
Afford	yastaṭīʿ an-nafaqa	يستطيع النفقة (يقدر على)
Affranchise	yukhalliṣ	يخلص (على بضاعة)
Affreightment	ʿaqd shaḥn	عقد شحن ـ بضاعة بالبحر
Afloat	ʿā'im	عائـــم
Afloat, to keep bills	yudāwil al-awrāq al-māliyya	يداول الأوراق المالية
After date	min tārīkhihi	من تاريخه

After hours	ba'd idawam	بعد الدوام
After sight	ba'd al-iṭṭilā'	بعد الاطلاع
Against	ḍidd	ضـــد (مقابل ، لقاء)
Age	'umr	عمـــر [الزمن الذى مضى على الأصل اعتبارا من تاريخ محدد]
Ageing of receivables	ta'mīr dhimam	تعمير الذمم المدينة [تحليل الذمم المدينة حسب قدمها]
Agency	wakāla	وكالـــة
Agencies, international	wakālāt duwaliyya	وكالات دولية
Agency fund	'uhdat al-wakāla	عهدة الوكالة
Agenda	jadwal a'māl	جدول أعمال (مفكرة ، يومية)
Agent	wakīl	وكيـــل
Agent de change	simsār burṣat awrāq māliyya	سمسار بورصة أوراق مالية
Agent, exclusive	wakīl ḥaṣrī	وكيل حصرى
Agent, forwarding	wakīl shaḥn	وكيل شحن
Agent, sole	wakīl waḥīd	وكيل وحيد
Agents of production	'awāmil al-intāj	عوامل الانتاج
Aggregate	ijmālī	اجمالي (مجموع)
Aggregate output	nātij ijmālī	ناتج اجمالي
Aggregate value	qīma ijmāliyya	القيمة الاجمالية
Aggregate weight	wazn ijmālī	الوزن الاجمالي
Aggregation	tajmī'	تجميع
Agio	muḍāraba	مضاربة (مصاريف قطع)
Agrarian	mukhtaṣṣ bi'l-arāḍī	مختص بالاراضي
Agrarian reform	iṣlāḥ zirā'ī	اصلاح زراعي
Agree	yuwāfiq	يوافـــق
Agreement	ittifāqiyya	اتفاقية
Agreement, gentleman's	ittifāq kalimat sharaf	اتفاق ، كلمة شرف
Agreement, mutual	ittifāq mutabādal	اتفاق متبادل
Agreement, verbal	ittifāq shafawī	اتفاق شفوى
Aid	musā'ada	مساعدة
Air freight	shaḥn jawwī	شحن جوى
A.J.E. (adjusting journal entry)	qayd ta'dīl	قيد تعديل
Aleatory	mukhāṭara	مخاطرة (مراهنة ، مجازفة) [تحت الربح والخسارة]
Aleatory contracts	'uqūd dhat mukhāṭara	عقود ذات المخاطرة
Algebraic progression	mutawāliya jabriyya	متوالية جبرية
Alienate	yanqul al-milkiyya	ينقل الملكية
Alienation	naql al-milkiyya	نقل الملكية
Alimentary debt	dayn nafaqa	دين نفقة
Allied company	sharika mutaḍāmina	شركة متضامنة (تابعة)

All-inclusive income statement	bayān al-arbāḥ wa'l-khasā'ir ash-shāmil	بيان الأرباح والخسائر الشامل
Allocate	1 yuḥammil	١ - يحمل
	2 yuwazzi'	٢ - يوزع
Allocation	taḥmīl	تحميل (تقييد في الحساب)
Allocation of resources	tawzī' al-mawārid	توزيع الموارد
Allot	yukhaṣṣiṣ	يخصص (يوزع)
Allottee	al-mukhaṣṣaṣ lahu	المخصص له
Allotment	tawzī'	توزيع
Allotment account	ḥisāb tawzī'	حساب توزيع
Allotment ledger	daftar ḥisābāt tawzī'	دفتر حسابات توزيع
Allotment letter	risālat takhṣīṣ	رسالة التخصيص [اشعار بقيمة حصص الأرباح أو عدد الأسهم]
Allow	1 yamnaḥ	١ - يمنح
	2 yukhaṣṣiṣ	٢ - يخصص
Allowable	masmūḥ bihi	مسموح به (مباح ، جائز)
Allowance	1 samāḥ	١ - سماح [المقدار المسموح به في مواصفات وكمية البضاعة]
	2 ḥasm	٢ - حسم [يوافق عليه لدى تسوية دين لقاء العطب أو التأخير]
	3 badal	٣ - بدل (علاوة)
Allowance for departure	badal safar	بدل سفر
Allowance for professional risks	badal akhṭār al-mihna	بدل أخطار المهنة
Allowance for representation	badal tamthīl	بدل تمثيل
Allowance for residence	badal iqāma	بدل اقامة
Allowance for tare	samāḥ 'ala 'l-'iyār	سماح على العيار [مقدار ما ينزله البائع للمشترين من وزن البضاعة لقاء وزن الاناء الذي يحتويها]
Allowances	'alāwāt	علاوات (مكافآت)
All-purpose financial statement	bayān mālī shāmil	بيان مالي شامل
All-round price	thaman shāmil	ثمن شامل
Alter	yu'addil	يعدل (يغير)
Alteration	ta'dīl	تعديل تغيير)
Altered cheque	shīk mu'addal	شيك معدّل
Alternative (adj.; v.)	badīl	بديل
Alternative cost	taklifa badīla	التكلفة البديلة
Amalgamate	yudmij	يدمج (يضم ، يوحد)
Amalgamation	damj	دمج [شركتين في شركة واحدة]
Amass	yajma'	يجمع (يحشد)

Amend	yuʿaddil	يعدل
Amendment	taʿdīl	تعديل (تصحيح)
Amendment of declaration	taṣ-ḥīh al-iqrār	تصحيح الاقرار
Amendment of taxes	taʿdīl aḍ-ḍarā'ib	تعديل الضرائب
Amercement	gharāma	غرامة
Amortisable	qābil li'l-iṭfā'	قابل للاطفاء
Amortisation	iṭfā'	اطفاء [الدين أو الموجود غير المنظور]
Amortisation schedule	jadwal al-iṭfā'	جدول الاطفاء
Amortise	yuṭfi'	يطفىء [بافراد مبالغ دورية تخصص لتسديده]
Amortised cost	taklifa muṭfa'a	التكلفة المطفأة
Amortisement	iṭfā'	اطفاء [دين تدريجيا بالسحب السنوى]
Amount (n.; v.)	mablagh	مبلغ (مقدار) ـ يبلغ
Amount covered	mablagh mughaṭṭa	المبلغ المغطي
Amount due	mablagh mustaḥaqq	المبلغ المستحق
Amount insured	mablagh mu'amman	المبلغ المؤمن
Amount of an annuity	qīmat ad-dafʿ as-sanawiyya	قيمة الدفعة السنوية
Amount, gross	mablagh ijmālī	المبلغ الاجمالي
Amounting to	al-bāligh qadruh	البالغ قدره
Analyse	yuḥallil	يحلل
Analysis	taḥlīl	تحليل (تفصيل)
Analysis sheet	kashf taḥlīl	كشف التحليل
Analyst	muḥallil	محلل
Analytic	taḥlīlī	تحليلي
Analytic report	taqrīr taḥlīlī	تقرير تحليلي
Analytic schedule	jadwal taḥlīlī	جدول تحليلي [لتقدير احتمالات الخطر في التأمين ضد الحريق]
Anchorage	rusūm al-marsā	رسوم المرسى
And co. (company)	wa-shurakāh	وشركاه [تظهر على الشك المسطر]
And reduced	mukhaffaḍ	المخفض [تظهر بعد اسم الشركة للدلالة على أن رأس مالها قد خفض حديثا]
Annex	yaḍumm	يضم (يلحق) ـ ملحق
Annexation	ḍamm	ضم (الحاق)
Annexed	murfaq	مرفق
Announce	yuʿlin	يعلن (يذيع)
Announcement	iʿlân	اعلان (بيان)
Annual	sanawī	سنوى
Annual Assembly	ijtimāʿ sanawī	اجتماع سنوى

Annual Audit	tadqīq sanawī	تدقيق سنوى
Annual closing	iqfāl sanawī	الاقفال السنوى ـ للقيود الختامية في نهاية السنة الماليــة
Annual consumption	istihlak sanawī	الاستهلاك السنوي الاستنفاذ (نتيجة تناقص الكمية بالاستعمال)
Annual declaration	iqrār sanawī	اقرار سنوى
Annual financial statement	bayānāt ḥisābiyya sanawiyya	بيانات حسابية سنوية (ختامية)
Annual report	taqrīr sanawī	تقرير سنوى
Annual return	at-taqrīr as-sanawī	التقرير السنوى [عن الاعضاء والرأسمال وخلافه]
Annual value	al-qīma as-sanawiyya	القيمة السنوية
Annually	sanawiyyan	سنويـــا
Annuitant	sanāhī	سناهي (صاحب مرتب سنوى)
Annuity	inad sanawī	ايراد سنوى
Annuity agreement or contract	itifāqiyyat ad-daf'a as-sanawiyya	اتفاقية الدفعة السنوية
Annuity certain	daf'a sanawiyya maḍmūna	الدفعة السنوية المضمونة
Annuity cost	taklifat ad-daf'a as-sanawiyya	تكلفة الدفعة السنوية
Annuity due	ad-daf 'a as-sanawiyya al-mustaḥaqqa	الدفعة السنويةالمستحقة
Annuity fund	'uhdat ad-daf'a as-sanawiyya	عهدة الدفعة السنوية
Annuity method	ṭarīqat ad-daf'a as-sanawiyya	طريقة الدفعة السنوية
Annuity system	niẓām ad-daf'a as-sanawiyya	نظام الدفعة السنوية
Annul	yafsakh	يفسخ (يلغي ، يبطل)
Annulment	faskh	فسخ (الغاء ، ابطال)
Anonymous	majhūl	مجهول (مُغْفَلْ ، بلا اسم)
Antedate	yu'arrikh musbaqan	يؤرخ مسبقا [أى بتاريخ سابق]
Anticipate	1 yatawaqqa'	١ - يتوقع
	2 yadfa'	٢ - يدفع ـ دينا قبل الاستحقاق
Anticipated cost	taklifa mutawaqqa'a	التكلفة المتوقعة
Anticipated interest	fā'ida mutawaqqa'a	الفائدة المتوقعة
Anticipated (or anticipatory) profit	ribḥ mutawaqqa'	الربح المتوقع
Anticipation	istīfā' ad-dayn qabl al-awān	استيفاء الدين قبل الاوان
Anticipation, in	muqaddaman	مقدما
Append	yulḥiq	يلحق (يضيف ، يلصق ، يرفق)
Appendage	mulḥaq	ملحق (اضافة ، حاشية ، تذييل)
Appendix	fahris	فهـرس (ملحق ، حاشية)
Applicant	ṭālib	طالب
Application	1 ṭalab	١ - طلب
	2 iktitāb fī as-hum	٢ - اكتتاب في أسهم
Application account	ḥisāb qisṭ al-iktitāb	حساب قسط الاكتتاب
Application for a post	ṭalab waẓīfa	طلب وظيفة
Application for shares	ṭalab as-hum	طلب أسهم
Application form	istimārat ṭalab	استمارة طلب

Application of law	taṭbīq al-qānūn	تطبيق القانون
Applied	taṭbīqī	تطبيقي
Applied cost	at-taklifa al-muṭabbaqa	التكلفة المطبقة
Applied economics	al-iqtiṣād at-taṭbīqī	الاقتصاد التطبيقي
Appoint	yu'ayyin	يعين (يوظف ، ينصب)
Appointment	1 ta'yīn	١ - تعيين (توظيف)
	2 maw'id	٢ - موعـد
Apportion	yuqassim	يقسم - إلى حصص
Apportionment	taqsīm	تقسيم (تخصيص)
Appraisal	taqdīr	تقدير (تثمين)
Appraisal leader	khabīr tathmīn	خبير تثمين
Appraisal method	uslūb at-tathmīn	اسلوب التثمين
Appraisal report	taqrīr tathmīn	تقرير تثمين - موجودات مؤسسة ما
Appraisal surplus	fā'iḍ at-taqdīr	فائض التقدير
Appraise	yuqaddir	يقدر (يثمن)
Appraised value	al-qīma al-muqaddara	القيمة المقدرة
Appraisement	taqdīr	تقدير (تثمين)
Appraiser	mukhammin	مخمن (مثمن)
Appreciation value	ziyādat qīmat al-amlāk	زيادة قيمة الاملاك
Appreciation of currency	irtifa' qīmat al-'umla	ارتفاع قيمة العملة
Appropriate (adj.)	munāsib	مناسب (لائق ، موافق)
Appropriate (v.)	yukhaṣṣiṣ	يخصص (يفرد)
Appropriated surplus	fā'iḍ mukhaṣṣaṣ	الفائض المخصص
Appropriation	māl mukhasṣṣaṣ	مال مخصص - لغرض ما
Appropriation account	ḥisāb at-takhṣīṣ	حساب التخصيص (حساب التوزيع)
Appropriation act	qarār at-takhṣīṣ	قرار التخصيص
Appropriation budget	mīzāniyyat al-mukhaṣṣaṣāt	ميزانية المخصصات
Appropriation ledger	ustādh ḥisābāt al-mukhaṣṣaṣāt	استاذ حسابات المخصصات
Appropriation of net income	tawzī' ar-ribḥ aṣ-ṣāfī	توزيع الربح الصافي
Appropriation period	muddat at-takhṣīṣ	مدة التخصيص
Appropriation receipt	īṣāl takhṣīṣ	ايصال تخصيص
Appropriation refund	radd mablagh at-takhṣīṣ	رد مبلغ التخصيص
Appropriation reimbursement	ta'wīḍ at-takhṣīṣ	تعويض التخصيص
Appropriation request	ṭalab at-takhṣīṣ	طلب التخصيص
Appropriation section	qism at-takhṣīṣ	قسم التخصيص
Approval of a balance sheet	i'timād al-mīzāniyya	اعتماد الميزانية
Approve	yuwāfiq 'ala	يوافق على (يعتمد ، يصدق على)
Approximate	taqrībī	تقريبي
Approximately	bi't-taqrīb	بالتقريب
Approximation	taqdīr taqrībī	تقدير تقريبي
Arbiter	ḥakam	حكم (وسيط ، مميز)
Arbitrage	1 taḥkīm	١ - تحكيم
	2 tarjih	٢ - ترجيح

		[بيع وشراء نفس السلعة في نفس الوقت في سوقين أو أكثر بقصد الاستفادة من الفروق الانية للأسعار]
Arbitrage of exchange	muwāzanat si'r aṣ-ṣarf	**موازنة سعر الصرف**
		[دفع ديـن في بلد ما بصـك مسحوب علـى بلـد آخر]
Arbitrary	i'tibāṭī	**اعتباطي**
		[لا على التعيين]
Arbitrate	yafṣil	**يفصل** (يتوسط ، يحكم)
Arbitration	taḥkīm	**تحكيم**
Arbitration award	qarār at-taḥkīm	**قرار التحكيم**
Arbitration board	hay'at at-taḥkīm	**هيئة التحكيم**
Arbitration of exchange	murājaḥa fi'ṣ-ṣarf	**المراجحة في الصرف**
Arbitrator	muḥakkam	**محكم** (وسيط)
Archives	maḥfūẓāt	**المحفوظات**
Archivist	amīn al-maḥfūẓāt	**أمين المحفوظات**
Are	ār	**آر**
		[مقياس سطحي فرنسي يساوى ١٠٠ متر مربـع]
Area	masāḥa	**مساحة**
Argument	ḥujja	**حجة** (مجادلة ، برهان)
Arithmetic	'ilm al-ḥisāb	**علم الحساب**
Arithmetic mean	al-mutawassiṭ al-hisābī	**المتوسط الحسابي**
Arithmetic progressions	mutawāliyāt 'adadiyya	**متواليات عددية**
Arm's length, at	'ala asās tijārī	**على أساس تجارى** (دون تحيز أو محاباة)
Arm's length transactions	mu'āmalāt 'ala asās tijārī	**معاملات على أساس تجارى**
Arrange	yurattib	**يرتب** (ينظم)
Arrangement	1 taswiya	**١ - تسوية ـ بين الدائن والمدين**
	2 tartib	**٢ - ترتيب**
Array	yurattib tasalsuliyyan	**يرتب تسلسليا**
		[مجموعة من أعداد مرتبة تصاعديا أو تنازليا]
Arrear	muta'akhir	**متأخر ـ عن الدفع**
Arrearage	raṣīd madīn	**رصيد مدين**
Arrears	baqāyā dayn	**بقايا دين**
Arrears of interest	fawā'id mut'akhkhira	**الفوائد المتأخرة**
Arrears of rent	ījār muta'akhkhir	**الايجار المتأخر**
Arrears, in	muta'akhkhir	**متأخر**
Arrival draft	saḥb	**سحب**
Arson	jarīmat al-ḥarq 'amdan	**جريمة الحرق عمدا**
Article	mādda	**مـــادة**
Articled	marbūṭ bi-shurūṭ	**مربوط بشروط**
Articled clerk	muḥāsib taḥt at-tamrīn	**محاسب تحت التمرين**
Articled, to be	yatamarran fī maktab muḥāsaba	**يتمرن في مكتب محاسبة**

Articles of association	niẓām ash-sharika al-asāsī	نظام الشركة الأساسي
Articles of incorporation	bunūd ta'sīs ash-sharika	بنود تأسيس الشركة
Articles of partnership	bunūd sharikat taḍāmun	بنود شركة تضامن
Articulation statement	kashf tafṣīlī	كشف تفصيلي
Artificial accounts	ḥisābāt mufta'ala	حسابات مفتعلة
Artificial person	shakhṣ i'tibārī	شخص اعتبارى
As at	kamā fī	كما في
As is	kamā huwa	كما هو (على علاته)
Ascertain	yataḥaqqaq	يتحقق من (يتأكد)
Ascertainable	mumkin at-taḥaqquq minhu	ممكن التحقق منه
Asking (or asked)	as-si'r al-maṭlūb	السعر المطلوب
Assembly	majlis	مجلس (جمعية)
Assembly costs	takālif at-tajmī'	تكاليف التجميع
Assembly, general	jam'iyya 'umūmiyya	جمعية عمومية
Assembly line	khaṭṭ at-tajmī'	خط التجميع
Assembly sheet	bayān tajmi'	بيان تجميع
Assent	yuwāfiq 'alā	يوافق على
Assert	yu'akkid	يؤكد
Assertion	ithbāt	اثبات (تأكيد)
Assess	yuqaddir ḍarība	يقدر ضريبة (يضع رسما)
Assessable	khāḍi' li 'ḍ-ḍarība	خاضع للضريبة
Assessable capital stock	ra's māl khāḍi' li'ḍ-ḍarība	رأسمال خاضع للضريبة
Assessed value	al-qīma 'l-muqaddara	القيمة المقدرة
Assessment	taqdīr	تقدير قيمة
Assessment list	qā'imat al-ashyā' al-khāḍi'a li'd-ḍarība	قائمة الأشياء الخاضعة للضريبة
Assessment of rates	taqdīr ujūr	تقدير الاجور
Assessment of taxes	taqdīr aḍ-ḍarā'ib	تقدير الضرائب
Assessor	mukhammin aḍ-ḍarā'ib	مخمن الضرائب
Assets	mawjūdāt	موجودات (اصول)
Assets, available	mawjūdāt ḥāḍira	موجودات حاضرة
Assets, circulating	mawjūdāt mutadāwala	موجودات متداولة
Assets, current	mawjūdāt mutadāwala	موجودات متداولة
Assets, fictitious	mawjūdāt wahmiyya	موجودات وهمية
Assets, fixed	mawjūdāt thābita	موجودات ثابتة
Assets, intangible	mawjūdāt ma'nawiyya	موجودات معنوية
Assets, liquid	mawjūdāt sā'ila	موجودات سائلة
Assets, other	mawjūdāt ukhrā	موجودات أخرى
Assets, real	mawjūdāt 'aqāriyya 'ayniyya	موجودات عقارية عينية
Assets, realisable	mawjūdāt qābila li'l-istibdāl	موجودات قابلة للاستبدال [أموال ممكنة الاستيفاء]
Assets, tangible	mawjūdāt malmūsa	موجودات ملموسة
Assets, wasting	mawjūdāt hālika	موجودات هالكة (مزرعة أخشاب) (فحم حجري)

Assign	yuḥawwil	**يحول** (ينقل)
Assignable	qābil li't-taḥwīl	**قابل للتحويل** (قابل للنقل)
Assignation	taḥwīl al-milkiyya	**تحويل الملكية** (نقل الملكية)
Assigned account	ḥisāb muḥawwal	**الحساب المحول** [الحساب المتنازل عنه ضمانا لقرض]
Assignee	mutanāzal ilayhi	**متنازل اليه**
Assigner	muḥawwil	**محول** (محيل ، مفوّض)
Assignment	taḥwīl 'amaliya	**تحويل أو عملية**
Assignment of lease	tanāzul 'an 'aqd ījār	**تنازل عن عقد ايجار**
Assignment, deed of	'aqd tanāzul	**عقد تنازل**
Assignor	mutanāzil li'l-ghayr	**متنازل للغير**
Assist	yusā'id	**يساعد** (يعاون)
Associate	sharīk	**شريك**
Associated company	sharika murtabiṭa bi-ukhrā	**شركة مرتبطة بأخرى**
Association	sharika	**شركة** (جمعية ، اتحاد ، رابطة)
Association, deed of	'aqd ta'sīs sharika	**عقد تأسيس شركة**
Assume	yaḍṭali' bi	**يضطلع ب** (يفترض) **ـ يتحمل**
Assumed liability	maṭlūbāt muḍṭala'bihā	**مطلوبات مضطلع بها**
Assumption of risk	taḥammul mas'ūliyyat al-mukhāṭara	**تحمل مسؤولية المخاطرة**
Assurance	ta'mīn	**تأمين** (كفالة ، ضمان)
Assurance, joint	ta'mīn mushtarak	**تأمين مشترك**
Assure	yu'akkid	**يؤكد** (يثبت ، يؤيد)
At a premium	bi-'a'lā min si'r al-iṣdār	**بأعلى من سعر الاصدار**
At a specified price	bi-si'r muḥaddad	**بسعر محدد**
At best	bi'l-aḥsan	**بالأحسن ـ في البورصة**
At call	'ind aṭ-ṭalab	**عند الطلب**
At par	bi-si'r al-iṣdār	**بسعر الاصدار**
At part	juz'iyyan	**جزئيا**
At sight	'inda'l-iṭ-ṭilā'	**عند الاطلاع**
Attach	yulḥaq bi	**يلحق ب** (يربط ، يصل)
Attaché	mulḥaq	**ملحق**
Attachment	ḥajz taḥaffuẓī	**حجز تحفظي** (تجميد ، توقيف)
Attachment against a third party	ḥajz mā li'l-madīn lada 'l-ghayr	**حجز ما للمدين لدى الغير**
Attendance fees	ujūr ḥuḍūr	**أجور حضور**
Attorney	muḥāmī	**محام** (وكيل دعاوى)
Attorney general	al-mudda'i 'l-'āmm	**المدعي العام**
Attorney, power of	wakāla	**وكالة** (تفويض) **ـ تفويض قانوني كامل**
Auction	mazād	**مزاد**
Auction fees	rusūm ad-dalāla	**رسوم الدلالة**
Auction sales	bay' bi'l-mazād al-'alanī	**بيع بالمزاد العلني**
Auctioneer	dallāl rasmī	**دلاّل رسمي**
Audit	yudaqqiq ḥisāban	**يدقق حسابا**

Audit adjustment	taswiyat al-murājaʿa	تسوية المراجعة
Audit certificate	shahādat al-murājaʿa	شهادة المراجعة
Audit notebook	daftar mulaḥazāt al-murājaʿa	دفتر ملاحظات المراجعة
Audit office	1 maktab murājaʿat al-ḥisābāt	١ - مكتب مراجعة الحسابات
	2 maḥkamat al-ḥisābāt	٢ - محكمة الحسابات (في المملكة المتحدة)
Audit period	muddat al-murājaʿa	مدة المراجعة
Audit programme	barnāmaj al-murājaʿa	برنامج المراجعة
Audit report	taqrīr al-murājaʿa	تقرير المراجعة
Audit standards	qawāʿid al-murajaʿa	قواعد المراجعة
Audit year	sanat al-murājaʿa	سنة المراجعة
Audit, annual	al-murājaʿa as-sanawiyya	المراجعة السنوية
Audit, complete	al-murājaʿa 'l-kāmila	المراجعة الكاملة
Audit, continuous	al-murājaʿa 'l-mustamirra	المراجعة المستمرة
Audit, final	al-murājaʿa 'n-hihā'iyya	المراجعة النهائية
Audit, interim	al-murājaʿa marhaliya	المراجعة المرحلية
Audit, internal	al-murājaʿa 'd-dākhiliyya	المراجعة الداخلية
Audit, partial	al-murājaʿa 'l-juz'iyya	المراجعة الجزئية
Audit, periodic	al-murājaʿa 'd-dawriyya	المراجعة الدورية
Audit, state-department	diwān al-muḥāsaba	ديوان المحاسبة
Audited voucher	mustanad mudaqqaq	مستند مدقق
Auditing	al-murājaʿa	المراجعة (فحص الحسابات)
Auditing of accounts	murājaʿat al-ḥisābāt	مراجعة الحسابات
Auditor	murājiʿ	مراجع (مدقق الحسابات)
Auditor, general	murājiʿ ʿāmm	مراجع عام
Auditor, internal	murājiʿ dākhilī	مراجع داخلي
Augment	yazīd	يزيـــد
Augmentation	ziyāda	زيـــادة
Authentic	ḥaqīqī	حقيقي (أصلي ، موثوق به)
Authenticated	muṣaddaq ʿalayhi	مصدق عليه
Authentication	muṣādaqa	مصادقـــة [شهادة بصحة الشيء]
Authenticity	mawthūqiyya	الموثوقية (صحة ، أصالة ، كون الشيء موثوقا بــه)
Authorise	yukhawwil	يخول (يمنح السلطة)
Authorisation	takhwīl	تخويل (تفويض ، ترخيص ، مأذونية)
Authorisation, absolute	tafwīḍ muṭlaq	تفويض مطلـــق
Authorised	mukhawwal	مخـــول (مفوض)
Authorised capital stock	ra's māl muṣarraḥ bihi	الرأسمال المصرح به
Authority	1 sulṭa	١ - سلطـــة
	2 marjiʿ	٢ - مرجـــع
Automatic machine	āla utūmātikiyya	آلة أوتوماتيكية
Automatic reinstatement	istimrār tilqā'ī	استمرار تلقائي [استمرار فعالية بوليصة التأمين بعد حدوث

		[خسارة معادلة لقيمة البوليصة الاسمية]
Automation	atmata	اتـــمتة
		[العمل بواسطة أجهزة أوتوماتيكية]
Auxiliary activities	ʻamaliyyāt farʻiyya	عمليات فرعية
Auxiliary equipment	muʻaddāt iḍāfiyya	معدات اضافية
Auxiliary service	khadamāt farʻiyya	خدمات فرعية
Avail	kafāla idāfiyya	كفالة اضافية
		[تضمن أحد الموقعين على سند تجارى]
Availability date	tārīkh as-saḥb al-mutawaqqaʻ	تاريخ السحب المتوقع
Available	mutawaffir	متوفر (موجود ، حاضر)
Available assets	mawjūdāt ḥāḍira	موجودات حاضرة
Available balance	raṣīd ḥāḍir	الرصيد الحاضر
Available cash	naqd ḥāḍir	النقد الحاضر
Available (earned) surplus	fā'iḍ ḥāḍir	الفائض الحاضر (المكتسب)
Average	mutawassiṭ	متوسط (معدل)
Average clause	sharṭ al-muʻaddal	شرط المعدل ـ في عقود التأمين
Average deviation	mutawassit al-inḥirāf	متوسط الانحراف (معدل الانحراف)
Average due date	mutawassiṭ tārīkh al-istihqāq	متوسط تاريخ الاستحقاق
Average life	al-ʻumr al-mutawassiṭ	العمر المتوسط
Average outgoing quality	muʻaddal newiya al-maṣrūf	معدل نوعية المصروف
Average price	as-siʻr al-mutawassiṭ	السعر المتوسط (متوسط السعر)
Average purchase price	mutawassiṭ siʻr ash-shirā'	متوسط سعر الشراء
Average sample number	muʻaddal raqam al-ʻayyina	معدل رقم العينة
Average statement	bayān tawzīʻ at-talaf al-baḥrī	بيان توزيع التلف البحرى
Average term of credit	mutawassiṭ muhlat ad-dafʻ	متوسط مهلة الدفع
Average, above	fawq al-mutawassiṭ	فوق المتوسط
Average, below	dūn al-mutawassiṭ	دون المتوسط
Award (n.; v.)	1 mukāfa'a	١ - مكافـــأة
	2 ḥukm	٢ - حكـــم
	3 yukāfi'	٣ - يكافىء
	4 yuṣdir ḥukman qaḍā' iyyan	٤ - يصدر حكما قضائيا
Axiom	badīha	بديهة (حقيقة مقررة)
Back (n.; v.)	1 matn	١ - متـن ـ الشيك أو البوليصة
	2 yuẓahhir	٢ - يظهـــر
		[يوقع على ظهر مستند اشعارا بالقبول]
Back a bill	yuẓahhir kumbiyāla	يظهر كمبيالة
Back interest	baqāyā fā'ida	بقايا فائدة
Back order	ṭalabiyya mutakhallifa	طلبية متخلفة
Back-bond	sanad tafwīḍ	سند تفويض
		[يعطى للضامن نظير ضمانة]

Back-door financing	tamwīl bi-ṭuruq ghayr ma'lūfa	تمويل بطرق غير مألوفة
Back-to-back credit	iʻtimād mustanid bi' ʻtimād ākhar	اعتماد مستند باعتماد آخر [عملية تتضمن اعتمادين يفتح الأول لمنفعة مستفيد لتوريد بضاعة ـ يعطي الأمر لمصرفه لفتح اعتماد ثان عن ذات البضاعة وفق شروط الاعتماد الأول مع بعض الاستثناءات التي لا تتعارض مع تلك الشروط]
Backwardation	1 gharāmat ta'khīr	١ - غرامة تأخير ـ عن تسليم أسهم
	2 dalāla	٢ - دلالة ـ لمقرض الأوراق المالية
Bad debt	dayn hālik	دين هالك
Bad money	ʻumla zā'ifa	عملة زائفة
Bail (n.; v.)	kafāla-yakful	كفالة ـ يكفل
Bail bond	ṣakk kafāla	صك الكفالة
Bailee	ḥāfiẓ al-wadīʻa	حافظ الوديعة [المؤتمن على حفظ الأمانات بموجب عقد]
Bailment	wadīʻa	وديعــة
Bailor	al-mudi'	المــودع [صاحــب الوديعــة]
Balance	1 raṣīd ḥisāb	١ - رصيد الحساب
	2 tawāzun hisāb	٢ - توازن الحساب
	3 yuwāzin ḥisāb	٣ - يوازن الحساب
Balance and debt system	tariqat ar-raṣīd wa'd-dayn	طريقة الرصيد والدين
Balance brought forward	raṣīd manqūl	رصيد منقول
Balance carried forward	raṣid muraḥḥal	رصيد مرحل
Balance of account	raṣīd ḥisāb	رصيد الحساب
Balance of payment	mīzān al-madfūʻat	ميزان المدفوعات
Balance of payment deficit	ʻajz fī mīzān al-madfūʻāt	العجز في ميزان المدفوعات
Balance of payment, unfavourable	mīzān madfūʻat ʻaksī	ميزان مدفوعات عكسي [ليس في صالح البلد]
Balance of trade	al-mīzān at-tijārī	الميزان التجارى
Balance of trade, adverse	mīzān tījarī ʻājiz	ميزان تجارى عاجز [في غير صالح البلد]
Balance record of raw material	sijill raṣīd al-mādda 'l-khām	سجل رصيد المادة الخام
Balance sheet	al-mīzāniyya	الميزانيــة
Balance sheet as at	al-mīzāniyya kamā fī	الميزانية كما في
Balance sheet audit	murājaʻat al-mīzāniyya	مراجعة الميزانية
Balance sheet item	band al-mīzāniyya	بنـد الميزانية
Balance sheet, aggregate	al-mīzāniyya 'l-ijmāliyya	الميزانية الاجمالية
Balance ticket	shahāda bi-raṣīd al-as-hum	شهادة برصيد الأسهم
Balance system	ṭarīqat ar-raṣd	طريقة الرصيد
Balance, in	mutawāzin	متـــوازن
Balance, out of	ghayr mutawāzin	غير متوازن
Balance, trial	mizān al-murajaʻa	ميزان المراجعة

Balancing	tarṣīd	ترصيـــد
Ballot	iqtirāʿsirrī	اقتراع سرى
Ballot box	ṣundūq al-iqtirāʿ	صندوق الاقتراع
Bank	maṣraf	مصــــرف
Bank account	ḥisāb maṣrafī	حساب مصرفي
Bank bill	sanad maṣrafī	سند مصرفي
		[مسحوب من مصرف على آخر]
Bank charges	rasūm maṣrafiyya	رسوم مصرفية
Bank charter	ʿaqd taʾsīs maṣraf	عقد تأسيس المصرف
Bank clearing	muqāṣṣa maṣrafiyya	مقاصة مصرفية ـ بين مصرف وآخر
Bank commission	ʿumūlat al-maṣraf	عمولة المصرف
Bank control	riqāba al-masarīf	رقابة المصارف
Bank credit	iʿtimād maṣrafī	اعتماد مصرفي
Bank discount	khaṣm maṣrafī	خصم مصرفي
Bank draft	ḥawāla maṣrafiyya	حوالة مصرفية
Bank guarantee	kafāla maṣrafiyya	كفالة مصرفية
Bank mortgage	rahn maṣrafī	رهن مصرفي
Bank notes	awrāq maṣraffiyya	أوراق مصرفية (بنكنوت)
Bank of issue	maṣraf al-iṣdār	مصرف الاصدار
Bank overdraft	tajāwuz maṣrafī	تجاوز مصرفي (حساب مكشوف)
		[تجاوز ما يسحب من البنك عن المبلغ المودع]
Bank rate of discount	muʿaddal al-khaṣm	معدل الخصم
Bank reconciliation	taswiyat ḥisāb al-maṣraf	تسوية حساب المصرف
		[يبين الفروق بين رصيد الحساب كما هو في حسابات المصرف وكما يظهر في دفاتر العميل]
Bank return	bayān waḍʿ al-maṣraf	بيان وضع المصرف
Bank statement	kashf ḥisāb maṣrafī	كشف حساب مصرفي
Bank stock	as-hum maṣraffiyya	أسهم مصرفية
Bank transfer	taḥwīl maṣrafī	تحويل مصرفي
Bank, central	al-maṣraf al-markazī	المصرف المركزى
Bank, investment	maṣārif istithmār	مصارف الاستثمار
Bankable paper	awrāq maqbūla	أوراق مقبولة
		[قابلة للحسم في المصرف]
Banker	ṣāḥib maṣraf	صاحب مصرف
Banker's acceptance	iʿtimād maṣrafī naqdī	اعتماد مصرفي نقدى
Banker's discount	al-ḥasm fi 'l-khārij	الحسم في الخارج
Banker's draft	ḥawāla maṣraffiyya	حوالة مصرفية
		[مسحوبة من مصرف على فرعة أو على مصرف آخر]
Banking	aʿmāl maṣraffiyya	أعمال مصرفية
Bankrupt (n.; v.)	muflis–yuflis	مفلس ـ يفلس

Bankruptcy	1 iflās	١ - افـــلاس
	2 taflīsa	٢ - تفليســـه
Bankruptcy by default	taflīs bi't-taqṣīr	تفليس بالتقصير
Bankruptcy by fraud	iflās mufta'al	افلاس مفتعل
Bankruptcy petition	ṭalab ishhār iflās	طلب اشهار افلاس
Bankruptcy, act of	fi'l mūjib li't-tāflīs	فعل موجب للتفليس [توقف عن الدفع]
Bankruptcy, court of	maḥkamat al-iflās	محكمة الافلاس
Bankruptcy, fraudulent	iflās iḥtiyālī	افلاس احتيالي
Bankruptcy, general	iflās 'umūmī	افلاس عمومي
Bargain (n.; v.)	musāwama–yusāwim	مساومة ـ يساوم
Bargaining, collective	musāwama jamā 'iyya	المساومة الجماعية
Barter (n.; v.)	1 mubādala	١ - مبادلة (مقايضة)
	2 yubādil	٢ - يبادل (يقايض)
Bartering	tijarat al-muqā-yaḍa	تجارة المقايضة
Base period	fatra qiyāsiyya	فترة قياسية
Base stock method	ṭarīqat al-makhzūn ath-thābit	طريقة المخزون الثابت
Basic budget	al-muwāzana 'l-asāsiyya	الموازنة الأساسية
Basic cost	taklifa asāsiyya	التكلفة الأساسية
Basic dimension	bu'd asāsī	البعد الأساسي
Basic pay	ajr asāsī	الأجر الأساسي
Basic point	an-nuqṭa' l-asāsiyya	النقطة الأساسية [المكان الجغرافي الذى يكون فيه السعر المعلن لسلعة ما هو الأساس الذى يتحدد بموجبه سعر السلعة نفسها في مكان آخر]
Basic point system	niẓām at-tas'īr al-asāsī	نظام التسعير الأساسي
Basic price	si'r asāsī	السعـر الأساسـي
Basic standard cost	taklifa mi'yāriyya asāsiyya	التكلفة المعيارية الأساسية
Basis	asās	الأساس [التكلفة أو القيمة المستخدمة كبديل عن التكلفة]
Basis of accounting	asās al-muḥāsaba	أساس المحاسبة
Basis of classification	asās at-taṣnīf	أساس التصنيف
Basis of comparison	asās al-muqārana	أساس المقارنة
Basket purchase	shirā' ijmālī	شراء اجمالي [شراء مجموعة متنوعة من الأصول بسعر قطعي اتفاقي]
Batch cost unit	taklifat al-majmū'a	تكلفة المجموعة
Batch costing	ḥisāb takālīf al-majmū'a	حساب تكاليف المجموعة
B.B.A. Bachelor of Business Administration	bakaluryus fī idārat al-a'māl	بكالوريوس في ادارة الاعمال
B.Com. Bachelor of Commerce	bakaluryus fi 't-tijāra	بكالوريوس في التجارة

Bear	yuʻḍārib	يضـــارب [لاحداث هبوط في السعر]
Bear interest (v.)	yu'ṭī fā'ida	يعطي فائدة
Bear market	sūq al-muḍāribīn	سوق المضاربين ـ البورصة النازلة
Bearer	ḥāmil	حامل ـ حوالة أو شيك
Bearer debentures	sanadāt li-ḥāmiliha	سندات لحاملها
Bearer securities	awraq māliyya tudfaʻ li-ḥāmilihā	أوراق مالية تدفع لحاملها
Bearer share	sahm li-ḥāmilihi	سهم لحامله
Bearer stock	sahm li-ḥāmilihi	سهم لحامله
Bearer, to	li-ḥāmilihi	لحاملـــه
Bearing of (the) tax	taḥammul aḍ-ḍarība	تحمل الضريبة
Bearish influences	mu'aththirāt nuzūliyya	مؤثرات نزولية ـ في البورصة
Bearish tendency	ittijah nuzūlī	اتجاه نزولي
Behalf, in – of	li-maṣlaḥat	لمصلحة
Behalf, on – of	bi 'n-niyāba ʻan	بالنيابة عن
Bell curve	munḥanā jarasī	منحني جرسي [خط بياني على شكل جرس]
Below par	aqall min al-qīma 'l-ismiyya	أقل من القيمة الاسمية
Beneficial	murbiḥ	مربـــح
Beneficial interest	ḥaqq al-intifāʻ	حـق الانتفاع
Beneficiary	mustafīd	المستفيد
Benefit (n.; v.)	manfaʻa–yastafīd	منفعة ـ يستفيد
Benefits	mazāyā	مزايـــا
Betterment	taḥsīn	تحسيـــن
Bias	taḥayyuz	تحيز (محابـــاة)
Bid (n.; v.)	'arḍ shirā–yaʻriḍ siʻran	عرض شراء ـ يعرض سعرا (يزايد)
Bid bond	khiṭāb ḍamān mabda'ī	خطاب ضمان مبدئي [يستعمل في العطاءات المحلية أو المقاولات الخارجية]
Bid book	sijill al-ʻurūḍ	سجل العروض
Bid price	siʻr al-ʻarḍ	سعر العرض
Bidding	muzāyada	مزايـــدة
Bidding, competitive	muzāyada tanāfusiyya	مزايدة تنافسية
Bilateral	thunā'ī	ثنائي (ذو طرفين)
Bilateral arrangement	ittifāq thunā'ī	اتفاق ثنائـــي
Bilateral trade agreements	ittifāqiyyāt tijāriyya thuna'iyya	اتفاقيات تجارية ثنائية
Bill (n.; v.)	1 fatūrat ḥisāb	١ - فاتورة حساب
	2 sanad	٢ - سند (كمبيالة)
	3 yursil fātūrat ḥisāb	٣ - يرسل فاتورة حساب
Bill book	daftar istiḥqāqāt al-kumbiyālāt	دفتر استحقاقات الكمبيالات
Bill broker	simsār awrāq māliyya	سمسار أوراق مالية
Bill discounted	kumbiyāla makhṣūma	كمبيالة مخصومة
Bill holder	ṣaḥib ḥawāla māliyya	صاحب حوالة مالية

Bill in abeyance	fātūra mustaḥaqqa	فاتورة مستحقة
Bill of exchange	kumbiyāla	كمبيالة (حوالة مالية ، سند سحب)
Bill of lading (b/l)	būlīṣat shaḥn	بوليصة شحن
Bill of materials	qā'imat al-ʻadad an-nawʻiyya	قائمة العدد النوعية
Bill of sale	sanad bayʻ	سند بيع
Bill of sight	taṣrīh muʻāyana	تصريح معاينة
Bill payable	waraqat dafʻ	ورقة دفع
Bill receivable	waraqat qabḍ	ورقة قبض
Bill to mature	kumbiyāla lam tustaḥaqq baʻd	كمبيالة لم تستحق بعد
Bill, claused or foul – of lading	būlīṣat shaḥn maʻ taḥaffuẓ	بوليصة شحن مع تحفظ [فيها اشارة لعيب في البضاعة]
Bill, clean – of lading	būlīṣat shaḥn bi-dūn taḥaffuẓ	بوليصة شحن بدون تحفظ [لا ذكر فيها لعيب في البضاعة]
Bill, foreign – of exchange	kumbiyāla khārijiyya	كمبيالة خارجية
Bill, inland – of exchange	kumbiyāla dākhiliyya	كمبيالة داخلية
Bill, long – of exchange	kumbiyāla ṭawīlat al-ajal	كمبيالة طويلة الأجل
Bill, meet a	yusaddid qīmat kumbiyāla	يسدد قيمة كمبيالة ـ عند الاستحقاق
Bill, retire a	yusaddid qīmat kumbiyāla qabl al-istiḥqāq	يسدد قيمة كمبيالة قبل الاستحقاق
Bill, short – of exchange	kumbiyāla qaṣīrat al-ajal	كمبيالة قصيرة الأجل
Bill, trade	kumbiyāla tijāriyya	كمبيالة تجارية
Bill, way	būlīṣat shaḥn bi's-sikka 'l-ḥadīdiyya	بوليصة شحن بالسكة الحديدية
Billing	iʻdād al-fawātīr	اعداد الفواتير
Billing machine	āla li-iʻdād al-fawātīr	آلة لاعداد الفواتير
Bills, past due	kumbiyālat maḍa istiḥqāquhā	كمبيالات مضى استحقاقها
Binary computer	kumbūtar thunā'ī	كومبيوتر ثنائي [عقل الكتروني ذو نظام ثنائي]
Binary system	an-niẓām ath-thunā'ī	النظام الثنائي
Binder	malaff	ملـــف
Binding	mulzim	ملـــزم
Black list	al-qā'ima as-sawdā'	القائمة السوداء
Black market	as-sūq as-sawdā'	السوق السوداء
Blank bill	kumbiyāla ʻalā bayāḍ	كمبيالة على بياض [خالية من اسم المستفيد]
Blank cheque	shīk ʻalā bayāḍ	شيك على بياض
Blank credit	kitāb iʻtimād maftūḥ	كتاب اعتماد مفتوح
Blank endorsement	tajyīr ʻalā bayāḍ	تجيير على بياض (تظهير مفتوح)
Blank transfer	taḥwīl ʻalā bayāḍ	تحويل على بياض
Blended fund	amwāl mukhtalaṭa	أموال مختلطة [حاصل مبيع الارث الذى يوزع على الورثة حسب تعليمات الموصي]
Blind entry	1 qayd ghāmiḍ	١ - قيد غامض (بدون شرح)

	2 tarḥīl mubāshir	٢ - ترحيل مباشر [بدون سند قيد]
Block	yujammid	يجمـــد
Block method	ṭariqat al-majmūʿāt	طريقة المجموعات [اسلوب مراجعة المستندات في مجموعات]
Block vouching	murājaʿa tafsīliyya	مراجعة تفصيلية [لاحدى مجموعات المستندات]
Blocked	mujammad	مجمـــد (موقوف)
Blocked account	hisāb mujammad	حساب مجمـد
Blocked currency	ʿumla mujammada	عمـــلة مجمدة
Blotter	1 daftar muswaddat al-quyūd	١ - دفتر مسودة القيود
	2 al-yawmiyya al-musāʿida	٢ - اليومية المساعدة [نوع من أنواع اليوميات تقسم عادة إلى أعمدة حتى يمكن أن تقيد العمليات المشابهة تباعا وبشكل متسلسل كل عملية في العمود الخاص بها ، الأمر الذى يمكن من استخراج مجموعها بشكل منفصل في آخر يوم]
Blue-sky law	qānun tanẓīm iṣdār as-sanadāt	قانون تنظيم اصدار السندات والأسهم (نظم في الولايات المتحدة بعد كارثة ١٩٣٠ المالية)
Board	majlis	مجلـــس
Board of directors	majlis idāra	مجلس ادارة
Board of trustees	majlis umanā’	مجلس الامناء
Body	hay’a	هيئـــة
Body corporate	shakhṣiyya iʿtibāriyya	شخصية اعتبارية
B.O.M. (beginning of month)	awwal ash-shahr	أول الشهر
Bon de sortie	khuluww rijl	خلو رجل
Bond	1 sanad dayn	١ - سند دين
	2 sanad taʿahhud	٢ - سند تعهد
Bond discount (and expense)	khaṣm iṣdār as-sanadāt	خصم اصدار السندات
Bond dividend	arbāḥ ʿalā shakl sanadāt	أرباح على شكل سندات
Bond fund	iʿtimād as-sanadāt as-ṣādira	اعتماد السندات الصادرة
Bond premium	mardūd as-sanad	مردود السند [المبلغ الزائد عن قيمة السند الاسمية]
Bond register	sijl sanadat	سجل سندات
Bond valuation	taqyīm as-sanad	تقييم السند
Bond(s), callable	sanadāt qābila li’l-istidʿā’	سندات قابلة للاستدعاء
Bond(s) called	sanadāt maṭlūba	سندات مطلوبة
Bonds first mortgage	sanadāt rahn awwal	سندات رهن أول
Bond(s) forged	sanadāt muzawwara	سندات مزورة
Bonded	maḍmūn	مضمون
Bonded debt	dayn maḍmūn bi-sanad	دين مضمون بسند
Bonds issue	iṣdār as-sanadāt	اصدار السندات
Bonds outstanding method	ṭarīqat tawzīʿ khaṣm as-sanad	طريقة توزيع خصم السند ـ على مدة الاصدار

Bonus	mukāfa'a	مكافــأة
Bonus share	sahm minhah	سهم منحة
Book account	quyūd daftariyya	قيود دفترية
Book debts	duyūn daftariyya	ديون دفترية
Book inventory	jard daftarī	الجرد الدفترى
Book of account	daftar ḥisābāt	دفتر حسابات
Book of final (secondary) entry	daftar al-ustādh	دفتر الاستاذ
Book of original entry	daftar al-yawmiyya	دفتر اليومية (القيد الاصلي)
Book profit	ar-ribḥ ad-daftarī	الربح الدفترى
Book surplus	al-fā'iḍ ad-daftarī	الفائض الدفترى
Book value	al-qīma 'd-daftariyya	القيمة الدفترية
		[التكلفة مطروح منها الاستهلاك المتراكم]
Bookkeeper	kātib ḥisābāt	كاتب حسابات
Bookkeeping	mask ad-dafātir	مسك الدفاتر
Bookkeeping by double entry	mask ad-dafātir bi-ṭarīqat al-qayd al-muzdawij	مسك الدفاتر بطريقة القيد المزدوج
Bookkeeping cycle	dawrat mask ad-dafātir	دورة مسك الدفاتر
Bookkeeping machine	āla li-mask ad-dafātir	آلة لمسك الدفاتر
Books	dafātir	دفاتر (سجلات)
Books, subsidiary	dafātir musā'ida	الدفاتر المساعدة
Boom	inti'āsh	انتعاش (رواج ، ازدهار)
Boot	'ilāwa	عــلاوة
Bordereau	kashf-lā'iḥa	كشف ، لائحة
Borrow	yaqtariḍ	يقتــرض
Borrowed capital	ra's māl muqtaraḍ	رأس مال مقترض
Boston ledger	daftar ustādh busṭun	دفتر استاذ بوسطن
		[دفتر استاذ يبين تغييرات الحساب افقيا وليس عموديا كما هو متبع]
Bounties	i'ānāt	اعانات (هبات مالية ، منح)
Bourse (Fr.); exchange	burṣa	البورصــة
B.O.Y. (beginning of year)	bidāyat al-'āmm	بدايــة العــام
Boycott (n.; v.)	muqāṭa'a-yuqāṭi'	مقاطعة ـ يقاطع
Branch	far'	فــرع
Branch accounts	ḥisābāt al-furū'	حسابات الفروع
Branch manager	mudīr al-far'	مدير الفرع
Branch offices	makātib al-furū'	مكاتب الفروع
Brand	'alāma	علامة (ماركة ، صنف)
Breach	mukhālafa	مخالفة (نقض ، انتهاك)
Breach of contract	mukhālafat shurūṭ al-'aqd	مخالفة شروط العقد
Break away	inhiyār fī as'ār al-awrāq al-māliyya	انهيار في أسعار الأوراق المالية
Breakdown	taḥlīl muḥāsabī	تحليل محاسبي
Break-even	ta'ādul	تعــادل
		[يغطى النفقات]

Break-even analysis	taḥlīl istīfā’ an-nafaqāt	تحليل استيفاء النفقات
Break-even chart	kharīṭat at-ta‘ādul	خريطة التعادل
		[تبين ربحية المشروع عند مستويات الطاقة المختلطة وتبين المستوى الذى لا يحقق عنده المشروع ربحا أو يحتمل خسارة أى تتعادل الايرادات مع النفقات]
Break-even point	nuqṭat at-ta‘adul	نقطة التعـادل
		[نقطة تقاطع منحنى النفقات مع منحنى الدخـــل]
Break-up value	qīmat ash-shay’ ka-khurda	قيمة الشيء كخردة
Bring a motion	yuqaddim iqtirāḥan	يقدم اقتراحا
Bring an action	yarfa‘ da‘wā	يرفع دعـوى
Bring forward	yuqadim	يقدم
		[ينقل عما قبله]
Broker	simsār	سـمسـار
Brokerage	samsara	سـمسـرة
Brokerage commission	‘umūlat as-samsara	عمولة السمسرة
Broker’s loan	qarḍ as-ṣimsār	قرض السمسار
Brought down	nuqila lima ba‘dahu	نقـل لما بعـده
Bubble company	sharika iḥtiyāliyya	شركة احتيالية
Budget	al-mīzāniyya at-takhtītiyya	الميزانية التخطيطية (الميزانية التقديرية)
Budget appropriations	mukhaṣṣaṣāt al-mizāniyya	مخصصات الميزانية
Budget committee	lajnat al-mīzāniyya	لجنة الميزانية
Budget document	wathīqat al-mīzāniyya‘al-ḥukūmiyya	وثيقة الميزانية الحكومية
Budget estimates	taqdīrāt al-mīzāniyya	تقديرات الميزانية
Budget expenditure	nafaqāt al-mīzaniyya	نفقات الميزانية
Budget period	fatrat al-mīzāniyya	فترة الميزانية
Budget speech	mūjaz al-mīzāniyya	موجز الميزانية
Budget surplus	fā’iḍ al-mīzāniyya	فائض الميزانية
Budget, bureau of the	dā’irat al-mīzāniyya	دائرة الميزانية
Budget, component	al-mīzāniyya ’anaser	الميزانية عناصر الميزانية
Budget, continuous	mīzāniyya mutaḥarrika	ميزانية متحركة
Budget, cyclical	mīzāniyyat ad-dawra al-iqtīṣādiyya	ميزانية الدورة الاقتصادية
Budget, extraordinary	mīzāniyya istithnā’iyya	ميزانية استثنائية
Budget, flexible	mīzāniyya marina	ميزانية مرنة
Budget, master	al-mīzāniyya al-‘āmma	الميزانية العامـة
Budget, operational	mīzāniyyat at-tashghīl	ميزانية التشغيل
Budget, production	mīzāniyyat al-intāj	ميزانية الانتاج
Budget, purchases	mīzāniyyat mushtarawāt	ميزانية مشتروات
Budget, sales	mīzaniyyat mabī‘āt	ميزانية مبيعات
Budgetary	khaṣṣ bi’l-mīzāniyya	خاص بالميزانية
Budgetary accounts	ḥisābāt al-mîzāniyya	حسابات الميزانية

Budgetary control	murāqabat al-mīzāniyya	مراقبة الميزانية
Budgetary deficit	'ajz al-mīzāniyya	عجز الميزانية
Budgetary receipts	wāridāt al-mīzāniyya	واردات الميزانية
Budgeted	marṣūd	مرصود (مضمن في الميزانية)
Budgeted (or planned) capacity	ṭaqat barnāmaj al-intāj	طاقة برنامج الانتاج
Budgeting	i'dād al-mīzāniyya	اعداد الميزانية
Bulk cargo	shaḥna sā'iba	شحنة سائبة [غير موضوعة في بالات]
Bull	muḍārib 'ala'l-irtifā' fi'l-burṣa	مضارب على الارتفاع في البورصة
Bulletin	nashra	نشرة
Bullion	sabīka	سبيكة ـ ذهب أو فضة
Bullion, gold standard	niẓām at-ta'āmul bi'dh-dhahab	نظام التعامل بالذهب
Burden	'ib'	عبء [نفقات انتاج رأسية]
Buoy (up)	yuda''im	يدعم (يعضد الأسعار)
Buoyancy	thabāt al-as'ār	ثبات الأسعار
Buoyant market	sūq mad'ūma	سوق مدعومة
Bureau	maktab	مكتب
Bureau de change	maktab taḥwuīl al-'umla	مكتب تحويل العملة
Burning ratio	nisbat al-iḥtīrāq	نسبة الاحتراق [نسبة الخسارة الفعلية الناجمة عن الاحتراق إلى قيمة الأملاك القابلة للحرق]
Business	1 mutajara	١ - متاجرة
	2 ta'āmul tijārī	٢ - تعامل تجارى
	3 mu'assasa tijariyya	٣ - مؤسسة تجارية
Business circles	awsāṭ tijāriyya	أوساط تجارية
Business combination	ittiḥād tijārī	اتحاد تجارى [من شركتين أو أكثر]
Business concern	maḥall tijārī	محل تجارى (مؤسسة تجارية)
Business connections	'alāqāt tijāriyya	علاقات تجارية
Business corporation	sharika ṣinā'iyya aw tijāriyya	شركة صناعية أو تجارية
Business cycle	ad-dawra 't-tijāriyya	الدورة التجارية
Business enterprise (or entity or unity)	1 kiyān qānūnī	١ - كيان قانونى
	2 al-a'māl 'umūman	٢ - الأعمال عموما
Business entity	ash-shakhṣiyya 'l-ma'nawiyya	الشخصية المعنوية
Business executive	mudīr a'māl	مدير الأعمال
Business hours	sā'āt ad-dawām	ساعات الدوام
Business interruption insurance	ta'mīn ta'aṭṭul al-'amal	تأمين تعطل العمل
Business management	idārt al-a'māl	ادارة الأعمال
Business premises	munshā'at al-shanika	منشآت الشركة
Business transaction	'amaliyya tijāriyya	عملية تجارية
Business trust	mu'assasat 'amaliyyāt mushtaraka	مؤسسة عمليات مشتركة
Businessman	rajul a'māl	رجل أعمال

Businessman's investment	istithmār rajul aʿmāl	**استثمار رجل الأعمال**
Business-type; cost-type	al-muḥāsaba ʿalā asās al-istiḥqāq	**المحاسبة على أساس الاستحقاق** [ينطبق هذا التعبير في المحاسبة الحكومية]
But–for income	īrād lawlā'ī	**ايـراد لولائـي** [جزء من ايراد ناجم عن منتجات احتسبت تكلفتها على أساس عنصر تكلفة اضافي زيادة عن العناصر التي تدخل في التكلفة عـادة]
Buyer's market	sūq al-mushtarī	**سوق المشترى** [الحالة الملائمة للمشترين حين يزداد العرض عن الطلب]
Buyer up	muḥtakir	**محتكر**
By-laws	anẓima dākhiliyya	**أنظمة داخلية** [لشركات أو جمعيات]
By-product	nitāj jānibī	**نتاج جانبي** (ثانوى)
C.A. Chartered Accountant – Scotland	muḥāsib qānūnī	**محاسب قانوني**
C.A.F. (continuous audit file)	malaff at-tadqīq ad-dā'im	**ملف التدقيق الدائم**
Calculable	yumkin iḥtisābuh	**يمكن احتسابه**
Calculate	yaḥsib	**يحسب**
Calculating machine	āla ḥāsiba	**آلة حاسبة**
Calculation	iḥtisāb	**احتساب**
Calculator	ḥāsib	**حاسب** (آلة حاسبة)
Call	1 daʿwa	**١ - دعـوة ـ لتسديد قيمة الأقساط**
	2 khayār	**٢ - خيـار ـ شراء أسهم بأسعار محددة**
Call account (Deposit)	wadīʿa taht al-talab	**وديعة تحت الطلب**
Call in	yasḥab min at-tadāwul	**يسحب من التداول**
Call loan	qarḍ ghibb aṭ-ṭalab	**قرض غب الطلب**
Call over	murājaʿa bi'l-munādāh	**المراجعة بالمناداة**
Call price	siʿr al-istidʿā'	**سعر الاستدعاء** [السعر الذى يستوفى به سند غب الطلب]
Call rate	muʿaddal al-fā'ida	**معدل الفائدة** [على قروض قصيرة الأجل]
Callable bond	sanad qābil li 'l-istidʿa	**سند قابل للاستدعاء**
Callable capital	ra's māl maṭlūb dafʿuh	**رأس مال مطلوب دفعه**
Calls in advance	aqsāṭ madfūʿa muqaddaman	**أقساط مدفوعة مقدما**
Calls in arrears	aqsāt muta'akhkhira	**أقساط متأخرة**
Cambist	ṣarrāf	**صـرّاف**
Cancel	yafsakh	**يفسخ** (يلغي ، يحذف)
Cancellation	1 inhā'	**١ - انهاء ـ عقد تأمين قبل انتهاء المدة المحددة**
	2 ilghā'	**٢ - الغـاء**

Cancelled cheque	shīk malghī	**شيك ملغى**
Capacity	ṭāqa	**طاقة** (قدرة ، مقدرة)
Capacity cost	taklifat tashghīl aṭ-ṭāqa 'l-kāmila	**تكلفة تشغيل الطاقة الكاملة**
Capacity ratio	nisbat aṭ-ṭāqa	**نسبة الطاقة**
		[نسبة الانتاج الفعلى إلى الحد الأعلى الممكن من الانتاج]
Capacity usage ratio	nisbat istighlāl aṭ-ṭāqa	**نسبة استغلال الطاقة**
Capital	1 ra's māl	**١ - رأس المال**
	2 al-māl al-mustathmar fī mashrūʿ	**٢ - المال المستثمر في مشروع**
Capital account	ḥisāb ra's al-māl	**حساب رأس المال**
Capital assets	mawjūdāt ra's māliyya	**موجودات رأسمالية** (رأس مال ثابت)
Capital bonus stock dividend (U.S.)	sahm munḥa	**سهم منحة**
Capital budget	muwāzanat ar-ra's māl	**موازنة الرأسمال** (موازنة الاستثمار)
Capital coefficient	muʿāmil ar-ra's-māl	**معامل الرأسمال**
		[الكلفة الوسطية للحصول على وحدة اضافية لتحقيق الطاقة الانتاجية السنوية]
Capital dividend	ḥiṣṣat ribḥ ar-ra's māl	**حصة ربح الرأسمال**
		[تدفع من الرأسمال المدفوع]
Capital expenditure	maṣraf ra's mālī	**مصروف رأس مالي**
Capital gains	arbāḥ ra'smāliyya	**أرباح رأسمالية**
Capital goods	wasā'il intāj	**وسائل انتاج**
		[رأس مال عدة وأدوات]
Capital income	ʿā'idāt ar-ra'smāl	**عائدات الرأس مال**
Capital investment	istithmār ar-ra'smāl	**استثمار الرأس مال**
Capital levy	ḍarībat ar-ra'smāl	**ضريبة الرأس مال**
Capital liability	qarḍ ṭawīl al-ajal	**قرض طويل الأجل**
Capital movement	ḥarakat ar-ra'smāl	**حركة الرأس مال** (تداول الأموال)
Capital outlay; capital expenditure	maṣrūf ra'smālī	**مصروف رأس مالي**
Capital paid in (up); paid-in capital	ar-ra'smāl al-madfūʿ	**الرأس مال المدفوع**
Capital-reconciliation statement	bayān taswiyat ar-ra'smāl	**بيان تسوية الرأس مال**
Capital reserve	iḥtiyāṭi ar-ra's māl	**احتياطي الرأس مال**
Capital stock	ra's māl ash-sharika	**رأس مال الشركة**
Capital sum	al-qīma 'l-aṣliyya	**القيمة الأصلية**
		[رأس مال أى استثمارا مالى مع الاضافات التى لا تتطلب التبويب ضمن بند الايرادات]
Capital surplus	fā'iḍ ar-ra'smāl	**فائض الرأس مال**
Capital turnover	dawrat ar-ra'smāl	**دورة الرأس مال**
Capital value	al-qīma ar-ra's maliyya	**القيمة الرأسمالية**
		[الاستثمار في موجودات ثابتة مقاسة على أساس الكلفة أو أى قيمة أخرى]
Capital, accumulation of	tarākum ar-ra'smāl	**تراكم الرأس مال**
Capital, authorised	ar-ra'smāl al-muṣarraḥ bihi	**الرأس مال المصرح به**

Capital, called up	ar-ra'smāl al-maṭlūb	الرأس مال المطلوب
Capital, circulation	ar-ra'smāl al-mutadāwal	الرأس مال المتداول
Capital, consumption	ar-ra'smāl al-istihlākī	الرأس مال الاستهلاكي
Capital, debenture	ra'smāl sanadāt	رأس مال سندات
Capital, declared	ar-ra'smāl al-mu'lan	الرأس مال المعلن
Capital, floating or unspecialised	ra'smal sā'ib	رأس مال سائب (غير مخصص أو مقيد)
Capital, free	ra'smāl ḥurr	رأس مال حـر
Capital, idle	ra'smāl 'āṭil	رأس مال عاطل
Capital, initial	ra'smāl mabda'ī	رأس مال مبدئي
Capital, issued	ra'smāl muṣdar	الرأس مال المصدر
Capital, long-term	ra'smāl ṭawīl al-ajal	رأس مال طويل الأجل
Capital, lucrative	ra'smāl murbiḥ	رأس مال مربح
Capital, marginal efficiency of	al-fa'āliya al-ḥaddiyya li'r-rāsmāl	الفعالية الحدية للرأس مال
Capital, marginal productivity of	al-intājiyya al-ḥaddiyya li'r-rasmāl	الانتاجية الحدية للرأس مال
Capital, nominal	ra'smāl ismī	رأس مال اسمي
Capital, outstanding	ra's māl ghayr muṣdar	رأس مال غير مصدر
Capital, rate of formation	nisbat takwīn ar-ra'smāl	نسبة تكوين الرأس مال
Capital, reduction	takhfīd ra'smāl	تخفيض رأس المال
Capital, registered	ar-ra'smāl al-musajjal	الرأس مال المسجَل
Capital, share	as-hum ra's al-māl	أسهم رأس المال
Capital, short-term	ra'smāl qaṣīr al-ajal	راس مال قصير الأجل
Capital, subscribed	ra'smāl muktatab bihi	رأس مال مكتتب به
Capital, sunk	ra'smāl maḥṣūr	رأس مال محصور
Capital, working	ra'smāl 'āmil	الرأس مال العامل(رأس مال التشغيل أو/الاستثمار)
Capitalisation	rasmala	رسملـة [تحويل إلى رأس مال أو تمويل]
Capitalisation unit	waḥdat at-taḥwīl ilā ra'smāl	وحدة التحويل الى رأس المال
Capitalise	yurasmil	يرسمـل [يحول إلى رأس مال]
Capitalised expense	maṣrūf murasmal	مصروف مرسمل [محول إلى رأس مال]
Capitalised leverage	arbāḥ murasmala	أرباح مرسملة [الارباح القابلة للتوزيع المضافة إلى الرأس مـال]
Capitalised surplus	al-fa'id al-muhawwal ila 'r-ra'smāl	الفائض المحول إلى الرأس مال
Capitalised value	al-qīma al-munasmala	القيمة المرسملة
Capitalism	ra'smāliyya	رأسمالية
Capitalist	1 ra'smālī	١ - رأس مالي
	2 mumawwil	٢ - ممّوَل
Captions	bunūd	بنـود (ابواب)
Card index	fahris al-biṭāqāt	فهرس الطاقات
Card ledger	sijill al-biṭāqāt	سجل البطاقات

Card of accounts	biṭāqat al-ḥisābāt	بطاقة الحسابات
Card time recorder	ālat tasjīl al-waqt	آلة تسجيل الوقت
Card, punched – system	ṭariqat al-biṭāqāt al-mathqubah	طريقة البطاقات المثقوبة
Cardex	nizam al-biṭāqāt	نظام البطاقات
Care of (c/o)	biwāsiṭat	بواسطة (بطرف)
Career	mihna	مهنـــة
Carriage charges (expenses)	maṣārīf an-naql	مصاريف النقل
Carriage forward	ujrat an-naql salafan	اجرة النقل سلفا
Carriage free	khaliṣ ujrat an-naql	خالص أجرة النقل
Carried forward	muraḥḥal limā ba'dahu	مرحل لما بعده (مدور)
Carried interest	al-fā'ida 'l-maḥmūla	الفائدة المحمولة
Carrier	nāqil	ناقــل (شركة نقل)
Carryback	khasāra murtaja'a	خسارة مرتجـعة [مبلغ صافي الخسارة الممكن تنقيصه من صافي دخل العامين السابقين]
Carry down	yunqal li-asfal	ينقل لأســفل
Carry on the books	yusajjal fi'd-dafātīr	يسجل في الدفاتر
Carry over	yudawwir	يـدوّر (يرحل)
Carrying charge	maṣārīf mutajaddida	مصاريف متجددة [تتعلق بالملكية وتقيد مصاريف جارية وتضاف أحيانا إلى قيمة الأصل]
Carry-over file; permanent file	al-malaff ad-dā'im	الملـف الدائـم
Cartel	takattul al-muntijīn	تكتل المنتجين
Cash (n.; v.)	naqd	نقد (صندوق ، خزينة ، فلوس ، دراهم)
Cash, to	yaqbiḍ	يقبــض
Cash account	ḥisāb aṣ-ṣundūq	حساب الصندوق
Cash advances	sulaf naqdiyya	سـلف نقديـة
Cash asset	amwal aṣ-ṣundūq	أموال الصندوق
Cash audit	murāja'a naqdiyya	مراجعة نقدية [مراجعة عمليات نقدية خلال مدة معينة]
Cash basis	al-asās an-naqdī	الأســاس النـقدى [طريقة تسجيل الايرادات والمصاريف فور استلامها ودفعها دون اعتبار المدة التي تشملها هذه المبالغ]
Cash book	daftar aṣ-ṣundūq	دفتـر الصندوق
Cash budget	taqdīr as-suyūla	تقديـر السيولة [تقدير مقبوضات ومدفوعات النقد خلال مدة معينة في المستقبل]
Cash count	jard an-naqdiyya	جـرد النقدية
Cash disbursement (C.D.)	madfū'āt naqdiyya	مدفوعات نقدية
Cash discount	khaṣm naqdī	خصم نقدى ـ لتعجيل الدفع
Cash dividend	arbāḥ naqdiyya	أرباح نقدية ـ عن الأسهم
Cash error account	az-ziyāda wa'n-naqṣ fi'ṣ-ṣundūq	الزيادة والنقص في الصندوق

Cash flow	as-suyūla an-naqdiyya	السيولة النقدية
Cash fund	aṣl naqdī	أصل نقــدى [قابل للتحويل إلى نقد بسهولة]
Cash in (at) bank	nuqūd mūda'a fi'l-bank	نقود مودعة في البنك
Cash in transit	naqd fi'ṭ-ṭarīq	نقـد في الطريق
Cash items	mufradāt naqdiyya	مفردات نقدية
Cash journal	yawmiyyat aṣ-ṣundūq	يومية الصندوق
Cash margin	at-ta'mīn an-naqdī	التأمين النقدى [مبلغ يحتجز في المصرف لضمان حرية تنفيذ عملية]
Cash offer	'arḍ fi'lī	عرض فعلي (حقيقي)
Cash on delivery (C.O.D.)	daf' 'inda 't-taslīm	دفع عند التسليم
Cash on hand	naqd fi 'ṣ-ṣundūq	نقد في الصندوق
Cash price	as-si'r naqdan	السعر نقـدا
Cash ratio	an-nisba 'n-naqdiyya	النسبة النقدية [معامل الأموال الموجودة (معامل الخزينة)]
Cash receipt	īṣāl naqdī	ايصال نقدى
Cash records	sijillāt an-naqd	سجلات النقد
Cash register	ālat tasjīl an-naqd	آلة تسجيل النقد
Cash reserve	iḥtiyāṭī naqdī	احتياطي نقدى
Cash revision	murāja'at aṣ-ṣundūq	مراجعة الصندوق
Cash sale	bay' naqdī	البيع النقدى
Cash surplus	fā'iḍ naqdī	الفائض النقدى
Cash surrender value	qīmat istirdād naqdī	قيمة استرداد نقدى ـ بوليصة تأمين على الحياة
Cash till	ṣundūq al-waḥdāt an-naqdiyya	صندوق الوحدات النقدية
Cash with order (C.W.O.)	ad-daf' 'inda 'ṭ-ṭalab	الدفع عند الطلب
Cash, counter – book	daftar muswaddat aṣ-ṣundūq	دفتر مسودة الصندوق
Cash, in	naqdan	نقــدا [عكس عينا]
Cash, petty	ḥisāb an-nathriyyāt	حساب النثريات
Cash, recovering – journal	daftar an-naqdiyya 'l-wārida	دفتر النقدية الواردة
Cashed cheque	shīk madfū' naqdan	شيك مدفوع نقدا
Cashier	amīn as-ṣundūq	أمين الصندوق
Cashing	ṣarf	صــرف
Cast (U.K.)	yajma'	يجــمع ـ أرقاما
Casual profit	ribḥ 'araḍī	ربح عرضي
Category	sharīḥa	شريحة (فئة ، باب ، صنف)
Ceiling price	al-ḥadd al-a'la li's-si'r	الحد الأعلى للسعر
Census	iḥṣā' as-sukkān	احصاء السكان
Cent, per (%)	bi 'l-mi'a	بالمئــة
Centre	markaz	مركز (مقر)
Central bank	al-maṣraf al-markazī	المصرف المركزى

Central reserve system	niẓām markāziyyat al-iḥtiyāṭī	**نظام مركزية الاحتياطي** [نظام ايداع احتياطي المصارف في البنك المركزى]
Central risk	markaziyyat al-makhāṭir al-masrafiyq	**مركزية المخاطر المصرفية** [تجميع كل الالتزامات على العميل لدى المصارف عن طريق إدارة المصرف المركزى بهدف تزويد المصارف باجمالي مخاطر كل عميل على حدة]
Centralisation	al-markaza	**المركـــزة**
Centralisation of authority	markaziyyat as-sulṭa	**مركزية السلطة**
Centralism	al-markaziyya	**المركـــزية**
Certificate	shahāda	**شـــهادة**
Certificate of deposit	shahādat īdā‘	**شهادة ايداع**
Certificate of discharge	shahādat khuluww ṭaraf	**شهادة خلو طرف**
Certificate of incorporation	rukhṣat ta’sīs sharika	**رخصة تأسيس شركة**
Certificate of indebtedness	shahādat ithbāt dayn	**شهادة اثبات دين**
Certificate of origin	shahādat mansha’	**شهادة منشأ**
Certificate of quality	shahāda naw‘iyya	**شهادة نوعيـــة**
Certificate of quantity	shahādat kammiyya	**شهادة كميـــة**
Certificate of registration of mortgage	ṣakk tasjīl rahn	**صك تسجيل رهن**
Certificate of shipment	wathīqat shaḥn	**وثيقة شـــحن**
Certificate, bankrupt's	wathīqat ṣulḥ iflās	**وثيقة صلح افلاس** (صك مصالحة)
Certificate, mill's	rukhṣat maṣna‘	**رخصة مصنع**
Certificate, registered	sanad ismī	**ســـند اســـمي**
Certificate, share	ṣakk bi-sahm	**صك بسهم** (سند بسهم)
Certified	mu‘tamad	**معتمد** (مجاز ، حامل شهادة)
Certified cheque	shīk muṣaddaq	**شيك مصدق** (معتمد من البنك)
Certified public accountant, C.P.A. (U.S.A.)	muḥāsib qānūnī mu‘tamad	**محاسب قانوني معتمد**
Certify	yuṣaddiq ‘ala	**يصدق على** (يوثق ، يضمن ، يشهد)
Certifying officer	al-mas’ūl‘an at-taṣdīq	**المسؤول عن التصديق**
Cession of property	tanāzul ‘an milkiyya	**تنازل عن ملكية**
Chairman	ra’īs	**رئيـــس**
Chairman of the board	ra’īs majlis idāra	**رئيس مجلس الادارة**
Chain discount	silsilat khuṣūmāt tijāriyya	**سلسلة خصومات تجارية**
Chamber of commerce	ghurfat at-tijāra	**غرفة التجارة**
Chancellor of the Exchequer (U.K.)	wazīr al-maliyya fī biriṭānya	**وزير المالية في بريطانيا**
Change	‘umla ṣaghīra	**عملة صغيرة** (فكّة ، صرافة)
Change of ownership	naql milkiyya	**نقل ملكية** (تغيير المالك)
Channel	majrā	**مجرى** (طريق التسلسل)
Channel discount	khaṣm tasalsul	**خصم تسلسل** [الخصم الممنوح على المبيعات للمؤسسات الحكومية أولمن يتمم صنع المنتوجات المباعة]

Channelling	tawzīʻ	توزيع (تحويل ، توجيه)
Charge (n.; v.)	nafaqa	نفقة (رسم) ـ يقيد على
Charge account	ḥisāb al-ʻamīl	حساب العميــل
Charge off	yuʻdim	يعــدم (يعامل كخسارة)
Charge and discharge statement	bayān ar-ra'smāl wa'd-dakhl	بيان الرأسمال والدخل
		[بيان موجز يبين الرأس مال والدخل بغرض اعطاء تقرير نهائى أو مؤقت عنهما]
Chargeable expenses	al-maṣrūfāt at-taḥmīliyya	المصروفات التحميلية
Chargee	dā'in mumtāz	دائـن ممتــاز
Charm price	siʻr ighrā'	سعــر اغــراء
		[السعر الذى ينقص جزؤه العشرى عن الدولار وينتهى بتسعة أو أى رقم قريب يلفت النظر مثال ٣,٩٨ ، ٤,٩٥]
Chart	rasm bayānī	رسم بياني (بيان ، جدول)
Chart for attributes	munḥana 'n-nawʻiyya	منحنى النوعيــة
		[نوع من المنحنى الاحصائي يستعمل لتحليل نوعية الانتاج]
Chart of accounts	jadwal taṣnif al-ḥisābāt	جدول تصنيف الحسابات
Charter (n.; v.)	rukhṣa	رخصة (براءة) ـ يستأجر
Chartered accountant	muḥāsib qānūnī	محاسب قانونــي
Chartered company	sharika mumtāza	شــركة ممتازة
		[شركة مرخص لها من مجلس الشعب ـ البرلمان]
Chartered parties	al-mutaʻāqidūn	المتعاقــدون
Chattels	amwāl manqūla	أموال منقولة
Check (n.; v.)	1 murājaʻa	١ - مراجعة (تدقيق)
	2 Yatahaqqaq	٢ - يتحقق من (يراجع)
Check against	muṭābaqa	مطابقة (مقابلة)
Check cut-offs	murājaʻat fatrat al-qaṭʻ	مراجعة فترة القطع
		[مراجعة قيود لفترة سابقة ولاحقة لتاريخ معيــن]
Check figure	raqm qiyāsī	رقم قياسي
		[رقم مشتق من رقم آخر ويمثله ويستعمل في التحقيق في العمليات الحسابية]
Check register	sijill ash-shīkāt al-muṣdara	سجل الشيكات المصدرة
Check up	yudaqqiq	يــدقق (يراجع) حساباً
Cheque	shīk	شيــك
Cheque to bearer	shīk li-ḥāmilihi	شيك لحاملة
Cheque to order	shīk li-amr	شيــك لأمــر
Cheque without funds	shīk duna raṣīd	شيك دون رصيد
Cheque, crossed	shīk musaṭṭar	شيك مسطّر
Cheque, dishonoured	shīk marfūd	شيك مرفوض
Cheque, open	shīk ʻādī	شيك عادى (غير مسطّر)

Cheque, stale	shīk mutaqādim	شيـك متقـادم
Cheque, stopped	shīk mujammad	شيـــك مجمّد
Cheque, traveller's	shīk siyāḥi	شيك سياحي
Chief accountant	ra'īs muḥāsaba	رئيس محاسبة
Chief creditor	ad-dā'in al-awwal	الدائـــن الأول
Chose	ḥuqūq i'tibāriyya	حقوق اعتبارية
Choses in action	1 ḥaqq mutanāza' fīh 2 amwāl manqūla waduyūn	١ - حق متنازع فيه ٢ - أموال منقولة وديون
Chronological	mu'arrakh bi-ḥasab at-tasalsul az-zamanī	مؤرخ بحسب التسلسل الزمني
C and F	c and f	ســـي آنـد اف [سعر البضاعة مضافا إليه أجور الشحن حتى ميناء الوصول المحددة]
C.I.F.	sīf	ســـيف [التكلفة والتأمين واجرة الشحن]
Circles, exchange	awsāṭ al-burṣa	أوساط البورصة
Circular	nashra dawriyya	نشرة دوريـــة
Circular letter of credit	kitāb i'timād dawrī	كتاب اعتماد دورى
Circularisation	tathbīt	تثبيت (عملية ارسال كتب تثبيت للذمم المدينة والدائنة)
Circulating assets (U.K.)	mawjūdāt mutadāwala	موجودات متداولة
Circulating capital	ra's-māl mutadāwal	رأس مال متداول
Circulation	tadāwul	تـــداول
Circulation of costs	tawzi' furūq at-takālīf	توزيع فروق التكاليف [طريقة توزيع فروق التكاليف بين التكلفة الثابتة والفعلية على المنتجات أو الاعمال التي نتجت عنها تلك الفروق]
Circulation of shares	tadāwul al-as-hum	تداول الأسهم
Claim	muṭālaba	مطالبة (ادعاء ، طلب)
Class interval	ar-raqm al-ladhī yushakkil zumra fi't-tawzī' at-takrārī	الرقم الذي يشكل زمرة في التوزيع التكراري
Classification	taṣnīf	تصنيـــف
Classification of accounts	taṣnīf al-ḥisābāt	تصنيـــف الحسابات
Classified trial balance	mīzān al-murāja'a 'l-muṣannaf	ميزان المراجعة المصنف
Classify	yuṣannif	يصنـــف
Clause	madda	مـــادة (بند ، فقرة)
Claused bill of lading	būlīṣat shaḥn bi-taḥaffuẓāt	بوليصة شحن بتحفظات
Clause of rejection	sharṭ fāsikh	شرط فاسخ
Clause, valeur given	sharṭ al-qīma 'l-muqaddara	شرط القيمة المقدرة
Clean bill of exchange	kumbiyāla naẓīfa	كمبيالة نظيفة [ليس عليها أى اشارة إلى مستندات]

Clean bill of lading	būlīṣat shaḥn naẓīfa	**بوليصة شحن نظيفة** [ليس فيها أية اشارة إلى عيب في البضاعة المشحونة]
Clean certificate	shahāda naẓīfa	**شهادة نظيفة** [تدل على خلو البضاعة من العيوب في الشحن]
Clean credit	i'timād naẓīf	**اعتماد نظيف** [اعتماد قبول كمبيالات دون ارفاقها بمستندات]
Clean draft	tasdīd 'ādī	تسديد عادى ـ للسند التجارى
Clean receipt	īṣāl dūna taḥaffuẓ	ايصال دون تحفظ
Clear a bill	yastabdil kumbiyāla bi-nuqūd	يستبدل كمبيالة بنقود
Clear an account	yusaddid ḥisāban	يسدد حسابا
Clear loss	khasāra wāḍiḥa	خسارة واضحة (لا تعوض)
Clear off a mortgage	yuḥarrir ar-rahn	يحرر الرهن
Clear profit	ribḥ ṣāfī	ربح صافي
Clearance	1 tasāmuḥ	١ - تسامح ـ بمبلغ
	2 fakk ar-rahn	٢ - فك الرهن
	3 muqāṣṣah	٣ - مقاصّة
Clearance sale	tanzīlat	تنزيلات (تصفية)
Clearing	taṣfiyat ḥisābāt	تصفية حسابات (تبرئة ذمة)
Clearing account	ḥisāb al-muqāṣṣa	حساب المقاصّة
Clearing house	ghurfat al-muqāṣṣa	غرفة المقاصّة
Clearing house statement	bayān ghurfat al-muqāṣṣa	بيان غرفة المقاصّة
Clearing office	maktab at-taṣfiya	مكتب التصفية
Clearing payment	daf'at al-muqāṣṣa	دفعة المقاصّة
Clearing sheet	ṣakk al-muqāṣṣa	صك المقاصّة
Clerical error	khaṭa' kitābī	خطأ كتابي [قيد غير صحيح]
Client	'amīl	عميل (زبون)
Clock card	biṭāqat ḥuḍūr	بطاقة حضور (يطبع عليها الوقت)
Clocking off	mi'ād intihā'	ميعاد انتهاء
Clocking on	mi'ād al-bad'	ميعاد البدء
Close	1 yuqfil	١ - يقفل ـ حسابا أو محلا تجاريا
	2 yaḍa' ḥaddan li's-si'r	٢ - يضع حدا للسعر ـ في البورصة
Close an account	yuqfil ḥisāban	يقفل حسابا
Closed corporation	sharika muqfala	شركة مقفلة
Close out (U.S.)	bay' taṣfiya	بيع تصفية (بسعر مخفض)
Closed account	ḥisāb muqfal	حساب مقفل
Closed end investment company	sharikat istithmār li-'adad maḥdūd min al-musāhimīn	شركة استثمار لعدد محدود من المساهمين
Closed mortgage (or bonds)	rahn bi ḥad aqsa	رهن بحد أقصى
Closing	iqfāl	اقفال (اغلاق أو اختتام)

Closing balance	raṣīd al-iqfāl	رصيد الاقفال (آخر المدة)
Closing date	tārīkh al-iqfāl	تاريخ الاقفال
Closing entry	qayd iqfāl	قيد اقفال
Closing price	si'r al-iqfāl	سعر الاقفال
Closing stock	biḍā'at al-iqfāl	بضاعة الاقفال (آخر المدة)
Closing the books	iqfāl ad-dafātir	اقفال الدفاتر
Closing trial balance	mīzan al-murāja'a 'l-khitāmī	ميزان المراجعة الختامي
C.O.D. (cash on delivery)	ad-daf' 'inda 'l-istilām	الدفع عند الاستلام
Code (n.; v.)	1 ramz	١ - رمز (اشارة) ـ يرمز (يضع رمزا)
	2 dalīl ar-rumūz	٢ - دليل الرموز
Code number	raqm tarmīz	رقم ترميز
Coded	murammaz	مرمز
Coefficient	mu'āmil	معامل
Coffer	sundūq ḥadīdī	صندوق حديدى
Coinsurance clause	band ta'mīn mushtarak	بند تأمين مشترك [بند تحديد نسبة الخسارة في التأمين]
Collapse in price	tadahwur al-as'ār	تدهور الأسعار
Collate	yujammi'	يجمع ـ عناصر مسألة أو قضية
Collateral	ḍamān	ضمان [ملك مرهون كضمان دين]
Collateral on a loan	ḍamān 'ala qârḍ	ضمانة على قرض
Collateral security	ḍamān iḍāfī	ضمان اضافي
Collateral trust bonds	sanadāt maḍmūna	سندات مضمونة بسندات أخرى
Collateralise	yaḍman daynan bi'r-rahn	يضمن دينا بالرهن
Collectibility	qābiliyyat at-taḥṣīl	قابلية التحصيل
Collecting charges	maṣārif at-taḥṣīl	مصاريف التحصيل
Collection items	awrāq bi-rasm at-taḥṣīl	أوراق برسم التحصيل
Collective action	'amal jamā'ī	عمل جماعي
Collective agreements	ittifāqiyya jamā'iyya	اتفاقية جماعية
Collective bargaining	musāwama jamā'iyya	مساومة جماعية
Collective bonus	mukāfa'a jamā'iyya	مكافأة جماعية
Collision insurance	ta'mīn ḍidd at-taṣādum	تأمين ضد التصادم
Column	'āmūd	عامود ـ في سجل الحسابات
Columnar journal	yawmiyya dhāt a'mida	يومية ذات أعمدة
Columnar system	niẓām al-a'mida 'l-muta'addida	نظام الأعمدة المتعددة
Collusion	tawāṭu'	تواطؤ
Combination	takattul	تكتل [اتفاقية تجمع شركتين أو أكثر لمنافع متبادلة]
Combine (U.S.)	ittiḥād	اتحاد (مجموعة شركات)
Combined depreciation and-upkeep method	ṭarīqat jam'al-istihlāk wa'ṣ-ṣiyāna	طريقة جمع الاستهلاك والصيانة
Combined financial statement	bayānāt ḥisābiyya mujamma'a	بيانات حسابية مجمعة
Commandité (Fr.)	shariket tawṣiya	شركة توصية

Commandité partner (Fr.)	sharīk muwaṣṣī	شريك موصّي
Commandité, société en (Fr.)	sharikat tawṣiya	شركة توصية
Commerce	1 tijāra	١ - تجـــارة
	2 ʿamal tijārī	٢ - عمل تجارى
Commercial	tijārī	تجـــارى
Commercial book	daftar tijārī	دفتر تجارى
Commercial branch	farʿ tijārī	فرع تجارى
Commercial case	daʿwa tijāriyya	دعوى تجارية
Commercial cost	at-taklifa ʾt-tijāriyya	التكلفة التجارية [الكلفة العامة لتشغيل مشروع تجارى]
Commercial debt	dayn tijārī	دين تجارى
Commercial director	mudīr tijārī	مدير تجارى
Commercial law	qānūn tijārī	قانون تجارى
Commercial paper	waraqa tijāriyya	ورقة تجارية ـ قابلة للتداول
Commercial practice	ʿurf tijārī	عـرف تجـــارى
Commercial register	sijill tijārī	سجل تجارى
Commercial representative	mumaththil tijārī	ممثل تجارى
Commercial treaty	muʿāhada tijāriyya	معاهدة تجارية
Commission	ʿumūla	عمـــولة
Commission agent	wakil bi'l-ʿumūla	وكيل بالعمولة
Commissioner	wakīl tijārī	وكيل تجارى
Commitment	iltizām	التزام (تعهد ، ارتباط)
Committee	lajna	لجنــــة
Committee of inspection	lajnat murāqabat ad-dāʾinīn	لجنة مراقبة الدائنين
Committee, auditing	lajnat murāqabat al-ḥisābāt	لجنة مراقبة الحسابات
Commodity	silʿa	سلعة (بضاعة)
Commodity credit	iʿtimād tijārī	اعتماد تجارى
Commidity exchange	burṣat al-baḍāʾiʿ	بورصة البضائع
Commodity, staple	muntajāt asāsiyya	منتجات أساسية
Common average	1 muʿaddal basīṭ	١ - معدل بسيط
	2 muʾaddal khaṣṣ	٢ - معدل خاص
Common cost	taklifa mushtaraka	تكلفة مشتركة
Common due date	tārīkh istiḥqāq mushtarak	تاريخ استحقاق مشترك
Common interests	maṣāliḥ mushtaraka	مصالح مشتركة
Common law	al-qānūn al-ʿāmm	القانون العام [قانون العرف والعادة]
Common law corporation	sharika musāhama ʿurfiyya	شركة مساهمة عرفية [تعمل بدون سلطة حكومية رسمية]
Common law trust	sharika iḥtikāriyya	شركة احتكارية
Common share	sahm ʿādī	سهم عادى
Common stock	sahm ʿādī	سهم عادى
Communication	ittiṣāl	اتصال (ابلاغ ، اعلام)

Community of interest	ta nasīq maṣāliḥ	تنسيق المصالح [التنسيق بين مصالح وعمليات مؤسستين أو أكثر بوسائل لا تصل إلى الرقابة الفعلية]
Community property	mulk mushtarak	ملك مشترك ـ بين الزوج والزوجة
Companies Act	qānūn ash-sharikāt	قانون الشركات
Companies articles	anẓimat ash-sharikāt	أنظمة الشركات
Companies, trust	ash-sharikāt al-muwaḥḥada	الشركات الموحدة
Company	sharika	شركـــة
Company contract	ʿaqd ash-sharika	عقد الشركة
Company promoter	mu'assis ash-sharika	مؤسس الشركة
Conpany, finance	sharika māliyya	شركة مالية
Company, holding	sharika qābiḍa	شركة قابضة
Company, joint stock	sharika musāhama taḍāmuniyya	شركة مساهمة تضامنية
Company, limited liability	sharika musāhama maḥdūda	شركة مساهمة محدودة
Company, private limited	sharika khāṣṣa dhāt mas'ūliyya maḥdūda	شركة خاصة ذات مسؤولية محدودة
Company, public	sharika ʿāmma	شركة مساهمة (شركة عامة)
Company, real estate	sharika ʿaqāriyya	شركة عقارية
Company, statutory	sharika ṣaḥibat imtiyāz	شركة صاحبة امتياز
Comparability	qābiliyyat al-muqārana	قابلية المقارنة
Comparative	muqāran	مقارن (قياسي)
Comparative balance sheets	mīzāniyyāt muqārana	ميزانيات مقارنة
Comparative cost	taklifa muqārana	تكلفة مقارنة
Comparative statement	bayān muqāran	بيان مقارن
Compensate	yuʿawwiḍ	يعـّوض
Compensation	taʿwīḍ	تعويـض
Compensation of damage	taʿwīḍ 'an at-talaf	تعويض عن التلف
Compensatory balance	ar-raṣīd al-mujzī	الرصيد المجزى [الحد الأدنى لرصيد حساب العميل الجارى والمساوى لنسبة مئوية متفق عليها من القرض الممنوح لذلك العميل]
Compete for	yatanāfas ʿala	يتنافس على
Competence	jadāra	جدارة (صلاحية ، اختصاص)
Competent	kuf'	كفـؤ (مختص ، جدير)
Competent authority	al-sulṭa 'l-mukhtaṣṣa	السلطة المختصة
Competition	munafasa	منافسة (مزاحمة)
Competitive price	siʿr tanāfusī	سعر تنافسي
Competitor	munāfis	منافـس
Compilation	jamʿal-bayānāt	جمع البيانات
Compilation of audit data, principles for	mabādi' jamʿ al-maʿlūmāt li-aghrāḍ at-tadqīq	مبادىء جمع المعلومات لأغراض التدقيق
Compile	yajmaʿ	يجمع (ينسق ، يصنف)
Complaint	shakwā	شكـوى

Complementary	takmīlī	تكميلي (ملحق ، متمم)
Complete audit	murāja'a kāmila	مراجعة كاملة
Complete payment (v.)	yusaddid ar-raṣīd	يسدد الرصيد
Completed transaction	'amaliyya muntahiya	عملية منتهية
Complex	murakkab	مركب (معقد ، مشبك)
Complex number	raqam murakkab	رقم مركب
Complexity	ta'qīd	تعقيد
Comply	yuṭābiq	يطابق (يماثل)
Component	'unṣur	عنصر (جزء)
Component budget (U.S.)	al-mīzāniyya 'l-asāsiyya	الميزانية الأساسية
Compose	yu'allif	يؤلف (يشكل)
Composite	murakkab	مركب
Composite life method (of depreciation)	ṭarīqat al-istihlāk al-murakkaba	طريقة الاستهلاك المركبة [الاستهلاك المحسوب على أساس استهلاك اصول ثابتة معتبرة ككل بنسبة المتوسط القياسي]
Composite policy	'aqd ta'mīn mushtarik bi'l-arbāḥ	عقد تأمين مشترك بالأرباح
Composite rate of depreciation	mu'addal al-istihlāk al-murakkab	معدل الاستهلاك المركب
Composition	1 taswiya	١ - تسوية (اتفاق)
	2 ṣulḥ al-muflis ma'a dā'inīh	٢ - صلح المفلس مع دائنيه
Composition tax	ḍarība thābita	ضريبة ثابتة
Compound	yuṣāliḥ	يصالح [يتفق على تسوية دين وديا]
Compound amount	mablagh murakkab	مبلغ مركب
Compound discount	khaṣm murakkab	خصم مركب
Compound interest	fā'ida murakkaba	فائدة مركبة
Compound journal entry	qayd yawmiyya murakkab	قيد يومية مركب [مؤلف من عدة عمليات]
Compound ratio	nisba murakkaba	النسبة المركبة
Compounding with creditors	muṣālaḥa ma' ad-dā'inīn	المصالحة مع الدائنين [الاتفاق بين المدين والدائنين على قبول جزء
	yastāmil nizam al-computer	من ديونهم]
Comprise	yushakkil	يشكل (يشمل ، يحتوى على)
Compromise	ḥull wasaṭ	حل وسط (تسوية)
Comptroller (controller)	murāqib mālī	مراقب مالي
Comptroller (controller) general	murāqib al-ḥisābat al-'āmm	مراقب الحسابات العام
Computation	iḥtisāb	احتساب (تقدير)
Compute	yaḥtasib	يحتسب
Computer	'aql iliktrūnī	العقل الالكتروني [آلة حاسبة اليكترونية]
Computerise	yastāmil nizam al-computer	يستعمل نظام الكمبيوتر
Concentration	tarkīz	تركيز (تكثيف)
Concentration of authority	tarkīz as-sulṭa	تركيز السلطة

Concept	mafhūm	مفهــوم (تصور)
Concern	wiḥda iqtiṣādiyya	وحدة اقتصادية (عمل تجارى مثلا)
Concern, going	al-estimrarīyah	الاستمرارية ، مبدأ محاسبي
Concession	1 imtyāz	١ - امتياز (رخصة ، تصريح)
	2 ṭakhfīḍ	٢ - تخفيض ـ ضرائب
Concession companies	sharikāt al-imtiyāz	شركات الامتياز
Concession rights	ḥuqūq al-imtiyāz	حقوق الامتياز
Concessionaire	ṣāhib al-imtiyāz	صاحب الامتياز
Concessionary	ṣāḥib imtiyāz	صاحب امتياز
Conciliation	muṣālaḥa	مصالحــة
Conclude	yakhtim	يختــم
Conclusion	natīja	نتيجة (ختام ، نهاية)
Conclusive	nihā'ī	نهائي (حاسم ، قطعي)
Condemn	yuṣādir	يصادر (للمصلحة العامة)
Condensed balance sheet	al-mīzāniyya 'l-mukaththafa	الميزانية المكثفة
		[الميزانية التي تدمج فيها البنود غير الأساسية حتى تسهل معرفة الوضع المالى]
Condition	1 sharṭ	١ - شــرط
	2 ḥāla	٢ - حالـة (ظرف)
Conditional acceptance	qabūl mashrūṭ	قبول مشروط
Conference	mu'tamar	مؤتمــر
Confidential	sirrī	ســرى
Confirm	yu'akkīd	يؤكــد (يثبت)
Confirmation	1 ta'kīd	١ - تأكيــد
	2 tathbīt	٢ - تثبيــت
Confirmation letter	kitab tathbīt	كتاب تثبيت
Confirmed banker's credit	i'timād maṣrafī muthbat	اعتماد مصرفي مثبت
Confirmed credit	i'timād mu'azzaz	اعتماد معزز (مثبت)
Confirmed letter of credit	kitāb i'timād muthbat	كتاب اعتماد مثبت
Confiscate	yuṣādir	يصــادر
Confiscation	muṣādara	مصــادرة
Conflict	yu'āriḍ	يعــارض
Conform	yuṭābiq	يطابق (يوافق)
Conformity, in – with the articles	wifqan li'n-niẓām	وفقا للنظام
Connections, business	'alāqat tijāriyya	علاقات تجارية
Consecutive	mutalāḥiq	متلاحق (متتالي)
Consensual contract	'aqd bi't-tarāḍī	عقد بالتراضي
Consensus	ijmā' ar-ra'y	اجماع الرأى
Consent (n.; v.)	muwāfaqa	موافقة (قبول) ـ يوافق (يقبل)
Consequential loss (insurance)	khasāra ghayr mubāshira	الخسارة غير المباشرة
		[الناتجة عن النار أو أى خطر مؤمن ضده]
Conservative estimate	taqdīr mutaḥaffiẓ	تقدير متحفظ
Conservatory procedure	ijrā' taḥaffuẓī	اجراء تحفظي

Consideration	dāfi' al-maṣlaḥa	**دافع المصلحة** [الذى دعا الفريق المتعاقد لابرام العقد وتكون على شكل وعد أو القيام بعمل أو الامتناع عن عمل]
Consign	yūdi'	**يودع ـ بضاعة برسم الأمانة**
Consignation	īdā'	**ايداع ـ بضاعة برسم الأمانة**
Consignee	muda' ladayhi	**المودع لديه**
Consignment	irsāliyyat biḍā'a	**ارسالية بضاعة** (شحنة)
Consignment account	hisāb biḍā'at al-amāna	**حساب بضاعة الأمانة**
Consignment, on	bi-rasm al-amāna	**برسم الأمانة**
Consignor (er)	mūdi'	**المـــودع**
Consistency	al-momathalah	**المماثلة** (انتظام ، ثبات) **مبدأ محاسبى**
Consistent buying	mushtarayāt motamathelah	**مشتريات متماثلة**
Consolidate	yuwaḥhid	**يوحد** (يدمج)
Consolidated account	ḥisāb muwaḥḥad	**حساب موحد**
Consolidated annuities	mawārid muwahhada	**موارد موحدة**
Consolidated balance sheet	mizāniyya muwaḥḥada	**ميزانية موحدة**
Consolidated financial statement	bayānat ḥisābiyya muwaḥḥada	**بيانات حسابية موحدة**
Consolidated goodwill	shuhra muda'ama	**الشهرة المدعمة** [ذلك الجزء من المبلغ الذى تدفعه الشركة الام مقابل استثمارها في شركة فرعية بالنظر إلى مقدرة تلك الشركة الفائقة على تحقيق الربح أو أى قيمة اخرى لا تسجل في دفاتر الشركة الفرعية]
Consolidated group	majmū'at sharikāt muwaḥḥadat al-mīzāniyya	**مجموعة شركات موحدة الميزانية**
Consolidated income statement	bayān ad-dakhl al-muwaḥḥad	**بيان الدخل الموحد** [لمشروع أو أكثر كوحدة اقتصادية واحدة]
Consolidated net earnings	ṣāfi'd-dakh al-muwaḥḥad	**صافي الدخل الموحد**
Consolidated surplus	fā'iḍ muwaḥḥad	**الفائض الموحد**
Consolidating financial statement	tawḥīd al-bayānat al-ḥisābiyya	**توحيد البيانات الحسابية** [ورقة عمل تظهر التفاصيل التي تدخل في البيان المالي الموحد]
Consolidation	1 tawḥīd	**١ - توحيد ـ شركتين أو أكثر**
	2 i'dād mīzāniyya muwaḥḥada	**٢ - اعداد ميزانية موحدة**
	3 wiḥda	**٣ - وحدة ـ من مجموعة مؤسسات**
Consols	amwāl maḍmūna	**أموال مضمونة ـ سندات دين الحكومة البريطانية**
Consortium	majmū'a	**مجموعـــة** [اتحاد مالي بين بعض المؤسسات المالية الكبرى لتحويل مشروعات تحتاج إلى رساميل ضخمة]
Constant cost	taklifa thābita	**تكلفة ثابتة**
Constituent	ta'sīsī	**تأسيسي** (مقوم)

Constituent assembly	majlis ta'sīsī	مجلس تأسيسي
Constituent company	sharika mukawwana	شركة مكونة
Constitute	yukawwin	يكون (يؤلف ، يشكل)
Constitution	qānūn asāsī	قانون أساسي (دستور)
Constitutional	qānūnī	قانوني (دستورى)
Construction	inshā'	انشــاء
Construction in progress	inshā' qayd al-injā	انشاء قيد الانجاز
Consular invoice	fātūra qunṣuliyya	فاتورة قنصلية [فاتورة تغطي بضائع مشحونة من بلد لآخر حسب نموذج معين تتطلبة البلد المشحونة إليها البضاعة ومصادق عليها من قبل موظف قنصلي مسؤول يعمل في البلد المصدر]
Consult	yastashīr	يستشير (يشاور ، يراجع)
Consultant	mustashār	مستشــار
Consultation	istishāra	استشــارة
Consultative	istishārī	استشــارى
Consume	yastahlik	يستهــلك
Consumer	mustahlik	مستهــلك
Consumer's co-operative societies	jam'iyya istihlākiyya ta'āwuniyya	جمعية استهلاكية تعاونية
Consumer credit	'i'timān istihlākī	الائتمان الاستهلاكي [القروض المصرفية الممنوحة لشراء السلع الاستهلاكية]
Consumer goods	baḍā'i' istihlākiyya	بضائع استهلاكية
Consumer industries	ṣinā'āt istihlākiyya	صناعات استهلاكية
Consumer price index	dalīl as'ār al-mustahlik	دليل أسعار المستهلك
Consumption credit	taslīf li'l-istihlāk	تسليف للاستهلاك
Contango	gharāmat ta'jīl	غرامة تأجيل [الفائدة أو النفقات الاخرى التي يدفعها المضارب لتأخره في استلام أو دفع قيمة الأسهم التي اشتراها بانتظار ارتفاع أسعارها]
Contents	muḥtawayāt	محتويــات
Contents of a bill of exchange	qīmat al-kumbiyāla	قيمة الكمبيالة
Contest (n.; v.)	yatanāza'	يتنازع - على دين قضية متنازع عليها
Contingency	ṭāri'	طــارىء
Contingency fund	ṣundūq aṭ-ṭawāri'	صندوق الطوارىء
Contingent annuity	daf'a dawriyya ṭari'a	دفعة دورية طارئة
Contingent asset	aṣl mashrūṭ	أصل مشروط
Contingent charge (or cost)	nafaqa mashrūṭa	نفقة (أو كلفة) مشروطة
Contingent liability	iltizām ṭāri'	التزام طارىء
Contingent on	1 iḥtiyāṭan li 2 ma' at-taḥaffuẓ	١ - احتياطا لـ ٢ - مع التحفظ

Contingent profit	ribḥ iḥtimālī	**ربح احتمالي** [ربح يعتمد تحقيقة على حدث غير مؤكد في المستقبل]
Contingent reserve	iḥtiyāṭī lil-ṭawāri'	**احتياطي للطوارىء**
Continuing appropriation	takhṣīs mudawwar	**تخصيص مدوّر** [تخصيص ينتقل رصيدة إلى السنة المالية الجديدة وبعدها يعتمد للصرف]
Continuity concept	mafhūm al-istimrāriyya	**مفهوم الاستمرارية** [افتراض استمرارية وحدة اقتصادية في جميع الظروف العتيادية]
Continuous audit	at-tadqīq al-mustamirr	**التدقيق المستمر**
Continuous inventory	al-jard al-mustamirr	**الجرد المستمر** [فحص الموجودات والتأكد من مساواة العدد الفعلي أو الوزن أو القياس الموجود فعلا وما يظهر على بطاقات الجرد]
Contra account	ḥisāb lahu muqābil	**حساب له مقابل**
Contra, as per	bi'l-muqābil	**بالمقابل** (بدلا من)
Contra charge	qayd lahu muqābil	**قيد له مقابل**
Contra entry	band ḥisāb bi-muqābil	**بند حساب بمقابل**
Contraband	1 tahrīb	**١ - تهريب**
	2 sil'a muharraba	**٢ - سلع مهربة**
Contract (n.; v.)	'aqd	**عقد - يتعاقد**
Contract a debt	yaqtariḍ	**يقترض** (يستدين)
Contracts authorisation	tafwīḍ bi-'aqd	**تفويض بعقد**
Contract of employment	'aqd istikhdām	**عقد استخدام**
Contract price	si'r al-'aqd	**سعر العقد** [السعر المنصوص عنه في عقد البيع أو الشراء]
Contracting parties	al-aṭrāf al-muta'āqida	**الأطراف المتعاقدة**
Contractor (er)	muqāwil	**مقاول** (متعهد)
Contradict	yunāqiḍ	**يناقض**
Contradiction	tanaquḍ	**تناقض**
Contrary	'ala 'aks	**على عكس**
Contribute	yus-him	**يسهم**
Contributed capital	ra's-māl musāham bihi	**الرأسمال المساهم به**
Contributed surplus	al-fā'iḍ al-madfū'	**الفائض المدفوع**
Contribution	1 hiba	**١ - هبة**
	2 musāhama	**٢ - مساهمة - بنفقات أو بمعدل خسارة**
	3 mablagh al-iktitāb bi-ashum	**٣ - مبلغ الاكتتاب بأسهم**
	4 manfa'a	**٤ - منفعة**
Contribution margin	'ā'id al-musāhama	**عائد المساهمة** (العائد الحدى) [الفرق بين قيمة المبيعات والتكاليف المتغيرة للمبيعات]

Contribution theory	naẓariyyat al-ishām	**نظرية الاسهام** [النظرية القائلة بأن بيع السلع والخدمات يكون مصدرها متفاوتا للتمويل وتدفع منه النفقات الرأسية وغيرها من النفقات]
Contributory insurance scheme	ta'mīnāt ijtimā'iyya	**تأمينات اجتماعية**
Control	1 ḍabṭ	**١ - ضبـــط**
	2 ḥālat at-tawāzun	**٢ - حالة التوازن** [حين تكون الانحرافات عن المعدل الاحصائي المعتاد ذات طبيعة عشوائية ودون سبب يمكن أن تعزى إليه]
	3 as-sayṭara	**٣ - السيطرة** [على اختيار أغلبية أعضاء مجلس الادارة لمؤسسة]
	4 aḍ-ḍabṭ ad-dākhilī	**٤ - الضبط الداخلي**
Control account	ḥisāb ḍabṭ	**حسـاب ضبـط** [حساب يشتمل بصورة أولية على اجمالي نوع أو أكثر من العمليات تظهر تفاصيلها في دفتر الاستاذ الفرعي]
Control chart	rasm riqāba bayānī	**رسم رقابة بياني**
Control techniques	funūn ar-riqāba	**فنون الرقابة** (أساليب الرقابة)
Controllable cost	takāliridiyya	**تكاليف ارادية** [يمكن التحكم بها من قبل الادارة]
Controllable cost variance	inḥirāf takālīf irādī	**انحراف تكاليف ارادي** [يمكن تحميل المسؤولية الاولى فيه على شخص معين]
Controlled company	sharika tabi'a	**شركات تابعة ـ لمراقبة شركة أم**
Controlled economy	iqtiṣād muwajjah	**اقتصاد موجّه**
Controller	murāqib	**مراقب حالي**
Controlling company	sharika mālika	**شركة مالكة ـ لشركة أخرى أو أكثر**
Controlling-company accounting	ṭarīqat muḥasabat ash-sharika '-mālika	**طريقة محاسبة الشركة المالكة** [الطريقة التي تتبعها الشركة الأم في قيد استثمارها وعملياتها مع الشركة الفرعية]
Controversy	jidāl	**جدال** (خلاف ، نزاع)
Convention	ittifaq	**اتفاق** (عقد) **ـ مؤتمر**
Convene	yad'ū ila 'jtimā'	**يدعو إلى اجتماع**
Conventional rate	as-si'r al-muttafaq 'alayhi	**السعر المتفق عليه**
Conversion	taḥwīl	**تحويـــل**
Conversion cost	takālif at-taḥwīl	**تكاليف التحويل** [مجموع الأجور والمصاريف المباشرة والتكاليف العامة لتحويل المواد الخام إلى منتجات جاهزة أو تحويل المادة من مرحلة انتاجية إلى أخرى]
Conversion loan	qarḍ taḥwīl	**قرض تحويل**

Conversion of reality into personality	taḥwīl al-ʿaqārāt ilā amwāl manqūla	تحويل العقارات إلى أموال منقولة
Conversion, fraudulent – of stocks	ikhtilas as-hum	اختلاس أسهم
Convert	yuḥawwil	يحــوّل
Convertibility	qābiliyyat at-taḥwīl	قابلية التحويل
Convertible	yumkin taḥwīluh aw ibdāluh	يمكن تحويله أو ابداله
Convertible bond	sanad qābil li'l-istibdāl	سند قابل للاستبدال بأسهم أو أوراق مالية أخرى
Convertible paper money	awrāq naqdiyya qabila li't-taḥwīl	أوراق نقدية قابلة للتحويل إلى عملات أجنبية
Convertible securities	awrāq māliyya sahlat at-taḥwīl	أوراق مالية سهلة التحويل الى نقد
Cook	yuzawwir	يــزوّر (يلفق)
Cook the balance sheet	mīzāniyya muzawwara	ميزانية مزورة
Cooling period	fatrat al-intiẓār	فترة الانتظار (في حالة الاضرابات العمالية)
Co-op	taʿāwuniyya	تعاونية
Co-operate	yataʿāwan	يتعــاون
Co-operation	taʿāwun	تعــاون
Co-operative	jamʿiyya taʿāwuniyya	جمعية تعاونية
Co-operative bank	masarf taʿāwunī	مصرف تعاوني
Co-operative Society	jamʿiyya taʿāwuniyya	جمعية تعاونية
Co-ordinate	yunassiq	ينســق
Co-ordination	tansīq	تنسيــق
Co-partner	sharīk	شريــك
Copy	nuskha	نسخة (صورة)
Copyright	ḥaqq an-nashr	حــق النشــر
Corporate action	qarār musāhimīn	قرار مساهمين [يتخذه أو يوافق عليه المساهمون أو مجلس الادارة ويتعلق بسياسة الشركة]
Corporate debt	duyūn sharikāt	ديون شركات
Corporate seal	khatam ash-sharika	ختم الشركة
Corporation stocks (U.K.)	qurūḍ baladiyya	قروض بلدية
Corpus	aṣl aw ra's māl	أصل أو رأسمال
Correlation	ʿalāqa mutabādala	العلاقة المتبادلة
Correlation coefficient	muʿāmil al-irtibāṭ	معامل الارتباط
Correlation ratio	nisbat al-irtibaṭ	نسبة الارتباط
Correlation table	jadwal al-irtibāṭ	جدول الارتباط
Correspondent bank	maṣraf murāsil	مصرف مراسل
Corresponding entry	qayd ḥisābī muṭābiq	قيد حسابي مطابق
Cost	taklifa	تكلفــة
Cost absorption	istīʿāb at-taklifa	استيعاب التكلفة
Cost account	ḥisāb at-takālif	حساب التكاليف
Cost accountancy	muḥāsabat at-takālīf	محاسبة التكاليف [علم تحديد تكلفة المنتجات والخدمات]

Cost accountant	muḥāsib at-takālīf	محاسب تكاليف
Cost accounting	ijrā'āt ḥisāb at-taklifa	اجراءات حساب التكلفة
Cost accounts	ḥisāb al-intāj wa't-tawzīʻ	حساب الانتاج والتوزيع
Cost allocation	takhṣīs at-taklifa	تخصيص التكلفة [تخصيص بنود التكاليف الخاصة على الوحدات المخصصة أو على مراكز التكلفة المتعلقة بها طبقا لما حدث فعلا]
Cost analysis	taḥlīl at-taklifa	تحليل الكلفة
Cost and freight (C/F)	al-kulfa wa'sh-shaḥn	الكلفة والشحن
Cost apportionment	tawzīʻ at-taklifa	توزيع التكلفة [توزيع بنود التكاليف على وحدات الانتاج والخدمات باستخدام معدلات تتناسب مع علاقة هذه البنود بوحدات الانتاج]
Cost audit	murājaʻat at-takālīf	مراجعة التكاليف
Cost basis (of accounting)	qawāʻid taqdīr wa-tasjīl al-maṣārīf	قواعد تقدير وتسجيل المصاريف
Cost centre (center)	markaz at-taklifa	مركز التكلفة
Cost classification	tabwīb ʻanāṣir at-takālīf	تبويب عناصر التكاليف
Cost code	dalīl at-takālīf	دليل التكاليف
Cost conscious	wāʻin li't-taklifa	واع للتكلفة [واع لضرورة عدم تجاوز الكلفة حدا معينا أو أن تكون أقل ما يمكن]
Cost consultant	mustashār takālīf	مستشار تكاليف
Cost control	muraqabat at-takālīf	مراقبة التكاليف
Cost curve	khaṭṭ at-taklifa 'l-bayānī	خط التكلفة البياني
Cost data	maʻlūmāt at-takālīf	معلومات التكاليف
Cost distribution	tawzīʻ at-taklifa	توزيع التكلفة
Cost elements	ʻanāṣir at-takālīf	عناصر التكاليف
Cost estimate sheet	qā'imat at-takālīf at-taqdīriyya	قائمة التكاليف التقديرية
Cost finding	taḥdīd at-taklifa	تحديد التكلفة
Cost fraction	taklifat wiḥdat intāj aw ʻamal	تكلفة وحدة انتاج أو عمل
Cost free	dūna takālīf	دون تكاليف
Cost, insurance and freight (C.I.F.)	sīf	سيــف [سعر البضاعة بما فيه التأمين والشحن]
Cost journal	yawmiyyat at-takālīf	يومية التكاليف
Cost ledger	ustādh at-takālīf	استاذ التكاليف
Cost of defectives	taklifat al-muntajāt al-maʻība	تكلفة المنتجات المعيبة
Cost of goods purchased	taklifat shirā' al-biḍāʻa	تكلفة شراء البضاعة [مضافا إليه تكلفة النقل والتخزين والتسليم وغيرهـــا]
Cost of living	takālīf al-maʻīsha	تكاليف المعيشة
Cost of living bonus	taʻwīḍ ghalā' al-maʻīsha	تعويض غلاء المعيشة
Cost of living index	ar-raqm al-qiyāsī li-nafaqāt al-maʻīsha	الرقم القياسي لنفقات المعيشة

Cost of production	taklifat al-intāj	**تكلفة الانتاج**
Cost of removal and betterment	taklifat an-naql wa't-taḥsīn	**تكلفة النقل والتحسين**
Cost of reproduction	taklifat at-tajdīd	**تكلفة التجديد** [التكلفة الحالية المقدرة لاستبدال أصل موجود بأصل آخر يماثله عندما كان حديثا]
Cost of sales	taklifat al-mabīʿāt	**تكلفة المبيعات**
Cost or less principle	mabda' khafḍ juz' min taklifat al-aṣl	**مبدأ خفض** (أو حذف) **جزء من تكلفة الأصل**
Cost or market, whichever is lower	siʿr as-sūq aw at-taklifa ayyuhumā aqall	**سعر السوق أو التكلفة أيهما أقل** [عند تقييم البضاعة في المخازن]
Cost plus	at-taklifa wa'r-ribḥ	**التكلفة والربح** [طريقة لتحديد سعر بيع بضائع أو خدمات بموجب عقد ينص على زيادة كلفة البضاعة أو الخدمات بمقدار زيادة على التكلفة متفق عليها]
Cost plus pricing	tasʿīr at-taklifa wa'r-ribḥ	**تسعير التكلفة والربح** [عملية تحديد سعر البيع علي أساس اضافة عامل ربح محدد الى التكاليف]
Cost price	1 at-taklifa 2 siʿr al-ʿaqd	**١ - التكلفة** **٢ - سعر العقد**
Cost rate; overhead rate	muʿaddal at-taklifa 'r-ra'siyya	**معدل التكلفة** (النفقات) **الرأسية**
Cost records	sijillāt at-takālīf	**سجلات التكاليف**
Cost recovery	istiʿāb at-takālif	**استيعاب التكاليف**
Cost recovery basis	asās istīʿāb at-takālīf	**أساس استيعاب التكاليف**
Cost reduction	takhfīḍ at-taklifa	**تخفيض التكلفة**
Cost saving	taqlīṣ at-taklifa	**تقليص التكلفة**
Cost sheet	qā'imat at-takālīf al-fiʿliyya	**قائمة التكاليف الفعلية**
Cost standard	siʿr at-taklifa 'l-miʿyāriyya	**سعر التكلفة المعيارية**
Cost system	niẓām at-takālif	**نظام التكاليف**
Cost type (accounting)	namaṭ at-taklifa 'l-mustaḥaqqa	**نمط التكلفة المستحقة** [المحاسبة المبنية على أساس المستحقات]
Cost unit	wiḥdat ḥisāb at-taklifa	**وحدة حساب التكلفة**
Cost unit rate	muʿaddal wiḥdat an-nashāṭ	**معدل وحدة النشاط** [معدل فعلى أو محدد مقدما لتوزيع التكاليف الاضافية على أساس مجموع عدد وحدات النشاط المنتجة]
Cost variance	inḥrāf at-taklifa	**انحراف التكلفة**
Cost/volume/profit relationship	ʿalāqat at-taklifa wa'l-intāj wa'r-ribḥ	**علاقة التكلفة والانتاج والربح**
Cost, actual	at-taklifa 'l-fiʿliyya	**التكلفة الفعلية**
Cost, at prime	bit-taklifa 'l-mubāshira	**بالتكلفة المباشرة**
Cost, comparative	at-taklifa 'n-nisbiyya	**التكلفة النسبية**
Cost, daily operating	taklifat at-tashghīl al-yawmiyya	**تكلفة التشغيل اليومية**
Cost, diminishing	at-taklifa 'l-mutanāqiṣa	**التكلفة المتناقصة**
Cost, fixed	at-taklifa ath-thābita	**التكلفة الثابتة**

Cost, joint	at-taklifa 'l-mushtaraka	التكلفة المشتركة
Cost, marginal	at-taklifa 'l-ḥaddiyya	التكلفة الحدية
Cost, prime	at-taklifa 'l-asāsiyya	التكلفة الأساسية
Cost, production	taklifat al-intāj	تكلفة الانتاج
Cost, replacement	si'r at-taklifa 'l-istibdāli	سعر التكلفة الاستبدالي
Cost, semi-variable	at-taklifa shibh al-mutaghayyira	التكلفة شبه المتغيرة
Cost, standard	at-taklifa 'l-mi'yāriyya	التكلفة المعيارية
Cost, unit	taklifat wiḥdat al-intāj	تكلفة وحدة الانتاج
Cost, utilities – accounting	muḥāsabat takālīf al-khadamāt al-intājiyya	محاسبة تكاليف الخدمات الانتاجية
Cost, variable	at-taklifa 'l-mutaghayyira	التكلفة المتغيرة
Costing	tathbīt si'r at-taklifa	تثبيت سعر التكلفة
Costs	takālīf	تكاليف
Count	ya'udd	يعد (يحصي)
Count sheet	qā'imat al-jard	قائمة الجرد
Counter entry	qayd 'aksī	قيد عكسي
Counter error	al-akhṭā' al-muta'ādila	الأخطاء المتعادلة (الأخطاء المتقابلة)
Counterbalance	yuqābil	يقابل (يوازن)
Counterfeit money	nuqūd muzayyafa	نقود مزيفة (مزورة)
Counterfoil	arūma	أرومة (كعب المستندات)
Countersign	yuṣādiq 'ala tawqī'	يصادق على توقيع
Coupons	qasā'im	قسائم
Covenant	ittifāq	اتفاق (عقد)
Covenantee	muta'ahhad lahu	متعهد له ـ مدين
Covenanter	muta'ahhid	متعهد (دائن)
Cover	yughaṭṭī	يغطي (يسدد ما عليه)
Cover into	yuḥawwil ila	يحوّل إلى [الأرصدة المحولة الى خزينة الولايات المتحدة]
Cover, ample	taghṭiya kāfiya	تغطية كافية
Coverage (U.S.)	1 majāl	١ - مجال
	2 mablagh at-taghṭiya	٢ - مبلغ التغطية
Coverage of circularisation	madā taghṭiyat at-ta'yīdāt	مدى تغطية التأييدات ـ الذمم
Covering	taghṭiya	التغطية [توفير وسيلة دفع لمواجهة التزامات معينة]
Covering entry	1 qayd shāmil	١ - قيد شامل [لجميع عناصر عملية ما]
	2 qayd taghṭiya	٢ - قيد التغطية [لاخفاء عملية عن طريق قيد عملية وهمية بقيمة مساوية]
Covering warrant	wathīqat taghṭiya	وثيقة تغطية
C.P.A. (Certified public accountant) (U.S.)	muḥāsib qānūnī mujāz	محاسب قانوني مجاز

Credit (n.; v.)	'i'timān maṣrafī	الائتمان المصرفي (التسليف) ـ يقيد بالحساب
Credit account	1 ḥisāb dā'in	١ - حساب دائن
	2 ḥisāb i'timād	٢ - حساب اعتماد
Credit advice	ish'ār bi'l-i'timād	اشعار بالاعتماد
Credit agency	wakālat al-'i'timān	وكالة الائتمان
Credit balance	1 raṣīd dā'in	١ - رصيد دائن
	2 raṣīd al-i'timād	٢ - رصيد الاعتماد
		[الرصيد المتبقي من الاعتماد]
Credit bureau	maktab 'i'timān	مكتب ائتمان
Credit card	biṭāqat istidāna	بطاقة استدانة (امريكان اكسبرس)
Credit contra accounts	ḥisābat niẓāmiyya dā'ina	حسابات نظامية دائنة
Credit co-operative societies	jam'iyyāt at-taslīf at-ta'āwuniyya	جمعيات التسليف التعاونية
Credit department	idārat al-'i'timān	ادارة الائتمان (التسليف)
Credit facility	tas-hīl 'i'timānī	تسهيل ائتماني
Credit line	tas-hīl mālī muḥaddad	تسهيل مالي محدد ـ يمنحه مصرف لعميل
Credit note	ish'ār dā'in	اشعار دائن
Credit rating	malā'a	مـــلاءة
Credit risk	makhāṭir al-'i'timān	مخاطر الائتمان
Credit sale	bay' ājil	بيـع آجـــل
Credit slip	1 ish'ār dā'in	١ - اشعار دائن
	2 qasīmat īdā'	٢ - قسيمة ايداع
Credit standing	raṣīd ad-dayn	رصيد الدين
Credit transaction	'amaliyya ājila	عملية آجلة
Credit union	niqābat taslīf	نقابة تسليف
Credit, acceptance	i'timād al-qabūl	اعتماد القبول
Credit, bad	dayn ma'dūm	دين معدوم
Credit, blank	i'timād 'alā bayāḍ	اعتماد على بياض (اعتماد مكشوف)
Credit, circular	i'timād dawrī	اعتماد دورى
Credit, confirmed	i'timād muṣādaq 'alayhi	اعتماد مصادق عليه
Credit, confirmed irrevocable	i'timād mu'azzaz	اعتماد معزز (غير قابل للالغاء)
Credit, documentary	i'timād mustandī	اعتماد مستندى
Credit, invalid letter of	kitāb i'timād lāghin	كتاب اعتماد لاغ
Credit, irrevocable documentary	i'timād mustandī mu'azzaz	اعتماد مستندى معزز (غير قابل للالغاء)
Credit, letter of	kitāb i'timād	كتاب اعتماد
Credit, long-term	i'timād ṭawīl al-ajal	اعتماد طويل الأجل
Credit, revocable	i'timād qābil li'l-ilghā'	اعتماد قابل للالغاء
Credit, revolving	i'timād mutakarrir	اعتماد متكرر
Credit, short-term	i'timād qaṣīr al-ajal	اعتماد قصير الأجل
Creditor	dā'in	دائـــــن
Creditor account	ḥisāb dā'in	حساب دائن
Creditor ledger	daftar ustādh ad-dā'inīn	دفتر استاذ الدائنين
Creditor, guaranteed	dā'in maḍmūn	دائن مضمون
Creditor, privileged	dā'in mumtāz	دائن ممتاز

Creditworthiness	malā'a	ملاءة
Cremation certificate	shahādat itlāf	شهادة اتلاف [قسم يؤديه الوصي أو الوكيل بأن الأوراق المالية التي سددت قد جرى اتلافها]
Crop insurance	ta'mīn al-maḥṣūl	تأمين المحصول
Cross action	da'wā muḍādda	دعوى مضادة
Cross rate	si'r aṣ-ṣarf al-mushtaqq	سعر الصرف المشتق [سعر الصرف بين عمليتين مشتقا من سعر صرف كل منهما لعملة ثالثة]
Cross-check	1 al-jam' al-mutaqāṭi'	١ - الجمع المتقاطع [أى الجمع الأفقي والرأسي]
	2 tadqiq	٢ - تدقيق [عملية ما عن طريق عملية أخرى]
Cross-entry	tas-hīh al-qayd al-mu'addal	تصحيح القيد المعدل
Cross-firing check	ash-shīkāt al-mutaqāṭi'a	الشيكات المتقاطعة [الوسيلة التي يلجأ اليها بعض العملاء في اظهار أرصدة رمزية في مقابل السحب على حسابين للعميل في مصرفين مختلفين]
Cross-foot	at-tajmī' ufuqiyyan	التجميع افقيا
Cross-reference	rabṭ	ربط ـ السابق واللاحق
Cross-section study	dirāsa maqṭa'iyya	دراسة مقطعية
Crossed cheque	shīk musaṭṭar	شيك مسطّر
Cum dividend	ma' ar-ribḥ	مع الربح [سعر اسهم متضمن حق استلام أرباحها المعلن عنها]
Cumulative dividend	arbāḥ as-hum tarākumiyya	أرباح أسهم تراكمية [أرباح على أسهم ممتازة تراكمية تدفع على فترات معينة وقبل توزيع أرباح الأسهم العادية]
Cumulative preferred capital stock	as-hum mumtāza dhāt arbāḥ tarākumiyya	أسهم ممتازة ذات أرباح تراكمية
Cumulative shares	as-hum tarākumiyya	أسهم تراكمية
Currency	1 'umla	١ - عملة
	2 tadāwul	٢ - تداول (رواج)
Currency account	ḥisāb qaṭ' ajnabī	حساب قطع أجنبي
Currency notes	nuqūd waraqiyya	نقود ورقية ـ حكومية
Currency principle	mabda' taqiyīd al-iṣdār	مبدأ تقييد الاصدار
Currency, hard	'umla ṣa'ba	عملة صعبة
Current	1 jārin	١ - جار
	2 mutadāwal	٢ - متداول
Current account	ḥisāb jārī	الحساب الجارى
Current asset	mawjūd mutadāwal	موجود متداول
Current balance	raṣīd ḥālī	رصيد حالي

Current budget	al-muwāzana 'l-jāriya	**الموازنة الجارية**
Current consumption	istihlāk ḥālī	**الاستهلاك الحالي**
Current cost	kulfa jāriya	**الكلفة الجارية**
Current expenditure	maṣānīf jāriya	**مصاريف جارية** [نفقات تغطي تكلفة التشغيل أو اضافة لموجودات المعمل خلال فترة محددة]
Current expenses	1 maṣārīf fatra ḥāliyya	**١ - مصاريف فترة حالية**
	2 maṣārīf tashghīl 'ādiyya	**٢ - مصاريف تشغيل عادية**
Current fund; general fund	aṣ-ṣundūq al-'āmm	**الصندوق العام**
Current income	dakhl jārī	**الدخل الجارى ـ خلال فترة محاسبية معينة**
Current investment	istithmār mu'aqqat	**استثمار مؤقت** (استثمار ذو مردود سريع)
Current liability	maṭlūb mutadāwal	**مطلوب متداول**
Current maturity	istiḥqāq jārī	**الاستحقاق الجارى** [جزء من دين طويل الأجل واجب التسديد خلال الاثنى عشر شهرا القادمة]
Current outlay cost	taklifa 'ājila	**تكلفة عاجلة** [تكلفة تتطلب انفاقا عاجلا]
Current price	as-si'r al-jārī	**السعر الجارى**
Current ratio	nisbat at-tadāwul	**نسبة التداول** [أى رأس المال العامل وهي نسبة الموجودات المتداولة إلى المطلوبات المتداولة]
Current return	'ā'id jārī	**العائد الجارى** [نسبة مئوية مبينة على أساس نسبة ربح السهم المدفوع خلال الاثنى عشر شهرا السابقة وسعر السوق للسهم الواحد في نهاية تلك الفترة]
Current standard	ma'āyīr jāriya	**المعايير الجارية**
Current standard cost	taklifa mi'yāriyya jāriya	**تكلفة معيارية جارية**
Current taxes	ḍarā'ib jāriya	**ضرائب جارية**
Curve	khaṭṭ bayānī	**خط بياني** (منحني)
Custodian	waṣi	**وصـــي** (أمين ، حارس)
Custody charges, safe	rasm al-ḥirāsa	**رسم الحراسة**
Custom duties	rusūm jumrukiyya	**رسوم جمركية**
Customer	'amīl	**عميــــل**
Customer ledger	daftar ustādh al-'umalā'	**دفتر استاذ العملاء**
Customer service	khidmat al-'amīl	**خدمة العميل**
Customs	jamārik	**جمـــارك**
Customs tariff	ta'rifa jumrukiyya	**تعرفة جمركية**
Cut-off	qaṭ'	**قطـــع** [تسجيل العمليات بغاية مقارنة السجلات مع الأرقام المتوفرة من مصادر خارجية]
Cut-off date	tārīkh al-qaṭ'	**تاريخ القطع** [بغية القيام بعملية تدقيق الحسابات]

Cut-off statement	kashf qaṭʻ	**كشف قطع**
		[بين طرفين يعده أحدهما بناء على طلب الآخر لغرض التدقيق]
Cycle	dawra zamaniyya	**دورة زمنية**
Cycle count	tiʻdād dawrī	**تعداد دوري**
Cyclical movement	ḥarakat ad-dawra 'l-iqtiṣādiyya	**حركة الدورة الاقتصادية**
Daily cash report	taqrīr an-naqd al-yawmī	**تقرير النقد اليومي**
Daily loans	qurūḍ ghibb at-talab	**قروض غب الطلب**
Daily time sheet	bayān al-awqāt al-yawmī	**بيان الأوقات اليومي**
Data	maʻlūmāt	**معلومات** (حقائق)
Date	tārīkh	**تاريخ** (موعد استحقاق)
Date of acquisition	tārīkh al-iqtinā'	**تاريخ الاقتناء**
Date, after	min tārīkhihi	**من تاريخه**
Date, due	tārīkh al-istiḥqāq	**تاريخ الاستحقاق**
Date, value	tārīkh al-qīma	**تاريخ القيمة**
		[تاريخ نفاذ مفعول تقدير القيمة]
Day bill	sanad tijārī	**سند تجاري** (سند محدد التاريخ)
	daftar muswadda	**دفتر مسودة** (دفتر يومية)
Day of maturity	tārīkh al-istiḥqāq	**تاريخ الاستحقاق**
Day price	siʻr al-yawm	**سعر اليوم**
Day to day loan or money	qarḍ yawmī	**قرض يومي**
		[تحت الطلب ويعطى عادة للسماسرة]
Day, exchange	yawm al-burṣa	**يوم البورصة**
		[يوم سوق الأوراق المالية]
Days of grace	fatrat as-samāḥ	**فترة السماح**
		[الفترة التالية لاستحقاق الكمبيالة والتى يمكن خلالها للمدين الوفاء دون التعرض للمهلة القانونية]
Dead loans	qurūd maʻdūma	**قروض معدومة**
		[قروض مضى ميعاد استحقاقها]
Dead loss	khasāra lā tuʻwwaḍ	**خسارة لا تعوض**
Dead stock	bidā'a tālifah	**بضاعة تالفة**
		[بضاعة لا يمكن بيعها]
Deadline	al-mawʻid al-aqṣā	**الموعد الأقصى**
Deadweight	ḥumūla sākina	**حمولة ساكنة**
		[وزن المركب بدون حمولة]
Deal	ṣafqa	**صفقة**
Deal with	yuʻāmil	**يعامل** (تجاريا)
Dealer	1 dallal	١ - **دلال** (في سوق الأوراق المالية)
	2 muwazziʻ	٢ - **موزع**
Dean schedule; analytic schedule	jadwal taḥlīlī	**جدول تحليلي** (في التأمين)

Dearness	ghalā'	غـــلاء
Death benefits	ta'wīḍat al-wafāh	تعويضات الوفاة
Debase	1 yukhaffiḍ	١ - يخفض (قيمة النقد)
	2 yaghish	٢ - يغش (النقد)
Debased currency	'umla mukhaffaḍat al-qīma	عملة مخفضة القيمة
Debasement	ghish al-'umla	غش العملة
Debenture	sanad tijārī	سند تجـــارى
Debenture (U.S.)	iqrāḍ bi-dayn	اقراض بدين
Debenture capital	ra'smāl sanadāt	رأسمال سندات
		[واردات ناتجة عن بيع سندات]
Debenture discount	khaṣm as-sanadāt	خصم السندات
Debenture holder	ḥāmil as-sanadāt	حامل السندات
Debenture loan	qarḍ sanadī	قـرض سـندى
Debenture premium	'alawat iṣdār as-sanadāt	علاوة اصدار السندات
Debenture redemption	istihlāk as-sanadāt	استهلاك السندات (استوفاء)
Debit	madīn	مدين - يقيد على الحساب
Debit account	ḥisāb madīn	حساب مديـن
Debit balance	raṣīd madīn	رصيد مديـن
Debit entry	qayd madīn	قيـد مديـن
Debit memorandum	mudhakkirat qayd madīn	مذكرة قيد مدين
Debit note	ish'ār madīn	اشعار مدين
Debit side	al-jānib al-madīn	الجانب المدين
Debit, pass or enter to the	yuqayyid 'alā	يقيـد علـى
		[ينقل إلى الحساب المدين]
Debt	dhimma	ذمـة (ديـن)
Debt book	daftar adh-dhimam	دفتر الـذمم
Debt collector	jābi' dh-dhimam	جابـي الـذمم
Debt conversion	taḥwīl ad-duyūn	تحويل الديـون
		[إلى ديون أخرى بشروط أحسن]
Debt financing	tamwīl ad-dayn al-'amm	تمويل الدين العام
Debt limit	al-ḥadd al-a'lā lil-dayn	الحد الأعلى للدين
		[لاستدانة أى دائرة حكومية]
Debt retirement	tāsdīd ad-dayn	تسديد الديـن
Debt service	ifā' ad-dayn	ايفاء الديـن
		[دفع الفائدة المستحقة والرأسمال]
Dept, acknowledge a	yuqirr bi-dayn	يقـر بديـن
Debt, active	1 dayn bi fā'ida	١ - دين بفائدة
	2 dayn mustaḥaqq al-adā'	٢ - دين مستحق الآداء
Debt, consolidate a	yuwaḥḥid ad-dayn	يوحد الدين
Debt, contract a	yastadīn	يستديـن
Debt, deny a	yunkir ad-dayn	ينكر الديـن
Debt, discharge of	istihlāk ad-dayn	استهلاك الدين - بتسديده
Debt, doubtful	dayn mashkūk fīhi	دين مشكوك فيه

Debt, due	dayn mustaḥaqq	دين مستحق
Debt, floating	yatrah sanadat ad-dayn	يطرح سندات الدين [دين عام طويل الأجل وغير مضمون]
Debt, frozen	dayn mujammad	ديـن مجـمد
Debt, incur a	yataḥammal ad-dayn	يتحمل الديـن
Dept, irrecoverable	dayn lā yusaddad	ديـن لايسـدد
Debt, irrevocable	dayn maḥtūm	دين محتوم (لا يسترد)
Debt, out of	khālin min ad-dayn	خال من الدين
Debt, outstanding	dayn muʿallaq	ديـن معلـق
Debt, redeem the	yastarridd ad-dayn	يسترد الدين
Debt, secured	dayn maḍmūn	ديـن مضمـون
Debt, sink a	yastahlik daynan	يستهلك دينا
Debt, write off a bad	yastabʿid daynan mayyitan	يستبعد دينا ميتا
Debtor	madīn	مـديـن
Debtors' accounts	ḥisābāt al-madīnīn	حسابات المدينين
Debtor country	balad madīn	بلد مدين
Decide	yattakhidh qarāran	يتخذ قرارا
Decimal	ʿashrī	عشـرى
Decimal currency	niẓām al-ʿumla'l-ʿashriyya	نظام العملة العشرى
Decimal equivalent	al-mukāfi' al-ʿashrī	المكافىء العشرى
Decimal fraction	kasr ʿashrī	الكسر العشرى
Decimal measure	qiyās ʿashrī	قياس عشرى
Decimal point	nuqṭa ʿashriyya	النقطة العشرية
Decimal scale	miqyās ʿashrī	مقياس عشرى
Decimal system	an-niẓām al-ʿashrī	النظام العشرى
Decimalise	aʿshar	أعشـر [يحول إلى النظام العشرى]
Decipherable	qābil l'l-ḥall	قابل للحل
Decision	qarār	قـرار
Decision-making	ittikhādh al-qarārāt	اتخاذ القرارات
Decisions of the general meeting	qarārāt al-jamʿyya 'l-ʿumūmiyya	قرارات الجمعية العمومية
Declarable	mumkin iʿlānuh	ممكن اعلانه
Declaration	1 taṣrīḥ	١ - تصريح (اعلان)
	2 qarār majlis al-idāra	٢ - قرار مجلس الادارة [بتحديد أرباح الاسهم]
Declaration of bankruptcy	ish-hār iflas	اشهار افلاس
Declared capital	ra'smāl muṣarraḥ bihi	الرأسمال المصرح به
Declared dividend	arbāḥ al-as-hum al-mu'lana	أرباح الأسهم المعلنة
Declared value	qīma muʿlana	القيمة المعلنة
Decline in economic usefulness	istihlāk	اسـتهلاك
Declining	ākhid fi 'l-inkhifāḍ	آخذ في الانخفاض
Declining-balance depreciation	istihlāk mutanāqiṣ	الاستهلاك المتناقص [طريقة الاستهلاك على أساس نسبة مئوية

		[من رصيد قيمة الأصل المستهلك]
Decrease	yunqiṣ	ينقص
Decreasing	mutanāqiṣ	متناقص
Decree in bankruptcy	qarār i'lān al-iflās	قرار اعلان الافلاس
Deduce	yastakhliṣ	يستخلص
Deduct	yakhṣum	يخصم
Deductible	qābil li'l-khaṣm	قابل للخصم
Deduction	1 khaṣm	١ - خصم (اقتطاع)
	2 istintāj	٢ - استنتاج
Deduction from gross income	khaṣm min ad-dakhl al-ijmālī	الخصم من الدخل الاجمالي
Deduction from income; income deductions	khaṣmiyyāt min ad-dakhl	خصميات من الدخل [المصاريف (بما فيها الخسائر) المستثناة من تكلفة التشغيل]
Deductions from net income	khaṣm min ṣāfi 'd-dakhl	الخصم من صافي الدخل [مثل مخصصات الاحتياطي وأرباح الأسهم]
Deed	ṣakk	صك (وثيقة ، حجة)
Deed of association	'aqd sharika	عقد شركة
Deed of mortgage	ṣakk rahn	صك رهن
Deed of partnership	'aqd sharāka	عقد شراكة
Deed of sale	'aqd bay'	عقد بيع
Deed of trust; trust deed	ṣakk wiṣāya	صك وصاية [نقل الملكية إلى وصي]
Defalcation	ikhtilās	اختلاس
Default	quṣūr	قصور (عن دفع دين)
Default of payment	takhalluf 'an ad-daf'	تخلف عن الدفع
Defeasance	faskh 'aqd	فسخ عقد
Defect	'ayb	عيب (خلل)
Defer	yu'ajjil	يؤجل (يرجىء الدفع)
Deferral (or deferment)	ta'jīl	تأجيل [معاملة الايراد محاسبيا على أنه استلم قبل انتسابه أو تحمل المصاريف قبل أن تظهر فائدتها]
Deferred annuity	daf'a sanawiyya mu'ajjala	دفعة سنوية مؤجلة
Deferred asset	maṣrūfāt mu'ajjala	مصروفات مؤجلة
Deffered charges (assets)	maṣrūfāt mu'ajjala	مصروفات مؤجلة
Deferred credit (revenue)	irad mu'ajjal	ايراد مؤجل
Deferred debits (assets)	maṣrūfāt mu'ajjala	مصروفات مؤجلة
Deferred dividends	arbāh mu'lana mu'ajjala	أرباح معلنة مؤجلة (الدفع)
Deferred liability	1 dayn mu'ajjal	١ - دين مؤجل
	2 iltizām ṭawīl al-'ajal	٢ - التزام طويل الأجل
	3 irād mu'ajjal	٣ - ايراد مؤجل
Deferred maintenance	ṣiyāna muta'akhkhira	صيانة متأخرة
Deferred payment sale	1 bay' bit-taqsīṭ	١ - بيع بالتقسيط

	2 bayʿli-ajal ṭawīl	٢ - بيع لأجل طويل
Deferred repairs (maintenance)	ṣiyāna muta'akhkhira	صيانة متأخرة
Deferred revenue (income)	irād mu'ajjal	ايـراد مؤجــل
Deferred shares	ashum mu'ajjalat ar-ribḥ	أسهم مؤجلة الربح
Deficiency	ʿajz	عجــز (نقص)
Deficiency account (or statement)	bayān ʿajz	بيان عجز (في ممتلكات المفلس)
Deficiency appropriation	mukhaṣṣaṣāt ʿajz	مخصصات عجز [أموال مخصصة لتغطية التزامات مترتبة زيادة عن مخصصات سابقة]
Deficit	ʿajz mālī	عجـز مالــي
Deficit account	ḥisāb al-ʿajz	حساب العجز (في دفتر الاستاذ)
Define	yuḥaddid	يحـدد (يعين ، يعرف)
Deflation	hubūṭ al-asʿār	هبـوط الأسعار
Deflation, currency	hubūṭ al-ʿumla	هبـوط العملـة
Defray	yusaddid an-nafaqāt	يسدد النفقات
De jure (iure)	sharʿī	شـــرعـي
Del credere agent	wakīl ḍamin	وكيل ضامن [وكيل يوافق على حماية موكله من الخسائر الناجمة عن تسليف طرف ثالث]
Delay (n.; v.)	1 muhla	١ - مهلــة
	2 ta'jīl	٢ - تأجيل ـ يؤجل
Delegate (n.; v.)	mufawwaḍ	مفوض (مندوب ـ يفوض)
Delegating responsibility	taḥwīl mas'ūliyyāt	تحويل المسؤوليات
Delegation of authority	tafwīḍ ṣalāḥiyyāt	التفويض بالصلاحيات
Delinquent	muta'akhkhir ad-dafʿ	متأخر الدفع
Delinquent account receivable	dayn mashkūk fī taḥṣīlihi	دين مشكوك في تحصيله
Delinquent taxes	ḍarā'ib muta'akhkhirat al-adā'	ضرائب متأخرة الاداء
Deliver	yusallim	يسلم ـ سلفا أو سندات
Deliverable	qābil li't-taslīm	قابل للتسليم
Delivered price	siʿr at-taslīm	سعر التسليم [يتضمن قيمة الشحن حتى ظهر الباخرة]
Delivery	taslīm	تسليم (تحويل)
Delivery note	ishʿār irsāl	اشعار ارسال
Delivery order (d/o)	amr taslīm	أمر تسليم ـ بورصة
Delivery, against	muqābil at-taslīm	مقابل التسليم
Delivery, cash on (c.o.d.)	ad-dafʿ ʿindat-taslīm	الدفع عند التسليم
Delivery, forward	taslīm 'ājil	تسليم آجــل
Delivery, prompt	taslīm fawrī	تسليم فــورى
Delivery, ready	taslīm sarīʿ	تسليم ســريــع
Demand	1 ṭalab	١ - طلـــب
	2 muṭālaba	٢ - مطالبـــة
Demand bill	sanad ʿind aṭ-ṭalab	سند عند الطلب
Demand curve	munḥana 'ṭ-ṭalab	منحني الطلب

Demand deposits	wadā'i' taḥt aṭ-ṭalab	ودائع تحت الطلب
Demand draft (d/d)	kumbiyālat ṭalab	كمبيالة طلب [أى تدفع عند الطلب]
Demand note	sanad 'ind aṭ-ṭalab	سند عند الطلب
Demand price	as-si'r al-maṭlūb	السعر المطلوب
Demand pull inflation	taḍakhkhum bi-sabab aṭ-ṭalab	تضخم بسبب الطلب
Demand rate	as-si'r'aind aṭ-ṭalab	السعر عند الطلب (سوق القطع الأجنبي)
Demand schedule	jadwal aṭ-ṭalab	جـدول الطلـب
Demand, alternate	aṭ-ṭalab al-badīl	الطلب البديل
Demand, contingent	ḥāja ṭāri'a	حاجة طارئة
Demand, in	maṭlūb	مطلوب (رائج)
Demonetisation	ibṭāl	إبطال (عملة أو طوابع من التداول)
Demurrage	arḍiyya	الأرضية (غرامة التأخير)
Denomination	fi'a	فئـة (عملة أو وزن أو مقياس أو طوابع)
De-obligation	ilghā' iltizaim	الغـاء التـزام
Department	dā'ira	دائرة (قسـم)
Department costs	takālīf al-aqsām	تكاليف الأقسام
Department head	ra'īs dā'ira	رئيس دائـرة
Department store	markaz tijārī	مركز تجاري (ذو أقسام عديدة)
Departmental charge	an-nafaqat al-muwazā āla al-aqsām	النفقات الموزعة على الأقسام
Departmental overhead	al-maṣrūfat ar-ra'siyya li'l-qism	المصروفات الرأسية للقسم
Departmental profit	arbaḥ al-qism	أرباح القسـم
Departmentalisation	at-tawzī' ila marākiz infāq	التوزيع إلى مراكز انفاق
Dependent variable	al-mutaghayyir al-murtabit	المتغير المرتبط (بعناصر أخرى متغيرة)
Depletable	'urḍa li'n-nafād	عـرضـة للنفاذ
Depleted cost	at-taklifa 'l-mutabaqqiya	التكلفة المتبقية [بعد خصم الاستنزاف المتراكم]
Depletion	nuḍūb	نضـوب (نفاذ)
Depletion unit method	ṭarīqat an-nuḍūb 'alā asās mu'addal al-istihlāk	طريقة النضوب على أساس معدل الاستهلاك
Deposit	wadī'a	وديعـــة
Deposit account	ḥisāb wadā'i'	حساب ودائع
Deposit banks	bunūk al-wadā'i'	بنوك الودائع
Deposit fees	rasūm idā'	رسوم ايداع
Deposit in transit	wadā'i' fiṭ-ṭarīq	ودائع في الطريق
Deposit insurance corporation	mua'assast ḍamān al-wadā'i'	مؤسسة ضمان الودائع [المؤسسة التي تقوم بضمان الودائع ضد توقف المصارف عن الدفع وذلك وفق شروط معينة]
Deposit rate	si'r al-fā'ida 'ala'l-īdā'āt	سعر الفائدة على الايداعات
Deposit receipt	īṣāl īdā'	ايصال ايداع
Deposit slip	qasīmat īdā'	قسيمة ايداع
Deposit, call	wadī'at ṭalab	وديعة طلب [وديعة تدفع عند الطلب]

Deposit, cash	wadīʿa naqdiyya	وديعة نقدية
Deposit, fixed	wadī ʿa marbūṭa	وديعة مربوطة [لمدة محددة]
Deposit, saving	wadīʿa 'd-dikhāriyya	وديعة ادخارية
Depositary	al-mūdaʿ ladyhi	المودع لديه
Depositor	al-mūdiʿ	المودع
Depositor's life insurance	ta'mīn ʿalā ḥayāt al-mūdiʿ	تأمين على حياة المودع [نوع من الودائع يمنح المودع تأمينا على حياته بدون تكاليف وتدفع قيمة الوديعة لورثة المودع في حالة الوفاة بالاضافة إلى مبلغ تأمين بحد أقصى يساوى قيمة الوديعة]
Depreciable	qābil li'l-istihlāk	قابل للاستهلاك
Depreciable cost	taklifa muwazzaʿa	التكلفة الموزعة [ذلك الجزء من تكلفة الأصل الثابت الذى يوزع على حياة الأصل النافعة]
Depreciable property	mawjūdāt qābila li'l-istihlāk	موجودات قابلة للاستهلاك
Depreciate	1 yatanāqas 2 yastahlik	١ - يتناقص ٢ - يستهلك
Depreciated cost	al-qīma 'd-daftariyya	القيمة الدفترية [التكلفة مطروحا منها الاستهلاك المتراكم]
Depreciated original cost	at-taklifa 'l-aṣliyya 'l-mustahlaka	التكلفة الأصلية المستهلكة [التكلفة الأصلية مطروحا منها الاستهلاك المتراكم]
Depreciation	1 istihlāk 2 tadahwur	١ - استهلاك (بسبب الاستعمال) ٢ - تدهور (سعر العملة في السوق)
Depreciation account	ḥisāb al-istihlāk	حساب الاستهلاك
Depreciation accounting	muḥāsabat al-istihlāk	محاسبة الاستهلاك
Depreciation adequacy	kifāyat al-istilhāk al-mutarākim	كفاية الاستهلاك المتراكم
Depreciation base	qāʿidat al-istihlāk	قاعدة الاستهلاك [قيمة الاستهلاك التي تخصم من قيمة الأصل الثابت دون النظر إلى قيمة بيع الأصل بعد استهلاكه تماما أو بعد استعماله لمدة معينة]
Depreciation expenses	maṣārīf al-istihlāk	مصاريف الاستهلاك
Depreciation fund	iḥtiyāṭi 'stibdāl	احتياطي استبدال [استثمارات بهدف استبدال أو المساعدة في استبدال الأصول عند استهلاكها]
Depreciation method	ṭarīqat al-istihlāk	طريقة الاستهلاك
Depreciation of currency	hubūt qīmat an-naqd	هبوط قيمة النقد
Depreciation of fixed assets	istihlāk al-mawjūdāt ath-thābita	استهلاك الموجودات الثابتة
Depreciation rate	muʿaddal al-istihlāk	معدل الاستهلاك
Depreciation reserve	iḥtiyāṭi 'l-istihlāk	احتياطي الاستهلاك

Depreciation unit	wiḥdat ḥisāb al-istihlāk	**وحدة حساب الاستهلاك** [قيمة الأصل الذى يحتسب على أساس معدل الاستهلاك]
Depression	rukūd	**ركود** (كساد ، هبوط)
Depression of prices	hubuṭ al-as'ār	**هبوط الأسعار**
Depression phase	marḥalat ar-rukūd	**مرحلة الركود**
Descriptive financial statement	bayān mālī waṣfī	**بيان مالي وصفي**
Descriptive statistics	iḥṣā'āt waṣfiyya	**احصاءات وصفية**
Destructible goods	baḍā'i' qābila li't-talaf	**البضائع القابلة للتلف**
Detail account	ḥisāb tafṣīlī	**حساب تفصيلي** [احد حسابات دفتر الاستاذ المساعد]
Detail progress sheet	qā'imat tashghil tafsīliyya	**قائمة تشغيل تفصيلية**
Detailed analysis	taḥlīl tafṣīlī	**تحليل تفصيلي**
Detailed audit	tadqīq mufaṣṣal	**تدقيق مفصل**
Details	tafāṣīl	**تفاصيل** (ايضاحات)
Detect	yaktashif	**يكتشف** (يلاحظ)
Determine	1 yuqarrir 2 yuṣaffī 'aqdan	**١ - يقـــرر** **٢ - يصفي عقدا**
Devaluate	yukhaffiḍ	**يخفض ـ قيمة العملة**
Devaluation	takhfīḍ	**تخفيض ـ قيمة العملة**
Develop	yuṭawwir	**يطـــور**
Development cost	takālīf taṭwīr	**تكاليف تطوير ـ المنتجات**
Development expense	maṣārīf at-taṭwīr	**مصاريف التطوير**
Deviation clause	sharṭ taghyīr al-itijāh	**شرط تغيير الاتجاه** [تغطية تأمين البضاعة مقابل قسط متفق عليه في حالات تحويل أو تغيير الطريق أو غير ذلك من تعديلات شركة النقل البحرية]
Devise	yūrith bi-waṣiyya	**يورث بوصية**
Devisee	al-muwaṣṣa lahu	**الموصى لـــه**
Devisor	al-muwaṣṣī	**الموصي**
Difference	ikhtilāf	**اختـــلاف**
Differential	tafāḍulī	**تفاضلـــي**
Differential costs	at-takālīf at-tafāḍuliyya	**التكاليف التفاضلية**
Digit	āḥādī	**آحـــادى** [أى من الأرقام صفر حتى ٩]
Dip	yukhaffid al-as'ar	**يخفض الأسعار** (في سوق الأوراق المالية)
Direct cost	at-taklifa al-mubāshira	**التكلفة المباشرة**
Direct costing method	ṭarīqat at-takālīf al-mubāshira	**طريقة التكاليف المباشرة**
Direct expenses	maṣārīf mubāshira	**المصاريف المباشرة**
Direct labour	ujūr mubāshira	**الأجور المباشرة** [أجور العمل المبذول في انتاج صنف ما]
Direct labour efficiency variance	mu'āmil fa'āliyat al-ujūr al-mubāshira	**معامل فعالية الأجور المباشرة** [ذلك الجزء من الأجور المباشرة الناتج عن

		الفرق بين مقياس ساعات العمل المقررة للعملية التي تمت وساعات العمل الفعلية التي صرفت]
Direct liability	iltizām mubāshir	**التزام مباشر**
Direct materials cost	taklifat al-mawādd al-mubāshira	**تكلفة المواد المباشرة**
Direct materials cost variance	inhirāf taklifat al-mawādd al-mubāshira	**انحراف تكلفة المواد المباشرة** [الفرق بين معيار تكلفة المواد المباشرة المخصصة للناتج الحاصل والتكلفة الفعلية بالمواد المباشرة المستعملة]
Direct materials mixture variance	inhirāf mazīj al-mawādd al-mubāshira	**انحراف مزيج المواد المباشرة** [ذلك الجزء من الاختلاف في استعمال المواد الناتج من الفرق بين تركيب المزيج المعيارى والفعلى]
Direct materials price variance	inhirāf si'r al-mawādd al-mubāshira	**انحراف سعر المواد المباشرة** [ذلك الجزء من الاختلاف في تكلفة المواد المباشرة الناتج من الفرق بين السعر المعيارى المحدد والسعر الفعلى المدفوع]
Direct materials usage variance	inhirāf istikhdām al-mawādd al-mubāshira	**انحراف استخدام المواد المباشرة** [ذلك الجزء من الاختلاف في تكلفة المواد المباشرة الناتج من الفرق بين الكمية المعيارية المحددة والكمية الفعلية المستعملة]
Direct materials yield variance	inhirāf mardūd al-mawādd al-mubāshira	**انحراف مردود المواد المباشرة** [ذلك الجزء من الاختلاف في استعمال المواد المباشرة الناتج من الفرق بين المنتوج المعيارى المحدد والمنتوج الفعلى الحاصل]
Direct relation	'alāqa mubāshira	**العلاقة المباشرة**
Direct shipment; drop shipment	shuḥna mubāshira	**شحنة مباشرة**
Direct verification	taḥaqquq mubāshir	**التحقق المباشر** [عملية يقوم بها مدقق الحسابات للتأكد من صحة البيانات والحسابات والبنود]
Direct wage rate variance	inhirāf mu'addal al-ujūr al-mubāshira	**انحراف معدل الاجور المباشرة** [ذلك الجزء من اختلاف الاجور المباشرة الناتج عن الفرق بين الاجر المعيارى والمعدل الفعلى الذى يدفع]
Direct wages; direct labour cost	ujūr mubāshira	**أجور مباشرة**
Direction of effort	al-hadaf al-manshūd	**الهدف المنشود** [تسمية أى توزيع للمصاريف بالاستناد إلى الفوائد المتحققة]
Directory	dalīl	**دليل**
Dirty bill of lading	wathīqat shaḥn ma' taḥaffuẓ	**وثيقة شحن مع تحفظ**
Disaffirm	yunkir	**ينكر** (ينقض عقدا)
Disallowance	man'	**منع** (حظر)
Disburse	yaṣrif	**يصرف** (يدفع)

Disbursement	dafʻ	**دفـــع** (نقدا أو بشيك)
Disbursement voucher	mustand ṣarf	**مستند صرف**
Disbursing officer	muwaẓẓaf aṣ-ṣarf	**موظف الصرف** [المخول بدفع قيمة الفواتير نقدا أو بشيكات]
Discharge	tasdīd dayn	**تسديد دين**
Disclaimer (of opinion)	ḥajb ar-ra'y	**حجب الرأى** [امتناع مدقق الحسابات عن ابداء الرأى في عدالة البيانات الحسابية الختامية أو في بيان منها دون الآخر]
Disclosure	iḍāḥāt	**ايضاحـــات** [حول البيانات الحسابية الختامية]
Discount	khaṣm	**خصـــم**
Discount a bill	yakhṣum kumbiyāla	**يخصم كمبيالة**
Discount allowed	khaṣm masmūḥ bihi	**خصم مسموح به**
Discount banks	bunūk al-khaṣm	**بنوك الخصم**
Discount earned	khaṣm muktasab	**خصم مكتسب**
Discount lost	khaṣm ḍā'iʻ	**خصم ضائع** [بسبب عدم دفع الثمن قبل انتهاء مدة الخصم]
Discount rate	muʻaddal al-khaṣm	**معدل الخصم**
Discount, allow a	yamnaḥ khaṣman	**يمنح خصما**
Discountable	qābil li'l-khaṣm	**قابل للخصم**
Discounted bill	kumbiyāla makhṣūma	**كمبيالة مخصومة**
Discovery period (insurance)	fatrat iktishāf al-khasāra	**فترة اكتشاف الخسارة** [الفترة المسموح بها للمؤمن بعد انتهاء عقد أو وثيقة التأمين ليكتشف خسارته أثناء التأمين وفي حدود الاتفاقية]
Discrepancy	mughāyara	**مغايرة** (اختلاف ، عدم تطابق ، فرق)
Discrimination, price	tamyīz fi's-siʻr	**تمييز في السعر**
Dishonour	imtināʻ ʻan ad-dafʻ	**الامتناع عن الدفع**
Disinvestment	ʻawdat ar-rasāmīl ilā maṣādirihā	**عودة الرساميل إلى مصادرها** [استثمار في الاتجاه المعاكس]
Disparity	tabāyun	**تباين** (بين سعرين)
Dispatch earning	tawfīr fī kulfat ash-shaḥn	**توفير في كلفة الشحن** [ناجم عن تفريغ الشحنة الفورى في مرفأ الوصول]
Dispatch note	biṭāqat taṣdīr	**بطاقة تصدير**
Dispersion	tashattut	**تشتـــت** [مقدار اختلاف مجموعة معلومات رقمية عن المعدل المعيارى]
Disposable income	ad-dakhl al-fardi 'ṣ-ṣāfī	**الدخل الفردى الصافي** [بعد طرح الضرائب والالتزامات الاخرى]

Disposition of net income (or net profit or net earnings)	al-tasaruf fi-d-dakhl as-ṣāfī	التصرف في الدخل الصافي [بيان مالي يظهر أحيانا في تقرير المدقق والتقارير السنوية إلى المساهمين أو الشركاء ويبين أرباح الاسهم المعلنة أو الأرباح المسحوبة واحتياطي الفائض المخصص أو العائد منه وغيرها من البنود مع الرصيد المضاف إلى الارباح المتراكمة أو الملكية]
Dissolution	ḥall sharika	حـلّ (تصفية) شركة
Dissolve	yaḥill	يحـل (شركة)
Distort	yuḥarrif	يحـرف (يشوه ، يضلل)
Distraint	hajz	الحجـز (لاستيفاء دين)
Distress	1 ḥajz iḥtiyāṭī 2 ʿusr	١ - حجز احتياطي ٢ - عسـر
Distress merchandise	biḍāʿa li't-taṣfiya	بضاعة للتصفية
Distribution	tawzīʿ	توزيـع
Distribution account	ḥisāb at-tawzīʿ	حساب التوزيع
Distribution expense (or cost)	taklifat at-tawzīʿ	تكلفة (مصروفات) التوزيع
Distribution of profits	tawzīʿ al-arbāḥ	توزيع الأرباح
Distribution of the dividend	tawzīʿ arbāḥ al-as-hum	توزيع أرباح الأسهم
Distribution, masked, veiled	tawzīʿ muqannaʿ	توزيع مقنع
Distributor discount; trade discount	khaṣm tijārī	الخصم التجارى
Distributor's price list	la'iḥat asʿār al-muwazziʿ	لائحة أسعار الموزع
Divided account	ḥisāb ismī	حساب اسمي [أى حساب يمثل تصنيفا جزئيا من حساب حقيقي كالايرادات والمصاريف بالنسبة للأرباح المحتفظ بها]
Dividend	ribḥ as-sahm	ربح السـهم [حصة السهم في الأرباح الموزعة]
Dividend announcement	iʿlān arbāḥ al-as-hum	اعلان أرباح الأسهم
Dividend income	īrād arbāḥ al-as-hum	ايراد أرباح الأسهم
Dividend payable	arbāḥ as-hum ghayr madfūʿa	ارباح أسهم غير مدفوعة
Dividend share	sahm iḍāfī	سـهم اضافـي [لا يستحق إلا بعض الربح لأنه اضيف إلى رأسمال الشركة المسدد بقيمة الأسهم العادية]
Dividend warrant	qasīmat ribḥ sābiq mutarākim	قسيمة ربح سابق متراكم
Dividends in arrears	arbāḥ lam tuqbaḍ	أرباح لم تقبض
Dividends in kind; property dividend	arbāḥ ʿayniyya	أرباح عينية
Divisible	qābil li'l-qisma	قابل للقسمة
Division of capital	taqsīm ra's al-māl	تقسيم رأس المال
Division of costs	marāḥil at-taklifa	مراحل التكلفة
Division of labour	taqsīm al-ʿamal	تقسيم العمل
Document	mustanad	مستند (وثيقة)
Documentary	mustanadī	مستندى (وثائقي)

Documentary bill	kumbiyāla mustanadiyya	**كمبيالة مستندية**
Documentary credit	iʿtimād mustanadī	**اعتماد مستندى**
Documentary draft	saḥb mustanadī	**سحب مستندى** (كمبيالة مستندية)
Documentation	daʿm bi'l-wathā'iq	**دعم بالوثائق**
Documents	mustanadāt	**مستندات**
Domestic	maḥallī	**محلي** (اهلي)
Domestic corporation	sharika maḥalliyya	**شركة محلية** [تؤسس حسب قوانين بلد معين]
Domicile	maqarr thābit	**المقر الثابت** [المكان الذى يتخذ منه الشخص أو الشركة مقرا رسميا ثابتا]
Domiciled bill	kumbiyāla muwaṭṭana	**كمبيالة موطنة** [ورقة تجارية معين فيها مكان الدفع]
Domiciliation	tawṭīn	**توطـين** [تعيين محل الوفاء]
Donate	yatabarraʿ	**يتبـرع** (يهب)
Donated surplus	fā'iḍ mawhūb	**الفائض الموهوب** [الناتج من هبات المساهمين وغيرهم]
Donations	hibāt	**هبات** (تبرعات ، عطايا)
Dormant account	ḥisāb sakin	**حساب ساكن** (غير مستعمل)
Dormant partner	sharīk muwaṣṣī	**شريك موصي**
Dormant warrant	kafāla ʿala bayāḍ	**كفالة على بياض**
Double (n.; v.)	ḍiʿf	**ضعف ـ يضاعف**
Double account form balance sheet	al-mīzāniyya dhāt al-ḥisābayn	**الميزانية ذات الحسابين** [الميزانية المعدة على أساس نظام الحساب المزدوج مستخدمة أحيانا في بريطانيا ولها قسمان الرأسمال أو التمويل وحساب التشغيل أو الحساب العام]
Double account system	niẓām al-ḥisāb al-muzdawaj	**نظام الحساب المزدوج**
Double distribution	tawzīʿ muzdawaj	**التوزيع المزدوج** [اعادة توزيع المصاريف حيث تنتقل التكلفة إلى حساب آخر أو توزيع على عدة حسابات]
Double entry	qayd muzdawaj	**قيد مزدوج**
Double entry bookkeeping	mask ad-dafātir bi'l-qayd al-muzdawaj	**مسك الدفاتر بالقيد المزدوج**
Double entry system	niẓām al-qayd al-muzdawaj	**نظام القيد المزدوج**
Double liability	iltizām muzdawaj	**الالتزام المزدوج** [التزام شخص يخص المساهمين والذى يقضي بمضاعفة الهبات التي دفعوها أو تعهدوا بدفعها]
Double sampling	ʿayyināt muzdawaja	**العينات المزدوجة** [طريقة تقسيم عملية أخذ العينات إلى

مرحلتين بحيث أنه بعد فحص العينة الأولى
تقبل المجموعة أو ترفض أو تعلق بانتظار
فحص العينة الثانية]

Double taxation	izdiwāj aḍ-ḍarība	ازدواج الضريبة
Doubtful account	ḥisāb mashkūk fī-taḥṣīlihi	حساب مشكوك في تحصيله
Doubtful debts	duyūn mashkūk fīhā	ديون مشكوك فيها
Doubtful notes and accounts (U.S.)	duyūn ghayr maḍmūnat al-istīfa'	ديون غير مضمونة الاستيفاء
Doubtful, reserve for – debts	iḥtiyāṭi 'd-dujūn al-mashkūk fīhā	احتياطي الديون المشكوك فيها
Downfall	inhiyār al-as'ār	انهيار الأسعار
Downstairs merger	damj ash-sharika 'l-umm bi'sh-sharika al-far'iyya	دمج الشركة الأم بالشركة الفرعية
Draft	1 muswadda	١ - مسودة
	2 kumbiyāla	٢ - كمبيالة
	3 hawāla	٣ - حوالـــة
Draft budget	mashrū' mīzāniyya	مشروع ميزانية
Draft, bank	ḥawāla maṣrafiyya	حوالة مصرفية
Draft, demand	kumbiyāla taḥt aṭ-ṭalab	كمبيالة تحت الطلب
Draft, sight	saḥb 'ind al-iṭṭilā'	سحب عند الاطلاع
Draft, time	ḥawāla lī-ajal	حوالة لاجل
Draw	yas-hab	يسحب (شيك أو كمبيالة أو نقود)
Draw on another	yas-hab ḥawāla 'alā ākhar	يسحب حوالة على آخر
Draw out	yas-hab mālan	يسحب مالا (من مصرف)
Draw up	yuḥarrir	يحرر (سندا)
Drawback	1 fawāt ribḥ	١ - فوات ربــح
	2 takhfīḍ	٢ - تخفيض (سعر)
	3 istirdād rusūm al-istīrād	٣ - استرداد رسوم الاستيراد (بعد تصدير المواد المستوردة)
Drawee	al-mas-ḥūb 'alayhi	المسحوب عليه
Drawer	as-sāḥib	الساحــب
Drawing account	ḥisāb al-mas-ḥūbāt	حساب المسحوبات
Drawings	mas-ḥūbāt	مسحوبـــات
Drawn	1 mas-ḥūb	١ - مسحوب (سند)
	2 maqbūḍ	٢ - مقبوض (القيمة)
Drop shipment	shaḥn mubāshir	شحـن مباشـر [من المصنع إلى تاجر المفرق]
Dual control system	niẓām ar-riqāba 'l-muzdawaja	نظام الرقابة المزدوجة
Dud cheque	shīk bi-dūn raṣīd	شيك بدون رصيد
Due	mustaḥiqq ad-daf'	مستحق الدفع
Due date	mī'ād al-istiḥqāq	ميعاد الاستحقاق
Due from banks	mustaḥiqq 'ala al-maṣārif	المستحق على المصارف (المصارف المدينة)

Due to	mustaḥiqq lahu	مستحق له
Due to banks	mustaḥiqq li'l-maṣārif	المستحق للمصارف (المصارف الدائنة)
Dues	1 rasm	١ - رسم (مرفأ)
	2 ḍarā'ib	٢ - ضرائب (على رخص أو أحواض سفن)
	3 ḥuqūq mutarattiba 'alā	٣ - حقوق مترتبة على
Duly	1 fī ḥīnihi	١ - في حينة
	2 ḥasab al-uṣūl	٢ - حسب الأصول
Duly accepted	tawqī' bi'l-qabūl	توقيع بالقبول
Duly acquitted	mu'ashshar 'alyhi bis-sadād	مؤشر عليه بالسداد
Dump	yughriq	يغرق (الاسواق الخارجية بالسلع بأسعار أرخص من سعر مكان المنشأ أى بخسارة)
Duplicate	ṣūra ṭibq al-aṣl	صورة طبق الأصل
Duplication	izdiwāj	ازدواج
Dutiable	khāḍi' li'r-rusūm	خاضع للرسوم (المكوس)
Duties	rusūm jumrukiyya	رسوم جمركية
Duty; tariff	ta'rifa	تعرفة
Duty drawback	istirdād ar-rasm al-jumrukī	استرداد الرسم الجمركي [استرداد كل أو بعض الرسوم التى يتقاضاها الجمرك عن مواد مستوردة لتصنيفها عند اعادة تصدير المصنع منها]
Duty free	mu'fā min ar-rusūm	معفى من الرسوم
E. & O. E. (errors & omissions excepted)	mā 'ada 's-sahw wa'l-khaṭa'	ماعدا السهو والخطأ
Earmarking	ḥajz mablagh	حجز مبلغ (من الحساب لتنفيذ عملية معينة)
Earn	yaksab	يكسب
Earned	muktasab	مكتسب
Earned income	1 īrād muktasab	١ - ايراد مكتسب [من خدمات شخصية مؤداة تميزا عن أنواع الايرادات الاخرى]
	2 īrād muḥaqqaq	٢ - ايراد محقق
Earned surplus	fā'iḍ muktasab	فائض مكتسب [صافي الربح المتراكم مطروحا منه ما وزع على المساهمين وما نقل إلى حساب حقوق المساهمين]
Earnest money	'arbūn	عربون (لعقد صفقة ما)
Earning capacity	qudrat al-kasb	قدرة الكسب
Earnings	1 īrādāt	١ - ايرادات (ربح أو دخل)
	2 ṣāfi 'l-arbāḥ	٢ - صافي الأرباح
	3 dakhl fardī	٣ - دخل فردى
	4 īrād muktasab	٤ - ايراد مكتسب

Earnings statement	1 bayān al-arbāḥ wa'l-khasā'ir	١ - بيان الأرباح والخسائر
	2 kashf taḥlīlī li'd-dakhl	٢ - كشف تحليلي للدخل
Easement	ḥaqq al-intifā'	حـــق الانتفاع [حق مالك الأرض بالاستفادة من طريق أو ماء أو طاقة كهربائية أو أية منفعة أخرى فى الأرض المجاورة]
Easy terms	shuruṭ sahla	شروط سهلة (تسهيلات بالدفع)
Eat off	ya'mal dūn intāj	يعمل (المصنع) دون انتاج
Eat up	ya'kul	يأكل (الرأسمال والعائدات)
Economic	iqtiṣādī	اقتصـــادى
Economic activity	1 nashāṭ iqtiṣādī	١ - النشاط الاقتصادى [انتاج وتوزيع البضائع والخدمات]
	2 al-is-ham fi 'l-intaj	٢ - الاسهام في الانتاج (السلع أو الخدمات)
Economic cost; current cost	at-taklifa 'l-ḥaliyya	التكلفة الحالية
Economic equilibrium	at-tawāzun al-iqtiṣādī	التوازن الاقتصادى
Economic good	sil'a iqtiṣādiyya	سلعة اقتصادية
Economic interest	milkiyyat maṣlaḥa	ملكية مصلحة [ملكية مؤسسة أو جزء منها]
Economic law	qānūn iqtiṣādī	قانون اقتصادى
Economic life	'umr iqtiṣādī	العمر الاقتصادى [المدة التي يستطيع الأصل الثابت خلالها أن يؤدى خدمات نافعة لصاحبه]
Economic lot size	al-ḥajm al-iqtiṣādī	الحجم الاقتصادى [عدد الوحدات المطلوبة في عملية شراء واحدة أو التي يتم انتاجها في دورة واحدة قبل تحويل الآلات إلى انتاج صنف آخر بحيث تحمل أقل نفقات ممكنة أو تتحقق أقصى الفوائد]
Economic unit	wiḥda iqtiṣādiyya	وحدة اقتصادية ١ - [أى فرد أو مجموعة لها هدف أو مصالح مشتركة مع الأخرى] ٢ - [مجموعة مؤسسات تعمل تحت اشراف واحـــد]
Economical	iqtiṣādī	اقتصـــادى
Economics	'ilm al-iqtiṣād	علم الاقتصاد
Economist	'ālim iqtiṣādī	عالم اقتصادى
Economy	1 iqtiṣād	١ - اقتصاد
	2 tawfīr	٢ - توفيـــر
Effective rate	mu'addal fa''āl	المعدل الفعال [نسبة الايراد الدورى المحقق الى القيمة السوقية للأموال المستثمرة]
Effects	1 mumtalakat shakhṣiyya	١ - ممتلكات شخصية (متاع)
	2 awrāq	٢ - أوراق

Effects not cleared	awrāq lam tuḥaṣṣal qīmatuha	أوراق لم تحصل قيمتها
Efficiency	fa'āliyya	فعاليــة
		١ - نسبة الانجاز
		٢ - نسبة المردود الى الزاد
		٣ - الانتاج بأقل تكلفة
		٤ - معدل الأربحية
		٥ - الوضعية المثلى للانتاج
Efficiency of estimates	kifayat-at-taqdīrāt	كفاية التقديرات
Efficiency ratio	mu'addal al-fa'āliya	معدل الفعالية
Efficiency variance	mu'āmil al-fa'āliya	معامل الفعالية
		[اختلاف ناتج عن أسباب غير التغيير في سعر المواد أو الأيدى العاملة]
Efficiency, marginal – of investment	al-kifāya 'l-ḥaddiyya li'l-istihimār	الكفاية الحدية للاستثمار
Elasticity	murūna	مـــرونة
Elasticity of demand	murūnat aṭ-talab	مرونة الطلب
Elasticity of supply	murūnat al-'arḍ	مرونة العرض
Elements	'anāṣir	عناصر (مواد)
Elements of cost	'anāṣir at-taklife	عناصر التكلفة
Embezzle	yakhtalis	يختلس (مالا)
Embezzlement	ikhtilās	اختلاس
Emolument	ta'wīḍ	تعويض (عن خدمات شخصية
Employ	yastakhdim	يستخدم
Employee	mustakhdam	مستخدم (بفتح الدال)
Employer	mustakhdim	مستخدم (بكسر الدال)
Employment	istikhdām	استخدام (توظيف)
Encash	yaqbiḍ	يقبض (قيمة شيك)
Enclose	yurfiq	يرفق (وثيقة برسالة)
Enclosures	murfaqāt	مرفقـــات
Encumber	yuthqil	يثقل (بالديون والرهونات)
Encumbrance	'ib'	عـــبء
	1 maṣroof mutawaqa'	١ - مصروف متوقع (المحاسبة الحكومية)
	2 iltizam	٢ - التـــزام
	3 rahn akari	٣ - رهن عقارى
End of month settlement	taṣfiyat nihāyat ash-shahr	تصفية نهاية الشهر
Ending balance	ar-raṣīd an-nihā'ī	الرصيد النهائي
Endorsable	qābil li't-tajyīr	قابل للتجيير (للتظهير)
Endorse	yujayyir	يجيّـر (يظهر)
Endorsee	al-mujayyar lahu	المجيّـر له (المظهر له)
Endorsement	tajyīr	تجيير (تظهير)
Endorsement in blank	tajyīr 'alā bayāḍ	تجيير على بياض
Endorsement without recourse	tajyīr waraqa dūn ḍamān daf'	تجيير ورقة دون ضمان دفع
Endorsement, conditional	tajyīr sharṭī	تجيير شرطي
Endorser	al-mujayyir	المجيـــر

Endow	yuqif mālan ʿalā	يقف مالا على
Endowment fund	ṣundūq li-mu'assasa khayriyya	صندوق لمؤسسة خيرية
Endowment policy method	ṭarīqat al-waqfiyya 'l-baḥta	طريقة الوقفية البحتة
		[حساب قسط الاهلاك على دفعات دورية متساوية طبقا لعقد تصفية بحتة على أن تكون حصيلة العقد في نهاية العمر الانتاجى للأصل مساويا للقيمة المهلكة للأصل]
Enface	1 yusajjil	١ - يسجل
	2 yuqayyid	٢ - يقيد (على وجه السند)
Enfacement	taqyīd as-sanad	تقييد السند
		[عبارة مسجلة على وجه السند]
Engrossment	bayʿ iḥtikārī	بيع احتكارى
		[شراء بضاعة معينة لاحتكارها وبيعها بأسعار يفرضها الشارى]
Enhance in price (v.)	yazīd al-asʿār	يزيد الأسعار
Enhancement	ziyādat al-asʿār	زيادة الأسعار
Enter	1 yuqayyid	١ - يقيد (في دفتر اليومية)
	2 yuraḥḥil	٢ - يرحـــل
Enterprise	1 mashrūʿ	١ - مشـــروع
	2 mu'assasa tijāriyya	٢ - مؤسسة تجارية
	3 sifat al-idāra 'n-nashitạ	٣ - صفة الادارة النشطة
Enterprise accounting	muḥasbat al-mu'assasa bi-ajma ʿihā	محاسبة المؤسسة بأجمعها
Enterprise cost	taklifat al-mushrūʿ	تكلفة المشروع
		[التكلفة التي تحملها مالكو الأصل الحاليون]
Enterprise value	qīmat al-aṣl	قيمـة الأصـل
		[قيمة أصل واحد أو صافي أصول المؤسسة على أساس افتراض استمرار نفع الأصل أو استمرار عمليات المؤسسة]
Entertainment expenses	maṣārīf diyāfa	مصاريف ضيافة
Entertainment tax	ḍarībat al-malāhī	ضريبة الملاهي
Entitled to	yastaḥiqq lahu	يستحق لـــه
Entrepreneur	ṣaḥib al-mushrūʿ	صاحب المشروع
Entries, adjustment	qu-yūd taʿdīl	قيود تعديل
Entries, closing	quyūd iqfāl	قيـود اقفـال
Entry	1 qayd ḥisābī	١ - قيد حسابي
	2 tarḥīl	٢ - ترحيـــل
	3 mādda	٣ - مادة (في حساب)
Entry, books of first	dafātir al-qayd al-awwalī	دفاتر القيد الأولى
Entry, double – system	nizām al-qayd al-muzdawij	نظام القيد المزدوج
Entry, single – system	niẓām al-qayd al-mufrad	نظام القيد المفرد
E.O.M. (end of month)	nihāyat ash-shahr	نهاية الشهر
E.O.Y. (end of year)	nihāyat al-ʿāmm	نهاية العام

Equal	muʻādil	**معـــادل** (مساو)
Equal annual payment method	ṭarīqat ad-dafʻa 's-sanawiyya l-mutasāwiya	**طريقة الدفعة السنوية المتساوية** [طريقة حساب احتياطي الاستهلاك على أساس تشغيل دفعة ثابتة سنويا بفائدة معينة بحيث أن المبلغ الاجمالي في نهاية المدة المقدرة كعمر انتاجي للموجود الثابت تعادل قيمة الموجود الثابت]
Equalisation	'amaliyyat at-ta'ādul	**عملية التعادل**
Equalisation point; basing point	mawqiʻ at-takāfu'	**موقع التكافؤ** (النقطة الأساسية) [المكان الجغرافي الذى يكون فيه السعر المعلن لسلطة ما هو الأساس الذى يتحدد بموجبه سعر السلعة نفسها في مكان آخر]
Equalisation reserve	iḥtiyāṭi 't-takafu'	**١ - احتياطي التكافؤ** [حساب استيعابى تقيد اليه دوريا مبالغ تغطي نفقات عمليات ذات حجم كاف لتغطية المصاريف التي صرفت بشكل غير منتظم خلال فترة محاسبية معينة] **٢ - احتياطي مختلط**
Equalising dividend	arbāḥ takāfu'	**أرباح تكافؤ** [الأرباح الموقوفة لتصحيح عدم الانصاف الناتج عن تغييرات في تاريخ توزيع الارباح المنتظمة]
Equality	musāwah	**مســـاواة**
Equals	al-aṭrāf al-muta'ādila	**الأطراف المتعادلة**
Equate	yuwāzin	**يوازن** (بين النفقات والواردات) ، **يسـوى**
Equation	1 taswiya 2 tawāzī 3 muʻādala	**١ - تسويـــة** **٢ - تـــوازى** **٣ - معادلـــة**
Equation of annuities	taswiyat ad-dafʻat as-sanahiya	**تسوية الدفعات السناهية**
Equation of debts	taswiyat ad-duyūn	**تسوية الديون**
Equation of exchange	muʻādalat al-mubādala	**معادلة المبادلة**
Equilibrium	tawāzun	**تـــوازن**
Equilibrium price	siʻr at-tawāzun	**سعر التوازن**
Equilibrium rate of interest	siʻr al-fā'ida 't-tawāzunī	**سعر الفائدة التوازني**
Equipment	muʻaddāt	**معـــدات**
Equipment trust certificate	wathīqat ṣundūqal-muʻaddāt	**وثيقة صندوق المعدات** [وثيقة بفائدة تثبت تملكا جزئيا لصندوق انشيء لغرض شراء المعدات وبيعها أو تأجيرها لمستعمليها]
Equipment, capital	ra'smāl tajhīz	**رأسمال تجهيز**
Equitable mortgage	rahn mustanad milkiyya	**رهن مستند ملكية** [ايداع مستندات ملكية كرهن لقرض مؤقت]
Equity	1 ḥaqq fī mawjudāt	**١ - حق في موجودات**

	2 ḥaqq ad-dā'inīn fī mawjūdāt	٢ - حق الدائنين في موجودات
	3 as-hum ʿādiyya	٣ - أسهم عادية
Equity financing	bayʿ as-hum	بيع أسهم [تقوم به الشركة صاحبة الأسهم]
Equity ownership	milkiyya	ملكيـــة [حصة المالك في ملكية أو في مؤسسة تخضع في حالة التصفية الى المطالبة المسبقة للدائنين]
Equity receiver	ḥaris gaḍā'ī	حارس قضائي
Equity security (U.S.)	as-hum ʿādiyya	أسهم عادية
Erroneous	khāṭi'	خاطيء (غير صحيح)
Error	khaṭa'	خطـأ
Error of estimates	khaṭa' at-taqdīrāt	خطـأ التقديرات
Error, standard	al-khaṭa' al-miʿyārī	الخطأ المعيارى
Errors of commission	akhṭā' irtikābiyya	أخطاء ارتكابية
Errors of omission	akhṭa' al-ḥadhf	أخطاء الحذف
Errors, rectification of	iṣlāh al-khaṭā'	اصلاح الاخطاء
Escapable cost	at-taklifa 'l-mumkin al-istighnā' ʿanhā	التكلفة الممكن الاستغناء عنها (في حالة تقلص حجم العمل)
Escape clause	shart insiḥāb	شرط انسحاب [شرط يسمح لطرف أو أكثر في اتفاقية بالانسحاب أو تعديل الانجاز المتعهد به]
Escrow	wathīqat ḍamān	وثيقة ضمان [موضوعة في مصرف لصالح شخص ثالث يسلم له عند تحقيق شرط معين]
Escrow funds	amwāl mawḍūʿa ka-wadīʿa qānūniyya	أموال موضوعة كوديعة قانونية
Establish	yuʿassis	يؤسس (ينشيء)
Establishment	1 munsha'a	١ - منشأة
	2 mu'assasa tijāriyya	٢ - مؤسسة تجارية
Establishment account	ḥisāb maṣārif at-ta'sīs	حساب مصاريف التأسيس
Establishment expenses	maṣārif at-ta'sīs	مصاريف التأسيس
Establishment of credit	fatḥ iʿtimād	فتـح اعتـماد
Estate	1 milkiyya	١ - ملكية (وبالأخص عقارية)
	2 tarika	٢ - تركـة
Estate accounting	muḥāsabat al-amlāk	محاسبة الأملاك [اعداد ومسك حسابات الأملاك الموضوعة في أيدى الاوصياء الذين عينتهم المحكمة]
Estate agent	simsār ʿaqārī	سمسار عقارى
Estate income	ribḥ aw irādʿ al-amlāk	ربح أو ايراد الاملاك [كما تحدده نصوص الوصية أو القانون]
Estate tax	ḍarība tarikāt	ضريبة تركات
Estate, personal	manqūlāt	منقولات (أموال منقولة)

Estate, real	ʿaqārāt	**عقارات** (مبنية وغير مبنية)
Estimate (n.; v.)	taqdīr	**تقدير** (تقييم) **ـ يقدر** (يقيّم)
Estimated cost	taklifa muqaddara	**تكلفة مقدرة**
Estimated profits	arbāḥ taqdīriyya	**أرباح تقديرية**
Estimated time	al-waqt al-muqaddar	**الوقت المقدر**
Estimated valuation	taqdīr juzāfī	**تقدير جزافي**
Estimating cost system	niẓām at-takālif at-taqdīrī	**نظام التكاليف التقديرى** [طريقة محاسبة تكون التكاليف المقدرة فيها هي الأساس للقيود على حسابات العمل قيد التنفيـذ]
Evade	yataharrab	**يتهرب** (من دفع الضرائب)
Evaluate	yuqaddir	**يقدر** (يقيّم)
Evaluation	taqdīr	**تقدير** (تقييم)
Evasion of taxes	taharrub min dafʿ aḍ-ḍarā'ib	**تهرب من دفع الضرائب**
Even	mutaʿādil	**متعادل** (متساو)
Even lot; round lot	kammiyya mi'awiyya	**كمية مئوية** [وحدة تتألف من مائة سهم أو مضاعفاته]
Events and conditions	ḥawādith wa-ẓurūf	**الحوادث والظروف** [ظواهر التغير الاقتصادى المعروفة في المحاسبة والتي تشكل موضوع العمليات]
Evidence	dalīl	**دليـل** (برهان ، بينة ، حجة)
Ex	1 bi-dūn	١ - **بـدون**
	2 khārij	٢ - **خـارج** (كذا)
	3 sābiq	٣ - **سـابق**
Ex allotment	bi-dūn tawziʿ arbah	**بدون توزيع أرباح** (الأسهم الخ)
Ex bond	li'l-wafā' ʿan dhimma	**للوفاء عن ذمة** (فلان)
Ex claim	dūn ḥaqq	**دون حـق**
Ex coupon	qasīma munfaṣila	**قسيمة منفصلة**
Ex dividend	bi-dūn ribḥ	**بـدون ربـح** [يطلق على سعر الورقة المالية المعروضة للبيع اذا احتفظ البائع بحقه في تحصيل أول ربح أو الفائدة المستحقة]
Ex interest	bi-dūn fawā'id mustaḥaqqa	**بدون فوائد مستحقة**
Ex new; ex rights	ḥuqūq munfaṣila	**حقوق منفصلة**
Ex ship	taslīm al-bākhira	**تسليم الباخرة** [السعر بجانب الباخرة في ميناء الوصول]
Ex works	taslīm al-maṣnaʿ	**تسليم المصنع** [السعر تسليم المصنع]
Exact interest	fā'ida basīṭa	**الفائدة البسيطة** (على أساس ٣٦٥)
Examination audit	1 faḥṣ	١ - **فحـص**
	2 tadqīq	٢ - **تدقيـق**
Examination report	taqrīr tadqīq	**تقرير تدقيق**
Examine	yudaqqiq	**يـدقـق**

Exceed	yatajāwaz	يتجاوز (يزيد عن)
Exception	1 taḥaffuẓ	١ - تحفظ (في تقرير مراقب الحسابات)
	2 ish'ār istifsār 'an nafqa	٢ - اشعار استفسار عن نفقة
	3 al-farq bayn at-taklifa' al-mi'yāriyya wa' t-taklifa 'l-fi'liyya	٣ - الفرق بين التكلفة المعيارية والتكلفة الفعلية
Exceptional profits	arbāḥ istithnā'iyya	أرباح استثنائية
Excess cash reserves	al-iḥtiyāṭi 'n-naqdi'l-fā'iḍ	الاحتياطي النقدى الفائض
Excess profits tax	ḍarā'ib 'ala 'l-arbāḥ az-zā'ida	ضرائب على الأرباح الزائدة
Excessive	zā'id	زائد (متجاوز الحد)
Exchange	1 muqāyaḍa	١ - مقايضة
	2 taḥwīl	٢ - تحويل (عملة)
	3 burṣa	٣ - بورصة (سوق)
Exchange at discount	si'r aṣ-ṣarf dūna't-ta'ādul	سعر الصرف دون التعادل (السعر الرسمي)
Exchange at par	si'r aṣ-ṣarf bit-ta'ādul	سعر الصرف بالتعادل
Exchange at premium	si'raṣ-ṣarf fawqa 't-ta'ādul	سعر الصرف فوق التعادل (أو السعر الرسمي)
Exchange cheque	shīk tabāduli	شيك تبادلي [الشيك المعطى مقابل نقد أو شيك آخر]
Exchange commission	'umūlat at-taḥwīl	عمولة التحويل
Exchange control	murāqabat aṣ-ṣarf al-ajnabī	مراقبة الصرف الأجنبي
Exchange cover	'taghṭiya bi'l-qaṭ' al-ajnabī	تغطية بالقطع الاجنبي
Exchange equalisation fund	ṣundūq muwāzanat al-'umla 'lajnabiyya	صندوق موازنة العملة الأجنبية [المال الذى تخصصه بعض الدول لمواجهة التغييرات الطارئة على سعر الصرف وتعهد به إلى هيئة خاصة]
Exchange fluctuations	taqallubāt as'ār taḥwīl al-'umla	تقلبات أسعار تحويل العملة
Exchange market	sūq tabādul al-'umla	سوق تبادل العملة
Exchange parity	ta'ādul si'r aṣ-ṣarf	تعادل سعر الصرف
Exchange position	waḍ' al-qaṭ' al-ajnabī	وضع القطع الأجنبي
Exchange quotations	as'ār al-awrāq an-naqdiyya	أسعار الأوراق النقدية (بورصة)
Exchange rate	si'r at-taḥwīl	سعر التحويل
Exchange, adverse	as'ār aṣ-ṣarf ghayr al-mulā'ima	أسعار الصرف غير الملائمة
Exchange, course of	khaṭṭ sayr al-qat' al-ajnabī	خط سير القطع الأجنبي
Exchange, foreign	qaṭ' ajnabī	قطع أجنبي
Exchange, foreign bills of	kumbiyāla khārijiyya	كمبيالات خارجية
Exchange, forward dealings	ṣafaqāt ṣirafa li-ajal	صفقات صرافة لأجل
Exchange, monetary	tabādul naqdī	التبادل النقدى
Exchange, security	tabādul al-awrāq al-māliyya	تبادل الأوراق المالية
Exchange, spot – dealings	safaqāt ṣirāfa naqdan	صفقات صرافة نقدا
Exchange, stock	sūq al-awrāq al-māliyya	سوق الأوراق المالية
Exchange, stock settlement	ayyām at-taṣfiya	أيام التصفية (بورصة)
Exchange, value of	qīmat istibdāl al-'umla	قيمة استبدال (العملة)
Exchangeable	qābil li'l-mubādala	قابل للمبادلة

Exchequer	1 wazārat al-māliyya	١ - وزارة المالية
	2 al-khazina 'l-'āmma	٢ - الخزينة العامة
Exchequer bills (bonds)	sanadāt 'ala 'l-khazīna	سندات على الخزينة
Excisable	khāḍi' li'ḍ-ḍarība	خاضع للضريبة
Excise duty	rasm intāj	رسم انتاج
Excise tax	ḍarībat intāj	ضريبة انتاج
Execution	tanfīdh	تنفيذ (انجاز ، اتمام)
Execution creditor	al-maḥjūz lahu	المحجوز له
Execution debtor	al-maḥjūz 'alayhi	المحجوز عليه
Executive (U.S.) (n.; adj.)	mudīr tanfīdhī	مدير تنفيذى (اجرائي)
Executive body	hay'a tanfīdhiyya	الهيئة التنفيذية
Executive function	waẓīfa tanfīdhiyya	وظيفة تنفيذية
Executive power	sulṭa tanfīdhiyya	سلطة تنفيذية
Executor	munaffidh al-waṣiyya	منفذ الوصية
Executory	mu'add li't-tanfīdh	معد للتنفيذ
Exempt	yu'fī	يعفي ـ من الضريبة
Exempt private company	sharika khāṣṣa mu'fāh	شركة خاصة معفاة
		[شركة من النوع العائلي معفاة من اعداد ميزانيتها]
Exemption	i'fā'	اعفـاء
Exemption limit	ḥadd al-i'fā'	حـد الاعفـاء
Exercise (n.; v.)	1 mumārasa	١ - ممارسـة
	2 yumāris	٢ - يمـارس
Exhaust	yastanfidh	يسـتنفذ
Exhaustion method	ṭarīqat al-istinfādh	طريقة الاستنفاذ
Exhibit (n.; v.)	1 bayān	١ - بيـان
	2 ya'riḍ	٢ - يعـرض
Expand	yatawassa'	يتوسـع
Expansion	tawassu'	توسـع
Expectancy; expected value	al-qīma 'l-mutawaqqa'a	القيمة المتوقعة
Expected standard	al-miqyās al-mutawaqqa'	المقياس المتوقع
Expedite	1 yanshaṭ	١ - ينشط (العمل التجارى)
	2 yursil	٢ - يرسل
	3 yu'ajjil	٣ - يعجّـل
Expediter	mursil	المرسـل
Expend	yaṣrif	يصـرف
Expandable fund	ṣundūq aṣ-ṣarf	صندوق الصـرف
		[صندوق يخصص لغرض معين]
Expenditure	1 infāq	١ - انفـاق
	2 maṣrūf	٢ - مصـروف
	3 taklifa	٣ - تكلفـة
Expenditure rate	al-ḥadd al-a'lā li'l-maṣārīf	الحد الأعلى للمصاريف
		[الذى تحدده الادارة لأى فترة من الزمن]

Expenditure, capital	al-maṣārīf ar-ra'smāliyya	المصاريف الرأسمالية
Expenditure, central	al-maṣārīf al-markaziyya	المصاريف المركزية
Expenditure, investment	al-infāq al-istithmārī	الانفاق الاستثماري
Expenditure, operating	nafaqāt at-tashghīl	نفقات التشغيل
Expenditure, revenue	maṣrūf īrādī	مصروف ايرادي
Expense	1 maṣrūf	١ - مصروف
	2 kulfat tashghīl	٢ - كلفة تشغيل
	3 nafaqa	٣ - نفقة
Expense analysis sheet	al-qā'ima 't-taḥlīliyya li'l-maṣārīf	القائمة التحليلية للمصاريف
Expense budget	mīzāniyya taqdīriyya li'l-maṣārīf	ميزانية تقديرية للمصاريف
Expense centre	markaz infāq	مركز انفاق
Expense control	ḍabṭ al-maṣārif	ضبط المصاريف [أي طريقة تهدف إلى ابقاء تكاليف المستقبل ضمن حدود معينة]
Expense distribution	tawzī' al-maṣrūf	توزيع المصروف (طبقا للغرض منه)
Expense price variance	inḥirāf mu'addal al-maṣārīf	انحراف معدل المصاريف
Expense utilisation variance	inḥirāf istikhdām al-maṣārīf	انحراف استخدام المصاريف
Expenses allocation account	ḥisāb tawzī' al-maṣrūfāt	حساب توزيع المصروفات
Expenses, accrued	maṣārīf mustaḥaqqa	مصاريف مستحقة
Expenses, administrative	maṣārīf idāriyya	مصاريف ادارية
Expenses, buying	maṣārif shirā'	مصاريف شراء
Expenses, contingent	msārīf tāri'a	مصاريف طارئة
Expenses, direct	maṣārif mubāshira	مصاريف مباشرة
Expenses, fixed	maṣārif thābita	مصاريف ثابتة
Expenses, general	maṣārif 'āmma	مصاريف عامة
Expenses, incidental	maṣārif 'araḍiyya	مصاريف عرضية
Expenses, indirect	maṣārīf ghayr mubashira	مصاريف غير مباشرة
Expenses, manufacturing	maṣārīf taṣnī'iyya	مصاريف تصنيعية
Expenses, overhead	maṣārīf ra'siyya	مصاريف رأسية
Expenses, petty	maṣārīf nathriyya	مصاريف نثرية
Expenses, running	nafaqāt jāriya	نفقات جارية
Expenses, selling	maṣārīf bay'	مصاريف بيع
Expenses, sundry	maṣārīf mutanawwi'a	مصاريف متنوعة
Expenses, tangible	maṣārif malmūsa	مصاريف ملموسة
Expenses, trading	maṣārīf tijāriyya	مصاريف تجارية
Expenses, travelling	nafaqāt safar	نفقات سفر
Experience	khibra	خبرة
Experienced	khabīr	خبير (محنّك)
Experiment	tajriba	تجربة (اختبار)
Experimental costs	takālīf tajārib	تكاليف تجارب
Expiration	1 inqiḍā'	١ - انقضاء
	2 istiḥqāq	٢ - استحقاق
Expired cost	taklifa muntahiya	تكلفة منتهية

		[المصرف الذى لا ينتظر من ورائه اية فائدة اخـــرى]
Expired utility	1 manfa'a muntahiya	١ - المنفعة المنتهية
	2 istihlāk mutarakim	٢ - الاستهلاك المتراكم
Explanatory	īḍāḥī	ايضاحي (تفسيرى)
Explicit	ṣarīh	صـــريح (بين ، جلي ، واضح)
Exploitation	istighlāl	استغلال (استثمار)
Exploitation operating account	ḥisāb al-istighlāl aw at-tashghīl	حساب الاستغلال أو التشغيل
Export (n.; v.)	taṣdīr	تصدير - يصدر
Export quota	ḥiṣṣat aṣ-ṣādirāt	حصة الصادرات (كوتا)
Exportable	qābil li-t-taṣdīr	قابل للتصدير
Exportations; exports	ṣādirāt	الصادرات
Exposition	sharḥ	شـــرح
Expropriate	yanzi' al-milkiyya	ينزع الملكية (يصادر)
Expunge	yashṭub	يشطب (يحذف)
Expunged, stock – from the list	sahm maḥdhūf min al-lā'iḥa	سهم محذوف من اللائحة
Ex-rights	ḥuqūq munqaḍiya	حقوق منقضية [مصطلح يدل على عدم أحقية المساهمين القدامى لشراء أسهم جديدة بالسعر السابق]
Extend	1 yumaddid	١ - يـمـــدد
	2 yabsuṭ al-arqām	٢ - يبسط الارقام (ينقل رقما إلى عامود آخر)
Extend an invoice (v.)	basṭ al-fātūra	بسط الفاتورة [يدرج الجمع المفصل لمفردات الفاتورة]
Extended coverage	tawsī' taghṭiyat būlīṣa	توسيع تغطية بوليصة (تأمين ضد الحريق بحيث تغطى الأخطار الناتجة عن العواصف والبرد والزلازل والمظاهرات وغيرها)
Extent	madā	مـــدى
External assets	mawjūdāt khārij al-balad	موجودات خارج البلد
External audit	tadqīq khārijī	تدقيق خارجي (من قبل طرف مستقل)
External auditor	mudaqqiq ḥisābāt	مدقق حسابات (خارجي)
External control	raqāba khārijiyya	الرقابة الخارجية
External trade	tijāra kharijiyya	تجارة خارجية
External transaction	'amaliyya ma ṭaraf khārijī	عملية مع طرف خارجي
Extinction of obligations	intihā' al-iltizāmāt	انتهاء الالتزامات
Extra dividend	arbāḥ as-hum iḍāfiyya	أرباح اسهم اضافية (دون ضمان استمرار دفعها)
Extract of account	mustakhraj ḥisāb	مستخرج حساب
Extraordinary depreciation	istihlāk ghayr 'ādī	الاستهلاك غير العادى
Extraordinary loss	khasāra ghayr 'ādiyya	خسارة غير عادية
Extraordinary revenue	īrādāt istithnā'iyya	ايرادات استثنائية
Extrapolation	tanabbu'	تنبـــؤ [خارج المعلومات الاحصائية المتوفرة]
Extravagant	bāhiẓ	باهـــظ (الثمن)

F.A.C.C.A. Fellow of the Association of Certified Accountants	zamīl fī jam'iyyat al-muḥasibīn al-mu'tamadīn al-qānūniyyin	زميل في جمعية المحاسبين المعتمدين القانونيين
Face amount (value)	al-qīma 'l-ismiyya	القيمة الاسمية
Face amount certificate	ta'ahhud bi'l-qīma 'l-ismiyya	تعهد بالقيمة الاسمية [صيغة عقد بين بعض الشركات الاستثمارية والمستثمرين يوافق بموجبها المستثمرون على تسديد جميع الاقساط المطلوبة إلى الشركة]
Facilities	1 tas-hīlāt	١ - تسهيلات
	2 marāfiq	٢ - مرافق (منشآت ثابتة)
Factor	1 wasiṭ tijārī bi'l-'amūla	١ - وسيط تجاري بالعمولة
	2 'āmil	٢ - عامل (في الرياضيات)
Factor, cost	'āmil al-kulfa	عامل الكلفة
Factorage	samsara	سمسرة (عمولة)
Factors of production	awāmil al-intāj	عوامل الانتاج
Factory	maṣna'	مصنع (معمل)
Factory cost; manufacturing cost	takālīf al-maṣna'	تكاليف المصنع
Factory expenses	maṣārif al-maṣna'	مصاريف المصنع [التي لا تشمل المواد الاولية والعمل المباشر]
Factory ledger	ustādh ḥisābāt al-maṣna'	استاذ حسابات المصنع [دفتر يشتمل على تكاليف التشغيل في مؤسسة صناعية مثل المواد والايدى العاملة والتكلفة العادية]
Factory prices	as'ār al-maṣna'	أسعار المصنع
Fail	1 yuflis	١ - يفلس
	2 yataqāas	٢ - يتقاعس
Fail, to – in one's engagements	yatakhallā an wafā' iltizāmātihi	يتخلى عن وفاء التزاماته
Failed firm (U.S.)	mu'assasa muflisa	مؤسسة مفلسة
Failing payment within	li-'adam ad-daf' fī muddat	لعدم الدفع في مدة .....
Failure	fashal	فشل
Failure to accept	'adam al-qabūl	عدم القبول
Failure of a firm	fashal al-munsha'a	فشل المنشأة
Fair	'ādil	عادل (مشروع قانوني)
Fair market value	qīmat as-sūq al-ādiyya	قيمة السوق العادية
Fair trade price	si'r al-bay' ath-thābit	سعر البيع الثابت [الذى يحدده منتج البضاعة لبائعي الجملة والمفرق منعا للمنافسة بينهم]
Fair value	al-qīma 'l-ma'qūla	القيمة المعقولة (العادلة)
Fairness (of financial statements)	'adāla	عـدالـة (البيانات الحسابية الختامية)
Fake (U.S.) (v.; adj.)	yulaffiq	يلفّق ـ ملفّق
Fall clause	sharṭ at-takāfu'	شرط التكافؤ [بين السعرين لورقة مالية]
Fall due	yastaḥiqqad-daf'	يستحق الدفع

Fall in prices	hubuṭ bi'l-as'ār	هبوط بالأسعار
Fall in value	hubuṭ bi'l-qīma	هبوط بالقيمة
Falsification	tazyīf	تـزييـــف
Family allowance	ta'wīḍ 'ā'ilī	تعويض عائلي
Family partnership	sharāka 'ā'iliyya	شراكة عائلية [شراكة ينتمي أعضاؤها إلى عائلة واحدة]
Fancy goods	sila' fakhma	ســلع فخــمة
Fancy price	thaman bāhiẓ	ثمــن باهــظ
Fare	ta'rifat naql	تعرفــة نقــل
Farm price method	tathmīn mawjūdāt al-muzāri'	تثمين موجودات المزارع
F.A.S. (free alongside ship)	al-biḍā'a bi-muhādhāt al-bākhira	البضاعة بمحاذاة الباخرة
F.A.S. price	si'r al-biḍ'a bi-ḥidhā' al-bākhira	سعر البضاعة بحذاء الباخرة
Fault, intentional	khaṭa' muta'ammad	خطــأ متعمــد
Favour, balance in your	raṣīd li-ṣāliḥika	رصيد لصالحك
Favourable balance	raṣid dā'in	رصيد دائـــن
Favourable difference (variance)	at-tafāwūt al-mulā'im	التفاوت الملائم [زيادة التكاليف المتوقعة عن التكاليف الفعلية أو العائدات الفعلية عن العائدات المتوقعة]
Favourable exchange	si'r aṣ-ṣarf al-mulā'im	سعر الصرف الملائم
Feedback	niẓām raf' at-taqārīr	نظام رفع التقارير [رفع التقارير إلى السلطات العليا]
Fees	ujūr	اجــور (أتعاب ، رسوم)
Fees, auctioneer's	rusūm dilāla	رسوم دلالـــة
Fees, registration	rusūm tasjīl	رســم تسجيـــل
Fees, transfer	rusūm taḥwīl	رســم تحويـــل
Fictitious assets	mawjūdāt wahmiyya	موجودات وهمية
Fictitious bill of exchange	kumbiyālat mujāmala	كمبيالة مجاملة
Fictitious depreciation	istihlāk wahmi	استهلاك وهمــي
Fictitious profits	arbāḥ wahmiyya	أرباح وهميـــة
Fictitious value	qīmah wahmiya	قيمـــة وهميـــة
Fidelity insurance	ta'mīn' i'timānī	تأمين ائتماني (ضد سوء الائتمان)
Fidelity insurance bond (U.S.)	wathīqat ta'mīn ḍidd sū' al-'i'timān	وثيقة تأمين (ضد سوء الائتمان)
Fiduciary	shakhṣ mu'taman	شخص مؤتمـــن [على وصاية او ادارة مؤسسة]
Fiduciary accounting	al-muḥasaba 'l-'i'timāniyya	المحاسبة الائتمانية [محاسبة الأملاك الموضوعة تحت إدارة وصي]
Fiduciary paper money	nuqūd waraqiyya 'i'timāniyya	نقود ورقية ائتمانية
Figure (n.; v.)	1 raqm	١ - رقــم
	2 yaḥsib	٢ - يحســب
File	malaff	ملـــف
File back	yu'īd ila 'l-malaff	يعيد إلى الملف
Fill up	yamla'	يمــلأ (استمارة)

Final account	ḥisāb khitāmī	حساب ختامي
Final dividend	ribḥ as-sahm ākhir al-ʿāmm	ربح السهم آخر العام
Final instalment	qisṭ akhīr	قسط أخيـــر
Finance (n.; v.)	tamwīl	تمويـــل ـ يمـــول
Finance company	sharikat tamwīl	شركة تمويـــل
Finance, public	al-māliyya 'l-ʿāmma	الماليـــة العامـــة
Financial	mālī	مالـــي
Financial accounting	al-muḥasaba 'l-māliyya	المحاسبة الماليـــة
Financial administration	al-idāra 'l-māliyya	الادارة الماليـــة
Financial adviser	mustashār mālī	مستشار مالـــي
Financial charges	aʿbā' māliyya	أعبـاء مالية
Financial circles	awsāṭ māliyya	أوساط مالية
Financial committee	lajna māliyya	لجنة مالية
Financial cost	maṣārif māliyya	المصاريف المالية
Financial crisis	azma māliyya	أزمة مالية
Financial interests	maṣāliḥ māliyya	مصالح مالية
Financial law	al-qānūn al-mālī	القانون المالي
Financial market	as-sūq al-māliyya	السوق المالية
Financial operation	ʿamaliyya māliyya	عملية ماليـــة
Financial opinion	al-awsāṭ al-māliyya	الأوساط المالية
Financial planning	at-takhṭiṭ al-mālī	التخطيط المالـــي
Financial position (condition)	al-markaz al-mālī	المركز المالي
Financial ratio	an-nisba 'l-māliyya	النسبة المالية (احدى النسب التي يستعملها المحاسبون وأصحاب البنوك لمعرفة وضع المؤسسة المالي)
Financial statement	bayān mālī	بيـــان مالـــي
Financial structure	al-haykal al-mālī	الهيكل المالي
Financial year	as-sana 'l-māliyya	السنة الماليـــة
Financier	1 mumawwil	١ - ممـــوّل
	2 khabīr mālī	٢ - خبير مالـــي
Financing	tamwīl	تمويـــــل
Findings of a report	natā'ij taqrīr	نتائج تقريـــر
Fine (n.; v.)	gharāma māliyya	غرامة ماليـــة ـ يغـــرّم
Finished goods (stock)	biḍāʿa tāmmat aṣ-ṣun'	بضاعة تامة الصنع
Firm	mu'assasa	مؤسسة (شركـــة)
Firm accounting releases (F.A.R.)	majmūʿat taʿlīmāt al-mu'assasa	مجموعة تعليات المؤسسة (بشأن المراجعة والمحاسبة)
Firm contract	ʿaqd mulzim	عقـد ملـزم
Firm offer	ʿarḍ thābit	عـرض ثابـت
Firm policy	siyāsat ash-sharika	سياسة الشركة (المتبعة)
Firm price	as-siʿr al-manṣūṣ	السعـر المنصوص [أى السعر المنصوص عليه في العقد]
First cost; original cost	at-taklifa 'l-aṣliyya	التكلفة الأصلية

First in first out (F.I.F.O.)	mā yarid awwalan yuṣraf awwalan	مايرد أولا يصرف أولا
First mortgage bonds	sanadāt maḍmūna bi-rahn min ad-daraja 'l-ūlā	سندات مضمونة برهن من الدرجة الاولى
Fiscal	mālī	مالـــي
Fiscal agent	wakīl mālī	الوكيل المالي [الجهة الموكل إليها إدارة إصدار أية أوراق مالية ودفع قيمتها وفوائدها في مواعيد الاستحقاق بالنيابة عن الجهة المصدرة للأوراق وتقوم المصارف غالبا بدور الوكيل المالي للمؤسسة التي تقترض عن طريق إصدار السندات]
Fiscal period	fatrā māliyya	الفتـرة الماليـة
Fiscal policy	siyāsa māliyya	السياسة الماليـة
Fiscal year	sana māliyya	السنة الماليـة
Fit	tālā'um	تـــلاؤم [العلاقة بين الفترة التي تتحقق فيها الفائدة من عملية ما والفترة التي تترتب فيها الفائدة وتسجل]
Fixed asset	1 mawjūd thabit 2 mawjūd ra'smālī	١ - موجـود ثابـت ٢ - موجود رأسمالي (غير متداول)
Fixed asset unit	wiḥdat al-mawjūdāt ath-thābita	وحدة الموجودات الثابتة [أصل أو مجموعة من الموجودات الثابتة المعترف بها في عمليات المحاسبة المتعلقة بالموجودات الثابتة لمشروع معين بالموجودات]
Fixed budget	al-muwāzana 'th-thabita	الموازنـــة الثابتـة
Fixed capital	ra's māl thābit	رأسمال ثابت
Fixed charges	nafaqāt thiābita	نفقات ثابتـــة
Fixed cost	taklifa thābita	تكلفـــة ثابتة
Fixed deposits	īdā'āt li-ajal	ايـداعات لأجـــل
Fixed income	dakhl thābit	دخـل ثـابت
Fixed instalment	qisṭ thābit	قســط ثابـت
Fixed liabilities	1 maṭlūbāt thābita 2 iltizāmat ṭawīlat al-ajal	١ - مطلوبات ثابتة ٢ - التزامات طويلة الأجل
Fixed overhead	maṣrūfat ra'siyya thābita	مصروفات رأسية ثابتة
Fixed period	ajal muḥaddad	أجـل محـددّ
Fixed price	si'r muḥaddad	سعـر محـدد
Fixed rate	si'r aṣ-ṣarf ath-thābit	سعر الصرف الثابت
Fixed resale price	si'r maḥaddad li'l-muwazzi'īn	سعر محدد للموزعين [أدنى سعر يحدده منتج البضاعة للموزعين لبيع البضاعة المشتراه منه]
Fixed trust	mu'assasa li's-tithmār al-amwāl al-mushtaraka	مؤسسة لاستثمار الأموال المشتركة
Fixtures	tarkībāt	تركـيبات (متاع ثابت)

Flash report	taqrīr mūjaz	**تقـريـر موجـز** [تقرير يبين عناصر الوضع المالي كليا أو جزئيا قبل اقفال الدفاتر]
Flat	ṣāfī	**صـــاف** (بدون اضافة الفائدة)
Flat cost	si'r al-kulfa	**سعر الكلفة**
Flat market	sūq rākida	**ســوق راكـــدة**
Flexibility	murūna	**مـرونـــة**
Flexible budget	muwāzana marina	**الموازنة المرنة**
Flexible standard	mi'yār marin	**معيار مـــرن** [التكلفة المعيارية لفئة معينة من المصاريف تضم مبلغا ثابتا مضافا إليه سعر معين لكل وحدة انتاج للقسم المتغير من المصاريف]
Float	1 yuqawwim	**١ - يقـــوم**
	2 yaṭraḥ as-human li'l-bay'	**٢ - يطرح أسهما للبيع**
Floatation	1 taqwīm	**١ - تقويـــم**
	2 ṭarḥ sandāt māliyya fi's-sūq	**٢ - طرح سندات مالية في السوق**
Floating assets; current assets	mawjūdāt mutadāwala	**موجودات متداولة**
Floating capital	rāsmāl mutadāwal	**رأس مال متداول**
Floating debt	iltizāmāt jāriya	**التزامات جارية** (وقصيرة الأجل)
Floating liabilities; current liabilities	maṭlūbāt mutadāwala	**مطلوبات متداولة**
Floating rate	si'r aṣ-sarf al-'ā'im	**سعر الصرف العائم**
Flow chart	bayān tadaffuqqī	**بيان تدفقـــي**
Flow of money	tadāwul an-naqd	**تداول النـقد**
Flow statement	kashf radaffuqī	**كشف تدفقي** [يبين تنبؤ بتحويل العمليات ضمن الحسابات]
Fluctuate	yataqallab	**يتقـــلب**
Fluctuation of prices	taqallubāt al-as'ār	**تقلبات الأسعار**
F.O.B. (free on board)	fub	**فـــوب** [السعر على أساس التسليم على ظهر الباخرة من ميناء الشحن المحدد]
F.O.B. price	as-si'r fub	**السعر فوب**
Folio	ṣafḥa	**صفحة** (من سجل تجارى)
Foot	yajma' arqām	**يجمع أرقـــام**
Foot the bill (v.)	yadfa' qīmat as-sanad	**يدفع قيمة السند**
Footing	waḍ'	**وضع** (مركز ، ظرف)
Force up prices (v.)	yarfa' al-as'ār	**يرفع الأسعار**
Forced loan	qarḍ ilzāmī	**قرض الزامي**
Forced sale value	qīmat bay' taṣfiya	**قيمة بيع تصفية**
Foreclosure	ḥajz	**حجز** (العقار المرتهن)
Foreign aid	musā'adāt ajnabiyya	**مساعدات أجنبية**
Foreign currency	'umla ajnabiyya	**عملة أجنبية**
Foreign exchange	mubādalat al-'umlat al-ajnabiyya	**مبادلة العملات الأجنبية**

Forfeit	1 suqūṭ ḥaqq	١ - سقوط حـــق
	2 gharāma	٢ - غـــرامة
Forgery	tazwīr	تزوير (تزييف)
Form (n.; v.)	1 namūdhaj	١ - نمـــوذج
	2 yu'assis	٢ - يؤسس (يشكل)
Formal	1 uṣūlī	١ - اصـــولي
	2 rasmī	٢ - رسمـــي
Formation expenses	maṣārīf ta'sīs	مصاريف تأسيس
Forward	li-ajal	لأجل (مقدما)
Forward accounting	muḥāsaba tanabbu'iyya	محاسبة تنبؤية [تشمل اعداد التكلفة المعيارية التكاليف والعائدات المقدرة والنقد السائل المطلوب والخطوط البيانية المظهرة لنقاط التعادل والبيانات المالية المتوقعة والدراسات المتعلقة بهـــا]
Forward delivery	taslīm ājil	التسليم الآجل
Forward exchange (covering)	at-taghṭiya li-ajal	التغطية لأجل [شراء عملة أجنبية بالسعر الحالي لمواجهة تقلبات أسعار الصرف]
Forward exchange market	sūq at-taslīf 'ala 'l-awrāq an-naqdiyya	سوق التسليف على الأوراق النقدية
Forward exchange rate	si'r aṣ-ṣarf li-ajal	سعر الصرف لآجل [السعر الذى تتم على أساسه عمليات الصرف التي تنفذ بعد عقدها بمدة معينة]
Forward price	si'r at-taslīm	سعر التسليم
Forward rates	as'ār 'amalyyāt al-būrṣa 'l-ājila	أسعار عمليات البورصة الآجلة
Forward sale	bay' li-ajal	بيـع لأجـــل
Forward transaction	ṣafqa li-ajal	صفقة لأجـــل
Forward, carry – the balance	yanqul ar-raṣīd	ينقل الرصيـــد
Foundation	mu'assasa	مؤسســـة
Founder	mu'assis	مـــؤسس
Founders' shares	as-hum al-mu'assisīn	أسهم المؤسسين
Fraction	kasr	كسر (جزء من عدد صحيح)
Framework	iṭār	إطـــار
Franchise (U.S.)	1 imtiyāz	١ - امتياز (ممنوح من الحكومة)
	2 wakālat ḥaṣr	٢ - وكالة حصر
	3 rukhṣat ta'sīs	٣ - رخصة تأسيس
	4 nisbat at-taḥammul	٤ - نسبة التحمل [وهي نسبة المخاطر التي تحدد الحد الأعلى للخسارة التي يتحملها المؤمن له فان زادت الخسارة عن هذا الحد تحمل المؤمن الخسارة كاملة]
Fraud	iḥtiyāl	احتيال (غش ، تدليس)

Fraud statements	bayānāt ghayr ṣaḥīḥa	بيانات غير صحيحة (مزيفة)
Fraudulent balance sheet	mīzāniyya mulaffaqa	ميزانية ملفقة
Fraudulent bankruptcy	iflās iḥtīyālī	افلاس احتيالي
Free	majjānan	مجـانـــا
Free and clear	bari' adh dhimma	برىء الذمة (غير مقيد برهن الخ)
Free competition	munāfasa ḥurra	منافسة حرة
Free currency	'umla ḥurra	العملة الحرة
Free enterprise; laissez faire	iqtiṣād ḥurr	الاقتصاد الحر
Free goods	baḍā'i' mu'fāh	بضائع معفاة (من رسوم الدخول)
Free imports	mustawradāt mu'fāh	مستوردات معفاة (من الضرائب الجمركية)
Free of charge	mu'fā min ar-rasm	معفي من الرسم
Free on quay	musallam 'ala 'r-raṣīf	مسلم على الرصيف
Free price	si'r ḥurr	سعـر حـــر
Free trade	tijāra ḥurra	تجـارة حـــرة
Freeze	yujammid	يجـــمد
Freight	1 ujrat shaḥn	١ - اجرة شحن
	2 ḥamūla	٢ - حمــولــة
Freight payable at destination	ujūr ash-shaḥn tudfa' fī mīnā' al-wuṣūl	أجور الشحن تدفع في ميناء الوصول
Freight pre-paid	ujūr ash-shaḥn madfū'a muqaddaman	أجور الشحن مدفوعة مقدما
Frequency	tikrār	تكــــرار
Frequency chart	rasm bayānī li-tawzī' tikrārī	رسم بيانـي لتوزيع تكراري
Frequency curve	munḥanā tikrārī	منحني تكراري
Frequency distribution	tawzī' tikrārī	توزيع تكراري
Fringe benefits	mīzāt iḍāfiyya	ميزات اضافية (للموظفين خلاف مرتباتهم)
Frozen assets	mawjūdat mujammada	موجودات مجمدة
Fulfil	1 tanfīdh	١ - تنفيــــذ
	2 yubri' dhimma	٢ - يبرىء ذمة
Full capacity	ṭaqa quṣwā	طاقة قصوى
Full co-ordination	tansīq tāmm	تنسيق تام
Full costing method	ṭarīqat at-takālīf al-kulliyya	طريقة التكاليف الكلية الاجمالية
Full employment	istikhdām kāmil	استخدام كامل
Full liability	iltizām fardī	التزام فردى (لا يشترك فيه أحد)
Fully paid capital stock	as-hum ra'smāl madfū'a bil-kāmil	أسهم رأس مال مدفوعة بالكامل
Fully subscribed capital	ra'smāl muktatab bihi bi'l-kāmil	رأسمال مكتتب به بالكامل
Function	waẓīfa	وظيفـــة
Function, by	bi-ḥukm al-waẓīfa	بحكم الوظيفة
Functional	waẓīfī	وظيفــــي
Functional accounting	al-muḥāsaba 'l-waẓīfiyya	المحاسبة الوظيفية
Functional statement	bayān waẓīfī	بيان وظيفي (بيان التكاليف مقسمة حسب الوظائف أو أقسام الوظائف)
Fund (n.; v.)	1 sundūq	١ - صنــدوق

	2 i' timād mālī	٢ - اعتماد مالى
	3 ra'smāl	٣ - رأسمال (يمول)
Fund account	ḥisāb ṣundūq	حساب صندوق (مخصص لغرض معين)
Fund asset	aṣl yakhuṣṣ ṣundūq mu'ayyan	أصل يخص صندوق معين
Fund balance sheet	mīzāniyyat ṣundūq	ميزانية صندوق (مخصص لغرض معين)
Fund control	riqābat amwāl	رقابة الأموال
Fund group	majmū'at ṣanādīq	مجموعة صناديق (لأغراض ادارية ولغرض رفع التقارير)
Fund liability	maṭlūbāt aṣ-ṣundūq	مطلوبات الصندوق
Fund pool	tajmī' al-amwāl li-gharaḍ al-istithmār	تجميع الأموال لغرض الاستثمار
Fund surplus	fā'iḍ aṣ-ṣundūq	فائض الصندوق [زيادة موجودات الصندوق على مطلوباته]
Fundamental	asāsī	أساسي (جوهرى)
Funded debt	dayn mughaṭṭā	دين مغطى (سندات أو أوراق طويلة الأجل)
Funded reserve	iḥtiyāṭī mughaṭṭā	احتياطي مغطي
Funding bonds	sanadāt tamwīl	سندات تمويل [لاستهلاك دين أو لتمويل المصاريف الجارية]
Fund statement; flow statement	bayān isti'māl al-amwāl	بيان استعمال الاموال
Furniture	athāth	أثـــاث
Furniture and fixtures	athāth wa tarkībāt	أثاث وتركيبات
Futures price	si'r ta'āqudī	سعر تعاقدى
Gain (n.; v.)	ribḥ	ربح (مكسب) ـ يربح (يكسب)
Gain or loss	ribḥ aw khasāra	ربح أو خسارة
Gamble	yuqāmir	يقامر
Gap	fajwa	فجوة (ثغرة)
Garnishee	1 amwāl maḥjūza bi-ḥawzat shakhṣ thālith	١ - أموال محجوزة بحوزة شخص ثالث
	2 al-maḥjuz ladayhi	٢ - المحجوز لديه
Garnisher	ḥājiz al-amwāl	حاجز الأموال
Garnishment	1 qarār ḥajz amwāl	١ - قرار حجز أموال
	2 ta'yīn shakhṣ thālith	٢ - تعيين شخص ثالث
	3 Da'wa i'tirāḍ ala hajz	٣ - دعوى اعتراض على حجز
General	'āmm	عـــام
General acceptance	qabūl bilā sharṭ	قبول بلا شــرط
General accountant	muḥāsib 'āmm	محاسب عام
General and administrative expenses	maṣārīf 'umūmiyya wa idāriyya	مصاريف عمومية وادارية
General audit	tadqīq 'āmm	تدقيق عـــام [لأخذ فكرة عن العمليات التجارية قبل تسويتها النهائية]

General average	muʿaddal ʿāmm al-khasāra	**معدل عام الخسارة** [خسارة ناجمة عن تضحية مقصودة من أجل دره خطر عام عن سفينة وحمولتها أو الأشخاص الموجودين عليها ويساهم الجميع في تحمل تلك الخسارة]
General balance sheet	mīzāniyya ʿumūmiyya shāmila	**ميزانية عمومية شاملة**
General contingency reserve	iḥtiyāṭī ʿāmm li'ṭ-ṭawāri'	**احتياطي عام للطوارىء**
General expense (burden)	nafqāt ʿāmma	**نفقات عامة** (نفقات ادارية)
General fixed assets fund	ṣundūq al-uṣūl ath-thābita 'l-ʿāmma	**صندوق الاصول الثابتة العامة** [عدا تلك المضمنة في الرأسمال العامل أو صندوق خدمات الجمهور]
General fund	ṣundūq ʿāmm	**صنـدوق عـــام** [الاصول والخصوم المخصصة للأهداف العامة]
General income	irād ʿāmm	**ايـــراد عـــام**
General journal	daftar yawmiyya ʿāmma	**دفتر يومية عامة**
General ledger	daftar al-ustādh al-ʿāmm	**دفتر الاستاذ العام**
General lien	1 hajz ʿāmm	**١ - حجز عام**
	2 ḥaqq ḥajz mumtalakāt al-madīn	**٢ - حق حجز ممتلكات المدين** [لوفاء الدين المستحق]
General obligation bonds	as-sanadāt al-maḍmūn tasdīdha	**السندات المضمون تسديدها** (من قبل المصدر)
General operating expenses	maṣārīf at-tashghīl al-ʿāmma	**مصاريف التشغيل العامة** [اصطلاح يقصد به المصاريف الادارية ومصاريف البيع وأحيانا تكلفة الانتاج والتكاليف الأخرى]
General overhead	maṣārif ra'siyya ʿāmma	**المصاريف الرأسية العامة**
General partner	sharik umūmī	**شريك عمومي**
General records	as-sijillāt al-ʿāmma	**السجلات العامة** [دفتر الاستاذ العام واليومية والسجلات والملفات التي تسنده]
General representation letter	kitāb at-tamthīl al-ʿāmm	**كتاب التمثيل العام**
General reserve	iḥtiyāṭi ʿāmm	**احتياطي عام**
Generality	shumūliyya	**شمولية** (عمومية)
Generally accepted accounting principles	uṣūl muḥāsabiyya mutaʿāraf ʿalayhā	**أصول محاسبية متعارف عليها**
Geometric mean	al-wasaṭ al-handasī	**الوسط الهندسي**
Geometric progression	mutawāliya handasiyya	**متوالية هندسية**
Gift	hiba	**هبـــة** (عطية)
Gilt-edged securities	al-as-hum al-maḍmūna	**الأسهم المضمونة** (في سوق الأوراق المالية) [الأسهم التي تمتاز بقوتها]
Give an account of (v.)	yurājʿ tafāṣīl ḥisāb	**يراجع تفاصيل حساب**
Give credit (v.)	yaftaḥ i'timad	**يفتـح اعتمادا**
Give for the call (v.)	yashtarī li-ajal fī mawʿid al-istilām	**يشترى لأجل في موعد الاستلام**

Give for the put (v.)	yashtarī li-ajal at-taslīm	يشترى لأجل التسليم
Give on stock (v.)	yastalif ʿala awrāq māliyya	يستلف على أوراق مالية
Give-away price	siʿr zahīd	سـعر زهيـد
Giving-effect statement	bayān mālī taṣawwurī	بيان مالي تصورى
Go down	yankhafiḍ	ينخفـض
Go into an account (v.)	yudaqqiq ḥisāb	يدقق حسابا
Going concern	mu'assasa ʿāmila	مؤسسة عاملة (يتوقع لها الاستمرار)
Going concern value	ḥuqūq al-mālik ad-daftariyya	حقوق المالك الدفترية [أى صافي اصول المؤسسة]
Going price	as-siʿr as-sā'id	السعر السائد
Going to press prices	al-as'ār al-akhīra	الأسعار الأخيـرة
Gold bullion standard	ʿiyār as-sabā'ik adh-dhahabiyya	عيار السبائك الذهبية
Gold exchange standard	ʿiyār aṣ-ṣirāfa 'dh-dhahabiyya	عيار الصرافة الذهبية
Gold premium	ʿilāwat adh-dhahab	علاوة الذهب [فرق قيمة العملة الرسمية والقيمة الذهبية]
Gold reserve	iḥtiyāṭi 'dh-dhahab	احتياطي الذهب
Gold standard	ʿiyār adh-dhahab	عيار الذهب
Goods account	ḥisāb as-silaʿ	حساب السلع
Goods in process (progress)	biḍaʿa taḥt at-tashghīl	بضاعة تحت التشغيل (بضاعة غير تامة الصنع)
Goods in stock	biḍāʿa fi 'l-mustawdaʿ	بضاعة في المستودع
Goods in transit	biḍāʿa biṭ-ṭarīq	بضاعة بالطريق
Goods on hand	baḍā'iʿ jāhiza	بضائـع جاهزة (في المتناول)
Goodwill	ash-shuhra	الشـــهرة
Government control	riqāba ḥukūmiyya	الرقابة الحكومية
Government finance	amwāl ʿāmma	أموال عامة (حكومية)
Government obligations	iltizāmāt al-ḥukūma	التزامات الحكومة
Government revenue	al-wāridāt al-ʿāmma	الواردات العامة
Government securities (stock)	sanadat ad-dawla'l-māliyya	سندات الدولة المالية
Governmental accounting	al-muḥasaba 'l-ḥukūmiyya	المحاسبة الحكومية
Grace	muhla	مهلـــة
Grace, days of	ayyām al-muhla	أيـام المهلـــة [لدفع السندات أو أقساط التأمين]
Grade (n.; v.)	1 daraja	١ - درجـــة (مرتبة)
	2 ṣinf	٢ - صنف (نوع) ـ يصنف (يبوب)
Graduated income tax	ḍarībat ad-dakhl at-taṣāʿudiyya	ضريبة الدخل التصاعدية
Grand total	al-majmūʿ al-kullī	المجموع الكلي
Grant (n.; v.)	1 minḥa	١ - منحـــة (هبة)
	2 takhwil ṣarf	٢ - تخويل صرف (محدد الهدف والقيمة والمدة)
Grant a loan	yamnaḥ qarḍ	يمنـح قرضـــا
Grant clean credit	yaftaḥ iʿtimādan ʿala 'l-makshūf	يفتح اعتمادا على المكشوف
Grantee	al-mamnūḥ lahu	الممنوح لــه
Granter (grantor)	al-māniḥ	المانـــح

Graph	khaṭṭ bayānī	خـط بيانـــي
Graphic curves	munḥanyāt bayāniyya	منحنيات بيانية
Gratis	majjānan	مجـانـــا
Gratuitous loan	qarḍ bi-dūn fā'ida	قرض بدون فائدة
Gross	ijmālī	اجـالـــي
Gross book value	qīmat al-aṣl ad-daftariyya	قيمة الأصل الدفترية (قبل الاستهلاك)
Gross cost of merchandise sold	al-qīma 'l-ijmāliyya li'l-biḍā'a 'l-mubā 'a	القيمة الاجمالية للبضاعة المباعة [تكلفة بيع البضاعة حسب الفاتورة بعد أية مرتجعات أو تعويضات واضافة الجمارك والرسوم والتأمين والنقل]
Gross earnings	īrādāt ijmāliyya	ايرادات اجمالية
Gross income	dakhl ijmālī	دخـل اجمالـــي
Gross interest	fā'ida ijmāliyya	الفائدة الاجمالية
Gross loss	khasāra ijmāliyya	الخسارة الاجمالية
Gross (merchandise) margin	hāmish al-biḍā'a 'l-ijmālī	هامش البضاعة الاجمالي [صافي المبيعات مطروحا منها تكلفة البضاعة المباعة]
Gross national product (G.N.P.)	ijmāli 'n-nātij al-qawmī	اجمالي الناتج القومي
Gross profit	ar-ribḥ al-ijmālī	الربح الاجمالي
Gross profit analysis	taḥlīl ar-ribḥ al-ijmālī	تحليل الربح الاجمالي
Gross profit method (of inventory)	ṭarīqat ar-ribḥ al-ijmālī fi 'l-jard	طريقة الربح الاجمالي في الجرد [طريقة تقدير قيمة بضاعة نهاية المدة عن طريق ايجاد تكلفة المبيعات بتطبيق نسبة اجمالي الأرباح المقدرة على المبيعات الصافية وطرح هذه التكلفة من مجموع بضاعة أول المدة والمشتريات]
Gross profit ratio	mu'addal ar-ribḥ al-ijmālī	معدل الربح الاجمالي [الربح الاجمالي مقسوما على صافي المبيعات]
Gross revenue (sales)	irādāt ijmāliyya	الايرادات الاجمالية
Gross sales	ijmāli 'l-mabī'āt	اجمالي المبيعات [أى اجمالي المبيعات قبل طرح المردودات والخصومات ولكن بعد طرح الخصومات التجارية والتعديلات الأخرى والضرائب الأخرى]
Group banking	al-majmū'a 'l-maṣraffiyya	المجموعة المصرفية
Group financial statement	bayān mālī jamā'ī	بيان مالي جماعي [بعدد من الشركات تملكها جهة واحدة وتزاول نفس الأعمال]
Group insurance	ta'mīn jamā'ī	التأمين الجماعي
Group price rate	ajr jamā 'ī	الأجر الجماعي
Group rate of depreciation	al-mu'addal al-jamā'ī li 'l-istihlāk	المعدل الجماعي للاستهلاك
Grouping financial statement	tajmī' al-ma'lumāt al-wārida fī bayānāt māliyya far'iyya	تجميع المعلومات الواردة في بيانات مالية فرعية

Growth	numuww	نمـو (تطور)
Growth curve	munḥana 'n-numuww	منحنى النمـو
Guarantee (n.; v.)	kafāla	كفالة ـ يكفل
Guaranteed bond	sanad maḍmụn	سند مضمون
Guaranteed dividend	arbāḥ ashum maḍmūna	أرباح أسهم مضمونة
		[أرباح دورية لأسهم شركة مضمونة من قبل شركة أخرى]
Guarantor	kafīl	كفيـــل
Guaranty	kafāla	كفالـــة
Hand tool	'udda yadawiyya	عـدة يدوية
Hand, at	fī mutanāwal al-yad	في متناول اليد
Hand, cash in	naqd fi 'ṣ-ṣundūq	نقد في الصندوق
Hand, in, on	fi 'l-mustawdaʿ	في المستودع
Hand, out of	khārij al-murāqaba	خارج المراقبة (خارج التفتيش أو المراجعة)
Hand, stock in	biḍāʿa makhzūna	بضاعة مخزونة
Handbook	dalīl	دليـــــل
Handling	1 muñawala	١ - مناولـــة
	2 muʿālaja	٢ - معالجة (الأمـــر)
Handsel	ʿurbūn	عربـــون
Hang up	yuʿalliq	يعـــلق
Head accountant	ra'īs muḥāsaba	رئيس محاسبة
Head cashier	amīn ṣundūq ra'īsī	أمين صندوق رئيسي
Head office	al-markaz ar-ra'īsī	المركز الرئيسي (للشركة)
Headquarters	maqarr ash-sharika	مقـر الشركة
Hedge	ṣafaqāt tawāzun	صفقات توازن
		[عمليات بيع أو شراء تهدف إلى ازالة الربح أو الخسارة الناجمين عن تذبذب الأسعار]
Hedger clause (U.S.)	sharṭ ḥimāya	شرط حماية
		[يرفق بالنشرات والاعلانات]
Hedging	taḥawwuṭ	تحـــوط
		[نوع من التأمين الاقتصادى يستعمله المتعاملون بالسلع والأوراق المالية]
Heritage	irth	ارث
Hidden reserve; secret reserve	iḥtiyāṭī sirrī	احتياطي سرى
Hire of money	fā'idat al-amwāl	فائدة الأموال
Hire purchase agreement	'aqd bay' bi't-taqsīṭ	عقد بيع بالتقسيط
Hire purchase credit	iʿtimād bi't-taqsīṭ	اعتماد بالتقسيط
Histogram	mudarraj tikrārī	مدرج تكرارى (احصاء)
Historical costs	takālīf tārikhiyya	تكاليف تاريخية (فعليـــة)
Hold a payment (v.)	yurji' dafʿa	يرجىء دفعـــة
Hold a security (v.)	yaḥfaẓ rahīna	يحفظ رهينة

Hold as security (v.)	yaḥjiz bi-ṣifat rahn	يحجز بصفة رهن
Hold harmless agreement	ittifāqiyyat taḥammul aḍ-ḍarar	اتفاقية تحمل الضرر [اتفاقية تنص على أن مسؤولية الضرر يتحملها طرف عن طرف آخر]
Hold over	yurji'	يرجـىء
Hold up	yūqif	يوقـف
Holder	ḥāmil	الحامل (الحائز ، المالك)
Holder of an account	ṣāḥib ḥisāb	صاحب حساب
Holding company	sharika qābiḍa	شركة قابضة
Honour	dafʿ	دفع (قيمة الورقة التجارية عند تقديمها)
Horizontal	ufuqī	افقـي
Horizontal co-ordination	tansīq ufuqī	تنسيق افقـي
Hot bill	sanad sarīʿ	سند سريع [أي يستحق في بضعة أيام]
Hot money	māl manqūl	مال منقـول
Hour, output per	al-mardūd bis-sāʿa	المردود بالساعة (الواحدة)
Hourly costs	at-takālīf fi's-sāʿa 'l-wāḥida	التكاليف في الساعة الواحدة
Hourly rate	al-muʿaddal fi's-sāʿa' l-wāḥida	المعدل في الساعة الواحدة
Housing allowance	taʿwīḍ sakan	تعويض سكن (علاوة)
Hypothecate	yarahan	يرهـن
Hypothecated assets	mawjūdāt marhūna	موجودات مرهونة
Hypothecation certificate	ṣakk rahn	صك رهـن
Hypothesis	farḍiyya	فرضيـة
Ideal standard cost	at-taklifa 'l-miʿyāriyya 'l-muthāliya	التكلفة المعيارية المثالية (أو الجارية)
Identical	mutamāthil	متماثل (متطابق)
Identify	yuʿayyin	يعين (الهوية)
Identity	1 ʿalāqa	١ - علاقة (بين وظيفتين رياضيتين أو تعبيرين منطقيين)
	2 huwiyya	٢ - هويـة
Idle	ʿāṭil	عاطل (عن العمل)
Idle capacity	ṭāqa ʿāṭila	طاقة عاطلة (غير مستغلة)
Idle capacity cost	taklifat aṭ-ṭāqa' 'l-ʿātila	تكلفة الطاقة العاطلة [الاختلاف الناجم عن عدم استعمال التسهيلات بالمعدلات المتوقعة]
Idle capital	ra'smāl ʿāṭil	الرأسمال العاطل
Idle facilities cost	taklifat aṭ-ṭāqa' 'l-ʿāṭila	تكلفة الطاقة العاطلة
Idle time	waqt ḍā'iʿ	الوقت الضائع
Illegal	ghayr qānūnī	غير قانوني
Illegal profits	arbāḥ ghayr mashrūʿa	أرباح غير مشروعة
Illicit	maḥẓūr	محظور (غير مشروع)
Illicit gains	kasb ghayr mashrūʿ	كسب غير مشروع

Illiquid	ghayr naqdī	**غير نقدى** (غير قابل للتحويل النقدى)
Illiquidity	fuqdān as-suyūla 'n-naqdiyya	**فقدان السيولة النقدية**
Imaginary number	raqm iftirāḍī	**رقم افتراضي** [عدد وهمي]
Imbalance	ikhtilāl tawāzun	**اختلال توازن**
Immediate	fawrī	**فوري**
Immediate delivery	taslīm fawrī	**تسليم فوري**
Immediate superior	ar-ra'īs al-mubāshir	**الرئيس المباشر**
Immobilise	yujammid	**يجمّد** [يزيل صفة السيولة عن نقد ما]
Immovable	1 ghayr manqūl	١ - **غير منقول** (ثابت)
	2 'aqār	٢ - **عقار**
Immunity	i'fā'	**اعفاء** (من الضرائب الخ)
Impair	yuḍ'if	**يضعف** (ينقص)
Impairment (of capital)	tadahwur ar-ra'smāl	**تدهور الرأسمال** ١ - [نقصان الرأسمال المصرح عنه بسبب توزيع الأرباح والخسائر] ٢ - [قيمة زيادة المطلوبات عن الموجودات بسبب الخسائر]
Impersonal account	ḥisāb ghayr shakhṣī	**حساب غير شخصي**
Implied contract	'aqd ḍimnī	**عقد ضمني**
Implied trust	sharika ḍimniyya	**شركة ضمنية** [تستنتج من العمليات التجارية بين الأطراف المعنية]
Imply	yataḍamman	**يتضمن** (يشمل)
Import (n.; v.)	istirād	**استيراد ـ يستورد**
Import credit	i'ti'mād li'l-istīrād	**اعتماد للاستيراد**
Import licence	i jāzat istīrd	**اجازة استيراد**
Import quota	ḥiṣṣat al-istīrād	**حصة الاستيراد** [الحد الأقصى من المواد المستوردة]
Import surplus	fā'iḍ al-mawādd al-mustawrada	**فائض المواد المستوردة**
Impose	yafriḍ	**يفرض** (ضريبة)
Impose fines	yafriḍ gharāmāt	**يفرض غرامات**
Impound	yuṣādir	**يصادر** (يحجز)
Imprest	sulfa	**سلفة**
Imprest basis	asās al-'uhda 'l-mustadīma	**أساس العهدة المستديمة**
Imprest cash (fund)	'uhda mustadīma	**العهدة المستديمة** (صندوق النثرية)
Imprest system	niẓām al-'uhda 'l-mustadīma	**نظام العهدة المستديمة**
Improvement	taḥsīn	**تحسين** (اصلاح)
Impute	yansib	**ينسب** (يعزى إلى)
Imputed cost	at-taklifa 'l-badīla	**التكلفة البديلة**
Imputed interest	īrād ar-ra'smāl	**ايراد الرأسمال** [الذى يشكل جزءا من صافي دخل المؤسسة]

In detail	bit-tafṣīl	بالتفصيل
In, kind	ʿaynan	عينا (غير نقدى)
In lieu	badīl	بديـــل
In short	bi'l-mukhtaṣar	بالمختصر
		[في عامود مجاور وتابع ويكون عادة على الشمال لتوضيح معلومات احصائية ومحاسبية]
Inaccuracy	ʿadam diqqa	عـدم دقـة
Inactive account; dormant account	ḥisāb ghayr mutaḥarrik	حساب غير متحرك
Inadequacy	ʿadam kifāya	عدم كفاية
Inadmitted asset	aṣl lā yadkhul ḍimn at-taṣfiya	أصل لا يدخل ضمن التصفية
Inalienability	khāṣṣiyyat ʿadam at-taḥwīl	خاصية عدم التحويل (في ملكية)
Inapplicability	ʿadam muṭābaqa	عـدم مطابقـة
Incapacity	ʿadam maqdira	عـدم مقـدرة
Incentive	ḥāfiz	حافـــز (دافع)
Incident	1 tāri'	١ - طارىء (محتمل حدوثه)
	2 mutawaqqif ʿalā	٢ - متوقف على
Incidental	ʿaradī	عرضـــي
Including	ḍimnan	ضمنا (بما فيه)
Inclusion	idrāj	ادراج (تضمين)
Inclusive	mushtamil ʿalā	مشتمل على
Inclusive acceptance	qabūl ḍimnī	قبول ضمني
Income	1 dakhl	١ - دخــــل
	2 īrād	٢ - ايـــراد
Income account	1 ḥisāb ad-adakhl	١ - حساب الدخل
	2 ḥisāb al-arbāḥ wa'l-hkasā'ir	٢ - حساب الأرباح والخسائر
	3 ḥisāb al-irādāt wa'l-maṣrūfāt	٣ - حساب الايرادات والمصروفات
Income after taxes	ad-dakhl baʿd aḍ-ḍarā'ib	الدخل بعد الضرائب
Income and expenditure; revenue and expenditure	al-īrādāt wa 'l-maṣrūfāt	الايرادات والمصروفات
Income bond	sanad dakhl	سند دخل
		[لا تدفع عليه فوائد الا اذا اكتسب]
Income deduction	ḥusūmāt ad-dakhl	حسومات الدخل
		[أحد المصاريف التي تدخل في حساب صافي دخل المؤسسة التي لا تشكل جزءا من مصاريف التشغيل]
Income earned	1 ad-dakhl al-muḥaqqaq	١ - الدخل المحقق
	2 ad-dakhl al-muktasab	٢ - الدخل المكتسب
		[من تقديم الخدمات]
Income realisation	taḥqīq ad-dakhl	تحقيق الدخل
Income sheet; income statement	bayān al-arbāḥ wa'l-khasāir	بيان الأربح والخسائر
Income tax	ḍarībat ad-dakhl	ضريبة الدخل
Income tax return	bayān ḍarībat ad-dakhl	بيان ضريبة الدخل
Income, additional	dakhl iḍāfī	دخل اضافي

Income, annual	dakhl sanawī	دخـل سنوى
Income, disposable	dakhl jāhiz	دخل جاهز (ممكن التصرف به)
Income, minimum	al-ḥadd al-adnā līd-dakhl	الحد الادنى للدخل
Income, real	dakhl fiʿlī	الدخل الفعلي
Incomings	1 īrādāt	١ - ايــرادات
	2 ʿā'idāt	٢ - عائــدات
	3 amwāl maqbūḍa	٣ - أموال مقبوضة
Incomputable	ghayr qābil li't-taqdīr aw al-ḥisāb	غير قابل للتقدير أو الحساب
Inconsumable	ghayr qābil li'l-istihlāk	غير قابل للاستهلاك
Inconvertible	ghayr qābil li't-taḥwīl	غير قابل للتحويل
Incorporate	1 yadmij sharika bi-sharika	١ - يدمج شركة بشركة
	2 yu'assis sharika	٢ - يؤسس شركة
Incorporated company	sharika mu'assasa	شركة مؤسسة
Incorporated company (U.S.)	sharika muqfala	شركة مقفلة
Incorporation	1 ta'sīs sharika	١ - تأسيس شركة
	2 shahkṣiyya iʿtibāriyya	٢ - شخصية اعتبارية
Increase of capital	ziyādat ar-ra'smāl	زيادة الرأسمال
Increase of price	ziyādāt as-siʿr	زيادة السعر
Increase of value	ziyādat al-qīma	زيادة القيمة
Increment	ʿalāwa	عــلاوة
Incremental cost	at-taghyīr fi 't-taklifa 'l-ijmāliyya	التغيير في التكلفة الاجمالية [نتيجة لاضافة أو حذف وحدة انتاج أو تغيير في العناصر التي تؤثر على التكلفة مثل النمط والحجم أو منطقة التوزيع]
Incur	yatakabbad at-taklifa	يتكبد التكلفة
In-cycle work	ʿamal dākhil ad-dā'ira	عمل داخل الدائرة [العمل الذى ينفذه المشغل عندما تكون الآلة مشتغلة بدورتها]
Indebted	madīn	مديـــن
Indebtedness	madyūniyya	مديونيــة
Indefinite	ghayr muʿayyan	غيــر معيــن
Indemnification	taʿwīḍ	تعويـــض
Indemnify	yuʿawwiḍ	يعـــوض
Indemnity	taʿwīḍ	تعويـــض
Indemnity bond	sanad taʿwīd	سند تعويض
Indemnity, cash	taʿwīḍ naqdi	تعويض نقدي
Indenture	ʿaqd matabādal-ash-shurūṭ	عقد متبادل الشروط (بين طرفين أو أكثر)
Independence	istiqlāliyyat al-mudaqqaq	استقلالية المدقق
Independent accountant; public accountant	muḥāsib qānūnī muʿtamad	محاسب قانوني معتمد
Independent audit	tadqīq mustaqill	تدقيق مستقل
Independent variable	mutaghayyir mustaqill	متغير مستقل
Index (n.; v.)	1 fahris	١ - فهرس (يفهرس)

	2 mu'ashshir	٢ - مؤشـــر (دلالة)
	3 uss	٣ - أس
Index numbers	arqām qiyāsiyya	أرقام قياسية
Index of correlation	mu'āmil al-irtibāṭ	معامل الارتباط
Index of quantity	ar-raqm al-qiyāsī li'lkammiyya	الرقم القياسي للكمية
Indexing	at-taṣnīf bi'l-arqām	التصنيف بالارقام
Indices (pl. of index)	usus	أســــس [جمــع اس]
Indices, price	al-arqām al-qiyāsiyya li'l-as'ār	الأرقام القياسية للاسعار
Indicate	yushīr ilā	يشير إلى
Indicator	mu'ashshir	مؤشـــر
Indirect	ghayr mubāshir	غير مباشر
Indirect cost	taklifa ghayr mubāshira	تكلفة غير مباشرة
Indirect expenses	maṣārīf ghayr mubāshira	مصاريف غير مباشرة
Indirect labour cost	ujūr ghayr mubāshira	أجور غير مباشرة
Indirect liability	iltizām ghayr mubāshir	التزام غير مباشر
Indirect material	taklifat al-mawādd ghayr al-mubāshira	تكلفة المواد غير المباشرة
Indirect wages	ujūr 'ummal ghayr mubāshira	أجور عمال غير مباشرة
Individual	1 wiḥda	١ - وحـــدة
	2 'unṣur	٢ - عنصـــر
Industrial	ṣinā'ī	صناعـــي
Industrial accident reserve	iḥtiyāṭī ḥawādith muwaẓẓafīn	احتياطي حوادث موظفين (وعمال)
Industrial bank	maṣraf sinā'ī	مصرف صناعي
Industrial shares	as-hum ṣinā'iyya	اسهم صناعية
Industrialisation	taṣnī'	تصنيـــع
Industry	ṣinā'a	صناعـــة
Industry producing capital goods	ṣinā'at wasā'il al-intāj	صناعة وسائل الانتاج
Inflate	yuḍakhkhim	يضخـــم
Inflated price	si'r mutaḍakhkhim	السعر المتضخم
Inflation	taḍakhkhum	تضخـــم
Inflow	tadaffuq	تدفـــق
Influence	ta'thīr	تأثير (نفوذ)
Influx	tadaffuq al-amwāl	تدفق (الأموال)
Inform	yukhbir	يخبر (يفيد)
Informal	ghayr rasmī	غير رسمي
Informal record	sijill ghayr rasmī	سجل غير رسمي
Information	1 ma'lūmāt	١ - معلومات
	2 i'lām	٢ - اعـــلام
Infringe	yukhālif	يخالـف
Infringe on	yukhill bi'l-'aqd	يخل بالعقد
Ingot	sabīka	سبيكـــة
Inherit	yarith	يـــرث

Inheritance	irth	إرث
	ḍarībat at-tarikāt	ضريبة التركات
Inheritance tax (U.S.)	1 awwalī	١ - أولـــي
Initial (n.; v.)	2 yuwaqqi' bil-ḥurūf al-	٢ - يوقع بالحروف الاولى
	'ūlā	رأسمال التأسيس (رأسمال أولي)
Initial capital	ra'smāl at-ta'sīs	نفقات التأسيس الأولية
Initial investment cost	nafaqāt at-ta'sīs al-awwaliyya	الحروف الاولى من الاسم
Initials	al-ḥurūf al-'ūlā min al-ism	يبادر (يستهل ، يباشر ، يبدأ)
Initiate	yubādir	١ - مبـــادرة
Initiative	1 mubādara	٢ - روح الابداع
	2 rūḥ al-ibdā'	دائرات الضرائب
Inland revenue	dā-irat aḍ-ḍarā'ib	احتياطي مستتر
Inner reserve	iḥtiyāṭī mustatir	١ - وسائل الانتاج الضرورية
Input	1 wasā'il al-intāj aḍ-ḍarūriyya	
	2 az-zād	٢ - الـــزاد
		[المادة أو المعلومات التي تزود بها الآلة
		الحاسبة أو الدماغ الالكتروني]
Inscribe	yusajjil	يسجل (يقيد ، يدون)
Inscribed stocks	as-hum musajjala	أسهم مسجلة (في دفاتر الشركة)
Insert	yudrij	يـــدرج (يدخل)
Insignificant	ḍa'īl	ضئيل (لا أهمية له)
Insolvable (U.S.)	'ājiz māliyyan	عاجز ماليا (غير مليء)
Insolvency	'ajz mālī	عجز مالي
		[عدم القدرة على الدفع]
Insolvent	muflis	مفلس (مدين)
Inspect	yafḥaṣ	يفحص (دفاتر)
Inspection certificate	shahādat faḥṣ	شهادة فحص (معاينة)
Instability	'adam ath-thabāt	عدم الثبات
Instalment	1 daf'a	١ - دفعة (جزء من دين)
	2 qist	٢ - قســط
Instalment buying	shirā' bi't-taqsīṭ	شراء بالتقسيط
Instalment method of accounting	ṭarīqat muḥāsabat at-taqsīṭ	طريقة محاسبة التقسيط
		[طريقة تسجيل ايرادات البيع بالتقسيط]
Instalment sale	bay' bi't-taqsīṭ	بيع بالتقسيط
Institution	mu'assasa	مؤسسة ـ معهد
Institution, credit	mu'assasat taslīf	مؤسسة تسليف (مؤسسة اعتماد)
Institution, investment	mu'assast istithmār	مؤسسة استثمار
		[مصرف توظيف أموال]
Institutional buyer	mustathmir mutamakkin	مستثمر متمكن
		[أى مؤسسة لديها مبالغ طائلة للاستثمار]
Instrument	1 wasīla	١ - وسيـــلة
	2 wathīqa	٢ - وثيقـــة
Instrument of credit	wasīlat i'timād	وسيلة اعتماد

Instrument of payment	adāt ad-daf'	اداة الدفع (وسيلة الدفع)
Instrument of transfer	ṣakk taḥwīl	صـك تحويل
Insufficient funds	raṣīd ghayr kāfī	رصيد غير كاف
Insurable	qābil li't-ta'mīn	قابل للتأمين
Insurable interest	fā'ida qābila li'ḍ-ḍamān	فائدة قابلة للضمان [مصلحة شخص بملكية آخر بحيث أن تلفها أو الاضرار بها يعود عليه بخسارة مالية]
Insurable value	al-qīma' l-mu'ammana	القيمة المؤمنة [تكلفة استبدال سلعة بأخرى جديدة ومماثلة مطروحا منها خصم معقول للاستهلاك]
Insurance	ta'mīn	تأميـــــن
Insurance certificate	shahādat ta'mīn	شهادة تأمين
Insurance charges	nafaqāt at-ta'mīn	نفقات التأمين
Insurance coverage	at-taghṭiya 't-ta'mīniyya	التغطية التأمينية
Insurance fee	rasm at-ta'mīn	رسم التأمين
Insurance fund	ṣundūq li-taghṭiyat al-khasā'ir	صندوق لتغطية الخسائر [التـــي يتحملها الشخص بنفسه]
Insurance policy	wathīqat ta'mīn	وثيقة تأمين (بوليصة تأمين)
Insurance premium	qisṭ aṭ-ta'mīn	قسط التأمين
Insurance register	sijill at-ta'mīn	سجل التأمين [سجل المعلومات الأساسية المتعلقة بالتأمين السارى المفعول]
Insurance reserve	iḥtiyāṭi 't-ta'mīn	احتياطي التأمين
Insure	yu'ammin 'alā	يؤمن على (يضمن)
Insured	al-mu'amman 'alayhi	المؤمن عليه
Insuree	al-mu'amman lahu	المؤمن لـه
Insurer	al-mu'ammin	المؤمن (شركة التأمين)
Intangible	ghayr malmūs	غير ملموس (وهمي ، غير مادى)
Intangible asset	aṣl ma'nawī	أصل معنوى
Intangible value	qīma ma'nawiyya	القيمة المعنوية [قيمة مؤسسة بكاملها لمؤسسة عاملة زيادة على صافي اصولها الحقيقية]
Integer	'adad ṣaḥīḥ	عدد صحيح (تام ، كامل)
Integral	mukammil	مكمل (متمم)
Integrate	yuwaḥḥid	يوحد (يكمل ، يتمم)
Integrated accounts	ḥisābāt muwaḥḥada	حسابات موحدة (متكاملة)
Integration	tawḥīd	توحيد (تكميل ، تتميم)
Integrity	1 tamām ash-shay'	١ - تمام الشـيء
	2 istiqāma	٢ - استقامة (أمانة)
Inter-bank agreement	ittifāqiyyat maṣārif	اتفاقية مصارف
Inter-bank transfers	taḥwīlāt bayn al-maṣārif	تحويلات بين المصارف
Inter-branch operations	'amaliyyāt bayn al-furū'	عمليات بين الفروع
Interchange (n.; v.)	istibdāl	استبدال (تغيير) ـ يستبدل

Interchangeable	qābil li'l-istibdāl	**قابل للاستبدال**
Interchangeable parts	al-ajzā' al-badīla	**الأجزاء البديلة** [أجزاء يمكن استبدال الواحدة بالأخرى بصورة اعتباطية دون أن يؤثر ذلك على عمل المجموعة التي تكونها هذه الأجزاء]
Inter-company	bayna sharika wa sharika	**بين شركة وشركة** (أو شركات أخرى)
Inter-company elimination	ḥadhf bayn ash-sharikāt	**حذف بين الشركات** [طرح الاستثمارات والذمم والمبيعات والمشتريات بين مجموعة شركات عند تحضير الميزانيات الموحدة وبيانات الأرباح والخسائر]
Inter-company profit	ribḥ mā bayna 'sh-sharikāt	**ربح ما بين الشركات** [الأرباح الدفترية التي تمثل زيادة تكاليف خدمات شركة لأخرى على تكلفتها لمجموعة الشركات ككل]
Inter-company transactions	al-ʿamaliyyāt at-tijāriyya bayn sharika wa ukhrā	**العمليات التجارية بين شركة وأخرى**
Inter-departmental profit	ar-ribḥ mā bayn ad-dawā'ir	**الربح ما بين الدوائر** [الزيادة على تكلفة البضاعة أو الخدمات التي يحملها قسم لآخر في مؤسسة واحدة]
Interest	1 fā'ida	**١ - فائــدة**
	2 'ā'id ar-ra'smāl al-mustathmar	**٢ - عائد الرأسمال المستثمر**
	3 maṣlaḥa	**٣ - مصلحــة**
Interest account	ḥisāb al-fā'ida	**حساب الفائدة**
Interest allowed on deposits	fā'idat al-īdāʿāt	**فائدة الايداعات**
Interest due but not collected	fā'ida mustaḥaqqa ghayr muḥaṣṣala	**الفائدة المستحقة غير المحصلة**
Interest in arrears	fā'idat mustahaqqa	**فائدة مستحقة**
Interest income	īrādāt fawa'id	**ايرادات فوائد**
Interest on capital	fā'idat ar-ra'smāl	**فائدة الرأسمال**
Interest rate	muʿaddal al-fā'ida	**معدل الفائدة**
Interest spread	ḥadd al-fā'ida	**حد الفائدة**
Interest table	jadwal al-fā'ida	**جدول الفائدة**
Interest, accrued	fā'ida mustaḥaqqa	**فائدة مستحقة**
Interest, annual	fā'ida sanawiyya	**فائدة سنوية**
Interest, compound	fā'ida murakkaba	**فائدة مركبة**
Interest, debit	fawā'id madīna	**فوائد مدينة**
Interest, default; **interest of default**	fawā'id at-ta'khir bi'd-dafʿ	**فوائد التأخير بالدفع**
Interest, deferred	fa'ida mu'ajjala	**فائدة مؤجلة**
Interest, interim	fa'ida iḍāfiyya	**فائدة اضافية** (بين الفوائد العادية)
Interest, nominal	fa'ida ismiyya	**فائدة اسمية**
Interest, outstanding	fā'ida mustaḥaqqa	**فائدة مستحقة**
Interest, simple	fā'ida basīṭa	**فائدة بسيطة**
Interest, usurious	fā'ida fāḥisha	**فائدة فاحشة** (فائدة مراب)

Interference	tadākhul	**تداخـــل** [مقدار واتجاه الانحراف عن بعد أساسي يعتبر مقبولا في مواصفات معينة]
Inter-fund transfer	taḥwīl bayn aṣ-ṣanādīq	**تحويل بين الصناديق** [المبلغ المحول من صندوق لآخر]
Interim	marḥalī	**مرحلـــي**
Interim audit	tadqīq marḥalī	**تدقيق مرحلي** [ذلك الجزء من التدقيق الجارى خلال فترة محاسبية لم تنته بعد]
Interim closing	iqfāl marḥalī	**اقفال مرحلي** [خلافا لاقفال نهاية السنة المالية]
Interim dividend	arbāḥ al-ashum al-marḥaliyya	**أرباح الأسهم المرحلية** [المعلنة خلال العام وقبل معرفة الأرباح النهائية]
Interim report	taqrīr marḥalī	**تقرير مرحلي** [يصدر في أى وقت سوى نهاية السنة المالية]
Interim statement	bayān marḥalī	**بيان مرحلـــي** [بيان يصدر في أى وقت خلال السنة المالية]
Internal auditing	tadqīq dākhilī	**التدقيق الداخلي**
Internal auditor	mudaqqiq dākhilī	**مدقق داخلي**
Internal check	ḍabṭ dākhilī	**الضبط الداخلي** [للعمليات المحاسبية عن طريق توزيع السلطات]
Internal control	riqāba dākhiliyya	**الرقابة الداخليـــة**
Internal reporting	taqārīr dākhiliyya	**التقارير الداخلية** [رفع التقارير ضمن نطاق الشركة]
Internal revenue	wāridāt aḍ-ḍarā'ib	**واردات الضرائب**
Internal transaction	qayd muḥāsabī dākhilī	**قيد محاسبي داخلي** [عكس القيد الناشىء عن عملية مع الخارج]
Interpolation	taqdīr qiyam mutawassiṭa	**تقدير قيم متوسطة** (على أساس مجموعة من المعلومات المتوفرة)
Interpret	yufassir	**يفســـر**
Interpretation	tafsīr	**تفسيـــر** [شرح يتضمن اعطاء معلومات تتعلق بفرض وسياق بيان ما أوما ينطوى عليه هذا البيان]
Interval	1 fatra 2 fāṣil	**١ - فتـــرة** **٢ - فاصـــل**
Inter-vivos trust	waṣiyya mawḍū'a bayn ashkhāṣ aḥyā'	**وصية موضوعة بين أشخاص أحياء**
Intestate	ghayr muwaṣṣī	**غير موصي** [المتوفي الذى لم يترك وصية]
Invalid	bāṭil	**باطل** (لاغ)

Invalidate a will	yubṭil wassiya	**يبطل (يلغي) وصية**
Inventory	1 al-biḍā'a	**١ - البضاعة**
		[مواد أولية ، بضاعة جاهزة أو تحت التشغيل المملوكة سواء كان ذلك في المخزن أو في الطريق أو لدى الغير]
	2 jard	**٢ - جـــرد**
Inventory book	daftar jard	**دفتر جـرد**
Inventory certificate	shahādat jard	**شهادة جـــرد**
		[تقدمه الادارة لمدقق الحسابات]
Inventory control	riqābat jard al-baḍā'i'	**رقابة جرد البضائع**
		[ضبط الموجودات بطرق محاسبية ومادية]
Inventory differences	furūqāt al-jard	**فروقات الجرد**
Inventory location	mawqi' biḍā'at al-jard	**موقع بضاعة الجرد**
Inventory pricing	tas'īr al-biḍā'a 'l-makhzūna	**تسعير البضاعة المخزونة**
Inventory profit	arbāḥ al-makhzūn	**أرباح المخزون**
		[زيادة تكلفة البضائع المخزونة خلال فترة إرتفاع الأسعار على أساس معدل ما يدخل أولا يخرج أولا على تكلفتها على أساس ما يدخل آخرا يخرج أولا]
Inventory records	sijillāt al-jard	**سجلات الجــرد**
Inventory reserve	iḥtiyāṭī taghyīr qīmat al-makhzūn	**احتياطي تغيير قيمة المخزون**
		[حساب تقييم يغطي التخفيض في تكلفة البضائع المخزونة إلى قيمتها السوقية أو إلى أقل من قيمة التكلفة بسبب إستعمال طريقة ما يدخل أولا يخرج أولا في تقييم الموجودات أو نزول الأسعار أو بطلان الاستعمال أو نقصان في المواد المطلوبة وغير ذلك]
Inventory sheets	kushūf al-jard	**كشوف الجــرد**
Inventory tags	biṭāqāt al-jard	**بطاقات الجــرد**
		[بطاقات تعريف بمواد البضاعة]
Inventory turnover	dawrat al-bidā'a	**دورة البضاعة**
Inventory valuation	taqyīm al-biḍā'a	**تقييم البضاعة**
Inventory variation	ikhtilāf qiyam al-biḍā'a	**إختلاف قيم البضاعة**
		[بين أول المدة وآخر المدة التي يغطيها بيان الأرباح والخسائر وإنعكاس ذلك على تكلفة المبيعات]
Inventory with valuation	jard ma' taqyīm	**جــرد مع تقييم**
Inventory, partial	jard juz'ī	**جــرد جزئي**
Inventory, perpetual	jard mustamirr	**جــرد مستمر**
Invest	yastathmir	**يستثمر (يوظف مالا)**
Invested capital	ra'smāl mustathmar	**الرأسمال المستثمر**
Investigate	yataḥarrā	**يتحـــرى (يستقصي)**

Investigation	faḥṣ khāṣṣ	فحص خاص
		[للدفاتر والسجلات لهدف محدد]
Investment	istithmār	استثمار (توظيف المال)
Investment account	ḥisāb al-istithmār	حساب الاستثمار
Investment adviser	khabīr al-istithmārāt	خبير الاستثمارات
Investment bank	bank istithmār	بنك استثمار
Investment banker	mu'assasat taswīq sanadāt	مؤسسة تسويق سندات
		[مؤسسة تشترى الأسهم أو السندات جميعها أو بعضها من الشركة التي تصدرها وتبيعها للمستثمرين بالمفرق أو الجملة]
Investment broker	simsār istithmār	سمسار استثمار
Investment companies	sharikāt istithmār	شركات استثمار
Investment credits	iʻtimād tathmīr	اعتماد تثمير
		[اعتماد توظيف أموال في مشروع]
Investment expenditure	infāq istithmārī	الانفاق الاستثمارى
Investment in default	istithmār madīn	استثمار مدين
		[ورقة مالية لم تسدد قيمتها أو فوائدها]
Investment in gilt-edged stock	istithmār fī sanadāt maḍmūna	استثمار في سندات مضمونة
Investment portfolio	maḥfaẓat al-awrāq al-māliyya	محفظة الأوراق المالية
Investment trust (company)	sharikat istithmār	شركة استثمار (مدخرات الأفراد)
Investment yield	ʻā'idāt al-istithmār	عائد الاستثمار
Investments, fixed	istithmārāt thābita	استثمارات ثابتة
		[توظيف بأموال غير منقولة]
Investments, short-term	istithmārāt qaṣīrat al-ajal	استثمارات قصيرة الأجل
Invoice	fātūra	فاتورة
Invoice amount	qīmat fātūra	قيمة فاتورة
Invoice register	sijill al-fawātīr	سجل الفواتير
Invoice, consignment	fātūrat biḍāʻat al-amāna	فاتورة بضاعة الأمانة
Invoice, customs	bayān rusūm jumrukiyya	بيان رسوم جمركية
Invoice, itemised	fātūra mufaṣṣala	فاتورة مفصلة (مفندة البنود)
Invoice, original	fātūra aṣliyya	فاتورة أصلية
Invoice, outgoing	fātūra ṣādira	فاتورة صادرة
Invoice, pro forma	fātūra ṣūriyya	فاتورة صورية
Invoicing	iʻdād al-fawātir	اعداد الفواتير
Involuntary conversion	istibdāl jabrī	الاستبدال الجبرى
		[استبدال جبرى لملكية ما باخرى نتيجة ظروف خارجة عن سلطة المالك]
Involvement	maṣāʻib māliyya	مصاعب مالية
Inward charges	nafaqāt dākhiliyya	نفقات داخلية
Inward cash transfer	taḥ-wīl māl wārid	تحويل مال وارد
I owe you (I.O.U.)	anā madīn lak	أنا مدين لك
		[وثيقة غير رسمية بدين نقدى]

Irredeemable bond	sanad lā yustahlak	سند لا يستهلك
		[سند لا يسترد قبل استحقاقه]
Irregular	ghayr ādi	غير عادي
Irregularity	shudhūdh	شـذوذ
		[أى خطأ في دفاتر الحسابات]
Irrevocable credit	iʻtimād ghayr qābil li'n-naqḍ	اعتماد غير قابـل للنقض
Irrevocable trust	waṣiyya ghayr qābilat al-ilghā'	وصية غير قابلة الالغاء
Issuance (U.S.)	iṣdār	اصدار (أسهم مثلا)
Issue	iṣdār	اصدار (سندات أو عملة)
Issue above par	iṣdār yafūq as-siʻr al-'smī	اصدار يفوق السعر الاسمى
Issue at par	iṣdār bi's-siʻr al-ismī	اصدار بالسعر الاسمى
Issue of a draft	iṣdār sanad	اصدار سنـد
Issue voucher	sanad ṣarf	سند صـرف
Issue, current	isdār jārī	اصدار جـار
Issue, rate of	siʻr al-iṣdār	سعر الاصدار
Issue, restricted	iṣdār maḥdūd	اصدار محدود
Issued capital	ra'smāl muṣdar	الرأسمال المصدر
Issuing bank	maṣraf iṣdār	مصرف اصدار
Issuing office	maktab iṣdār	مكتب اصدار (حوالات)
Item	1 mādda	١ - مـادة
	2 band	٢ - بنـد
Items, balance sheet	bunūd al-mīzāniyya	بنـود الميزانية
Items, cash	mufradāt aṣ-ṣundūq	مفردات الصندوق
Item, credit	al-band al-dā'in	البنـد الدائـن
Item, debit	al-band al-madīn	البند المديـن
Itemised	mufannad	مفنـد (مفصـل)
Itemised balance sheet	mīzāniyya mufaṣṣalat al-bunūd	ميزانية مفصلة البنود
Job	ʻamal	عمـل
Job analysis	taḥlīl al-waẓā'if	تحليـل الوظائف
Job card	biṭāqat ʻamal	بطاقـة عمـل
Job costing; job order costing	taḥdīd taklifat al-ʻamal	تحديـد تكلفة العمـل
Job costs	takālīf alʻamaliyya	تكاليف العمليـة
Job estimates	taqdīrāt al-ʻamaliyya	تقديرات العملية
Job in process (progress)	ʻamaliyya taḥt at-tashghīl	عملية تحت التشغيل
Job ledger	ustādh al-ʻamaliyyāt	استاذ العمليات
Job order	amr ʻamal	أمـر عمـل
Job order record	sijill awāmir al-ʻamal	سجل أوامر العمل
Job time ticket	biṭāqat awqāt al-ʻamal	بطاقة أوقات العمل
Job work	ʻamal bi'l-qiṭʻa	عمل بالقطعة (عمل محدد الاجرة)
Job, by the	bi'l-qiṭʻa	بالقطعة (بالمقاولة)
Jobber	1 wasīṭ	١ - وسيـط

	2 tājir jumla	٢ - تاجر جملة
Jobbery	muḍāraba	مضاربة (بأسعار السندات العاملة)
Jobless	bi-dūn ʿamal	بدون عمل (عاطـــل)
Join	yanḍamm ila	ينضـــم إلـــى
Joint	mushtarak	مشترك (عمومـــي)
Joint account	ḥisāb mushtarak	حساب مشترك (جماعي)
Joint action	ʿamal mushtarak	عمل مشترك
Joint adventure; joint venture	mashrūʿ mushtarak	مشروع مشترك
Joint adventure society	sharikat muḥāṣṣa	شركة محاصـــة
Joint and several	taḍāmun	تضامن (تكافل)
Joint and several co-debtor	madīn mushtarik bi't-taḍāmun	مدين مشترك بالتضامن
Joint and several liability	iltizām mushtarak bi't-taḍāmun	التزام مشترك بالتضامن
Joint charges	maṣrūfāt mushtaraka	مصروفات مشتركة
Joint cost	taklifa mushtaraka	التكلفة المشتركة
Joint creditors	da'inūn mutaḍāminūn	دائنون متضامنون
Joint debtors	madīnūun mutaḍāminūn	مدينون متضامنون
Joint facilities income	īrādāt al-marāfiq al-mushtaraka	ايرادات المرافق المشتركة [الايرادات الناتجة عن استعمال مرافق مشتركة لانتاج نوعين او أكثر من الخدمات]
Joint guarantee	kafālat taḍāmun	كفالة تضامن
Joint liability	iltizām mushtarak	التزام مشترك
Joint ownership	milkiyya mushtaraka	ملكية مشتركة (ملكية مشاع)
Joint property	milk mushtarak	ملك مشترك
Joint responsibility	mas'ūliyya mushtaraka	مسؤولية مشترك
Joint services	khadamāt mutarābiṭa	خدمات مترابطة
Joint stock association (or company)	sharika musāhama maḥdūda	شركة مساهمة محدودة
Joint variance	inḥirāf mukhtalaṭ	الانحراف المختلط
Jointly	bi't-taḍāmun wa 't-takāful	بالتضامن والتكافل
Journal	daftar yawmiyya	دفتر يومية
Journal entry	qayd fī daftar yawmiyya	قيد في دفتر يومية
Journal items	bunūd al-yawmiyya	بنود اليومية
Journal voucher	sanad qayd yawmiyya	سند قيد يومية
Journal, bought	daftar yawmiyyat al-mushtarayāt	دفتر يومية المشتريات
Journal, subsidiary	daftar al-yawmiyya 'l-musāʿid	دفتر اليومية المساعد
Journalisation	mask daftar al-yawmiyya	مسك دفتر اليومية
Journalise	yuqayyid fī daftar al-yawmiyya	يقيد في دفتر اليومية
Judgement	ḥukm	حكـــم
Judgement creditor	dā'in qānūnī	دائن قانوني
Judgement debtor	madīn qānūnī	مدين قانوني
Judicial	qaḍa'ī	قضائـــي
Judicial factor (U.S.)	wakīl muf-lis	وكيل مفلس

Jump	qafza	قفزة ـ في الأسعار
Junior	ḥadith fi 'l-mihna	حديث في المهنة
Junior accountant	muḥāsib mubtadi'	محاسب مبتدىء
Just price	si'r 'ādil	السعر العدل
Just wage	ajr 'ādil	الأجر العدل
Justifiable	qābil li't-tabrīr	قابل للتبرير
Justification	tabrīr	تبريـــر [سرد تحليلي لحاجة أحد الوكالات الحكومية لتمويل أحد المشاريع]
Kardex	niẓam al-biṭāqāt	نظام البطاقات (كاردكس)
Keen prices	adna 'l-as'ār	أدنى الأسعار
Keep a book	yamsik daftaran	يمسك دفترا
Keep a current account	yaftaḥ ḥisābān jāriyan	يفتح حسابا جاريا
Keep down	yaḥfaẓ nuzūlan	يحفظ نزولا [يمنع الأسعار من الارتفاع]
Keep the cash (v.)	yamsik aṣ-ṣunduq	يمسك الصندوق
Keep up	yaḥfaẓ ṣu'ūdan	يحفظ صعودا [يمنع (الأسعار) من الهبوط]
Kerb-stone broker	simsār khārij al-burṣa	سمسار خارج البورصة (سمسار السوق السوداء)
Kind	ṣanf	صنف (نوع ، جنس)
Kite	kumbiyāla ṣūriyya	كمبيالة صورية (سند وهمي)
Kite flyer	ṣāḥib as-sanad al-wahmī	صاحب السند الوهمي (دون تغطية)
Knock off	yunqiṣ	ينقـــص (من قيمة الفاتورة)
Knock-down	1 yursī	١ - يرســـي [يعلن عن رسو السلعة على مزايد]
	2 yukhaffiḍ	٣ - يخفض (الأسعار)
Knock-out price	si'r bakhs	سعر بخس (يتحدى كل مزاحمة)
Kurtosis	darajat al-irtifa' ila 'l-qimma	درجة الارتفاع إلى القمة [التركيز حول القيمة المركزية في التوزيع الاحصائي]
Label (n.; v.)	biṭāqa	بطاقة ـ يصنف بالبطاقة
Label, accounting	biṭāqat ḥisāb	بطاقة حساب
Label, tie-on	biṭāqa mathqūba	بطاقة مثقوبة
Labelling	taṣnīf bi'l-biṭāqāt	تصنيف بالبطاقات
Labour	1 yad 'āmila	١ - يد عاملة
	2 'amal	٢ - عمـــل
Labour cost	taklifat al-aydi 'l-'āmila	تكلفة الأيدى العاملة
Labour cost analysis sheet	sijill taḥlīl kulfat al-'amal	سجل تحليل كلفة العمل

Labour hour	sāʿat ʿamal	ساعة عمل
Labour hour rate	taklifat sāʿat ʿamal	تكلفة ساعة عمل
Labour market	sūq al-yad al-ʿāmila	سوق اليد العاملة
Labour saving	tawfīr bi'l-aydi 'l-ʿāmila	توفير بالأيدى العاملة
Labour time record	sijill sāʿāt al-ʿamal	سجل ساعات العمل
Labour, cost of	taklifat al-yad al-ʿāmila	تكلفة اليد العاملة
Labour, direct	ujūr mubāshira	أجور مباشرة
Labour, indirect	ujūr ghayr mubāshira	أجور غير مباشرة
Labourer	ʿāmil	عـامـــل
Lack of capital	ḥaja ila 'r-r'smāl	الحاجة إلى الرأسمال
Ladder	sullam	سلم (الأجور مثلا)
Lade	yuḥammil	يحمل (يشحن)
Lading, bill of	būlīṣat shaḥn	بوليصة شحن
Lag	fāṣil zamanī	الفاصل الزمني [بين حوادث متلاحقة ومترابطة مثل إستلام النقود وإيداعها]
Land	arḍ	أرض [الاستثمار في أراضي محسنة دون الأبنية]
Land agent	simsār arāḍī	سمسار أراضي
Land improvements	ʿamaliyyāt taḥsīn al-arāḍī	عمليات تحسين الأراضي
Land owner	ṣāḥib al-arḍ	صاحب الأرض
Land security	ta'mīn ʿaqārī	تأمين عقارى
Land shares	as-hum ʿaqārāt ghayr mabniyya	أسهم عقارات غير مبنية
Land tax	ḍarība ʿaqāriyya	ضريبة عقارية
Landed	ʿaqārī	عقـــارى
Landing	tafrīgh	تفريغ (على اليابسة)
Landing charges	nafaqāt tafrīgh	نفقات تفريغ
Landlord	ṣāḥib al-milk	صاحب الملك
Lapping	ikhtilās	اختـــلاس [تلاعب أمين الصندوق بنقد تسلمه من عميل دون أن يسجله لحساب العميل إلا بعد فترة أخرى عند تسلمه نقدا من عميل آخر يغطى به حساب العميل الأول]
Lapse	suquṭ al-ḥaqq bi't-taqādum	سقوط الحق بالتقادم
Lapsing schedule	jadwal tawzīʿ	جدول توزيع (تكلفة الموجودات الثابتة) [جدول يبين تكاليف الموجودات الثابتة كل بمفرده ويبين غالبا مجموع ما أضيف إلى الموجودات الثابتة سنويا ومعها تفاصيل توزيع تكاليفها على الفترات المحاسبية التي تتبع تاريخ شرائها]
Larceny	ikhtilās	اختلاس (سرقة)
Last in first out (L.I.F.O.)	mā yarid akhīran yuṣraf awwalan	ما يرد أخيرا يصرف أولا
Law suit	daʿwā	دعوى (قضائية)

Lawful	qānūnī	قانونــي
Lawyer	muḥāmī	محامــي
Lay by	yaddakhir	يدخــر (يقتصد)
Lay days	ayyām ar-rusuww	أيام الرســو [أيام تفريغ وتحميل السفينة في الميناء بدون جزاء]
Lay in	1 yakhzin	١ - يخــزن
	2 yaddakhir	٢ - يدخــر
Laying off	tasrīḥ	تسريح (عمال أو مستخدمين)
Laying out	saḥb māl	سحب مال (للتسديد)
Lead schedule	jadwal ra'īsī	جدول رئيسي (في التدقيق)
Lead sheet	waraqat ʿamal ra'īsiyya	ورقة عمل رئيسية (في التدقيق)
Leader	al-awrāq al-qudwa	الأوراق القدوة (في سوق البورصة)
Leading shares	al-ashum al-mashhūra	الأسهم المشهورة (بورصة)
Lease (n.; v.)	1 ʿaqd ījār	١ - عقد ايجار
	2 isti'jār	٢ - استئجار
	3 muddat ījār	٣ - مدة ايجار
Leasehold	arḍ musta'jara	أرض مستأجرة
Leasehold improvements	iṣlāḥāt al-arḍ al-mu'ajjara	اصلاحات الأرض المؤجرة
Leaseholder	musta'jir	مستأجــر
Leave	ijāza	اجــازة
Leave, annual	ijāza sanawiyya	اجازة سنــوية
Leave, on	fī ijāza	في اجــازة
Leave, sick	ijāza maraḍiyya	اجازة مرضية
Ledger	al-ustādh	الاســتاذ [الدفتر الرئيسى الذى يحتفظ به بالحسابات الأساسية والحسابات الضابطة للدفاتر المساعدة]
Ledger account	ḥisāb ustādhī	حساب اســتاذى [الحساب المحفوظ في دفتر الاستاذ]
Ledger asset	aṣl ustādhī	أصل استاذى [أى أصل مسجل في دفتر الاستاذ (في التأمين)]
Ledger control	raqīb ustādhī	رقيب استاذى [ضبط حسابات سجل مساعد للاستاذ عن طريق استعمال حساب الرقيب في الاستاذ]
Ledger folio	ṣafḥat al-ustādh	صفحة الاستاذ
Ledger journal	sijill mutaʿaddid al-aʿmida	سجل متعدد الأعمدة [يستعمل كدفتر يومية ودفتر استاذ معا]
Ledger work	mask daftar al-ustādh	مسك دفتر الاستاذ
Ledger, general	daftar al-ustādh al-ʿāmm	دفتر الاستاذ العام
Ledger, goods purchased	ustādh al-mushtarayāt	استاذ المشتريات
Ledger, goods sold	ustādh al-mabīʿāt	استاذ المبيعات

Legacy	mirāth bi-waṣiyya	ميراث بوصية
Legacy duty	ḍarībat at-tarikāt	ضريبة التركات
Legal	qānūnī	قانوني (شرعي)
Legal accounts	ḥisābāt muntaẓima	حسابات منتظمة
Legal capacity	ahliyya qānūniyya	أهلية قانونية
Legal capital; legal value	ar-ra'smāl al-muṣarraḥ bihi qānūnan	الرأسمال المصرح به (قانونيا)
Legal charges	nafaqāt qaḍā'iyya	نفقات قضائية
Legal debt margin	hāmish ad-dayn al-masmuḥ bihi	هامش الدين المسموح به [زيادة الدين المسموح به عن الدين المستحق]
Legal entity	kiyān qānūnī	كيان قانوني
Legal liability	mas'ūliyya qānūniyya	مسؤولية قانونية
Legal reserve	al-iḥtiyāṭi al-qānūnī	الاحتياطي القانوني (الاجباري ، الالزامي)
Legal tender	naqd qānūnī	نقد قانوني (له القوة الابرائية المطلقة)
Legal tender currency	al-ʻumla 'l-qānūniyya	العملة القانونية [النقود التي يحددها القانون للتداول والتي يجب على الدائن قبولها من المدين وفاء لدينه]
Legalise	yajʻal sharʻiyyan	يجعل شرعيا
Legality	sharʻiyya	شرعية
Legally	sharʻiyyan	شرعيا (قانونيا)
Legatee	al-mūṣā lahu	الموصى له (الوارث بوصية)
Legator	al-mūṣī	الموصي (المورث بوصية)
Lend	1 yuqriḍ	١ - يقرض
	2 yuwaẓẓif mālan	٢ - يوظف مالا
Lend money on contango	yuwaẓẓif mālan bi't-taslīf ʻalā awrāq māliyya	يوظف مالا بالتسليف على اوراق مالية (بورصة)
Lend money on mortgage	yuqriḍ mālan bi-rahn	يقرض مالا برهن
Lendable	qābil li'l-iqrāḍ	قابل للاقتراض
Lender	muqriḍ	المقرض
Lender on security	muqriḍ bi-kafāla	المقرض بكفالة
Lending	iqrāḍ aw tawẓīf	اقراض أو توظيف
Lending institution	mu'assasat iqrāḍ	مؤسسة اقراض
Less	adnā	ادنى (أقل)
Lessee	musta'jir	مستأجر (عقار مبني)
Lessen	yuqallil	يقلل (يخفض)
Lessor	mu'ajjir al-ʻaqār	مؤجر العقار
Letter of acceptance	kitab qabūl	كتاب قبول
Letter of acknowledgement	kitāb iqrār	كتاب اقرار
Letter of advice	kitāb ikhṭār	كتاب اخطار
Letter of allotment	ishʻār takhṣīṣ	اشعار تخصيص (اسهم)
Letter of confirmation	kitāb tathbīt	كتاب تثبيت
Letter of credit	kitāb iʻtimād	كتاب اعتماد
Letter of guarantee	khiṭāb ḍamān	خطاب ضمان (كفالة مصرفية)

Letter of hypothecation	ṣakk kafāla	صك كفالة (صك رهن)
Letter of indication	kitāb ithbāt huwiyya	كتاب اثبات هوية
Letterhead	1 tarwīsa	١ - ترويسة
	2 waraq khiṭābat murawwas	٢ - ورق خطابات مروس
Level	mustawā	مستوى
Leverage	al-munḥana 'l-'aksī	المنحني العكسي [اتجاه صافي الدخل لانه يتغير عكسيا مع المبيعات]
Leviable	qābil li't-taklīf aḍ-ḍarā'ibī	قابل للتكليف الضرائبي
Levy (n.; v.)	1 yuqaddir aḍ-ḍarā'ib	١ - يقدر الضرائب
	2 yaṭlub ziyādat ra'sal-māl	٢ - يطلب زيادة رأس المال
Liability	iltizām	التزام
Liability certificate	shahādat iklā' mas'ūliyya	شهادة اخلاء مسؤولية
Liability dividend	arbāḥ ashum dhimamiyya	أرباح أسهم ذممية [الأرباح التي تدفع بواسطة اصدارما يثبت المديونية]
Liability for endorsement	iltizām at-taẓhīr	التزام التظهير [التزام طارىء ناتج عن تظهير التزام للغير ويستمر إلى أن يثبت أن المدين الأصلي قد قام بتسديده أو أخفق في ذلك]
Liability reserve; accrued liability	maṭlūbāt mustaḥaqqa	مطلوبات مستحقة
Liability to an outsider	iltizam li-ṭaraf khārijī	التزام لطرف خارجي
Liabilities	maṭlūbāt	مطلوبات
Liabilities payable at sight	duyūn tudfa' ghibb aṭ-ṭalab	ديون تدفع غب الطلب
Liabilities, bonded	duyūn mu'amman 'alayha bi-rahn	ديون مؤمن عليها برهن
Liabilities, circulating	maṭlūbāt mutadāwala	مطلوبات متداولة
Liabilities, contingent	iltizāmāt ṭāri'a	التزامات طارئة
Liabilities, current	maṭlūbūt mutadāwala	مطلوبات متداولة
Liabilities, fixed	maṭlūbāt thābita	مطلوبات ثابتة
Liabilities, long term	duyūn ṭawīlat al-ajal	ديون طويلة الأجل
Liable	1 mas'ūl taḍāmunī	١ - مسؤول تضامني
	2 mas'ūl qānūniyyan	٢ - مسؤول قانونيا
	3 madīn	٣ - مدين
	4 mukallaf	٤ - مكلف
Liable, jointly and severally	mas'ūl bi't-takāful wa't-taḍāmun	مسؤول بالتكافل والتضامن
Licence (n.)	ijāza	اجازة (رخصة ، تصريح ، اذن)
License (v.)	yujīz	يجيز (يرخص ، يصرح بـ ، يأذن)
Licensed public accountant	mudaqqiq 'umūmī mujāz	مدقق عمومي مجاز
Licensee	al-murakhkhaṣ lahu	المرخص له
Licensing authority	as-sulṭā al-murakhkhiṣa	السلطة المرخصة
Lien	ḥaqq ḥajz	حق حجز (الممتلكات لوفاء دين)
Lienee	1 ar-rāhin	١ - الراهن
	2 al-madīn	٢ - المدين (بأجرة الشحن أو بقيمة السلع الخ)

Lienor	1 al-murtahin	١ - المــرتــهن
	2 ṣāḥib ad-dayn al-mumtāz	٢ - صاحب الدين الممتاز
Life annuitant	sanāhī	سناهي (ذو ايراد مدى الحياة)
Life annuity	mawrid mada 'l-ḥayāh	مورد مدى الحياة
Life estate	milkiyya mada 'l-ḥayāh	ملكية مدى الحياة
Life insurance	ta'mīn ʿala 'l-ḥayāh	تأمين على الحياة
Life table	jadwal al-ajal	جــدول الأجل
Life tenant	mustafīd mada 'l-ḥayāh	مستفيد مدى الحياة [الفرد الذى يحق له إستعمال أملاك أو الاستفادة من إيرادها طيلة حياته]
L.I.F.O. (Last in first out) (U.S.)	mā yarid akhīran yuṣraf awwalan	ما يرد أخيرا يصرف أولا
Limit (n.; v.)	ḥadd-yuḥaddid	حــد ـ يحــدد
Limit of credit	saqf al-iʿtimād	سقف الاعتماد (الحد الأعلى للاعتماد)
Limited audit	tadqīq maḥdūd	تدقيق محــدود [من حيث الطبيعة أو المدة التي يغطيها]
Limited cheque	shīk maḥdūd	شيك محــدود [شيك محدود بالنسبة للمبلغ ويستعمل في الغالب لصرف المرتبات حيث يذكر الحد الأقصي للمبلغ على وجه الشيك منعا لمحاولات زيادة مبلغه]
Limited company	sharika maḥdūda	شركة محدودة
Limited liability	mas'ūliyya maḥdūda	مسؤولية محدودة
Limited liability company	sharika dhāt mas'ūliyya maḥdūda	شركة ذات مسؤولية محدودة
Limited life asset	aṣl maḥdūd al-fā'ida	أصل محدود الفائدة (والعمر)
Limited partner	sharīk muṣī	شريك موصي
Limited partnership; société en commandité simple	sharikat tawṣiya basīṭa	شركة توصية بسيطة
Limited private company	sharika khaṣṣa dhāt mas'ūliyya maḥdūda	شركة خاصة ذات مسؤولية محدودة
Limited responsibility	mas'ūliyya maḥdūda	مسؤولية محدودة
Line of credit	tashīlāt muʿtamada	التسهيلات المعتمدة [التسهيلات الممنوحة من قبل المصرف وفقا لشروط معينة]
Liner terms	aʿrāf an-naql al-baḥrī	أعراف النقل البحرى
Liquid assets	mawjūdāt sā'ila	موجودات سائلة [أمــوال جاهــزة]
Liquid debt	dayn sā'il	ديــن ســائل
Liquid funds	amwāl sā'ila	أموال سائلة
Liquid reserve	iḥtiyāṭī ḥurr	احتياطي حــر
Liquid resources	mawārid jāhiza	مــوارد جاهــزة
Liquidate	yuṣaffī	يصفّــــي
Liquidate a company (v.)	yuṣaffī sharika	يصفّي شركة
Liquidating dividend	ḥiṣṣat at-taṣfiya	حصة التصفية

Liquidation	1 tasdīd ad-dayn	١ - تسديد الدين
	2 at-taḥwīl ilā naqd	٢ - التحويل إلى نقد
	3 taṣfiya	٣ - تصفية (الحسابات أو الأشغال)
Liquidation value	qīmat at-taṣfiya	قيمة التصفية
Liquidation, compulsory	taṣfiya ijbāriyya	تصفية اجبارية
Liquidation, voluntary	taṣfiya ikhtiyāriyya	تصفية اختيارية
Liquidator	ma'mūr at-taṣfiya	مأمور التصفية
Liquidity	suyūla	سيولة
Liquidity difficulties	ṣu'ūbat as-sayūla 'n-naqdiyya	صعوبات السيولة النقدية
Liquidity of investment	suyūlat al-istithmār	سيولة الاستثمار
Liquidness	suyūla	سيولة
List	qā'ima	قائمة
List price	as-si'r al-mu'lan 'anhu	السعر المعلن عنه
Listed	mudraj	مدرج
Listed securities	al-awrāq al-māliyya 'l-mudraja	الأوراق المالية المدرجة [في قائمة السوق]
Listed stock	al-as-hum al-mudraja	الأسهم المدرجة (في التسعيرة الرسمية)
Living allowance	t'wīḍ ma'īsha	تعويض معيشة
Living wage	al-ḥadd al-adnā li'l-ujūr	الحد الأدنى للأجور
Load factor pricing	as-si'r at-tafāḍulī	السعر التفاضلي [تغاير التسعيرة في أوقات مختلفة بقصد الاستخدام الأقصى لوسائل الانتاج]
Loading	taḥmīl nafaqāt	تحميل نفقات
Loading expenses (charges)	nafaqāt at-taḥmīl	نفقات التحميل
Loan (n.; v.)	qarḍ	قرض - يقرض
Loan account	ḥisābāt al-qurūḍ	حسابات القروض
Loan amortisation	iṭfā' al-qarḍ	اطفاء القرض
Loan at a notice	qarḍ li-ajal	قرض لأجل
Loan at call	qarḍ ghibb aṭ-ṭalab	قرض غب الطلب
Loan bank	maṣrif al-qurūḍ	مصرف القروض
Loan ceiling	saqf al-qarḍ	سقف القرض (الحد الأعلى للقرض)
Loan certificate	sanad qarḍ	سند قرض
Loan fund	ṣundūq al-qurūḍ	صندوق القروض
Loan interest	fā'ida 'ala 'l-qurūḍ	فائدة على القروض
Loan on collateral	qarḍ bi-rahn aw kafāla	قرض برهن أو كفالة
Loan on mortgage	qarḍ bi-rahn	قرض برهن
Loan on overdraft	qarḍ makshūf	قرض مكشوف (قرض دون ضمان)
Loan on stock	taslīf 'alā awrāq māliyya aw as-hum	تسليف على أوراق مالية أو أسهم (بورصة)
Loan value	qīmat al-qarḍ	قيمة القروض [الحد الأعلى للمبلغ الممكن اقراضه من المؤمن على بوليصة التأمين]
Loan, bottomry	qarḍ ''lā rahn al-bākhira	قرض على رهن الباخرة
Loan, consolidated	qarḍ maḍmūn	قرض مضمون

Loan, conversion	qarḍ taḥwīl	قـرض تحويــل
Loan, debenture	qarḍ ilzāmī	قرض الزامي [بموجب القانون مع سند استرداد القيمة]
Loan, long-dated	qarḍ ṭawīl al-ajal	قرض طويل الأجل
Loan, perpetual	qarḍ dā'im	قرض دائم
Loan, premium	qarḍ taslīf li-ajal	قرض تسليف لاجل ـ بورصة
Loan, redemption	qarḍ istihlāk	قرض استهلاك
Loan, secured	qarḍ maḍmūn	قرض مضمون
Loan, simple	qarḍ istihlāk ʿādī	قرض استهلاك عادى (اعتياد شراء سلع)
Loanable	mumkin iqtirāḍuh	ممكن اقتراضه
Loanee	muqtariḍ	مقتــرض
Loaner	muqriḍ	مقــرض
Loaning	iqrāḍ	اقــراض
Loans against credit balances	qurūḍ bi-ḍamān al-arṣida al-dā'ina	قرض بضمان الأرصدة الدائنة
Local	maḥallī	محلــي
Local improvement fund	ṣundūq tamwīl at-taḥsīnāt al-maḥalliyya	صندوق تمويل التحسينات المحلية
Lock up (n.; v.)	tajmīd	تجميد (رساميل) ـ يجمد مالا
Lock-out	ighlāq al-ʿamal	اغلاق العمل [يقوم به أرباب العمل لاخضاع العمال بنتيجة البطالة]
Lock-up capital	ra'smāl mujammad	رأسمال مجمد
Loco price	as-siʿr fī makān al-intāj	السعر في مكان الانتاج
Lodge	1 yudiʿ	١ - يــودع
	2 yuqaddim shakwā	٢ - يقدم شكوى
Lodge securities as collateral	yūdiʿ awrāq māliyya bi-ṣifat kafāla	يودع أوراقا مالية بصفة كفالة
Logarithm	lūgharithm	لوغاريثم
Long	muḍārib bi'l-irtifāʿ	مضارب بالارتفاع (بورصة)
Long-form procedures	ijrā'āt ṭawīla wa mufaṣṣala	اجراءات طويلة ومفصلة
Long-form report	taqrīr at-tadqīq al-muṭawwal	تقرير التدقيق المطول
Long-standing	mundh tārīkh qadīm	منذ تاريخ قديم
Long-standing accounts	ḥisābāt mustaḥaqqa mundhu mudda ṭawīla	حسابات مستحقة منذ مدة طويلة
Long-term	ṭawīl al-ajal	طويل الأجل
Long-term contract	ʿaqd ṭawīl al-ajal	عقد طويل الأجل
Long-term debt	dayn ṭawīl al-ajal	دين طويل الأجل
Long-term investment	istithmārāt ṭawīlat al-ajal	استثمارات طويلة الأجل
Long-term lease	ījar li-mudda ṭawīla	ايجار لمدة طويلة
Long-term liability	maṭlūbāt ṭawīlat al-ajal	مطلوبات طويلة الأجل
Long-term loan	qarḍ ṭawīl al-ajal	قرض طويل الأجل
Look into	1 yafḥaṣ	١ - يفحــص
	2 yaṭṭaliʿ ʿalā	٢ - يطلع على
Look over	1 yurājiʿ	١ - يراجــع

	2 yudaqqiq	٢ - يدقــق
	3 yataṣaffaḥ	٣ - يتصفّــح
Loose	sā'ib	سائب (غير ثابت)
Looseleaf ledger	daftar ustādh bi-awrāq sā'iba	دفتر استاذ بأوراق سائبة
Lop off	1 yunqiṣ	١ - ينقص
	2 yuqallil	٢ - يقلل (عتادا أو دينا)
Loss	khasāra	خســـارة
Loss, at a	bi-khasāra	بخســـارة
Loss and gain; profit and loss	al-arbāḥ wa 'l-khasā'ir	الأرباح والخسائر
Loss balance	raṣīd khāsir	رصيد خاسر
Loss carried forward	khasāra muraḥḥala	خسارة مرحلة
Loss on exchange	khasārat ṣarf an-naqd	خسارة صرف النقد
Loss ratio	nisbat al-khasā'ir	نسبة الخسائر [التي يدفعها المؤمن إلى الأقساط التي يقبضها خلال سنة]
Lost	mafqūd	مفقود (ضائع)
Lost discount	al-khaṣm aḍ-ḍā'i'	الخصم الضائع [الخصم على الشراء الذى لم ينتفع به بسبب عدم التسديد خلال الفترة المحددة]
Lost usefulness	al-fā'ida'ḍ ḍā'i'a	الفائدة الضائعة (الاستهلاك)
Lot	majmū'a	مجموعة (جملة ، كمية ، رزمة)
Lot acceptance sampling	akhdh 'ayyināt al-qabūl	أخذ عينات القبول
Lot tolerance per cent defective	an-nisba 'l-maqbūla li'l-mawādd at-tālifa	النسبة المقبولة للمواد التالفة
Lower of cost or market	sir as-suq aw al-kulfa ayyuhumā aqall	سعر السوق أو الكلفة أيهما أقل
Lower the currency (v.)	yukhaffiḍ qīmat an-naqd	يخفض قيمة النقد
Lucrative	murbiḥ	مربــح (مكسب)
Lucrative capital	ra'smāl kāsib	رأسمال كاسب
Lucrative prices	as'ār murbiḥa	أسعار مربحة
Lump sum	mablagh ijmālī	مبلغ اجمالي
Lump sum of appropriation (or allotment)	takhṣiṣ al-mablagh al-ijmālī	تخصيص المبلغ الاجمالي
Lump sum purchase	shirā' ijmālī	شراء اجمالي [دون تفصيل سعر كل سلعة بمفردها]
Lump sum sale	bay' ijmālī	بيع اجمالي [دون تفصيل سعر كل سلعة بمفردها]
Lump sum settlement	tasdīd ijmālī	تسديد اجمالي [بدفعة اجمالية دون ذكر التفاصيل]
Lump tare	wazn ijmālī	الوزن الاجمالي (الوزن القائم)
Luxury articles	sila' kamāliyya	سلع كمالية
Luxury goods; luxuries	kamaliyyāt	كماليـــات
Luxury tax	ḍarībat al-kamāliyyāt	ضريبة الكماليات

Luxury trade	tijārat al-kamāliyyāt	تجارة الكماليات
Machine hour rate	muʿaddal sāʿat al-āla	معدل ساعة الآلة [أى كلفة عملها في الساعة الواحدة]
Machine work	ʿamal bil-āla	عمل بالآلة
Machinery	ālāt	آلات
Machinery and equipment	ālāt wa-mu'iddāt	آلات ومعدات
Mail (n.; v.)	barīd	بريد (يرسل بالبريد)
Mail credit	iʿtimād barīdī	اعتماد بريدى
Mail order	ṭalab barīdī	طلب بريدى (سلع)
Mail order business	ḥānūt li'l-bayʿ bi'l-murāsala	حانوت للبيع بالمراسلة
Mail transfer	ḥawāla barīdiyya	حوالة بريدية
Mail transfer order	amr dafʿ barīdī	أمر دفع بريدى
Maintain	1 yughadhdhī	١ - يغذى (صندوقا)
	2 yaṣūn	٢ - يصون (يحفظ)
Maintenance	ṣiyāna	صيانــة
Maintenance allowance	taʿwīḍ ṣiyāna	تعويض صيانة
Maintenance and repairs	ṣiyāna wa-taṣlīḥāt	صيانة وتصليحات
Maintenance charges	nafaqāt ṣiyāna	نفقات صيانة
Maintenance cost	taklifat aṣ-ṣiyāna	تكلفة صيانة
Maintenance order	amr aṣ-ṣiyāna	أمر الصيانة
Maintenance reserve	iḥtiyāṭi 'ṣ-ṣiyāna	احتياطي الصيانة
Majority	aktharityya	أكثرية (أغلبية)
Majority owned subsidiary	sharika tābiʿa mamlūka bi-akthariyya	شركة تابعة مملوكة بأكثرية [تملك الشركة الام أكثر من ٥٠٪ من أسهمها]
Make (n.; v.)	1 yaṣnaʿ	١ - يصنــع
	2 yu'assis	٢ - يؤســس
	3 yuḥarrir	٣ - يحــرر
Make out a cheque	yuḥarrir shīkan	يحرر شيكا
Make a loan (v.)	yaḥṣul ʿalā qarḍ	يحصل على قرض
Make a settlement	yujrī taswiya	يجري تسوية
Maker	munshi'	منشىء (صانع)
Maker of a promissory note	mutaʿahhid bi'd-dafʿ fi 'l-kumbiyāla	متعهد بالدفع في الكمبيالة (السند)
Make-ready time	waqt al-iʿdād	وقت الاعداد [الوقت المصروف لاعداد الآلات قبل البدء بالانتاج]
Make-up of balance	mukawwināt ar-raṣīd	مكونات الرصيد
Making an entry	ʿamal qayd	عمــل قيــد [تسجيل مفردة حساب]
Making over	1 taḥwīl	١ - تحويــل (ملكية)
	2 taghyīr waḍʿ	٢ - تغيير وضع (دين)

Making over a debt	taḥwīl dayn	تحويل دين
Making up	1 taʻwīḍ	١ - تعويـــض
	2 iʻdād	٢ - اعداد (ميزانية)
	3 tasdīd	٣ - تسديد (حساب)
Making up for losses	taʻwīḍ al-khasā'ir	تعويض الخسائر
Maladjustment	1 ʻadam taṭābuq	١ - عدم تطابق
	2 ikhtilāl	٢ - اختلال (في جهاز)
Maladjustment in the balance of payments	ikhtilāl fī mizān al-madfūʻāt	اختلال في ميزان المدفوعات
Malfeasance	sū' istiʻmāl	سوء استعمال
Malpractice	sū' taṣarruf	سوء تصرف (تقصير معتمد)
Malversation	1 ikhtilās amwāl	١ - اختلاس أموال
	2 ʻadam dafʻ	٢ - عدم دفع
Malversation of public funds	ikhtilās amwāl al-ḥukūma	اختلاس أموال الحكومة
Man days	ayyām rajul	أيام رجل [أيام عمل رجل واحد]
Man hours	sāʻāt rajul	ساعات رجل [ساعات عمل لرجل واحد]
Man weeks	asābīʻ rajul	أسابيع رجل [أسابيع عمل لرجل واحد]
Manage	yudīr	يديـــر (يوجه)
Managed economy	iqtiṣād muwajjah	اقتصاد موجه
Management	idāra	ادارة ١ - [السلطة التنفيذية التي ترسم السياسة وتعمل على تنفيذها] ٢ - [رئيس المؤسسة أو الرئيس والجهاز الادارى]
Management account	ḥisāb al-idāra	حساب الادارة
Management accounting	muḥāsaba idāriyya	محاسبة ادارية
Management expenses	nafaqāt idāriyya	نفقات ادارية
Management investment company	sharikat idārat istithmār	شركة ادارة استثمار [لادارتها الحق في بيع وشراء الأوراق المالية]
Management science	ʻilm al-idāra	علم الادارة
Management services	al-khadamāt al-idāriyya	الخدمات الادارية
Manager	1 mudīr	١ - مديـــر
	2 ra'īs	٢ - رئيـــس
	3 wakil aʻmāl	٣ - وكيل أعمال
Managerial	idārī	ادارى
Managerial expenses	nafaqāt idāriyya	نفقات ادارية
Managing director	ʻuḍw muntadab	عضو منتدب
Mandate	1 tafwīḍ	١ - تفويض (توكيل)
	2 ʻaqd wakāla	٢ - عقد وكالة
Mandatory	ilzāmī	الزامـــي

Manifest	bayān ash-shaḥn	بيان الشحن
Manifesto	bayān rasmī	بيان رسمي (اعلان رسمي)
Manipulate	1 yusawwī	١ - يسوى (يرتب حسابا)
	2 yatalā'ab bi	٢ - يتلاعب بـ
Manipulation	1 talā'ub bi'l-as'ār	١ - تلاعب بالأسعار
	2 munāwarat fi 'l-burṣa	٢ - مناورات في البورصة
Manipulations	muḍārabāt mufta'ala	المضاربات المفتعلة
Manipulator	muḍārib bi'l-awrāq al-māliyya	مضارب بالأوراق المالية
Manpower (U.S.)	al-quwa 'l-'āmila	القوى العاملة
		[عدد الموظفين والمستخدمين في منشأة]
Manual	1 yadawī	١ - يــدوى
	2 dalīl	٢ - دليــل
Manual of accounting	dalīl al-muḥasaba	دليل المحاسبة
Manual of procedures	dalīl al-ijrā'āt	دليل الاجراءات
Manufacture (n.; v.)	1 sinā'a	١ - صناعــة
	2 taṣnī'	٢ - تصنيع ـ يصنع
Manufacturer's price	as-si'r fi 'l-maṣna'	السعر في المصنع
Manufacturer's warranty	ḍamān aṣ-ṣāni'	ضمان (كفالة) الصانع
Manufacturing account	ḥisāb at-taṣnī'	حساب التصنيع
Manufacturing burden	a'bā' at-taṣnī'	أعباء تصنيع
Manufacturing cost; factory cost	kulfat al-maṣna'	كلفة المصنع
Manufacturing expenses	al-maṣrūfāt aṣ-ṣinā'iyya	المصروفات الصناعية
		[عدا عن المواد الخام والاجور المباشرة]
Manufacturing statement	kashf at-taṣnī'	كشف التصنع
		[أى بيان تكلفة المواد المصنوعة]
Margin	1 ribḥ ijmālī	١ - الربح الاجمالي
	2 hāmish aḍ-ḍamān	٢ - هامش الضمان
	3 ta'mīn naqdī	٣ - تأمين نقدى
Marginal	1 hāmishī	١ - هامشــي
	2 ḥaddī	٢ - حــدى
Marginal analysis	taḥlīl ḥaddī	تحليل حدى
Marginal balance	ar-raṣīd al hāmishī	الرصيد الهامشي
		[زيادة الايراد على التكلفة المتغيرة]
Marginal cost	at-takālif al-ḥaddiyya	التكاليف الحدية (التزايدية ، التفاضلية ، المباشرة)
		[الزيادة أو النقصان في التكلفة الناتجة عن اختلاف بسيط في المدود]
Marginal costing	at-taklīf al-ḥaddī	التكليف الحدى
		[تخصيص التكاليف الحدية أو المتغيرة إلى عملية أو دائرة أو محصول تمييزا لها عن التكليف الاستيعابي والتكليف المباشر]
Marginal efficiency of capital	al-kifāya 'l-ḥaddiyya li 'r-ra'smāl	الكفاية الحدية للرأسمال
Marginal efficiency of investment	al-kifaya 'l-ḥaddiyya li'l-istithmār	الكفاية الحدية للاستثمار

Marginal income	al-īrād al-ḥaddī	**الايراد الحدى** [زيادة المبيعات على التكاليف المباشرة لتلك المبيعات]
Marginal income ratio	nisbat al-īrād al-ḥaddī	**نسبة الايراد الحدى** [النسبة المئوية المتوفرة من كل دينار مبيعات لتغطية التكاليف الثابتة والارباح بعد خصم النسبة المئوية اللازمة للتكاليف المتغيرة]
Marginal productivity	ṭāqat al-intāj al-ḥaddiyya	**طاقة الانتاج الحدية** [الزيادة في القيمة النقدية الناتجة عن زيادة وحدة انتاجية في كمية أحد عوامل الانتاج المستخدمة في أى برنامج أو عملية]
Marginal return	intaj haddī	**انتاج حدي** [تتساوى نفقات الانتاج مع ما ينتج]
Marginal unit cost	at-taklifa ’l-ḥaddiyya li’l-wiḥda	**التكلفة الحدية للوحدة**
Marginal worker	al-ʿāmil al-ḥaddī	**العامل الحدى** [العامل الذى يكون أجره مساويا لما انتجه]
Mark (n.; v.)	siʿr	**سعر** (بورصة) **- يسعّر**
Mark-down (n.; v.)	1 takhfīd	١ - **تخفيض** [مثلا تخفيض سعر البيع أو قيمة الموجودات]
	2 iʿādat taqiyīm as-sanadāt	٢ - **اعادة تقييم السندات** [بالاستناد إلى هبوط أسعارها في السوق]
Mark-down cancellation	ilghā’ at-takhfīḍ	**الغاء التخفيض**
Market	sūq	**سوق**
Market cost rate	muʿaddal taklifat as-sūq	**معدل تكلفة السوق**
Market price; current price	siʿr as-sūq	**سعر السوق** (السعر الجارى)
Market rate of discount	siʿr al-khasm as-sūqī	**سعر الخصم السوقي** [أى السائد في السوق]
Market research	dirāsat as-sūq	**دراسة السوق**
Market value	siʿr as-sūq	**سعر السوق**
Marketable	rā’ij fi ’s-sūq	**رائج في السوق**
Marketable securities	awrāq māliyya mutadāwala	**أوراق مالية متداولة**
Marketability	rawāj	**رواج** [صلاحية السلعة للبيع]
Marketing	taswīq	**تسويق** (تصريف البضائع)
Marketing cost	taklifat at-taswīq	**تكلفة التسويق**
Marking	tathbīt al-asʿār	**تثبيت الأسعار** [في سوق الأوراق المالية]
Mark-on	iḍāfa	**اضافة** [المبلغ المضاف إلى التكلفة عند تحديد أسعار البيع لتغطية مصاريف التشغيل وحد الأرباح]
Mark-up (U.S.)	iḍāfa	**اضافة** [المبلغ المضاف لسعر مبيع بقصد تحديد سعر أعلى جديد]

Marshal	yuṣannif al-mawjūdāt wa 'l-maṭlūbāt	**يصنف الموجودات والمطلوبات** [طبقا لمبدأ السيولة والاستحقاق]
Master budget	al-muwāzana ash-shāmila	**الموازنة الشاملة**
Master control account	ḥisāb raqīb ʿāmm	**حساب رقيب عام**
Matching	muṭābaqa	**مطـابقـــة** [مبدأ مقابلة الايرادات والمصاريف المرتبطة ببعض مع نفس الفترة المحاسبية ، أى تحديد البنود التي يجب أن تدخل في بيان الأرباح والخسائر]
Material	1 mādda 2 māddī	**١ - مـــادة** **٢ - مـــادى (هـام)**
Material in process; goods in process	mawādd qayd aṣ-ṣunʿ	**مواد قيد الصنع**
Materials	lawāzim	**لوازم** (أدوات)
Materials abstract	mulakhkhaṣ li'l-khāmāt al-maṣrūfa	**ملخص للخامات المصروفة**
Materials accounting	muḥāsabat al-mawādd	**محاسبة المواد** (أو اللوازم)
Materials and services	al-mawādd wa 'l-khadamāt	**المواد والخدمات**
Materials control	murāqabat al-mawādd	**مراقبة المواد**
Materials cost	taklifat al-mawādd	**تكلفة المواد**
Materials cost percentage rate	an-nisba 'l-mi'awiyya min al-mawādd al-mubashara	**النسبة المئوية من المواد المباشرة** [معدل فعلي أو محدد مقدما لتوزيع التكاليف الاضافية على أساس تكلفة المواد المباشرة]
Materials cost variance	inḥirāf taklifat al-mawādd	**انحراف تكلفة المواد**
Materials issue analysis sheet	kashf taḥlīl al-mawādd al-munṣarifa	**كشف تحليل المواد المنصرفة**
Materials mixture variance	inḥirāf khalṭat al-mawādd	**انحراف خلطة المواد**
Materials price variance	inḥirāf siʿr al-mawādd	**انحراف سعر المواد**
Materials usage variance	inḥirāf kammiyyat al-mawādd	**انحراف كمية المواد**
Materiality	mabda' al-mādiyya fi'l-muhāsabah	**مبدأ المادية في المحاسبة**
Mathematical	riyāḍī	**رياضـــي**
Mathematical programming	al-barmaja 'r-riyāḍiyya	**البرمجة الرياضية**
Mature	yastaḥiqq	**يستحق**
Matured liability	iltizām mustaḥiqq	**التزام مستحق**
Maturing liability	iltizām sawfa yastaḥiqq baʿd waqt qaṣīr	**التزام سوف يستحق بعد وقت قصير**
Maturity advice	ishʿār al-istiḥqāq	**اشعار (اخطار) الاستحقاق**
Maturity basis	asās al-istiḥqāq	**أساس الاستحقاق** [اساس احتساب قيم السندات ومعدل المردود على فرض أن السندات ستحفظ حتى تاريخ الاستحقاق]
Maturity date	tārikh al-istiḥqāq	**تاريخ الاستحقاق**
Maturity slip	qasīmat al-istiḥqāq	**قسيمة الاستحقاق**
Maximise profit	aqṣa r-ribḥ	**أقصى الربح** [يزيد الربح إلى الحد الأقصى ، يطور حجم الانتاج إلى الحد الذى تتساوى فيه تكلفة

انتاج وحدة جديدة مع صافي الوارد الحاصل
منها]

Maximum capacity	aṭ-ṭāqa 'l-quṣwā	**الطاقة القصوى**
Mean	mutawaṣṣit	**متوسـط**
Means	wasīla	**وسيلة** (واسطة)
Measurable	qābil li'l-qiyās	**قابل للقياس**
Measure (n.; v.)	1 qiyās	**١ - قياس ـ يقيس**
	2 ijrā'	**٢ - اجـراء**
Measurement	qiyās	**قيـاس**
Mechanical accounting	al-muḥāsaba 'l-āliyya	**المحاسبة الآلية**
Media	wasā'il	**وسائـل**
Median	mutawassiṭ	**متوسـط**
Medium of exchange	wasīlat ṣarf	**وسيلة صرف**
Medium-term loan	qarḍ mutawassiṭ al-ajal	**قرض متوسط الأجل**
Meet	1 yusaddid	**١ - يسدد ـ القيمة الكاملة**
	2 yuwājih	**٢ - يواجه ـ بطريقة مرضية**
Meet one's commitments (v.)	yusaddid iltizāmātihi	**يسدد التزاماته ـ كاملة**
Meeting	1 ijtimā'	**١ - اجتماع** (جلسة)
	2 jam'iyya	**٢ - جمعية ـ مساهمين**
Member	'uḍw	**عضـو**
Member of the board	'uḍw majlis idāra	**عضو مجلس ادارة**
Membership	1 'uḍwiyya	**١ - عضوية**
	2 shuruṭ al-qabūl	**٢ - شروط القبول**
Memorandum	mudhakkira	**مذكـرة**
Memorandum of association	'aqd at-ta'sīs	**عقد التأسيس**
Mercantile	tijārī	**تجارى** (مختص بالتجارة)
Mercantile bills	awrāq tijāriyya	**أوراق تجارية** (سندات تجارية)
Mercantile credit	i'timād tajārī	**اعتماد تجاري**
Merchandise	baḍā'i'	**بضائع** (سلع)
Merchandise account	ḥisāb al-biḍā'a	**حساب البضاعة**
Merchandise cost	taklifat al-fātura	**تكلفة الفاتورة** [ناقصا الخصم المكتسب]
Merchandise inventory	jard al-biḍā'a	**جرد البضاعة**
Merchandise procurement cost	taklifat shirā' al-biḍā'a	**تكلفة شراء البضاعة**
Merchant	tājir	**تاجـر**
Merchant bank	maṣrif tijārī	**مصرف تجارى**
Merge	1 yudmij	**١ - يدمـج**
	2 yandamij	**٢ - يندمـج**
Merger	damj	**دمـج** [اتحاد شركتين أو أكثر]
Merit bonus	mukāfa'at al-mardūd	**مكافأة المردود** [مكافأة على المردود والانتاج الجيد]
Merit rating	at-taqyīm wifqan li' l-jadāra	**التقييم وفقا للجدارة**

Metage	1 wazn	١ - وزن (عملية الوزن الرسمي)
	2 rasm al-wazn	٢ - رسم الوزن
Method	ṭarīqa	طريقة (اسلوب ، نسق)
Method of operation	ṭarīqat at-tashghīl	طريقة التشغيل
Method of payment	ṭarīqat ad-daf'	طريقة الدفع
Method variance	inḥirāf ṭarīqat at-taṣnī' al-juz'ī	انحراف طريقة التصنيع الجزئى
Method, deductive	aṭ-tarīqa 'l-istidlāliyya	الطريقة الاستدلالية
Methodical	manhajī	منهجي (منظم ، مرتب)
Metre	1 mitr	١ - متـــر
	2 'addād	٢ - عـــداد
Metric system	an-niẓām al-mitrī	النظام المترى
Microfilm	sharīṭ majharī	شريط مجهرى (مايكروفيلم) [شريط تصوير مستندات للحفظ]
Middleman	wasīṭ	وسيط (سمسار)
Millnet price	as-si'r al-muwajjah	السعر الموجه [سعر وحدة من السلع يتحدد فيها الثمن المدفوع أو يتأثر إلى حد كبير بأحد العوامل الموجهة]
Minimise	yukhaffiḍ ila 'l-ḥadd al-adnā	يخفض إلى الحد الأدنى
Minimum	ḥadd adnā	حـــد أدنـى
Minimum and maximum basis	niẓām al-ḥadd al-adnā wa 'l-ḥadd al-aqṣā	نظام الحد الأدنى والحد الاقصى
Minimum rate	al-ḥadd al-adnā li'l-ujūr	الحد الأدنى للأجور
Minimum value	al-qīma 'd-dunyā	القيمة الدنيا
Minor	1 far'ī	١ - فرعي (ثانوى)
	2 qāṣir	٢ - قاصـــر
Minority	aqalliyya	أقليـــة
Minority interest	musāhamat al-aqalliyya	مساهمة الأقلية
Minus	nāqiṣ	ناقـــص
Minute	maḥḍar jalsa	محضر جلسة
Misapplication of public funds	ikhtilās amwāl 'āmma	اختلاس أموال عامة
Miscalculate	yukhṭi' at-taqdīr	يخطىء التقدير (أو الحساب)
Miscarriage	1 ḍayā'	١ - ضياع ـ سلع أثناء النقل
	2 ikhfāq mashrū'	٢ - اخفاق مشروع
	3 sū' naql	٣ - سوء نقل
Miscellaneous	mutanawwi'	متنـــــوع
Miscellaneous assets	mawjūdāt ukhrā	موجودات أخرى [لا تصنف مع أى من مجموعات الموجودات الرئيسية]
Miscellaneous expenses	maṣārīf mutanawwi'a	مصاريف متنوعة
Miscellaneous income	īrādāt mutanawwi'a	ايرادات متنوعة
Miscellaneous revenue	irādāt mutanawwi'a	ايرادات متنوعة
Miscount (n.; v.)	khaṭa' ḥisābī	خطأ حسابي ـ يخطىء حسابيا

Misdeliver	yukhṭi' bi't-taslīm	**يخطىء بالتسليم**
Misenter	yuqayyid aksiyyan	**يقيد عكسيا ـ بندا حسابيا**
Misentry	tasjīl 'aksī	**تسجيل عكسي** (بصورة مخالفة)
Misfeasance	sū' istimāl as-sulṭa	**سوء استعمال السلطة**
Mislay	yuḍayyi'	**يضيع** (يفقد)
Mislead	yuḍallil	**يضلل** (يخدع)
Misleading	muḍallil	**مضلل** (خادع)
Misrepresent	yuḥarrif	**يحرف** (يفسد)
Misrepresentation	bayān khaṭi'	**بيان خاطىء ـ عن ميزانية**
Missed discount	khaṣm mafqūd	**خصم مفقود** [خصم نقدى على مشتريات لم يستغل لأن المشترى لم يدفع خلال فترة الخصم]
Missing	mafqūd	**مفقود** (ضائع)
Misstatement	bayān kādhib	**بيان كاذب** (زور)
Mistake	khaṭa'	**خطـأ** (غلط)
Misuse	sū' isti'māl	**سوء استعمال**
Misuse, fraudulent – of funds	ikhtilās amwāl	**اختلاس أموال**
Mixed inventory	makhzūn mukhtalaṭ	**مخزون مختلط**
Mixed reserve	iḥtiyāṭī mukhtalaṭ	**احتياطي مختلط** [حساب دائن يمثل مزيجا من التزام ما واستدراك وفائض موزع أو أى اثنين منهم]
Mixed surplus	al-fā'iḍ al-mukhtalaṭ	**الفائض المختلط** [حساب حقوق الملكية يحوى ليس فقط الايراد المحتجز ولكن أيضا عناصر الرأسمال المدفوع أو الزيادة في التقويم أو كليهما]
Mnemonic system	niẓām tadhkīrī	**نظام تذكيرى** [تصنيف الحسابات أو مجموعات الحسابات باستعمال حروف أو مجموعة حروف تدل على اسمها أو طبيعتها]
Mode	1 minwāl	**١ - منــول** [العدد الاكثر تكرارا بين مجموعة أرقام]
	2 uslub	**٢ - اسلوب** (طراز)
Model	namūdhaj	**نمــوذج** (نمط)
Moderate	mu'tadil	**معتــدل**
Moderate income	dakhl mu'tadil	**دخل معتدل**
Modernise	yujaddid	**يجــدد** (يحدّث) [يجعل الشىء متمشيا مع العصر]
Modification	tadīl	**تعــديل**
Momentary partnership	sharika taḍāmuniyya mu'aqqata	**شركة تضامية مؤقته**
Monetary	naqdī	**نقــدى**
Monetary fund	ṣundūq an-naqd	**صندوق النقد**
Monetary income	dakhl naqdī	**دخل نقدى**
Monetary market	sūq an-naqd	**سوق النقد**

Monetary standard	qāʻidat an-naqd	قاعدة النقد
Monetary transactions	ṣafaqāt naqdiyya	صفقات نقدية
Monetary unit	wiḥda naqdiyya	وحدة نقدية
Monetary value	qīma naqdiyya	قيمة نقدية
Money	1 'umla	١ - عملة
	2 naqd	٢ - نقد
Money at call	naqd taḥt aṭ-ṭalab	نقد تحت الطلب
		[نقد يدفع عند الطلب]
Money at short notice	naqd bi-ishʻār qaṣīr	نقد باشعار قصير
Money capital	ra'smāl naqdī	رأسمال نقدى
Money changer	ṣarrāf	صراف (صيرفي)
Money deposit	wadiʻa naqdiyya	وديعة نقدية
Money equivalent	al-muʻādil an-naqdī	المعادل النقدي
		[القيمة المقدرة للأملاك أو الخدمات الحاصلة نتيجة لعملية تجارية أو جزء منها لا يتضمن استلام نقود أو تعهد بالدفع]
Money in hand	naqd fi 'ṣ-ṣundūq	نقد في الصندوق
Money lender	muqriḍ an-nuqūd	مقرض النقود
Money rate	siʻr an-naqd	سعر النقد
		[قياسا على تعادل القوة الشرائية]
Money's worth; money equivalent	al-muʻādil an-naqdī	المعادل النقدى
Moneys	dafaʻāt	دفعات (نقدية)
Monopolisation	iḥtikār	احتكار
Monthly (adj.; adv.)	shahrī	شهرى ـ شهريا
Monthly report	taqrīr shahrī	تقرير شهرى
Monthly statement	bayān shahrī	بيان شهرى
Mortality	qābiliyyat al-istihlāk	قابلية الاستهلاك
Mortality curve	munḥana 'l-ajal	منحني الاجل
		[منحنى يبين امتداد الحياة الفعلية أو المقدرة لعدد كبير من الأفراد أو الاشياء]
Mortality rate	muʻaddal al-wafayāt	معدل الوفيات
Mortality statistics	iḥṣā'iyyāt al-wafayāt	احصائيات الوفيات
Mortality table	jadwal taqquʻāt al-ḥayāh	جدول توقعات الحياة
Mortgage (n.; v.)	1 rahn	١ - رهن
	2 rahn ʻaqārī	٢ - رهن عقارى
	3 ṣakk ar-rahn	٣ - صك الرهن ـ يرهن
Mortgage bank	maṣrif ar-ruhūnāt	مصرف الرهونات
Mortgage bond	sanad rahn	سند رهن
Mortgage credit	taslīf ʻaqārī	تسليف عقارى
Mortgage debenture	sanad dayn mu'amman bi-rahn	سند دين مؤمن برهن
Mortgage debt	dayn bi-rahn	دين برهن
Mortgage deed	ṣaq rahn	صك رهن
Mortgage loan	dayn maḍmūn bi-rahn	دين مضمون برهن

Mortgage, blanket	rahn ʿāmm	رهن عام
Mortgage, chattels	rahn amwāl manqūla	رهن أموال منقولة
Mortgage, equitable	rahn li-ḍamān i'timād maṣrafi	رهن لضمان اعتماد مصرفي
Mortgage, foreclose a	yughliq ar-rahn	يغلق الرهن [ينزع ملكية الشيء المرهون]
Mortgage, open-ended	rahn maftūḥ	رهن مفتوح
Mortgage, redemption of	fakk ar-rahn	فك الرهن
Mortgageable	qābil li'r-rahn	قابل للرهن
Motion	iqtirāḥ	اقتراح
Movable property	amwāl manqūla	أموال منقولة
Movables	manqūlāt	منقولات
Move	1 yaqtariḥ	١ - يقترح
	2 yatarāwaḥ	٢ - يتراوح ـ في سعر البورصة
Movement	1 ḥaraka	١ - حركة
	2 tadāwul	٢ - تداول
Moving average	mutawassiṭ mutaḥarrik	المتوسط المتحرك
Moving budget; continuous budget	mizāniyya mutaḥarrika	ميزانية متحركة
Moving projection	tanabbu' mustamirr	تنبؤ مستمر
Multilateral	mutaʿaddid al-aṭrāf	متعدد الاطراف
Multilateral agreement	ittifāqiyya bayn ʿiddat aṭrāf	اتفاقية بين عدة أطراف
Multiphase sampling	ikhtibār ʿayyināt mutaʿaddid al-marāḥil	اختبار عينات متعدد المراحل
Multiple	mutaʿaddid	متعدد
Multiple costs	takālīf murakkaba	التكاليف المركبة
Multiple product pricing	tasʿīr muntajāt mutaʿaddida	تسعير منتجات متعددة [طريقة لتحديد أسعار من يبيع سلعتين أو أكثر]
Multiple sampling	ikhtibār mutaʿaddid li'l-ʿayyināt	اختبار متعدد للعينات
Multiplication	1 aḍ-ḍarb al-ḥisābī	١ - الضرب الحسابي
	2 takāthur	٢ - تكاثر
Multiply	1 yaḍrib ʿadadan	١ - يضرب عددا
	2 yataḍāʿaf	٢ - يتضاعف
Multistage sampling	ikhtiyār mutaʿaddid al-marāḥil il'l-ʿayyināt	اختيار متعدد المراحل للعينات
Municipal dues	rusūm baladiyyāt	رسوم بلديات
Municipality	baladiyya	بلدية
Mutilated notes	awrāq naqd tālifa	أوراق نقد تالفة (بالية)
Mutual corporation	sharika mutabādala	شركة متبادلة [تقتصر على بنوك التوفير وشركات التأمين]
Mutual debts	duyun mutabādala	ديون متبادلة
Mutual fund	mu'assasat istithmār mushtaraka	مؤسسة استثمار مشتركة

Nail, pay on the	yadfaʻ fawran	يدفع فورا (دون تأخير)
Naked	dūn ḍamān	دون ضمان
Name	1 ism	١ - اسم
	2 ʻunwān	٢ - عنوان
Name a person in a deed	yusammī shakhṣan bi-ṣakk	يسمي شخصا بصك
Name a price	yuḥaddid siʻran	يحدد سعرا
Name of firm	1 ism ash-sharirka	١ - اسم الشركة
	2 ʻunwān ash-sharika	٢ - عنوان الشركة
Narration of a journal entry	bayān qayd yawmiyya	بيان قيد يومية
Narrative form	uslūb as-sard	اسلوب السرد [الطريقة التي يقدم بها بيان الارباح والخسائر مثلا مبتدئا من أعلى بالمبيعات ومنتهيا في الاسفل بصافي الربح]
National bank	1 al-maṣrif al-ḥukūmī	١ - المصرف الحكومي
	2 al-maṣrif al-waṭanī	٢ - المصرف الوطني
National debt	ad-dayn al-ʻāmm	الدين العام
National income	ad-dakhl al-qawmī	الدخل القومي
Nationalisation	ta'mīm	تأميم
Nationalise	yu'ammim	يؤمم
Natural	ṭabīʻī	طبيعي
Natural business year	sana māliyya ṭabīʻiyya	سنة مالية طبيعية [سنة مالية منتهية بانتهاء الفصل أو عند الحد الادنى من العمليات]
Natural person	shakhṣ ṭabīʻī	شخص طبيعي
Natural tolerance	at-tasāmuḥ aṭ-ṭabiʻī	التسامح الطبيعي [اصطلاح يستعمل في الاحصاء ويتعلق بالرسم البيانى الذى يراقب المتحولات ليصف طاقة مراحل التصنيع]
Nature of business	ṭabīʻat al-ʻamal	طبيعة العمل
Nature of contents	waṣf al-muḥtawayāt	وصف المحتويات
Necessity condition	sharṭ lāzim	الشرط اللازم
Negative confirmation	ta'yīd salbī	تأييد (تثبيت) سلبي
Negative goodwill	shuhra salbiyya	شهرة سلبية [زيادة قيمة الأسهم الدفترية يوم اقتنائها عن التكلفة التي حصلت عليها الشركة الام لأسهم بعض الشركات الفرعية منزلا منها اقساط شراء الأسهم الأخرى]
Negligence	ihmāl	اهمال (تقصير)
Negligible	ghyr dhī bāl	غير ذى بال (ممكن اسقاطه من الحساب لقلته)
Negligible error	khaṭa' ṭafīf	خطأ طفيف
Negotiability	qābiliyyat at-taḥwīl	قابلية التحويل
Negotiability of a bill	qābiliyyat as-sanad li't-taʻāmul at-tijārī	قابلية السند للتعامل التجارى

Negotiable	qābil li't-tadāwul	قابل للتداول
Negotiable instrument	awrāq tijāriyya qābila li't-taḥwīl	أوراق تجارية قابلة للتحويل
Negotiable papers	awrāq qābila li'taḥwīl	أوراق قابلة للتحويل
Negotiable securities	awrāq māliyya qābila li't-taḥwīl	أوراق مالية قابلة للتحويل
Negotiable title	sanad qābil li't-taḥwīl	سند قابل للتحويل
Negotiate	1 yu'āmil tijāriyyan 2 yaḥsim sanadan	١ - يعامل تجاريا ٢ - يحسم سندا
Negotiate a bargain	yufāwiḍ 'alā ṣafqa	يفاوض على صفقة
Negotiate a bill	yakhṣim kambiyāla	يخصم كمبيالة
Negotiate a loan	ya'qid qarḍan	يعقد قرضا
Negotiation of documents	tadāwul al-mustanadāt	تداول المستندات (شراء المستندات)
Net (n.; v.)	ṣāfī	صاف (يعطي ربحا صافيا)
Net assets	ṣafi 'l-mawjūdāt	صافي الموجودات
Net avails	al-qīma al-fi'liyya	القيمة الفعلية ـ لكمبيالة مخصومة
Net book value	ṣāfi 'l-qīma' d-daftariyya	صافي القيمة الدفترية
Net cash	ad-daf' naqdan	الدفع نقدا
Net cash, 30 days	ad-daf' naqdan khilāl thalāthīn yawman	الدفع نقدا خلال ٣٠ يوما
Net cost	ṣāfi 't-taklifa	صافي التكلفة
Net current assets	ar-ra'smāl al-'āmil	الرأسمال العامل
Net earnings	ṣāfi 'd-dakhl	صافي الدخل
Net income	īrād ṣāfī	ايراد صاف
Net interest	fā'ida ṣāfiya	فائدة صافية
Net investment coefficient	ṣāfī mu'āmil al-istithmār	صافي معامل الاستثمار
Net loss	ṣāfi 'l-khasāra	صافي الخسارة
Net national product	ad-dakhl al-qawmi 'ṣ-ṣāfī	الدخل القومي الصافي
Net operating profit	ṣāfī ribḥ at-tashghīl	صافي ربح التشغيل
Net output	ṣāfi 'l-intāj	صافي الانتاج
Net premium	ṣāfi 'l-qisṭ	صافي القسط
Net products	nātij ṣāfī	الناتج الصافي
Net profit	arbāḥ ṣāfiya	الأرباح الصافية
Net profit on sales	ṣāfī ribḥ al-mabī'āt	صافي ربح المبيعات
Net purchases	ṣāfi 'l-mushtarayāt	صافي المشتريات
Net realisable value	al-qīma 'ṣ-ṣāfiya 'l-mutaḥaqqiqa	القيمة الصافية المتحققة [عند بيع شيء ما]
Net revenue	ṣafi al-irad	صافي الايراد
Net sales	ṣāfi 'l-mabī'āt	صافي المبيعات
Net work	shabaka	شبكـــة
Net working capital; working capital	ra'smāl 'āmil	الرأسمال العامل
Net worth	ḥuqūq ash-shurakā'	حقوق الشركاء
Net yield	ḥaṣil ṣāfī	الحاصل الصافي
Nominal	ismī	اسمي (اعتباري)

Nominal account	ḥisāb ismī	**حساب اسمي** [حساب الأشياء : الارباح والخسائر ، تمييزا عن الحساب الشخصى]
Nominal capital	ra'smāl ismī	**رأسمال اسمي**
Nominal debenture	sanad ismī	**سند اسمي**
Nominal element	al-ʿunṣur al-ismī	**العنصر الاسمي** [ذلك الجزء من حساب الأصل أو الالتزام الذى يعكس التكلفة المستحقة أو الايراد المتحقق الذى يمكن أن ينقل إلى حساب الأرباح والخسائر]
Nominal interest	fā'ida ismiyya	**فائدة اسمية**
Nominal partner	sharīk ismī	**شريك اسمي**
Nominal share	sahm ismī	**سهم اسمي**
Nominal value	qīma ismiyya	**قيمة اسمية**
Nominal value; face value (of money)	al-qīma al-ismiyya aw al-qānūniyya li'n-nuqūd	**القيمة الاسمية أو القانونية للنقود**
Nominal wage	1 ajr naqdī	**١ - أجر نقدى**
	2 ajr ramzī	**٢ - أجر رمزى**
Nominate	1 yurashshiḥ	**١ - يرشح**
	2 yusammī	**٢ - يسمّي** (يعيّن)
Nomination	1 tarshīḥ	**١ - ترشيح**
	2 tasmiya	**٢ - تسمية**
Non-acceptance	ʿadam qabūl	**عدم قبول** (سند)
Non-apportionable	1 ghayr mumkin at-tawzīʿ	**١ - غير ممكن التوزيع**
	2 ghayr qābil ad-dafʿ	**٢ - غير قابل الدفع**
Non-assessable	ghayr mashmūl bi'ḍ-ḍarība	**غير مشمول بالضريبة**
Non-assessable capital stock	ar-ra'smāl al-madfūʿ kāmilan	**الرأسمال المدفوع كاملا** [لا يخضع لالتزامات المساهمة المزدوجة أو الاخرى]
Non-bank borrowing	iqtirāḍ ghayr maṣrafī	**اقتراض غير مصرفي**
Non-cash	ghayr naqdī	**غير نقدى**
Non-cash income	dakhl lā yudfaʿ naqdan	**دخل لا يدفع نقدا**
Non-controllable cost	taklifa lā irādiyya	**تكلفة لا ارادية**
Non-current assets	mawjūdāt ghayr mutadāwala	**موجودات غير متداولة**
Non-current liabilities	maṭlūbat ghayr mutadāwāla	**مطلوبات غير متداولة**
Non-cumulative dividend	ribḥ sahm ghayr tarākumī	**ربح سهم غير تراكمي**
Non-deductible	ghayr qābil li'l-ḥasm	**غير قابل للحسم**
Non-durable	hālik	**هالك** (تالف)
Non-expendable fund	amwāl lā yajūz al-masās bihā	**أموال لا يجوز المساس بها**
Non-feasance	taqāʿus	**تقاعس** [عدم تأدية الواجب المطلوب]
Non-interest bearing account	ḥisāb ghayr muntij fā'ida	**حساب غير منتج فائدة**
Non-ledger assets	mawjūdāt ghayr daftariyya	**الموجودات غير الدفترية**

		[الموجودات أو زياداتها التي لا تشمل عادة في الدفاتر]
Non-liability clause	sharṭ ʿadam al-masʾūliyya	**شرط عدم المسؤولية**
Non-negotiable	ghayr qābil li't-taḍāwul	**غير قابل للتداول** (للتعامل التجارى)
Non-operating	lā tashghīlī	**لا تشغيلي** [ناتج عن عملية عرضية]
Non-operating company	sharika ghayr ʿāmila	**شركة غير عاملة**
Non-operating expenses	maṣārif lā tashghī liyya	**مصاريف لا تشغيلية**
Non-operating income	īrād lā tashghīlī	**ايراد لا تشغيلي**
Non-operating profits	arbāḥ lā tashghīliyya	**أرباح لا تشغيلية**
Non-operating revenue	īrād lā tashghīlī	**ايراد لا تشغيلي**
Non-price competition	al-tanāfus bi-ghayr al-asʿār	**التنافس بغير الأسعار** (التنافس في الجودة والخدمات)
Non-productive	ghayr muntij	**غير منتج**
Non-profit corporation	mussasa lā tastahdif ar-ribḥ	**مؤسسة لا تستهدف الربح**
Non-recurrent	ghayr mutakarrir	**غير متكرر**
Non-recurring charges	aʿbāʾ nādira	**أعباء نادرة** (غير متكررة)
Non-recurring expenses	maṣārīf nādira	**مصاريف نادرة** (غير متكررة ، استثنائية)
Non-reimbursable	la yustaradd	**لا يسترد** (لا يعوض)
Non-revenue receipts	maqbūḍāt ghayr īrādiyya	**مقبوضات غير ايرادية** [في المحاسبة الحكومية كاسترداد القروض مثلا]
Non-standard material	mawādd mukhalifa li'n-namūdhaj	**مواد مخالفة للنموذج**
Non-standard method	ṭarīqa ghayr munāsiba	**طريقة غير مناسبة**
Non-stock corporation	sharika bi-lā ashum	**شركة بلا أسهم**
Non-taxable	ghayr khāḍiʿ li'ḍ-ḍarība	**غير خاضع للضريبة**
Non-transferable	1 ghayr qābil li't-taḥwīl 2 ismī	**١ - غير قابل للتحويل** **٢ - اسمي**
Non-transferable debentures	sanadāt ismiyya	**سندات اسمية** [لا يجوز تحويلها]
Non-variable expenses	nafaqāt ghayr mutaghayyira	**نفقات غير متغيرة**
Non-voting share	sahm ṣāmit	**سهم صامت** [لا يخول صاحبه حق التصويت]
No-par-value capital stock	ashum ra'smāl bi-dūn qīma ismiyya muḥaddada	**أسهم رأسمال بدون قيمة اسمية محددة**
Norm	miʿyār	**معيار**
Normal cost	taklifa ʿādiyya	**تكلفة عادية**
Normal curve	munḥanā ṭabīʿī	**منحني طبيعي**
Normal distribution	tawzīʿ ṭabīʿī	**توزيع طبيعي**
Normal price	siʿr ʿādī	**سعر عادى**
Normal return	al-ʿāʾid al-ʾādī	**العائد العادى** [ايرادات (الأموال المستثمرة) بفائدة عادية]
Normal standard	al-muʿaddal al-miʿyārī	**المعدل المعيارى** [خلال دورة تجارية]

Normal standard cost	taklifa miʿyariyya iʿtiyādiyya	تكلفة معيارية اعتيادية
Normal table	jadwal ṭabīʿī	جدول طبيعي
		[لائحة قيم مختارة محسوبة من المنحني الطبيعي]
Normal value	al-qīma 'ṭ-ṭabīʿiyya	القيمة الطبيعية
Nostro account	ḥisāb na ladaykum	حسابنا لديكم
		[الحساب الذى يفتحه مصرف محلي لدى مصرف في الخارج بعملة أجنبية]
Notarial seal	khātim tawthīqī	خاتم توثيقي
Notary	kātib al-ʿadl	كاتب العدل
Notary act	ʿaqd rasmī	عقد رسمي
Notary's deed	ṣakk muwaththaq	صك موثق
		[لدى كاتب العدل]
Note	kumbiyāla	كمبيالة
Note payable	kumbiyālat dafʿ	كمبيالة دفع
Note receivable	waraqat qabḍ	ورقة قبض
Note receivable discounted	waraqat qabḍ makhṣūma	ورقة قبض مخصومة (مباعة أو مجيرة)
Note to financial statements	īḍāḥ ḥawla 'l-bayānāt al-ḥisābiyya 'l-khitamiyya	ايضاح حول البيانات الحسابية الختامية
Note, advice	kitāb ishʿār maṣrafi	كتاب اشعار - مصرفي
Note, bank	waraqa māliyya	ورقة مالية (بنكنوت)
Note, consignment	bayān shaḥn	بيان شحن
Note, cover	ishʿār ta'mīn	اشعار تأمين
Note, credit	1 ishʿār dā'in	١ - اشعار دائن
	2 bayan bi'l 'itimad	٢ - بيان بالاعتماد
Note, debit	ishʿār madīn	اشعار مدين
Note, discount	kashf bi'l-khuṣūmāt	كشف بالخصومات
Note, promissory	kumbiyāla	كمبيالة
		[سند للأمر]
Notification	tablīgh	تبليغ (اخبار ، اشعر)
Noting a bill	ʿamal brutistu	عمل بروتستو - على ظهر الكمبيالة
Noting charges	maṣārif al-brutistu	مصاريف البروتستو
N.S.F. (not sufficient funds)	ḥisāb bi-dūn raṣīd	حساب بدون رصيد
		[الرصيد لا يغطي الشيك]
Nuisance value	qīmat taḍarrur	قيمة تضرر
		[القسط الزائد عن القيمة العادلة الواجب دفعها ثمنا لأصل أو ادعاء]
Null	bāṭil	باطل (لاغ)
Null and void	lāghin wa bātil	لاغ وباطل
Nullify	yubṭil	يبطل (يلغي)
Nullity of a contract	buṭlān ʿaqd	بطلان عقد
Number (n.; v.)	1 ʿadad	١ - عدد
	2 raqm	٢ - رقم

Number, even	ʿadad zawjī	عدد زوجي
Number, odd	ʿadad mufrad	عدد مفرد
Number, voucher	raqm as-sanad	رقم السند
Numbering	tiʿdād	تعداد (ترقيم)
Numerical	ʿadadī	عددى
Numerical measure	miqyās ʿadadī	مقاس عددى
Numerical scale	miqyās ʿadadī	مقياس عددى
Numerical value	qima ʿadadiyya	قيمة عددية

Object	hadaf	هدف (مقصد ، غرض)
Objection	iʿtirāḍ	اعتراض
Objective (adj.; n.)	mawḍūʿī	موضوعي (هدف)
Objective statement	bayān mawḍūʿī	بيان موضوعي [بيان مصاريف حسب نوعها (مباشرة وغير مباشرة)]
Objective value	qīma mawḍūʿiyya muḥaddada	القيمة الموضوعية المحددة
Objective, accidental	hadaf ʿaraḍī	هدف عرضي
Objective, designated	hadaf muʼayyan	هدف معين (محدّد)
Objective, ultimate	hadaf nihāʼī	هدف نهائي
Obligate	yulzim	يلزم (يفرض ، يوجب)
Obligated balance	mukhaṣṣaṣāt mulzimat al-infūq	مخصصات ملزمة الانفاق
Obligation	iltizām	التزام (موجب)
Obligation, fulfil one's	yafī bi'l-tizāmātihi	يفي بالتزاماته
Obligation, imperfect	iltizām adabī	التزام أدبي
Obligation, joint and several	iltizām bi't-takāful wa 't-taḍāmun	التزام بالتكافل والتضامن
Obligation, meet one's	yafī bi'ltizāmātihi	يفي بالتزاماته
Obligation, perfect	iltizām qānūnī	التزام قانوني
Obligation, release from an	yubriʼ min iltizām	يبرى من التزام
Obligation, undertake an	yartabiṭ bi'l-tizām	يرتبط بالتزام
Obligation, withdraw from one's	yansaḥib min iltizām	ينسحب من التزام
Obligations, incurred	iltizāmāt mutarattiba	الالتزامات المترتبة
Obligations, outstanding	iltizāmāt muʿallaqa	الالتزامات المعلقة
Oblige	yulzim	يلزم (يجبر ، يرغم)
Obliterate	1 yaṭmis	١ - يطمس (يمحو)
	2 yulghī	٢ - يلغي
Observance	murāʿāh	مراعاة (تقيد بنظام أو قانون)
Observations	1 mulāḥazāt	١ - ملاحظات
	2 mushāhadāt	٢ - مشاهدات
	3 iʿtirāḍāt	٣ - اعتراضات
Observed depreciation	istihlāk mutarākim	الاستهلاك المتراكم [المحدد بالمعاينة المادية أو تقييم الوضع في حالة العمل]

Obsolete (U.S.)	bāṭil al-istiʿmāl	باطل الاستعمال
Obsolete stocks	biḍāʿa qadīma	البضاعة القديمة
		[البضاعة غير الصالحة للاستعمال]
Obtain advances of money	yaḥṣul ʿalā sulfa naqdiyya	يحصل على سلفة نقدية
Obtainable	mumkin iḥrāzuh	ممكن احرازه
Occasional	ʿaraḍī	عرضي (ظرفي)
Occasional income	īrad ʿraḍī	ايراد عرضي
Occupancy	1 ishghāl	١ - اشـــغال
	2 tamalluk bi-waḍʿal-yad	٢ - تملك بوضع اليد
Occupancy expense	maṣārīf ishghāl ʿaqār	مصاريف اشغال عقار
Occupation	1 mihna	١ - مهنـــة
	2 shughl	٢ - شـــغل
Odd	1 mufrad	١ - مفـــرد
	2 shādhdh	٢ - شـــاذ
Odd lot (U.S.)	majmūʿa shādhdha	مجموعة شاذة
		١ - [وحدة تجارية أصغر من المعتاد]
		٢ - [صفقة بأقل من مئة سهم ـ بورصة]
Offer (n.; v.)	ʿaraḍ	عرض ـ يعرض
Offer, excess	ʿarḍ zā'id	عرض زائد
Offer, firm	ʿarḍ thābit	عرض ثابت
Offer, verbal	ʿarḍ shafahī	عرض شفهي
Offering price	al-siʿr al-maʿrūḍ	السعر المعروض
Office	1 maktab	١ - مكـــتب
	2 waẓīfa	٢ - وظيفة (منصب)
	3 markaz	٣ - مركـــز
Office equipment	muʿaddāt maktab	معـدات مكـــتب
Office expenses	maṣārīf maktab	مصاريف مكتب
Office furniture and equipment	athāth wa muʿaddāt maktab	أثاث ومعدات مكتب
Office hours	sāʿāt al-ʿamal	ساعات العمل
Office maintenance account	ḥisāb ṣiyānat al-maktab	حساب صيانة المكتب
Office manager	mudīr maktab	مدير مكتب
Office, central	al-maktab al-markazī	المكتب المركزى
Office, head	al-maktab ar-ra'īsī	المركز الرئيسي
Officer	ʿuḍw idārī	عضو اداری
Official	rasmī	رسمي (قانوني)
Official documents	wathā'iq rasmiyya	وثائق رسمية
Official estimate	taqdīr rasmī	تقدير رسمي
Official extract	mustakhraj rasmī	مستخرج رسمي
Official journal	jarīda rasmiyya	جريدة رسمية
Official notification	ishʿār rasmī	اشعار رسمي
Official price	as-siʾr ar-rasmī	السعر الرسمي ـ للأوراق المالية
Official quotation	as-siʾr ar-rasmī	السعر الرسمي (المعلن)
Official rate	si'r al-khaṣm ar-rasmī	سعر الخصم الرسمي ـ في المصرف

Officially	rasmiyyan	رسميا (بطريقة رسمية)
Offset (n.; v.)	1 muqāṣṣa	١ - مقاصة
	2 yuwāzin	٢ - يـوازن (يقابـل)
Offset account	ḥisāb tawāzunī	حساب توازني
Offsetting error	khaṭa' muwāzan	خطأ مـوازن
Offtake	rawāj	رواج ـ البضائع
Ogive	munḥanā tikrār tarākumī	منحني تكرار تراكمي [على شكل S]
Oil and gas payment	ḥiṣṣat an-nafṭ wa'l-ghāz	حصة النفط والغاز [حصة من يضخ الزيت من انتاج الزيت الخام والغاز من بئر معين أو قطعة أرض]
Oligopoly price	si'r at-taḍakhkhum	سعر التضخم [السعر حين يزيد الطلب على العرض]
Oligopsony price	si'r al-inkimāsh	سعر الانكماش [السعر حين يزيد العرض على الطلب]
Omission	ḥadhf	حـذف (اغفال ، اسقاط)
Omit	yaḥdif	يحـذف (يغفل ، يسقط)
On account	'ala 'l-ḥisāb	على الحساب
On change	fi 'l-burṣa	في البورصة
On consignment	bi'l-amāna	بالامانـــة [بضاعة مودعة للبيع بالامانة]
On cost (U.K.)	taklifa ghayr mubāshira	تكلفة غير مباشرة
On credit	bi'd-dayn	بالديـــن
On delivery	'ind at-taslīm	عند التسليم
On demand	'ind aṭ-ṭalab	عند الطلب
On hand	taḥt al-yad	تحت اليد (موجود)
On joint account	li-ṣāliḥ al-ḥisāb al-mushtarak	لصالح الحساب المشترك
On receipt of	'ind istilām	عند استلام
On request	'ind aṭ-ṭalab	عند الطلب
On sale or return	li'l-bay' aw li'r-rad	للبيع أو للرد
Onus	mas'ūliyya	مسؤوليـــة
Open (v.; adj.)	yaftaḥ	يفتح ـ مفتوح
Open account	1 ḥisāb maftūḥ	١ - حساب مفتوح
	2 qarḍ ghayr maḍmūn	٢ - قرض غير مضمون
Open cheque	shīk maftūḥ	شيك مفتوح (غير مسطر)
Open credit	i'timād makshūf	اعتماد مكشوف
Open end investment company	mu'assasat istithmār mushtaraka	مؤسسة استثمار مشتركة
Open (end) mortgage (or bond)	rahn maftūḥ	الرهن (أو السند) المفتوح
Open market policy	siyāsat as-sūq al-ḥurra	سياسة السوق الحرة
Open the books	fatḥ ad-dafātir	فتح الدفاتر
Opening balance	ar-raṣid al-iftitāḥī	الرصيد الافتتاحي [رصيد أول المدة]
Opening bid	al-'arḍ al-aṣlī	العرض الاصلـي

Opening capital	ar-ra'smāl al-awwalī	**الرأسمال الأولي** [رأسمال افتتاح المشروع]
Opening (a) credit	fatḥ iʿtimād	**فتـح اعتـماد**
Opening entry	qayd iftitāḥī	**قيد افتتاحي**
Opening price	siʿr al-iftitāḥ	**سعر الافتتاح** [عند مباشرة السوق نشاطها]
Operating	tashghīl	**تشغيل ـ مشروع تجارى**
Operating budget	mīzāniyyat at-tashghīl	**ميزانية التشغيل**
Operating capital	ra'smāl at-tashghīl	**رأسمال التشغيل**
Operating characteristic curve	munḥana 'ḥtimāl al-qabūl	**منحني احتمال القبول**
Operating company	sharika ʿāmila	**شركة عاملة**
Operating costs (or expenses)	takālīf at-tashghīl	**تكاليف** (نفقات) **التشغيل**
Operating cycle	dawrat at-tashghīl	**دورة التشغيل** [الوقت الضائع بين شراء مواد المخزون مثل المواد الخام وتحويلها إلى نقد]
Operating deficit	ʿajz at-tashghīl	**عجز التشغيل**
Operating effectiveness (or competence)	kafā'at at-tashghīl	**كفاءة التشغيل**
Operating expense ledger	ustādh maṣārīf at-tashghīl	**استاذ مصاريف التشغيل**
Operating income (or profit)	arbāḥ at-tashghīl	**أرباح التشغيل**
Operating ledger	ustādh ḥisābāt at-tashghīl	**استاذ حسابات التشغيل** [أى ايرادات ومصاريف التشغيل]
Operating leverage	munḥana 't-tashghīl al-ʿaksī	**منحني التشغيل العكسي** [ميل صافي الربح إلى التغير عكسيا مع المبيعات]
Operating performance income statement	bayān al-arbāḥ wa 'l-khasā'ir at-tashghīlī	**بيان الأرباح والخسائر التشغيلي** [بيان الأرباح والخسائر الذى يظهر الايرادات وتكاليف عناصر التشغيل العادية فـقط]
Operating ratio	muʿāmil at-tashghīl	**معامل التشغيل** [نسبة المصاريف الى المبيعات]
Operating report	taqrīr at-tashghīl	**تقرير التشغيل** [يبين التكاليف حسب الميزانية والتكاليف المعيارية والتكاليف الفعلية]
Operating reserve	iḥtiyāṭi 't-tashghīl	**احتياطي التشغيل**
Operating results	natā'ij at-tashghīl	**نتائج التشغيل** [صافي الربح أو صافي الخسارة]
Operating revenue	ṣāfī īrādāt at-tashghīl	**صافي ايرادات التشغيل**
Operating statement	bayān at-tashghīl	**بيان التشغيل**
Operation cost centre	markaz taklifat ʿamaliyyāt	**مركز تكلفة عمليات**
Operational	1 yataʿallaq bi-ʿamaliyya 2 qābil li't-tanfīdh	**١ - يتعلق بعملية** **٢ - قابل للتنفيذ**
Operational decision	qarār khāṣṣ bi'l-ʿamaliyyāt	**القرار الخاص بالعمليات**

Operations	'amaliyyat al-mu'assasa	عمليات المؤسسة
Operations research	dirāsat al-'amaliyyāt	دراسة العمليات
Operative	1 'amalī	١ - عملـــي
	2 nafidh al-maf'ūl	٢ - نافذ المفعول
Operator	1 muḍārib fi 'l-burṣa	١ - مضارب في البورصة
	2 'āmil tashghīl	٢ - عامل تشغيل
Opinion	ra'y mihanī li-murāqib al-ḥisābāt	الرأى المهني لمراقب الحسابات
Opportunity	furṣa	فرصة (امكانية)
Opportunity cost	at-taklifa 'l-badīla	التكلفة البديلة [التغير المتوقع في التكلفة بعد استخدام آلة أو طريقة أو مواد خام أو مواصفات أو عمليات بديلة]
Opportunity cost method	ṭarīqat at-taklifa 'l-badīla	طريقة التكلفة البديلة
Opposite side of an account	al-jānib al-muqābil min ḥisāb	الجانب المقابل من حساب
Optimum	al-amthal	الأمثل (الأفضل ، الأحسن)
Optimum output	al-intāj al-amthal	الانتاج الامثل
Option	khiyār	خـيـــار
Option bargain	1 ṣafqa sharṭiyya	١ - صفقة شرطية ـ في البورصة
	2 ṣafqa li-ajal	٢ ـ صفقة لأجل
	3 ṣafqa ḥurra	٣ - صفقة حرة
Option deal	'amaliyya khiyāriyya	عملية خيارية
Option money	1 mablagh al-bay' ash-sharṭī	١ - مبلغ البيع الشرطي
	2 qisṭ mumtāz	٢ - قسط ممتاز
Option order	ḥawāla sharṭiyya	حوالة شرطية
Option price	si'r sharṭī	السعر الشرطي
Optional	ikhtiyārī	اختيـــارى
Optional dividend	ar-ribḥ al-ikhtiyārī	الربح الاختيارى [الربح المخول دفعه بأكثر من طريقة مثلا نقدا أو على شكل أسهم]
Options market	1 sūq sharṭiyy aw li-ajal	١ - سوق شرطية أو لأجل
	2 burṣat al-ḥubūb	٢ - بورصة الحبوب
Order	1 ṭalab al-biḍā'a	١ - طلب البضاعة
	2 ḥawāla	٢ - حـوالـــة
Order book	sijill aṭ-ṭalabāt at-tjāriyya	سجل الطلبات التجارية
Order to pay	amr ad-daf'	أمر الدفع
Order, back	ṭalab muta'akkir	طلب متأخر
Order, book an	yusajjil ṭalab	يسجل طلب ـ بضائع الخ
Order, money	ḥawāla māliyya	حوالة مالية
Order, payable to	yadfa' li-amr	يـدفع لأمـــر
Order, postal	ḥawāla barīdiyya	حوالة بريدية
Order, revoke an	yulghī ṭalab	يلغـي طــلب
Ordinary annuity	daf'a sanawiyya 'ādiyya	دفعة سنوية عادية [أى تتم في نهاية كل فترة]

Ordinary bills	awrāq tijāriyya	أوراق تجارية (سندات تجارية)
Ordinary creditor	dā'in 'ādī	دائـن عــــادى [تمييزا عن الدائن الممتاز]
Ordinary depreciation	istihlāk 'adī	الاستهلاك العادى [فقدان منفعة الأصل الثابت بسبب الهلاك العادى والتقادم وغيره]
Ordinary interest	fā'ida 'āadiyya	الفائدة العاديــة [الفائدة البسيطة محتسبةعلي أساس ٣٦٠ يومــا]
Ordinary shares	ashum 'ādiyya	أسهم عادية
Organisation	1 tanẓīm	١ - تنظيــم
	2 hay'a	٢ - هيئة (جمعية ، منظمة ، مؤسسة)
Organisation and methods analysis	taḥlīl al-anẓima wa'l-asālīb	تحليل الأنظمة والأساليب
Organisation chart	mukhaṭṭaṭ tanẓīmī	المخطط التنظيمي (الهيكل الادارى)
Organisation cost (or expense)	takālīf at-ta'sīs	تكاليف التأسيس
Organisation manual	dalīl ash-sharika	دليل الشركة
Organisation unit	wiḥda idāriyya	وحدة ادارية [أى قسم ادارى في مؤسسة]
Organised efficiency	kifāya munaẓẓama	الكفايةالمنظمة
Original capital	ra'smāl aṣlī	الرأسمال الأصلي [الرأسمال المدفوع عند التأسيس]
Original copy	nuskha aṣliyya	نسخة أصلية (صورة أصلية)
Original cost	taklifa aṣliyya	التكلفة الأصلية
Original entry	qayd aṣlī	قيــد أصلــي [قيد في صيغة صحيحة لترحيله إلى دفتر الاستاذ]
Other assets	mawj ūd āt ukhr ā	موجودات أخرى (اصول أخرى)
Other deductions	1 nafaqāt ukhrā	١ - نفقات أخرى
	2 iqtiṭā'āt	٢ - اقتطاعات
Other income (or revenue)	īrādāt ukhrā	ايرادات أخرى
Other liabilities	maṭlūbāt ukhrạ	مطلوبات أخرى
Out of date	1 mutaqādīm	١ - متقــادم
	2 bāṭil	٢ - باطــل
Out-of-pocket expenses	maṣārīf jayb	مصاريف جـيب
Outbalance	yurajjiḥ	يرجح (يفوق على ، يزيد)
Outbargain	yaghlib fi 'l-musāwama	يغلب في المساومة
Outbid	yuzāyid	يزايد (في مزاد علني)
Out-cycle work (U.S.)	'amal khārij ad-dā'ira	عمل خارج الدائرة [العمل الذى ينفذه المشغل عندما تكون الآلة متوقفة]
Outgo	maṣrūfāt	مصروفات
Outlay	1 infāq	١ - انفــاق
	2 taklifa	٢ - تكلفــة

Outlay cost	taklifa musajjala	التكلفة المسجلة
Outlay expiration	takhfīḍ an-nafaqa	تخفيض النفقة [نتيجة لحادث أو ظرف متعلق بالأصل]
Outlet	1 makhraj	١ - مخرج (منفذ)
	2 majāl ḥayawī	٢ - مجال حيوى [لسلعـــة مـــا]
Outline	1 mujmal	١ - مجمـــل
	2 al-khuṭūṭ al-asāsiyya	٢ - الخطوط الأساسية (الخطوط العريضة)
Output	al-mardūd	المردود (الانتاج)
Output account	ḥisāb al-intāj	حساب الانتاج
Output cost	taklifat al-intāj	تكلفة الانتاج
Output–input analysis	taḥlīl al-mardūd wa'z-zad	تحليل المردود والزاد (الداخل)
Outsale	1 bay' bi'l-mazād	١ - بيع بالمزاد
	2 mazād	٢ - مـــزاد
Outstanding	aghayr musaddad	غيـر مســـدد
Outstanding capital stock	ra'smāl ashum bi't-tadāwul	رأسمال أسهم بالتداول
Outstanding cheque	shīk mawqūf	شيك موقوف (لم يصرف بعد)
Outstanding debts	duyūn ghayr musaddada	ديون غير مسددة
Outstanding expenses	nafaqāt mustaḥiqqat ad-daf'	نفقات مستحقة الدفع
Outstanding payment	daf'a muta'akhkhira	دفعة متـــأخرة
Outturn (output)	mardūd	مردود (انتاج ، محصول)
Outward consignment	biḍā'at amāna khārija	بضاعة أمانة خارجة
Over or under absorbed overhead; burden over or under applied	takālīf ra'siyya muḥammala bi'ziyāda aw an-naqṣ	التكاليف الرأسية المحملة بالزيادة أو النقص
Overabsorption	istī' āb zā'id	استيعاب زائـــد [زيادة القيود الدائنة في حساب الاستيعاب على مجموع الحساب نفسه]
Overage (U.S.)	fā'iḍ	فائض (مفرط ، زائد)
Overall basis	asās ijmāli	الأساس الاجمالي (العام)
Overall deficit	'ajz ijmālī	العجز الاجمالي
Overall gain	kasb ijmālī	الكسب الاجمالي
Overall loss	khasāra ijmāliyya	الخسارة الاجمالية
Overall surplus	fā'id ijmālī	الفائض الاجمالي
Over and short	ziyādat wa 'ajz aṣ-ṣundūq	زيادة وعجز الصندوق
Overcharge (n.; v.)	ziyāda faḥisha li'l-as'ār	زيادة فاحشة للأسعار
Overdraw (n.; v.)	saḥb 'ala 'l-kushūf	سحب على الكشوف
Overassessment	irhāq ḍarā'ibī	ارهاق ضرائبي (اجحاف بفرض الضرائب)
Overdraft	saḥb 'ala 'l-makshūf	سحب على المكشوف
Overdraft account	ḥisāb jārī madīn	الحساب الجارى المدين
Overdrawn account	ḥis āb makshūf	حساب مكشوف
Overdue	muta'akhkhir bi'd-daf'	متأخر بالدفع
Overdue payment	daf'a muta'akhkhira	دفعة متأخرة
Overestimate	yufriṭ fi 't-taqdīr	يفرط في التقرير

Overhaul (v.)	1 yafḥaṣ li't-tarmīm	١ - يفحص للترميم
	2 yurammim	٢ - يرمـــم
Overhead	maṣārīf ra'siyya	المصاريف الرأسية [وهي المصاريف غير المباشرة التي لا يمكن ربطها مع أى انتاج أو مشروع ومن هذه المصاريف ما هو ثابت لايتغير سواء كان هناك انتاج أم لا]
Overhead allocation	tawzī ʿal-maṣārīf ar-ra'siyya	توزيع المصاريف الرأسية [على وحدات التكلفة]
Overhead costs	takālīf ra'siyya	تكاليف رأسية
Overhead rate	muʿaddal al-maṣārīf ar-ra'siyya	معدل المصاريف الرأسية
Overhead variance	inḥirāf at-takālif ar-ra'siyya	انحراف التكاليف الرأسية
Overlap (n.; v.)	tadākhul	تداخـــل
Overlapping debt	dayn mutadākhil	الدين المتداخل
Overlook	1 yurāqib	١ - يراقب
	2 yuhmil	٢ - يهمل
Overpay	yadfaʿ bi'z-za'id	يدفع بالزائـــد [يدفع أكثر من اللازم]
Over-production	ifrāṭ fi 'l-intāj	افراط في الانتاج
Overrate	yubāligh fi 't-taqdīr	يبالغ في التقدير
Override	1 yatjāwaz	١ - يتجاوز
	2 yulghī	٢ - يلغي (يبطل)
Oversell	yabiʿ bi 'z-zā'id	يبيع بالزائـــد [يبيع بسعر فاحش أو يبيع كمية تزيد عما يمكن تسليمه]
Oversight	1 sahw	١ - سهو
	2 riqāba	٢ - رقابة (وصاية)
Overspending	1 ma'zaq mālī	١ - مأزق مالي
	2 ṣarf bāhiz	٢ - صرف باهظ [تجاوز حدود المبالغ المخصصة]
Overstock	ziyādat al-makhzūn	زيادة المخزون
Overtax	yufriṭ bi'ḍ-ḍarība	يفرط بالضريبة [يرهق في فرض الضريبة]
Overtime	waqt iḍāfī	وقت اضافـــي [ساعات عمل اضافية]
Overtime premium	badal waqt iḍāfī	بدل وقت اضافي
Over-valuation	ifrāṭ fi 't-tathmīn	افراط في التثمين
Owe	madīn	مـديـــن [أى في ذمته]
Owing	mustaḥaqq ad-dafʿ	مستحق الدفع
Own	yamtalik	يمتلك (يحوز)
Owner	mālik	مالك (صاحب الشيء)
Ownership	milkiyya	ملكية (حق الملك)

Pack	1 yaḥzim	١ - يحـــزم
	2 yu'abbi'	٢ - يعبـــىء
Package	1 ta'bi'a	١ - تعبئـــة
	2 ṭard	٢ - طـــرد (رزمـة)
Package charges	nafaqāt at-ta'bi'a	نفقات التعبئة
Packing charges	mafaqāt taghlīf	نفقات تغليف
Packing and dispatch department	qism al-ḥazm wa al-shahn	قسم الحزم والشحن
Packing list	qā'imat ta'bi'a	قائمة تعبئة
Packing material	mawādd taghlīf	مواد تغليف
Paginate	yuraqqim tasalsuliyyan	يرقم تسلسليا [صفحات دفتر تجارى]
Pagination	tarqīm mutasalsil	ترقيم متسلسل
Paid	1 madfū'	١ - مدفوع
	2 ma'jūr	٢ - مأجور (مستخدم)
Paid bills	sanadāt musaddada	سندات مسددة
Paid in advance	madfū' muqaddaman	مدفوع مقدما
Paid in capital	ra'smāl mu'ddā	رأسمال مؤدى [مجموع ما يؤديه المساهمون الى الشركة من مبالغ نقدية وممتلكات وخدمات] وخدمات]
Paid in surplus	fā'iḍ madfū'	فائض مدفوع [رأسمال يؤديه المساهمون ويسجل في حساب غير حساب قيمة الأسهم]
Paid up capital	ra'smal madfū'	الرأسمال المدفوع
Paper	waraqa māliyya	ورقة مالية (سند ، وثيقة)
Paper currency	'umla waraqiyya	عملة ورقية
Paper money	nuqūd waraqiyya	نقود ورقية
Paper profit	ribḥ wahmī	ربح وهمي (ربح مأمول)
Paper securities	awrāq māliyya	أوراق مالية
Paper, bearer	waraqa li-ḥāmilihā	ورقة لحاملها
Paper, commercial	waraqa tijāriyya	ورقة تجارية
Paper, negotiable	waraqa qābila li't-tadawul at-tijārī	ورقة قابلة للتداول التجارى
Paper, short	sanad qaṣīr al-ajal	سند قصير الأجل
Par	as-si'r al-ismī	السعر الاسمي [سعر المساواة لسند ما]
Par of exchange	si'r ṣirāfa mutakāfi'	سعر صرافة متكافىء
Par value	al-qīma 'l-ismiyya	القيمة الاسمية (القيمة الأصلية)
Par value capital stock	al-qīma 'l-ismiyya li-ashum ra's al-māl	القيمة الاسمية لأسهم رأس المال
Par, above	fawq al-qīma 'l-ismiyya	فوق القيمة الاسمية (فوق سعر المساواة)
Par, at	bi'l-qīma 'l-ismiyya	بالقيمة الاسمية (بسعر المساواة)
Par, below	aqall min al-qīma 'l-ismiyya	أقل من القيمة الاسمية
Parcel post	ṭard barīdī	طـــرد بريدى

Parent company	ash-sharika 'l-umm	الشـــركة الأم
		[وهي التي لها شركات تابعة]
Parity	1 takāfu'	١ - تكافـــؤ
	2 taʻādul	٢ - تعـــادل
		[سعر الصرف في سوقين]
Parity between two rates	taʻādul bayn siʻrayn	تعادل بين سعرين
Parity price	siʻr at-ta'ādul	سعر التعادل
Part time	dawām juz'ī	دوام جزئـــي
Partial	juz'ī	جزئي (غير تام)
Partial acceptance	qabūl juz'ī	قبول جزئي
Partial loss	khasāra juz'iyya	خسارة جزئية
Partial payment	sadād juz'ī	سداد جزئي
Partial shipment	shaḥn juz'ī	شحن جزئي
Participant	1 mushtarik	١ - مشترك
	2 musāhim	٢ - مساهم
Participate	1 yushārik	١ - يشارك
	2 yusāhim	٢ - يساهم
Participating capital stock	sahm mumtāz	السهم الممتاز
		[بالاضافة إلى نسبة الربح الثابتة التي يتمتع بها يشترك أيضا مع الأسهم العادية في الأرباح]
Participating dividend	arbāh alʼ as-hum al-mumtāza	أرباح الأسهم الممتازة
Participation	1 mushāraka	١ - مشاركـــة
	2 musāhama	٢ - مساهمـــة
Participation in profits	naṣīb fi 'l-arbāḥ	نصيب في الأرباح
Participation loan	qarḍ musāhama	قـــرض مساهمة
Particular lien	hajz khāṣṣ	حجز خاص
Particular partnership	sharika muḥāṣṣa	شركة محاصة
Particular power	wakāla khāṣṣa	وكالة خاصة
		[تعطى لمحام]
Particulars	tafāṣīl	تفاصيل (مفردات)
Particulars of an account	mufradāt ḥisāb mā	مفردات حساب ما
Particulars of sale	shurūt-al biaʻ	شروط البيع
Partly	juz'iyyan	جـزئيـــــا
		[بصورة جزئية]
Partly paid up shares	as-hum madfūʻa juz'iyyan	أسهم مدفوعة جزئيا
Partly secured creditor	dā'in maḍmūn juz'iyyan	دائن مضمون جزئيا
Partner	sharīk	شـــريـــك
Partner in joint account	sharīk fī ḥisāb mushtarak	شريك في حساب مشترك
Partner, active	sharīk ʻāmil	شريك عامل
		[في شركة توصية]
Partner, commandité	sharīk mūṣī	شريك موص (شريك برأسماله)
Partner, dormant	sharīk mūṣī	شريك موص

Partner, general	sharīk 'umūmī	شريك عمومي
Partner, incoming	sharīk jadīd	شريك جديد
Partner, junior	ash-sharīk al-aṣghar	الشريك الأصغر
Partner, limited	sharīk dhū mas'ūliyya maḥdūda	شريك ذو مسؤولية محدودة
Partner, managing	ash-sharīk al-mudīr	الشريك المدير [أى المكلف بالادارة]
Partner outgoing	sharīk munfakk	شريك منفك
Partner, senior	ash-sharīk al-akbar	الشريك الأكبر
Partner, sleeping	sharīk mūṣī	شريك موص
Partnership	1 sharāka	١ - شراكـــة
	2 sharikat taḍāmun	٢ - شركة تضامن
Partnership debt	dayn sharāka	دين شراكة
Partnership deed	'aqd ta'sīs sharika	عقد تأسيس شركة (عقد شراكة)
Partnership limited by shares	sharikat tawṣiya bi'l-as-hum	شركة توصية بالاسهم
Partnership, particular	sharikat ashkhāṣ	شركة أشخاص (شركة خاصة)
Partnership, simple limited	sharikat tawsiya basīṭa	شركة توصية بسيطة
Partnership, special	sharāka khāṣṣa	شراكة خاصة
Party	farīq	فريق (طرف)
Pass	1 yudāwil	١ - يـــداول
	2 yumarrir	٢ - يمرر (يسجل)
	3 yu'ayyid	٣ - يـؤيـــد
	4 yuṣawwit	٤ - يصـّــوت
Pass a dividend (v.)	yuthbit ribhan	يثبت ربحـا
Pass a transfer	yarudd taḥwīlan	يـــرد تحويلا [إلـى المحـــول]
Pass an entry	yumarrir qaydan	يمـرر قيـــدا [يقيد مادة في حساب ما]
Pass an item to current account	yusajil bandan fi ḥisāb jarī	يسجل بندا في الحساب الجارى
Passbook	daftar ḥisābāt	دفتر حسابات [مـع مصـــرف]
Passed dividend	ribḥ ghayr mu'lan	ربـح غيـر معلـــن [في التاريخ المعتاد لتوزيع أرباح الأسهم]
Passive bonds	sanadāt bi-dūn fawā'id	سندات بدون فوائد
Passive debt	dayn bi-dūn fawā'id	دين بدون فوائد
Past due	mustaḥiqq sābiqan	مستحق سابقا [متأخر من تاريخ استحقاق الدفع]
Past due account	ḥisāb mustaḥiqq sābiqan	حساب مستحق سابقا [حساب فات موعد استحقاقه]
Past due bills	awrāq mustaḥiqqa sābiqan	أوراق مستحقة سابقا [أوراق مستحقة ولم تدفع]
Patent	barā'at ikhtirā'	براءة اختراع (امتياز)
Patent fees	rusūm tasjīl barā'at al-ikhtirā'	رسوم تسجيل براءة الاختراع
Patent infringement suit	da'wa 'ntihāk barā'at ikhtirā'	دعوى انتهاك براء اختراع

Patent office	maktab barā'āt al-ikhtirā'āt	مكتب براءات الاختراعات
Patent right	ḥaqq al-ikhtirā'	حق الاختراع
Patentee	ṣāḥib al-barā'a	صاحب البراءة
Patron	'amīl	عميل (زبون)
Patronise	yu'āmil	يعامل (يتعامل مع)
Pattern	namaṭ	نمط (نموذج ، مثال)
Pawn (n.; v.)	rahn	رهن - يرهن
Pawn, securities in	sanadāt marhūna	سندات مرهونة
Pawnee	al-murtahin	المرتهن
Pawner	ar-rāhin	الراهن [المدين برهن]
Pay (n.; v.)	1 ujra	١ - اجرة
	2 yadfa'	٢ - يدفع (يسدد)
Pay (the) balance	yadfa' ar-raṣīd	يدفع الرصيد (يرصد دينا)
Pay (to) bearer	idfa' li-ḥāmilihi	ادفع لحامله
Pay day	yawm daf' ar-rawātib	يوم دفع الرواتب
Pay for	yadfa' thaman	يدفع ثمن
Pay in	yadfa'	يدفع (يسلم مالا)
Pay in advance	yadfa' muqaddaman	يدفع مقدما
Pay in cash	yadfa' naqdan	يدفع نقدا
Pay in full	yadfa' kāmilan	يدفع كاملا
Pay in funds	yadfa' amwālan	يدفع أموالا
Pay in kind	yadfa' 'aynan	يدفع عينا
Pay list	kashf ad-daf'	كشف الدفع
Pay off	1 yubri' dhimma	١ - يبرىء ذمة (يسدد دينا)
	2 yafukk rahnan	٢ - يفك رهنا
Pay off a creditor	yusaddid dā'inan	يسدد دائنا
Pay on delivery	yadfa' 'ind at-taslīm	يدفع عند التسليم
Pay on demand	yadfa' 'ind aṭ-ṭalab	يدفع عند الطلب
Pay on the nail	yadfa' fawran	يدفع فورا
Pay one's debts	yusaddid duyūnahu	يسدد ديونه
Pay out	yadfa'	يدفع (يسلم مالا)
Pay rate	mu'addal al-ujra	معدل الأجرة
Pay roll	jadwal ar-rawātib	جدول الرواتب
Pay roll account	ḥisāb ar-rawātib	حساب الرواتب
Pay roll distribution	tawzī' ar-rawātib	توزيع الرواتب
Pay roll receipt	īṣāl ar-rawātib	ايصال الرواتب
Pay roll records	sijillāt ar-rawātib	سجلات الرواتب
Pay roll register (P.R.)	sijill ar-rawātib	سجل الرواتب
Pay sheet	istimārat ar-rawātib	إستمارة الرواتب
Pay slip	qasīmat al-īdā'	قسيمة الايداع
Pay up	yusaddid	يسدد [يحرر سندات من التزامات بالتسديد]

Pay up a share	yusaddid qīmat sahm	يسدد قيمة سهم
Payable	yastaḥiqq ad-daf'	يستحق الدفع
Payee	al-madfū' lahu	المدفوع له (المستفيد ، المستلم)
Payer	ad-dāfi'	الدافـــع
Payment	daf'a	دفعـــة
Payment agreement	ittifāqiyyat madfū'āt	اتفاقية مدفوعات
Payment of money	daf'at nuqūd	دفعة نقود
Payment of taxes	adā' aḍ ḍarā'ib	أداء الضرائب
Payment on account	daf' 'ala 'l-ḥisāb	دفع على الحساب
Payment, put off	yu'ajjil ad-daf'	يؤجل الدفع
Payment, suspend	yu'alliq ad-daf'	يعلق الدفع
Peak	adh-dhurwa	الذروة (الحد الأقصى)
Peak hours	dhurwat an-nashāṭ al-yawmī	ذروة النشاط اليومي
Peak off	sa'āt khumūd an-nashāṭ	ساعات خمود النشاط
Peak output	mustawa 'l-intāj al-qiyāsī	مستوى الانتاج القياسي
Pecuniary	naqdī	نقدى (مالي)
Pecuniary benefit	al-mu'ādil an-naqdī	المعادل النقدى [المتبقي من عملية تجارية بعد خصم التكاليف]
Pecuniary legacy	ḥiba māliyya fī waṣiyya	هبة مالية في وصية
Pecuniary losses	khasārāt naqdiyya	خسارات نقدية
Pecuniary rights	ḥuqūq māliyya	حقوق مالية
Peg	yuthabbit as-si'r	يثبت السعر
Peg the market	yuthabbit as-sūq	يثبت السوق
Pegging	1 tathbīt al-as'ār	١ - تثبيت الأسعار [خلال فترة توزيع السندات]
	2 rabṭ as-si'r	٢ - ربـط السعـــر [تثبيت سعر صرف عملة بالنسبة لعملة أخرى]
Pending	mu'allaq	معلّـــق (غير جازم)
Pending accounts	ḥisābāt mu'allaqa	حسابات معلقة
Pending receipt of	bi'ntiẓār istilām	بانتظار استلام
Pension	1 ma'āsh	١ - معـــاش
	2 taqā'ud	٢ - تقاعـــد
Pension contributions	'ā'idāt taqā'udiyya	عائدات تقاعدية [المقتطع من مرتبات الموظفين]
Pension fund	ṣundūq ma'āshāt at-taqā 'ud	صندوق معاشات التقاعد
Pension plan	niẓām at-taqā'ud	نظام التقاعد
Pension reserve	iḥtiyāṭit-taqā'ud	احتياطي التقاعد
Pension, retirement	murattab at-taqā'ud	مرتب التقاعد
Pensionable	ṣāḥib ḥaqq fi 't-taqā'ud	صاحب حق في التقاعد
Pensioner	mataqā'id	متقاعـــد
Pensioning; pensioning off	iḥāla ila 't-taqā'ud	إحالة إلى التقاعد

Per	1 li-kull	١ - لكـــل
	2 bi-wāsiṭat	٢ - بواسطــة
	3 wifqan li	٣ - وفقا لــ
	4 bi-ḥasab	٤ - بحســب
Per annum	sanawiyyan	سنــويـــا
Per capita	li'l-fard al-wāḥid	للفـرد الواحــد
Per capita consumption	al-istihlāk li-kull nasma	الاستهلاك لكل نسمة
Per cent (centum)	bi'l-mi'a	بالمائــة (٪)
Per contra	1 lahu muqābil	١ - لـه مقابـل
	2 bi'l-'aks	٢ - بالعكـــس
Per day (diem)	yawmiyyan	يــوميـــا [فــي اليــوم]
Per day (per procurationem)	bi'n-niyāba 'an	بالنيابة عن
Percentage	nisba mi'awiyya	نسبة مئوية
Percentage depletion	nisbat al-istinfādh al-mi'awiyya	نسبة الاستنفاذ المئوية [محسوبة كنسبة من اجمالي الايرادات]
Percentage of profits	an-nisba 'l-mi 'awiyya min al-arbāh	النسبة المئوية من الأرباح
Percentage standard cost	taklifa mi'yāriyya muthlā	تكلفة معيارية مثلى
Percentage statement	kashf an-nisab al-mi' awiyya	كشف النسب المئوية [يحوى النسبة المئوية لكل بند في بيان الدخل أو التشغيل أو الميزانية إلى مجموع معين في ذلك البيان وذلك بالاضافة إلى مبالغ البيانات]
Perform	yunjiz	ينجز (يقوم ، ينفذ)
Performance	injāz	انجاز (تنفيذ)
Performance bond	kafālat tanfīdh	كفالة تنفيذ [كفالة نهائية لتمكين المقاولين من توقيع العقد لتنفيذ العملية المتعاقد عليها]
Performance budget	mīzāniyyat barāmij	ميزانية برامج [ميزانية إحدى دوائر الحكومة التي هي تقدير لحسابات الدائرة في المستقبل على أساس التراكم]
Peril	mujāzafa	مجازفة (مخاطرة)
Perils of the sea	akhṭār al-baḥr	أخطار البحر
Period	fatra	فترة (مدة ، زمن ، دورة)
Period cost (or charge or expense)	nafaqāt dawriyya	نفقات دورية
Periodic	dawrī	دورى
Periodic audit	tadqīq dawrī	تدقيق دورى
Periodic income	īrād dawrī	ايراد دورى
Periodic interest	fā'ida dawriyya	فائدة دورية
Periodic payment accumulating to '1'	daf'a dawriyya mutarākimā ila wāḥid	دفعة دورية متراكمة إلى (١) [المبلغ المطلوب ايداعه دوريا بفائدة مركبة حتى يصل إلى (١) في وقت معين]

Periodic payment with present value '1'	daf'a dawriyya qīmatuha 'l-ḥāliyya wāḥid	دفعة دورية قيمتها الحالية (١) [إحدى الدفعات المتساوية المطلوبة لتصفية دين حالي قيمته (١) حين يكسب الرصيد فائدة]
Periodic test check	1 al-faḥṣ al-ikhtibāri' d-dawrī	١ - الفحص الاختبارى الدورى
	2 al-jard al-fi'li 'd-dawri	٢ - الجرد الفعلي الدورى
Perish	yatlaf	يتلف (يتلاشى ، يضمحل)
Perishable goods	baḍā'i' sarī'at at-talaf	بضائع سريعة التلف
Permanent	dā'im	دائم (ثابت)
Permanent asset	1 aṣl ra'smālī	١ - أصل رأسمالي
	2 arḍ	٢ - أرض
Permanent credit	i'timād dā'im	اعتماد دائم
Permanent file	malaff tadqīq dā'im	ملف تدقيق دائم
Permanent investments	istithmārāt ṭawīlat al-ajal	استثمارات طويلة الأجل
Permissive	masmūḥ bihi	مسموح به (مرخص ، مجاز)
Permit (n.; v.)	rukhṣa	رخصـــــة
Permit, export	ijāzat taṣdīr	اجازة تصدير
Permit, import	ijāzat istīrād	اجازة استيراد
Perpetual	dā'im	دائم (مستمر)
Perpetual annuity	ma'āsh ṭūl al-ḥayāh	معاش طول الحياة
Perpetual inventory	jard mustamirr	الجرد المستمر
Perpetual inventory records	sijillāt al-jard al-mustamirr	سجلات الجرد المستمر
Person	1 shakhṣ	١ - شخـــــص
	2 sharika dhāt ḥuqūq wa-mas'ūliyyāt	٢ - شركة ذات حقوق ومسؤوليات
Person, fictitious	shakhṣ i'tibārī	شخص اعتبارى
Person, natural	shakhṣ ṭabī'ī	شخص طبيعي (شخص حقيقي)
Personal account	ḥisāb khāṣṣ	حساب خاص (شخصي)
Personal allowance	takhfīḍ shakhṣī	تخفيض شخصي [في ضريبة الدخل]
Personal credit	i'timād shakhṣī	اعتماد شخصي
Personal effects	amti'a shakhṣiyya	أمتعة شخصية
Personal estate	amlāk manqūla	أملاك منقولة
Personal holding company	sharika qābiḍā shakhṣiyya	شركة قابضة شخصية [شركة يملك معظم اسهمها عدد قليل من الأفراد]
Personal income	dakhl fard	دخـل فـــرد
Personal liability	iltizām shakhṣī	التزام شخصي
Personal property	milkiyya fardiyya	ملكية فردية
Personal selling	bay' mubāshir li'l-mustahlik	بيع مباشر للمستهلك
Personal service corporation	sharikat khadamāt shakhṣiyya	شركة خدمات شخصية
Personal tax	ḍarība shakhṣiyya	ضريبة شخصية

Personnel	muwaẓẓafūn	موظفــــون
		[هيئة الموظفين والمستخدمين في مكتب أو دائرة]
Personnel department	dā'irat shu'ūn al-muwaẓẓafīn	دائرة شؤون الموظفين (الذاتية)
Personnel manager	mudīr adh-dhātiyya	مدير الذاتية
Personnel record	sijill adh-dhātiyya	سجل الذاتية
Petition	1 ʿarīdat aṭ-ṭaʿn	١ - عريضة الطعن
	2 iltimās	٢ - التمــاس
Petitioning creditor	ṭalib ishhār al-iflās	طالب إشهار الافلاس
Petty cash	ṣundūq an-nathriyya	صندوق النثرية
Petty cash book	daftar ṣundūq an-nathriyya	دفتر صندوق النثرية
Petty cash fund	ṣundūq an-nathriyya	صندوق النثرية
Petty expenses	maṣārīf nathriyya	مصاريف نثرية
Photostat	yansakh ṣūra	ينسخ صورة
Physical asset	aṣl ḥaqīqī	أصل حقيقي (ملموس)
Physical budget	mīzāniyya ʿayniyya	ميزانية عينية
Physical count	jard fiʿlī	جرد فعلي
Physical depreciation	istihlāk māddī	استهلاك مادى
		[مثل التآكل والتلف]
Physical inventory	jard al-biḍʿa 'l-fiʿli	جرد البضاعة الفعلي
Physical life	al-ʿumr al-māddī	العمر المادى
		[مجموع سنوات حياة التشغيل الممكنة]
Physical test checks	ikhtibārāt fiʿliyya	اختبارات فعلية
Pick up	1 yartafiʿ	١ - يرتفــع
	2 yastaʿīd	٢ - يستعيــد
		[تأثيره أو سعره في السوق]
Piece costs	takālif al-qiṭʿa 'l-muntaja	تكاليف القطعة المنتجة
Piece price	siʿr al-qiṭʿa	سعر القطعة
Piece rate	ujrat al-qiṭʿa	اجرة القطعة
Piece wage system	niẓām al-ujūr bi'l-qiṭʿa	نظام الأجور بالقطعة
Piece work	al-ʿamal bi'l-qiṭʿa	العمل بالقطعة
Piece work card	biṭāqat al-intāj bi'l-qiṭʿa	بطاقة الانتاج بالقطعة
Piece work rate	siʿr ash-shughl bi'l-qiṭʿa	سعر الشغل بالقطعة
Pier	raṣif al-mīnā'	رصيف الميناء
Pier dues	rusūm raṣīf	رسوم رصيف
Pierage	ḍarībat raṣīf al-mīnā'	ضريبة رصيف الميناء
Pig on pork	sanad lāghī	ســند لاغ
Place	1 makān	١ - مكــان
	2 ʿamal	٢ - عمــل (وظيفة)
Place an order	yaṭlub shirā' biḍʿa	يطلب شراء بضاعة
Place shares	yaṭrah as-human li'l-iktitāb	يطرح أسهما للاكتتاب
Plan	khuṭṭa	خطـــة
Plan of action	khuṭṭat al-ʿamal	خطــة العمــل

Plant	maṣnaʿ	مصنـــــع
Plant fund	amwāl al-maṣnaʿ	أموال المصنع
		[الأموال المخصصة للحصول على الأرض والأبنية وإجراء التحسينات واقتناء الآلات]
Plant manager	mudīr al-maṣnaʿ	مدير المصنع
Plant purchasing officer	mudīr mushtarayāt al-maṣnaʿ	مدير مشتريات المصنع
Plant records	sijillāt al-maṣnaʿ	سجلات المصنع
Plant site	mawqiʿ al-maṣnaʿ	موقع المصنع
Pledge (n.; v.)	1 rahn	١ - رهـــن
	2 kafāla	٢ - كفالة (ضمان ، تعهد)
Pledge for a debt	rahn muqābil dayn	رهن مقابل دين
Pledge one's property	yarhīn mumtalakātihi	يرهن ممتلكاته
Pledged asset	aṣl marhūn	أصل مرهون
Pledged, hypothecation	rahn ḥiyāzī	رهن حيازى
Pledging	ʿamaliyyat ar-rahn	عملية الرهن
Plunge	yuḍārib	يضـــارب
		[بأموال كثيرة ـ بورصة]
Plunger	muḍārib	مضـــارب
Plus	1 zā'id	١ - زائـــد
	2 ijābī	٢ - ايجابـي
Point	1 wiḥda	١ - وحـــدة
		[من وحدات الأسعار في البورصة]
	2 daraja	٢ - درجـــة
	3 ḥadd	٣ - حـــد
Point sheet	waraqat mulāḥaẓāt	ورقة ملاحظات
Policy	1 siyāsa	١ - سياسة
	2 ʿaqd ta'min	٢ - عقد تأمين
Policy cost	taklifat tanfīdh as-siyāsa	تكلفة تنفيذ السياسة
Policy duty	rasm ta'mīn	رسم تأمين
Policy holder	mu'amman ʿalayhi	مؤمن عليه
Policy to order	ʿaqd ta'mīn li-amr	عقد تأمين لامر
Policy, all risks	ʿaqd ta'īn ḍidd jamīʿ al-akhṭār	عقد تأمين ضد جميع الأخطار
Policy, floating	ʿaqd ta'mīn bi'l-ishtirāk	عقد تأمين بالاشتراك
Policy, insurance	ʿaqd ta'mīn	عقد تأمين
Policy, open	ʿaqd ta'mīn maftūḥ	عقد تأمين مفتوح
Policy, paid up	ʿaqd ta'mīn madfūʿ al-qīma	عقد تأمين مدفوع القيمة
Policy, participating	ʿaqd ta'mīn mushtarik bi'l-arbāḥ	عقد تأمين مشترك بالأرباح
Pool (n.; v.)	1 tajammuʿ muntijīn	١ - تجمع منتجين
	2 ittifāq ḥaṣrī	٢ - اتفاق حصرى
		[بين شركات للقضاء على المنافسة]
	3 ittifāq al-muḍāribīn fi 'l-burṣa	٣ - اتفاق المضاربين في البورصة
	4 tajammuʿ sharikāt	٤ - تجمع شركات
	5 yus-him	٥ - يسهم (يشترك)

Pool funds	amwāl mushtaraka	**أموال مشتركة**
Pool risks	akhṭār mushtaraka	**أخطار مشتركة**
Pooling of interest	tajmīʿ al-maṣāliḥ	**تجميع المصالح**
		[اتحاد شركتين أو أكثر بحيث تبقى القيمة الدفترية لحصة كل شركة في الرأسمال المدفوع والأرباح المتراكمة في الشركة الجديدة دون تغيير يذكر]
Popular co-operative organisation	mu'assasa ta'āwuniyya shaʿbiyya	**مؤسسة تعاونية شعبية**
Popular prices	asʿār shā'iʿa	**أسعار شائعة**
Population	1 sukkān	**١ - السكان**
	2 majmūʿat ma'lūmāt	**٢ - مجموعة معلومات**
		[تؤخذ منها العينات]
Port	mīnā'	**ميناء**
Port charges (dues)	rusūm mīnā'	**رسوم ميناء**
Port of arrival	mīnā' al-wuṣūl	**ميناء الوصول**
Port of departure (embarkation)	mīnā' al-ibḥār	**ميناء الابحار**
Port of discharge	mīnā' at-tafrīgh	**ميناء التفريغ**
Port of entry	mīnā al-wuṣūl	**ميناء الوصول**
Port of loading	mīnā' ash-shaḥn	**ميناء الشحن**
Porterage	ujrat al-ʿitāla	**أجرة العتالة**
Portfolio	1 sanadāt tijāriyya	**١ - سندات تجارية**
	2 ḥaqībat awrāq wa-wathā'iq	**٢ - حقيبة أوراق ووثائق**
Portion	1 juz'	**١ - جزء**
	2 ḥiṣṣa	**٢ - حصة**
Position	1 ḥāla	**١ - حالة** (وضع)
	2 markaz	**٢ - مركز** (منصب)
Position book	daftar al-awḍāʿ al-māliyya	**دفتر الاوضاع المالية**
Position bookkeeping	muḥāsabat al-waḍʿ al-mālī	**محاسبة الوضع المالي**
Position of an account	ḥālat ḥisāb	**حالة حساب** (وضع حساب)
Positive	ijābī	**ايجابي**
Positive confirmation	tathbīt ijābī	**تثبيت ايجابي**
		[يرد الجواب سواء كان الرصيد مطابقا أم لا]
Possessions	mumtalakāt	**ممتلكات** (أموال مملوكة ، أملاك)
Possession, put in the – of	yumallik	**يملّك** (يخوّل)
Possession, take – of	yastawlī ʿalā	**يستولى على** (يضع يده على)
Possessory	tamalluki	**تملكي** (اقتنائي)
Possessory lien	rahn ḥiyāzī	**رهن حيازى**
		[حيازة الشيء لحين دفع المستحق عليه]
Post (n.; v.)	1 barīd	**١ - بريد**
	2 waẓīfa	**٢ - وظيفة** (منصب)
	3 yuraḥḥil bi'l-ḥisāb	**٣ - يرحّل بالحساب**
Postage	ujrat barīd	**أجرة بريد**
Postal	barīdī	**بريدى**

Postal cheque	shīk barīdī	شيك بريدى
Postal checking account	ḥisāb saḥb barīdī	حساب سحب بريدى
Post-audit	tadqīq lāḥiq	تدقيق لاحق [للحسابـــات]
Post-closing balance sheet	al-mīzāniyya ba'd al-iqfāl	الميزانية بعد الاقفال
Post-closing trial balance	mīzan al-murāja'a ba'd al-iqfāl	ميزان المراجعة بعد الاقفال
Post-date	tārīkh lāḥiq	تاريخ لاحق
Post-entry	nafdha lāḥiqa	نفذة لاحقة [نفذة حسابية مدونة بعد تاريخها]
Posting	tarḥīl	الترحيـــل
Posting to an account	tarḥīl ilā ḥisāb	الترحيل الى الحساب
Potential	kāmin	كامن (محتمل الوقوع)
Potential profit	ribḥ muḥtamal	ربح محتمل
Potentialities	imkāniyyāt	امكانيات
Pound	1 raṭl 2 junayh	١ - رطـــل ٢ - جنيـــه
Pound sterling	junayh istarlīnī	جنيه استرليني
Poundage	1 'umūla 2 rusūm	١ - عمـــولة ٢ - رســـوم
Power of attorney	wakāla	وكالة (تفويض) كاملة
Power of a liquidator	ṣalāḥiyat al-muṣaffī fi 'l-būrṣa	صلاحية المصفي في البورصة
Power, blank	wakāla 'ala bayāḍ	وكالة على بياض
Power, general	wakāla 'amma	وكالة عامة
Pre-audit	faḥṣ musbaq	فحص مسبق [فحص جميع الذمم المدينة قبل دفعها أو فحص عمليات البيع قبل أو عند التسليم]
Precede	yasbiq	يسبـــق
Precedent	sābiqa	سابقـــة
Preceding	sābiq	سابـــق
Pre-date	yasbiq at-tārīkh	يسبق التاريخ
Predecessor company	al-mu'assasa as-sābiqa	المؤسسة السابقة
Pre-determined costs	takālīf muḥaddada muqaddaman	التكاليف المحددة مقدما
Predict	yatanabba'	يتنبـــأ
Predicted cost	at-taklifa 'l-mi'yāriyya	التكلفة المعيارية
Prediction	tanabbu'	تنبـــؤ
Pre-emption	ash-shuf'a	الشفعـــة
Pre-emptive right	ḥaqq ash-shuf'a	حق الشفعة
Pre-emptor (U.S.)	ash-shafī'	الشفيـــع
Preference	afḍaliyya	أفضلية (أولوية)
Preference accumulative shares	as-hum mumtāza mutarākimat al-arbāḥ	أسهم ممتازة متراكمة الأرباح
Preference bonds	sanadāt mumtāza	سندات ممتازة
Preferential	imtiyāzī	امتيـــازى

Preferential shareholders	musāhimūn mumtāzūn	مساهمون ممتازون
Preferential tariff	at-ta'rifa 't-tafḍīliyya	التعرفة التفضيلية
Preferred capital stock	as-hum mumtāza	أسهم ممتازة
Preferred creditor	dā'in mumtāz	دائن ممتاز
Preferred share	sahm mumtāz	سهم ممتاز
Preferred stock	as-hum mumtaža	أسهم ممتازة
Preferred (stock) dividend	arbāḥ as-hum mumtāza	أرباح أسهم ممتازة
Pre-investment	mā qabl al-istithmār	ما قبل الاستثمار
Preliminary	tamhīdī	تمهيدى (أولي)
Preliminary audit	tadqīq awwalī	تدقيق أولي
Preliminary balance sheet	mīzāniyya awliyya	ميزانية أولية
Preliminary expenses	nafaqāt ta'sīs	نفقات تأسيس
Premature	sābiq li-awānihi	سابق لأوانة
Prematurely	qabl al-awān	قبل الأوان
Premises	1 mabnā	١ - مبنـــى
	2 muqaddimat al-'aqd	٢ - مقدمة العقد
	3 ḥaythiyyat al-qarār	٣ - حيثيات القرار
Premium	1 qist	١ - قسط
	2 'alāwa	٢ - علاوة (مكافأة)
		[فرق ثمن الأسهم أو الأصول عن علاوة القيمة الأسمية أو قيمة الاصدار أو قيمة السوق]
Premium amortisation	iṭfā' al-'alāwa	اطفاء العلاوة
		[استهلاك علاوة السعر المدفوعة عند شراء السندات باقتطاعها على أقساط متساوية من أصل الفوائد المقبوضة خلال المدة الباقية لاستحقاق السندات]
Premium bonds	sanadāt li-ajal	سندات لأجل
Premium insurance	qisṭ at-ta'mīn	قسط التأمين
Premium issue	'alāwat iṣdār	علاوة اصدار
Premium loan	qarḍ li-ajal	قرض لأجل
Premium reserve	iḥtiyāṭi' l-'alāwa	احتياطي العلاوة
Premium (redemption)	alāwat tasdīd	علاوة تسديد
Pre-paid	khāliṣ al-ujra	خالص الأجرة
Pre-paid asset; pre-paid expense	maṣārif madfū'a muqaddaman	مصاريف مدفوعة مقدما
Pre-paid income	īrādāt maqbūḍa muqaddaman	ايرادات مقبوضة مقدما
Prepared by client (P.B.C.)	jahhazaha 'l-'amil	جهزها العميل
Pre-pay	yadfa' al-ujra muqaddaman	يدفع الأجرة مقدما
Pre-payment	daf'a salafan	دفعة سلفا
Pre-production costs	takālīf mā qabl al-intāj	تكاليف ما قبل الانتاج
Prescriptive period	muddat at-taqādum	مدة التقادم
Present	yuqaddim	يقـــدم

Present value (or worth)	al-qīma 'l-ḥāliyya	**القيمة الحالية** [القيمة المعجلة لمبلغ معين يستحق الدفع في تاريخ لاحق]
Present value of '1'	al-qīma 'l-ḥāliyya li wahid	**القيمة الحالية لـ (١)** [المبلغ الحالي الذى إذا أودع بربح مركب معين لمدة معينة يعطي مردودا قدرة (١)]
Presentation	1 ʿarḍ	**١ - عـرض** [بيانات حسابية ختامية]
	2 tāqdīm	**٢ - تقديـم** [الورقة التجارية للقبول أو الدفع]
Presenter of a bill	muqaddim sanad	**مقدم سند**
Prevailing	sā'id	**سائـد**
Previous	sābiq	**سابـق**
Previous quotation	tasʿīra sābiiqa	**تسعيرة سابقة**
Price (n.; v.)	siʿr	**سعـر**
Price bid	as-siʿr al-maṭlūb	**السعر المطلوب**
Price bulletin	kashf asʿār	**كشف أسعار**
Price control	murāqabat asʿār	**مراقبة الأسعار**
Price current (P.C.)	as-siʿr al-ḥālī	**السعر الحالي** (سعر السوق)
Price cutting	muḍāraba bi's-siʿr	**المضاربة بالسعر**
Price discrimination	muḥābah bi's-siʿr	**المحاباة بالسعر**
Price elasticity	murūrūnat as-siʿr	**مرونة السعر**
Price fixing	taḥdīd al-asʿār	**تحديد الأسعار**
Price fluctuations	taqallubat al-asʿar	**تقلبات الأسعار**
Price freezing	tajmīd al-asʿār	**تجميد الأسعار**
Price index	dalīl al-asʿār	**دليل الأسعار** [رقم قياسي يستخدم للدلالة على صفات عامة في مجموعة من البنود]
Price inflation	taḍakhkhum al-asʿār	**تضخم الأسعار**
Price leader	ṣinf muḍāraba	**صنف مضاربة** [صنف بضاعة مسعرة بسعر منخفض جدا بقصد جذب العملاء]
Price leadership	qiyādāt al-asʿār	**قيادة الأسعار** [الأسعار الرائدة التي تحددها شركة كبيرة وتتبعها شركات صغرى في تبني الأسعار]
Price level	mustawa 'l-asʿār	**مستوى الأسعار**
Price list	qā'imat al-asʿār	**قائمة الأسعار** (تسعيرة)
Price maintenance	taḥdīd as-siʿr	**تحديد السعر** [تحديد تاجر الجملة أو المنتج للحد الأدني لسعر بيع بضاعته]
Price of call	siʿr aṭ-ṭalab	**سعر الطلب - في البورصة**
Price of option	siʿr al-ikhtiyār	**سعر الاختيار - في البورصة**
Price offered	as-siʿr al-maʿrūḍ	**السعر المعروض**

Price reduction	takhfīḍ as-siʻr	تخفيض السعر
Price stabilisation	tathbīt al-asʻār	تثبيت الأسعار
Price system	niẓām al-saʻar	نظام الأسعار
Price variance	ikhtilāf al-asʻār	اختلاف الأسعار
		[تغيير في سعر المواد أو الأيدى العاملة]
Price, actual	as-siʻr al-fiʻli	السعر الفعلي
Price, administered	as-siʻr al-muwajjah	السعر الموجه
		[سعر وحدة من السلع يتحدد فيها الثمن المدفوع أو يتأثر إلى حد كبير بأحد العوامل الموجهة]
Price, average	as-siʻr al-mutawassiṭ	السعر المتوسط
Price, cash	as-siʻr an-naqdī	السعر النقدى
Price, closing	siʻr al-iqfāl	سعر الاقفال ـ بورصة
Price, commodity	siʻr as-sila'	سعر السلع
Price, competitive	siʻr al-muzāḥama	سعر المزاحمة
Price, cost	siʻr at-taklifa	سعر التكلفة
Price, exorbitant	thaman fāḥish	ثمن فاحش
Price, fictitious	thaman ṣūrī	ثمن صورى
Price, fixed	siʻr maḥdūd	سعر محدود
Price, inclusive	siʻr shāmil	سعر شامل
Price, invoice	siʻr al-fātūra	سعر الفاتورة
Price, issue	siʻr al-iṣdār	سعر الاصدار
Price, market	siʻr as-sūq	سعر السوق
Price, nominal	siʻr ismī	السعر الاسمي
Price, opening	siʻr al-iftitāḥ	سعر الافتتاح
Price, purchase	siʻr ash-shirā'	سعر الشراء
Price, put and call	siʻr al-ikhtiyār	سعر الاختيار ـ بورصة
Price, quote a	yaʻriḍ siʻran	يعرض سعرا
Price, retail	siʻr al-mufarraq	سعر المفرق
Price, ruling	as-siʻr as-sā'id	السعر السائد
Price, sale	siʻr al-bay'	سعر البيع
Price, selling	siʻr al-mabī'	سعر المبيع
Price, set a	yusaʻir	يسعّر
Price, settled	siʻr muʻayyan	سعر معين (محدد)
Price, spot	siʻr at-taslīm al-fawrī	سعر التسليم الفورى (السعر النقدى)
Price, stock-taking	siʻr al-jard	سعر الجرد
Price, wholesale	siʻr al-jumla	سعر الجملة
Priceless	lā yuqaddar bi-thaman	لا يقدّر بثمن
Pricing	tasʻīr	تسعير
Pricing committee	lajnat at-tasʻīr	لجنة التسعير
Pricing policy	siyāsat at-tasʻīr	سياسة التسعير
Primary costs	ʻanāṣir at-takālif al-asāsiyya	عناصر التكاليف الاساسية
Primary deposit	wadīʻa awwaliyya	وديعة أولية

Primary liability	iltizām awwalī	**التزام أولي** [التزام الشخص بدفع قيمة السند المالي القابل للتداول والموقع باسمه]
Prime cost	at-taklifa 'l-awwaliyya	**التكلفة الاولية** [تكلفة المواد المباشرة والأيدى العاملة المباشرة التي تدخل في صناعة المنتوج]
Prime rate (U.S.)	si'r al-ḥasm al-awwalī	**سعر الحسم الاولى** [لدى المصارف الكبيرة للسلف غير المكفولة]
Prime trade bills	awrāq tijāriyya ghayr maṣrafiyya	**أوراق تجارية غير مصرفية**
Principal	1 ra'smāl	**١ - رأسمال**
	2 muwakkil	**٢ - موكل**
	3 rabb-'amal	**٣ - رب عمل**
Principal budget factor	al-āmil al-asāsi 'l-muwajjih li'l-mizāniyya	**العامل الأساسي الموجة للميزانية**
Principle	1 mabda'	**١ - مبدأ**
	2 qā'ida	**٢ - قاعدة**
Prior	sābiq	**سابق**
Priority	awlawiyya	**أولوية**
Priority of mortgage	awlawiyyat ar-rahn	**أولوية الرهن**
Private account	ḥisāb khaṣṣ	**حساب خاص**
Private accountant	muḥāsib khāṣṣ	**محاسب خاص** [مختص بحسابات شركة واحدة]
Private company	sharikat ashkhāṣ	**شركة اشخاص** (ذات مسؤولية محدودة)
Private corporation	sharika khāṣṣa	**شركة خاصة** [غير حكومية]
Private investments	istithmārāt khāṣṣa	**استثمارات خاصة** [توظيف الاموال في القطاع الخاص]
Private ledger	daftar ustādh khāṣṣ	**دفتر استاذ خاص** [تحفظ فيه الحسابات السرية أو الخاصة]
Private limited company	sharika khaṣṣa maḥūdat al-'ḍā'	**شركة خاصة محدودة الأعضاء**
Private offering	'aṭā' khāṣṣ	**عطاء خاص** [بيع اصدار السندات من قبل مصدرها بدلا من بيعها بواسطة شركة استثمار أموال]
Privilege	imtiyāz	**امتياز**
Privileged creditors	dā'inūn mumtāzūn	**دائنون ممتازون**
Privileged debt	dayn mumtāz	**دين ممتاز** [له الأسبقية على الديون العادية عند الآداء]
Pro rata	bi't-tanāsub	**بالتناسب**
Probability	iḥtimāl	**احتمال**
Probability sample	'ayyina 'ashwā'iyya	**عينة عشوائية** [يمكن احتساب خطأ اختيارها]

Probable life	al-ʿumr al-muḥtamal	العمر المحتمل [العمر الحالي مضافا اليه الحياة المتوقعة]
Probable life curve	munḥana 'ḥtimāl al-ʿumr	منحني احتمال العمر [يتوصل اليه من دراسة توزيعات تكرارية لاستعمال الآلات ومما يقترن بها من قابلية للاستهلاك]
Probate duty	ḍarībat at-tarika	ضريبة التركة
Problems	mashākil	مشاكل (مسائل ، قضايا)
Procedural review	al-marāja'a 'l-ijrā'iyya	المراجعة الاجرائية
Procedure	1 uṣūl al-muḥākamāt	١ - اصول المحاكمات
	2 ijrā'	٢ - اجـــراء
Procedures flowchart	mukhaṭṭaṭ ijrā'at tasalsulī	مخطط اجراءات تسلسلي
Proceed	yubāshir	يباشــــر
Proceedings	1 ijrā'āt	١ - اجـــراءات
	2 daʿwā	٢ - دعـــوى
Proceeds	1 ʿā'idāt	١ - عائـــدات
	2 ar-ribḥ aṣ-ṣāfī	٢ - الربح الصافي
Process (n.; v.)	1 ʿamaliyya	١ - عمليـــة
	2 daʿwā qaḍā'iyya	٢ - دعوى قضائية
	3 yuʿālij ṣināʿiyyan	٣ - يعالج صناعيا
	4 yulāḥiq qaḍa'iyyan	٤ - يلاحق قضائيا
Process control	dabṭ iḥṣā'i	الضبط الاحصائي [طريقة استخدام علم الاحصاء وغيره لتحليل عمليات الانتاج لكشف وتجنب المشاكل أثناء الانتاج]
Process cost centre	markaz taklifat tashghīl	مركز تكلفة تشغيل
Process costing	muḥāsabat at-takālif aṣ-ṣināʿiyyạ	محاسبة التكاليف الصناعية
Process costs	takālīf al-marāḥil aṣ-sināʿiyya	تكاليف المراحل الصناعية
Process of co-ordination	ʿamliyyaṭ at-tansīq	عملية التنسيق
Processed	muʿāmal	معامـــل [اخضع لسلسلة من عمليات التصنيع]
Processing	muʿāmala	معاملة (معالجة ، تحويل)
Procuration	wakāla	وكالـة (تفويض)
Procurator	muʿtamad	معتمـد (وكيل)
Procurement	1 shirā'	١ - شراء (تحصيل ، تدبير)
	2 qism at-ta'thīth aw at-tamwīn	٢ - قسم التأثيث أو التموين [في مخزن كبير]
Produce (n.; v.)	1 intāj	١ - انتاج (منتجات ، سلع)
	2 maḥṣūl	٢ - محصـــول
	3 yuntij	٣ - ينتج (يغل ، يثمر)
Produce exchange	burṣat al-baḍā'iʿ	بورصة البضائع
Producer	muntij	منتـــج
Producer ('s) capital (or goods)	wasā'il al-intāj	وسائل الانتاج

Producer's co-operative	at-ta'āwuniyya al-intājiyya	**التعاونية الانتاجية**
Producer's risk	iḥtimāl ar-rafḍ	**احتمال الرفض** [احتمال محسوب بموجب طريقة معينة لاخذ العينات بأن كمية ذات نوعية معينة سترفض بموجب هذه الطريقة]
Producer's credit	i'timād al-muntijīn	**اعتماد المنتجين**
Product	1 muntaj 2 natīja	**١ - منتـــج** **٢ - نتيجـــة**
Product cost	takālīf al-intāj	**تكاليف الانتاج**
Product differentiation	tanawwu' al-intāj	**تنوع الانتاج**
Product group cost unit	taklifat al-majmū'āt	**تكلفة المجموعات**
Production	intāj	**انتاج** (محصول ، غلة)
Production card	biṭāqat al-intāj	**بطاقة الانتاج**
Production centre	markaz intāj	**مركز انتاج**
Production control	murāqabat al-intāj	**مراقبة الانتاج**
Production cost	taklifat al-intāj	**تكلفة الانتاج**
Production department	dā'irat al-intāj	**دائرة الانتاج**
Production director	mudīr al-intāj	**مدير الانتاج**
Production engineering	handasat al-intāj	**هندسة الانتاج**
Production expenses	maṣārif al-intāj	**مصاريف الانتاج**
Production function	mu'ashshir al-intāj	**مؤشر الانتاج** [قائمة تبين العلاقة بين كميات عوامل الانتاج المستخدمة وبين كميات المنتوجات المعدة للبيع]
Production hour method	ṭarīqat mu'addal as-sā'a	**طريقة معدل الساعة** [حساب قسط الاستهلاك على دفعات دورية تمثل كل دفعة منها حاصل ضرب عدد الوحدات المنتجة خلال الفترة في معدل ثابت للاستهلاك محسوبا على أساس كل وحدة انتاج]
Production index	mu'ashshir al-intāj	**مؤشر الانتاج**
Production labour	u'māl al-intāj	**عمال الانتاج**
Production manager	mudīr al-intāj	**مدير الانتاج**
Production method of depreciation	ṭarīqat al-istihlāk al-intājiyya	**طريقة الاستهلاك الانتاجية** [طريقة احتساب الاستهلاك بواسطة نسبة ثابتة لكل ساعة انتاج]
Production order	amr intāj	**أمر انتاج**
Production planning	takhṭīṭ al-intāj	**تخطيط الانتاج**
Production processes	al-'amaliyyāt al-intājiyya	**العمليات الانتاجية**
Production statement	khulāṣat al-intāj	**خلاصة الانتاج** [ملخص للعناصر التي تشكل كميات الانتاج والتكاليف لمؤسسة أو لقسم منها خلال مدة معينة]

Production unit	wiḥda intājiyya	وحدة انتاجية
Production unit method	ṭarīqat al-wiḥda 'l-intājiyya	طريقة الوحدة الانتاجية [طريقة لاحتساب الاستهلاك بواسطة نسبة ثابتة لكل وحدة انتاجية وتحسب بقسمة قيمة الاصل على العدد المقدر للوحدات التي سيتم انتاجها أثناء حياة الأصل]
Productive	muntij	منتــج
Productive assets	uṣūl intājiyya	اصول انتاجية
Productive capital	ra'smāl muntij	رأسمال منتج
Productive labour (U.S.)	al-yad al-ʿāmila 'l-muntija	اليد العاملة المنتجة [الأجور المباشرة]
Productivity	intājiyya	انتاجية (قوة الانتاج) [نسبة المردود الى الزاد]
Profession	mihna	مهنــة
Professional	mihanī	مهنــي
Professional accountant	muḥāsib mihanī	محاسب مهني
Professional fees	atʿāb fanniyya	أتعاب فنية
Professional standards	uṣūl mihaniyya	أصول مهنية
Proficiency	mahāra	مهارة (براعة ، تفوق)
Profit	ribḥ	ربــح
Profit and loss account	ḥisāb al-arbāḥ wa'l khasā'ir	حساب الأرباح والخسائر
Profit and loss statement (or statement of profit and loss)	bayan al-arbāḥ wa'l-khasā'ir	بيان الارباح والخسائر
Profit graph	munḥana 'r-ribḥ	منحني الربح
Profit margin	hāmish ar-ribḥ	هامش الربح
Profit planning	takhṭīṭ ar-rabḥ	تخطيط الربح
Profit prior to consolidation	arbāḥ mā qabl at-tawḥīd	أرباح ما قبل التوحيد
Profit prior to incorporation	arbāḥ mā qabl at-ta'sīs	أرباح ما قبل التأسيس
Profit sharing	mushāraka fi'l-arbāḥ	مشاركة في الأرباح
Profit sharing scheme	nahj al-ishtirāk bi'r-ribḥ	نهج الاشتراك بالربح
Profit variance	inḥirāf ar-ribḥ	انحراف الربح
Profit, annual	ribḥ sanawī	الربح السنوى
Profit, cash	arbāḥ maqbūḍa	الأرباح المقبوضة
Profit, clear	ribḥ ṣāfī	الربح الصافي
Profit(s), divisible	arbāḥ qābila li't-tawzīʿ	أرباح قابلة للتوزيع
Profits, earned	arbāḥ muktasaba	أرباح مكتسبة
Profits, fictitious	arbāḥ ṣūriyya	أرباح صورية
Profitability	arbaḥiyya	أربحيــة
Profitable	murbiḥ	مربح (مفيد ، مكسب)
Profiteer	istighlālī	استغلالــي [من يربح ربحا فاحشا]
Profitless	ghayr murbiḥ	غير مربح (عديم النفع)
Proforma	ṣūrī	صــورى (شكلي)

Proforma balance sheet	mīzāniyya ṣūriyya	**ميزانية صورية** [ميزانية تحت الدراسة قد تشتمل على مبالغ افتراضية أو بدون مبالغ لاظهار طريقة العرض أو قد تشتمل على معاملات لم تتم بعد كتمويل مقترح]
Proforma entry	qayd ṣūrī	**قيد صورى**
Proforma invoice	fātūra mabda'iyya	**فاتورة مبدئية** (قائمة أولية)
Proforma statement	kashf mālī ṣūrī	**كشف مالي صورى**
Programme	barnāmaj	**برنامـــج** (منهاج)
Programme budget	mizāniyyat 'amal ḥukūmī	**ميزانية عمل حكومي**
Progress (n.; v.)	taqaddum	**تقدم** (رقي) **ـ يتقدم** (يرتقي)
Progress report	taqrīr at-taqaddum	**تقرير التقدم** [تقرير عن سير العمل]
Progression	1 tadarruj	**١ - تدرج** (تسلسل)
	2 mutawāliya	**٢ - متواليـــة**
Progressive	mutadarrij	**متدرج** (متزايد)
Progressive average	mu'addal taṣā'udī	**معدل تصاعدى** (معدل متدرج)
Progressive increase	ziyāda taṣā'udiyya	**زيادة تصاعدية**
Progressive rate	nisba taṣā'udiyya	**نسبة تصاعدية**
Progressive schedule	jadwal taṣā'udī	**جدول تصاعدى** [جدول لمقارنة المعلومات المالية أو التشغيلية تضاف اليه المعلومات الجديدة حين توفرها]
Progressive tax	ḍarība taṣā'udiyya	**ضريبة تصاعدية**
Prohibit	yamna'	**يمنـــع** (يحظّر)
Prohibited	mamnū'	**ممنوع** (محظور ، محرم)
Prohibitive prices	as'ār fāḥisha	**أسعار فاحشة** [مرتفع الى حد يمنع الشراء]
Project	mashrū'	**مشـــروع**
Projected financial statement	bayān mālī mustaqbalī	**بيان مالي مستقبلي**
Prolong	yumaddid	**يمـــدد**
Proling a bill	yumaddid istiḥqāq sanad	**يمدد استحقاق سند**
Prolong the time of payment	yumaddid muhlat ad-daf'	**يمدد مهلة الدفع**
Promise (n.; v.)	wa'd	**وعـــد ـ يعـــد**
Promise of shares	iltizāmāt al-as-hum	**التزامات الأسهم**
Promise to pay	ta'ahhud bi'd-daf'	**تعهد بالدفع**
Promissory	ta'ahhudī	**تعهدى** (التزامي)
Promissory note	sanad li-amr	**سند لأمر** (سند اذني)
Promote	1 yu'assis	**١ - يؤسس ـ شركة**
	2 yurawwij	**٢ - يروج** (ينشط ، يشجع)
	3 yuraqqī	**٣ - يرقـــي** (يرفع)
Promoter	mu'assis	**مؤسس** (منشىء)
Promoter's shares	as-hum mu'assis	**أسهم مؤسس**
Promotion	1 ta'sīs	**١ - تأسيـــس**

	2 tarwīj	٢ - ترويــج
	3 tarqiya	٣ - ترقيــة
Promotion expense	maṣārīf ta'sīs	مصاريف تأسيس
Prompt	fawrī	فــوري
Prompt cash	naqd li'l-istiʻmāl	نقد للاستعمال [تمييزا له عن نقد الميزانية أو الصندوق]
Prompt delivery	taslīm fawrī	تسليم فـوري
Prompt payment of bills	dafʻ al-kumbiyālāt fawran	دفع الكمبيالات فورا
Proof	burhān	برهان (اثبات ، دليل ، بينة)
Proof of loss	wathīqat ithbāt al-khasāra	وثيقة اثبات الخسارة
Propaganda	diʻāya	دعـايــة
Proper	munāsib	مناسب (ملائم ، مضبوط)
Properly	uṣūliyyan	اصوليا (بدقة)
Property	milk	ملك (عقار ، ملكية)
Property account (U.S.)	ḥisāb al-mawjūdat ath-thābita	حساب الموجودات الثابتة
Property accountability (U.S.)	mas'ūliyyat murāqabat al-mawjūdāt ath-thābita	مسؤولية مراقبة الموجودات الثابتة
Property dividend	arbāḥ naw'iyya	أرباح نوعية [ربح يدفع بتمليك عقار دون النقد أو الأسهم]
Property forwarded for a debit	dayn maḍmūn bi-rahn ʻaqārī	دين مضمون برهن عقاري
Property ledger; plant ledger	ustādh al-mawjūdāt ath-thābita	استاذ الموجودات الثابتة
Property management	idārat al-mumtalakāt	ادارة الممتلكات
Property, plant and equipment	mumtalakāt wa munsha'āt wa muʻaddāt	ممتلكات ومنشآت ومعدات
Property reserved (U.K.)	al-istihlāk al-mutarākim	الاستهلاك المتراكم (اصطلاح بريطاني)
Property seizure	ḥajz ʻaqārī	حجز عقاري
Property taxes	ḍarā'ib al-amlāk	ضرائب الأملاك
Property, immovable	amlāk ghayr manqūla	أملاك غير منقولة
Property, mortgaged	amlāk marhūna	أملاك مرهونة
Property, movable	amlāk manqūla	أملاك منقولة
Property, private	milkiyya khāṣṣa	ملكيــة خاصــة
Property, public	amlāk ʻāmma	أمـلاك عامــة
Property, real	ʻaqārāt thābita	عقارات ثابتة (أملاك غير منقولة)
Property, unalienable	ʻaqārāt ghayr qābila li't-taḥwīl	عقارات غير قابلة للتحويل
Proportion	nisba	نسبة (حصة ، جــزء)
Proportional	nisbī	نسبـــي
Proportional tax	ḍarība nisbiyya	ضريبة نسبية
Proportionately (or proportionally)	nisbayyan	نسبيا (بصورة نسبية)
Proposal	1 ʻarḍ	١ - عــرض
	2 iqtirāḥ	٢ - اقتـراح
Propose	1 yaʻriḍ	١ - يعــرض
	2 yaqtariḥ	٢ - يقتــرح

Proposition	taṣrīh	**تصريـــــح**
Proprietary	milkī	**ملكـي** (متعلق بالملكية)
Proprietary accounts	ḥisābạt al-mālkīn	**حسابات المالكين**
Proprietary company	ash-sharika 'l-mālika	**الشركة المالكــة**
		[لحق الاختراع أو المال أو لحق معلوم]
Proprietary interest	ḥuqūq ash-shuraka'	**حقوق الشركاء**
		[زيادة الموجودات على المطلوبات]
Proprietor	mālik	**مالك** (صاحب ملك)
Proprietorship	1 ḥuqūq ash-shurakā	١ - **حقوق الشركاء** (صافي الموجودات)
	2 milkiyya fardiyya	٢ - **ملكية فردية**
	3 mu'assasa fardiyya	٣ - **مؤسسة فردية**
Proprietorship account	ḥisāb al-mālik al-fard	**حساب المالك الفرد**
		[يحفظ لحقوق المالك الوحيد لمؤسسة]
Prorate	yuzzi' nisbiyyan	**يوزع نسبيا**
		[يوزع وفقا للحصص]
Prorateable	nisbī	**نسبي** (منسوب الى)
Prospect (n.; v.)	1 tawaqqu'	١ - **توقع** (تطلع ، تبصر)
	2 yunaqqib	٢ - **ينقب** (يبحث)
Prospectus	bayān	**بيان** (منشور)
		[نشرة أولية عن مشروع]
Prosper	yazdahir	**يـزدهــر**
Prosperity	izdihār	**ازدهـــار**
Prosperous	muzdahir	**مـزدهــر**
Protest	iḥtijāj	**احتجاج** (بروتستو ، شكوى قضائية)
Protest charges	nafaqāt iḥtijāj	**نفقات احتجاج**
Protest fee	rasm iḥtijāj	**رسم احتجاج**
Protest for non payment	iḥtijāj li-'adam ad-daf'	**احتجاج لعدم الدفع**
Prove	yubarhin	**يبرهن** (يفحص ، يثبت)
Proven	thābit	**ثابت** (مؤكد)
Provide	1 yuzawwid	١ - **يـــزود**
	2 yashtariṭ	٢ - **يشتـــرط**
	3 yaḥtāṭ	٣ - **يحتـــاط**
	4 yanuṣṣ	٤ - **ينص** (يحدد)
Provide a reserve	yukhaṣṣiṣ iḥtiyāṭīyyan	**يخصص احتياطيا**
Provided	sharīṭat an	**شريطة أن** (بشرط)
Provident fund	sundūq taw reā	صندوق توفير
Provision	1 mukhaṣṣaṣ	١ - **مخـــصص**
	2 iḥtiyāṭī	٢ - **احتياطي**
	3 mu'ūna	٣ - **مؤونة** (تغطية ، تمويل)
	4 naṣṣ	٤ - **نـــص**
Provision for depreciation	mukhaṣṣaṣ al-istihlāk	**مخصص** (احتياطي) **الاستهلاك**
Provisional	mu'aqqat	**مـؤقـــت**
Proviso	band sharṭī	البند الشرطي

Proxy	tawkīl	تـوكيــــل
Proxy voting	taṣwīt bi'n-niyāba	تصويت بالنيابة
Proxy, by	bi'l-wakāla	بالوكالة (بالنيابة)
Prudent investment	istithmār ḥakīm	استثمار حكيــم
Public	'āmm	عــام (حكومـي)
Public accountant (U.S.)	muḥāsib qānūnī	محاسب قانوني
Public accounting	al-muḥāsaba 'l-qānūniyya	المحاسبة القانونية
Public administration	al-idāra 'l-'āmma	الادارة العامة
Public auction	mazād 'alanī	مزاد علني
Public auditor	murāji''qānūnī	مراجع قانوني
Public bond	sanad 'āmm	سنـد عــام [تصدره الحكومة]
Public corporation (or company)	sharika 'āmma	شركة عامة
Public funds	1 amwāl 'āmma 2 sanadāt 'āmma	١ - أموال عامة ٢ - سندات عامة
Public liability	mas'ūliyya 'āmma	مسؤولية عامة [مسؤولية مدنية تجاه الغير]
Public offering	bay' as-hum li'l-jumhūr	بيع أسهم للجمهور
Public policy	siyāsa 'āmma	سياسة عامة
Public property	milkkiyya 'āmma	ملكية عامة
Public relations	'alāqāt 'āmma	علاقات عامة
Public revenue	wāridāt ad-dawla	واردات الدولة
Public sector deposits	wadā'i' al-qiṭā' al-'āmm	ودائع القطاع العام
Public service (or utility) company	mu'assasa dhāt naf' 'āmm	مؤسسة ذات نفع عام
Public utilities	marāfiq 'āmma	مرافق عامة
Public utility stocks	as-hum al-marāfiq al-'āmma	أسهم المرافق العامة
Punch	yathqub	يثقب (بطاقة أو شريط آلة حاسبة)
Punched cards	biṭqāt mathqūba	البطاقات المثقوبة
Punched card system	niẓām al-biṭāqāt al-mathqūba	نظام البطاقات المثقوبة
Purchase (n.; v.)	shirā'	شراء ـ يشترى
Purchase book	daftar al-mushtarayāt	دفتر المشتريات
Purchase by instalment	shirā' bi't-taqsīṭ	شراء بالتقسيط
Purchase commitment	iltizām bi'sh-shirā'	التزام بالشراء
Purchase contract	shirā' ta'āqudī	شراء تعاقدى [شراء بين مصدر السندات وضامنها بشراء جميع السندات التي لا يشتريها المساهمون]
Purchase cut-off	fatrat qaṭ' ash-shirā'	فترة قطع الشراء [مشتريات لفترة لاحقة وسابقة لتاريخ معين]
Purchase money obligation	iltizām bi-thaman ash-shirā'	التزام بثمن الشراء
Purchase on credit	shirā' ājil	شراء آجل
Purchase order	amr shirā'	أمر شراء (أمر توريد)
Purchase records	sijillāt al mushtarayāt	سجلات المشتريات
Purchase requisition	ṭalab shirā'	طلب شراء

Purchasing agent	wakīl mushtarayāt	وكيل مشتريات
Purchasing committee	lajnat mushtarayāt	لجنة مشتريات
Purchasing department	dā'irat mustarayāt	دائرة مشتريات
Purchasing power	quwwa shirā'iyya	قوة شرائية
Purchasing procedures	ijrā'at as-shirā	اجراءات الشراء
Pure	ṣāfī	صـــاف
Pure interest	fā'ida ṣāfiya	الفائدة الصافية
Pure premium	qisṭ ṣāfī	القسط الصافي
Pure profit	ribh ṣāfī	الربح الصافي
Pursuance	binā'an 'ala	بنـاء علـــى (طبقا لـ ، تنفيذ لـ)
Put	1 yuwaẓẓif mālan	١ - يوظف مالا
	2 yuḍārib fi 'l-burṣa	٢ - يضارب في البورصة
Put and call	al-ikhtiyār fi 's-si'r ash-sharṭī	الاختيار في السعر الشرطي [عملية بيع سلعة ما تتم في وقت معين وبسعر محدد]
Qualification	1 taḥaffuẓ	١ - تحـفـــظ [يرد في تقرير مدقق الحسابات ليوجه الانتباه إلى قيود فرضت على فحصه أو شكله وعدم موافقته على أى بند في البيانات]
	2 ahliyya	٢ - أهلية (كفاءة)
Qualified	1 taḥaffuẓī	١ - تحفظي
	2 mu'ahhal	٢ - مـؤهـــل
	3 mukhaffaf	٣ - مخفف (ملطف)
Qualified acceptance	qabūl sharṭī	قبول شرطي (قبول مع التحفظ)
Qualified report (or certificate)	taqrīr taḥafuẓẓī	تقرير تحفظي
Qualify	1 yataḥaffaẓ	١ - يتحــفظ
	2 yu'ahhil	٢ - يـؤهـــل
Qualifying reserve	ḥisāb taqyīm	حساب تقييم [حساب له علاقة بحساب آخر أو أكثر مثل حساب احتياطي الاستهلاك وحساب الديون المعدومة]
Qualitative	naw'ī	نوعي (وصفي)
Qualitative control	riqāba naw'iyya	الرقابة النوعية
Quality	naw'iyya	نـوعيـــة
Quality control	murāqabat naw'iyyat al-intāj	مراقبة نوعية الانتاج
Quantitative	kammī	كمــــي
Quantitative control	riqāba kammiyya	الرقابة الكمية
Quantity	kammiyya	كميـــــة
Quantity discount	khaṣm 'ala 'l-kammiyya	خصم على الكمية
Quarterly	rub' sanawī	ربـع ســنوى

Quasi	shibh	شبه (كما لو ، بمثابة)
Quasi-partner	sharīk bi'l-ism	**شريك بالاسم**
Quasi-public company	sharika shibh ʿāmma	**شركة شبه عامة**
Quasi-rent	dakhl al-fa'āliya	**دخل الفعالية**
		[ذلك الجزء من الدخل الاجمالي للمنتج يعزى لقيامه بعمليات فريدة من نوعها أو نتيجة لعنصر تكلفة منخفضة غير متوفرة للمنافسين]
Quasi-reorganisation	i'ādat tamwīl ash-sharika	**إعادة تمويل الشركة**
		[بغرض استيعاب عجز]
Quay	raṣif al-mīnā'	**رصيف الميناء**
Quayage	rasm ar-raṣīf	**رسم الرصيف**
Quick asset	mawjūd mutadāwal	**موجود متداول**
Quittance	barā'at dhimma	**براءة ذمة مالية**
Quota	ḥiṣṣa nisbiyya	**حصة نسبية** (كوتا)
Quota system	niẓām al-ḥiṣṣa 'n-nisbiyya	**نظام الحصة النسبية**
Quotation (bid)	1 ʿard	**١ - عرض**
	2 tasʿīr	**٢ - تسعير**
Quotation record	sijill at-tasʿīr	**سجل التسعير**
Quotations	tasʿīrāt	**تسعيرات** (أسعار معروضة)
Quotation(s), forward	siʿr li-ajal	**سعر لأجل**
Quotations, list of	jadwal al-asʿār	**جدول الأسعار**
Quote	1 yusaʿʿir	**١ - يسعّر**
		[يعطي السعر الجارى]
	2 yaqtabis	**٢ - يقتبس**
Quote a price (v.)	yuʿayyin siʿran	**يعين سعرا**
Quoted securities	sanadāt musaʿʿara	**سندات مسعرة**
Quotient	an-nātij	**الناتج**
		[خارج القسمة في الحساب]
Raise	1 yarfa'	**١ - يرفع** (يزيد)
	2 yujammi'	**٢ يجمّع** (يحشد ، يحصّل)
	3 yurabbī	**٣ - يربي**
	4 yazraʿ	**٤ - يزرع**
	5 yuthīr	**٥ - يثير**
Raise a loan (v.) (U.S.)	yuṣdir qarḍan	**يصدر قرضا**
Raise funds (U.S.)	yajmaʿ amwālan	**يجمع أموالا**
Raising	1 rafʿ asʿār	**١ - رفع ـ أسعار**
	2 jamʿ amwāl	**٢ - جمع ـ أموال**
Rally	irtifāʿ ath-thaman	**ارتفاع الثمن**
		[عودة الأسعار إلى الارتفاع]

Ramp	taḍakhkhum	تضخـــــم [زيادة باهظة في الأسعار]
Random	'ashwā'ī	عشوائي (جزافي ، اتفاقي)
Random numbers	arqām 'ashwā'iyya	أرقام عشوائية
Random sample	'ayyina 'ashwā'iyya	عينة عشوائية
Random variation	inḥirāf 'ashwā'ī	انحراف عشوائي
Range	madā	مـــــدى
Range of goods	tashkīlat baḍā'i'	تشكيلة بضائع
Rank	rutba	رتبة (درجة ، مرتبة)
Rank of mortgage	darajat ar-rahn	درجة الرهن
Rateable	1 qābil li't-tas'īr	١ - قابل للتسعير
	2 qābil li't-taklīf aḍ-ḍarā'ibī	٢ - قابل للتكليف الضرائبي
	3 nisbī	٣ - نسبـــي
Rate	1 mu'addal	١ - معـــــدل
	2 si'r	٢ - سعـــــر
Rate of contango	si'r at-taslīf 'ala 'l-awrāq al-māliyya	سعر التسليف على الأوراق المالية - بورصة
Rate of conversion of money	si'r taḥwīl an-naqd	سعر تحويل النقد
Rate of discount	si'r al-khaṣm	سعر الخـــصم
Rate of exchange	si'r aṣ-ṣarf	سعر الصرف
Rate of interest	si'r al-fā'ida	سعر الفائدة
Rate of pay	mu'addal al-ajr	معدل الأجر
Rate of return	nisbat al-'ā'id	نسبة العائد
Rates of return pricing	tas'īr mu'addal al-murdūd	تسعير معدل المردود [طريقة لتحديد الأسعار باضافة زيادة على التكلفة تنتج عائدا معلوما مسبقا على الأموال المستثمرة]
Rate of turnover	mu'addal dawrān	معدل دوران
Rate of wages	mu'addal al-ujūr	معدل الاجور
Rate, flat	si'r wahed	سعر واحد
Rate, forward	si'r ājil	السعر الآجل
Rate, market – of interest	si'r as-sūq li'l-fā'ida	سعر السوق للفائدة
Rate, office	as-si'r ar-rasmī	السعر الرسمي
Rate, piece	al-ajr bi'l-qiṭ'a	الأجر بالقطعة
Rate, standard	ta'rifa muwaḥḥada	تعرفة موحدة
Rate, surplus	nisbat al-fā'iḍ	نسبة الفائض
Rate, tariff	fi'at at-ta'rīfa 'l-jumrukiyya	فئة التعريفة الجمركية
Ratification	muṣādaqa	مصادقة
Ratification documents	wathā'iq taṣdīq	وثائق تصديق
Ratify	yuṣādiq 'alā	يصادق على
Rating	taqyīm	تقييم (تقدير ، تعيين)
Ratio	nisba	نسبـــة
Ratio test	ikhtibār nisba	اختبار نسبة

Ratio, cash	an-nisba 'n-naqdiyya	النسبة النقدية [نسبة الاحتياطى النقدى]
Ratio, current	nisbat at-tadāwul	نسبة التداول (بنسبة رأس المال العامل) [نسبة الموجودات المتداولة إلى المطلوبات المتداولة]
Ratio, liquidity	nisbat as-suyūla	نسبة السيولة
Ratio, operating (U.S.)	nisbat at-tashghīl	نسبة التشغيل (معامل الاستثمار)
Ratio, reserve	nisbat al-iḥtiyaṭī	نسبة الاحتياطي
Raw materials	mawādd khāmm	مواد خام (مواد أولية)
Reacquired stock	as-hum mustaradda	اسهم مستردة
Readjust	yu'addil	يعدل (يصحح)
Readjustment	1 taṣḥīḥ	١ - تصحيح
	2 taswiya	٢ - تسوية
Ready assets	mawjūdāt jāhiza	موجودات جاهزة (موجودات تحت اليد)
Ready made	jāhiz	جاهز
Ready money	suyūla naqdiyya	سيولة نقدية (مال نقدى)
Real account	ḥisāb ḥaqīqī	حساب حقيقي [حساب في الاستاذ ينقل رصيده إلى فترة مالية تالية اي كل حساب يظهر في الميزانية]
Real cost	1 at-taklifa bi'l-wiḥdāt al-qiyāsiyya	١ - التكلفة بالوحدات القياسية
	2 at-taklifa 'l-ḥaqīqiyya	٢ - التكلفة الحقيقية
Real estate	'aqārāt	عقارات
Real estate bank	maṣrif 'aqārī	مصرف عقارى
Real estate company	sharika 'aqāriyya	شركة عقارية
Real guarantee	ḍamān 'aynī	ضمان عيني
Real income	dkahl ḥaqīqī	دخل حقيقي (ايراد فعلي)
Real interest	fā'ida ḥaqīqiyya	فائدة حقيقية
Real price	qīma fi'liyya	قيمة فعلية
Real property	amlāk ghayr manqūla	أملاك غير منقولة (عقارات ، مباني)
Real tax	ḍariba 'ayniyya	ضريبة عينية
Real value	qīma ḥaqīqiyya	قيمة حقيقية
Real wage	ajr ḥaqīqī	الأجر الحقيقي
Realisable	1 qābil li't-taḥqīq	١ - قابل للتحقيق
	2 qābil li't taḥwīl	٢ - قابل للتحويل (للتصرف به)
Realisable assets	amwāl qābila lit-taḥwīl	اموال قابلة للتحويل
Realisation	taṣfiya	تصفية (تحويل) [تحويل الموجودات إلى نقود]
Realisation account	ḥisāb at-taṣfiya	حساب التصفية
Realisation of pledge	taṣarruf bi-rahn ma	تصرف برهن ما
Realisation value	qīmat at-taṣfiya	قيمة التصفية
Realise	yuḥaqqiq	يحقق [يحول المتاع إلى نقود]

Realised appreciation	ziyāda muḥaqqaqa	**الزيادة المحققة** [الزيادة في الأصول الجارية نتيجة للانتاج أو البيع]
Realised revenue (or profit)	ribḥ muḥaqqaq	**الربح المحقق**
Rebate	1 khaṣm	**١ - خصـــم**
	2 tanzīl	**٢ - تـنـزيـــل** [من الدين حين يسدد قبل الاستحقاق]
Rebound	'awdat al-irtifā'	**عودة الارتفاع** [عودة ارتفاع الأسعار بعد انخفاضها]
Recap (recapitulation)	ikhtiṣār	**اختصار** (تلخيص)
Recapitalisation	i'ādat takwīn ar-ra'smāl	**اعادة تكوين الرأسمال** [تغير رئيسي في طبيعة ومقدار الرأسمال غير المدفوع أو علاوة الاصدار يتضمن استيعاب العجز]
Recapitulate	yakhtaṣir	**يختصر** (يلخص)
Recash	yu'īd ila 'ṣ-ṣundūq	**يعيد إلى الصندوق**
Recategorisation	i'ādat at-taṣnīf	**اعادة التصنيف**
Recede	yatrāja'	**يتراجع** (ينسحب) [عن تعهد أو اتفاق]
Receipt	1 istilām	**١ - استلام**
	2 īṣāl istilam	**٢ - ايصال استلام**
Receipts	maqbūḍāt	**مقبوضات** (متحصلات ، ايرادات)
Receipts and expenditures	al-wāridāt wa'n-nafaqāt	**الواردات والنفقات**
Receipts book	daftar īṣālāt	**دفتر ايصالات**
Receipts, cash and payments	maqbūḍāt wa madfū'āt aṣ-ṣundūq	**مقبوضات ومدفوعات الصندوق**
Receipts, daily	wāridāt yawmiyya	**واردات يومية**
Receivable (adj.; n.)	mumkin qabduh	**ممكن قبضه** (قابل للاستلام)
Receivables (U.S.)	1 sanadāt mu'adda li'l-qabḍ	**١ - سندات معدة للقبض**
	2 dhimam madīna	**٢ - ذمم مدينة**
Receivables, ageing of	ta'mīr adh-dhimam	**تعمير الذمم** [تحليل الذمم المدينة حسب قدمها]
Receive	yatasallam	**يتســـلم**
Receiver	mustalim	**مستـــلم** [الفرد المكلف باستلام الاموال أو أشياء عينية بالأمانة
Receiver's certificate	shahādat al-mustalim bi'l-amāna	**شهادة المستلم بالأمانة** [اثبات مديونية يصدره المستلم بالأمانة يضمن من عائدها الأموال الضرورية لحفظ أو تشغيل الأملاك المسؤول عنها]
Receivership	1 jamā'at ad-dā'inīn	**١ - جماعة الدائنين**
	2 ḥirāsa qaḍā'iyya	**٢ - حراسة قضائية**
Receiving stores	makhāzin al-biḍā'a 'l-wārida	**مخازن البضاعة الواردة**
Reception	1 istilām	**١ - استلام** (قبض)

	2 istiqbāl	٢ - استقبال
Recipient	1 mustalim	١ - المستلم
	2 mustafīd	٢ - المستفيد
Reciprocal	mutabādal	متبـــادل
Reciprocity	tabādul	تبـــادل [المنافع والخدمات]
Reckon	1 yaḥsib	١ - يحســب
	2 yuḥāsib	٢ - يحاســب
Reckon extra charges	yaḥsib an-nafaqāt az-zā'ida	يحسب النفقات الزائدة
Reckon in	yuqaddir	يقـــدر (يعتبر)
Reckon off	1 yaṭraḥ	١ - يطرح
	2 yaqtaṭi'	٢ - يقتطع ـ مبلغا من حساب
Reckon up	1 yaḥsib	١ - يحســب
	2 yuqaddir	٢ - يقـــدر
Reckon up the receipts and expenses	yaḥsib al-wāridāt wa 'n-nafaqāt	يحسب الواردات والنفقات
Reckoner	1 ḥāsib	١ - حاســب
	2 muḥāsib	٢ - محاســب
	3 jadāwil al-ḥisābāt	٣ - جداول الحسابات
Reckoning	1 ḥisāb	١ - حســاب
	2 iḥṣā'	٢ - احصـــاء
Reclassification	i'ādat taṣnīf	اعادة تصنيف
Recognition	1 i'tirāf	١ - اعتـــراف
	2 qabūl	٢ - قبـــول
	3 taslīm	٣ - تســليم
Recognise	1 ya'tarif	١ - يعتـــرف
	2 yataḥaqqaq min	٢ - يتحقق من [يتحقق من قيمة عملية وتوقيتها وتصنيفها وشروطها الأخرى قبل قبولها وتثبيتها في دفاتر الحسابات]
Recommend	yūṣī	يوصـــي
Recommendation	tawṣiya	توصـــية
Recommendation, submit a – of dividend	ya'riḍ iqtirāḥ tawzī' al-arbāḥ	يعرض اقتراح توزيع الأرباح
Recompensation	ta'wīḍ	تعويـــض
Recompense	yu'awwiḍ	يعـــوض [عن خسارة]
Recompute	yu'īd at-taqdīr aw al-ḥisāb	يعيد التقدير أو الحساب
Reconcile	yuṭābiq	يطابق (يسوى)
Reconciliation	muṭābaqa	مطابقة (تسوية)
Reconciliation of surplus	taswiyat al-fā'iḍ	تسوية الفائض [بيان التغييرات في حسابات الفائض خلال فترة محاسبية]
Reconciliation statement	bayān taswiya	بيان تسوية

Reconciling item	aḥad bunūd at-taswiya	**أحد بنود التسوية**
Reconsider	yu'īd an-naẓar fī	**يعيد النظر في**
Reconsolidation of two companies	i'ādat damj sharikatayn	**اعادة دمج شركتين**
Reconvey	yurji'	**يرجـــع** [يعيد ملكا إلى صاحبه الأصلي]
Reconveyance	irjā'	**ارجـــاع** [رد ملك إلى صاحبه الأصلي]
Record	sijill	**سجـــل**
Record date	tārīkh tawzī' al-arbāḥ	**تاريخ توزيع الأرباح**
Recording medium	wāsiṭat tasjīl	**واسطة تسجيل** [كسند قبض أو قيد أو أى سند آخر تسجل بموجبه عملية تجارية]
Recount	yaḥsib min jadīd	**يحسب من جديد**
Recoup	yastaridd	**يسترد** (يعوض)
Recourse	ḥaqq ar-rujū'	**حق الرجوع** [حق الدائن في الرجوع على جميع الأطراف المعنيين في حالة عدم الوفاء]
Recover	1 yasta'īd 2 yuḥaṣṣil 3 yuḥawwil	١ - **يستعيد** (يسترد) ٢ - **يحصّـــل** ٣ - **يحول إلى ـ نقد أو موجودات متداولة**
Recover a debt	yastaridd daynan	**يسترد دينا**
Recover damages and costs	yuḥassil al-'uṭl wa'ḍ-ḍarar wa 'l-maṣārīf	**يحصّل العطل والضرر والمصاريف**
Recovery	1 taghṭiya 2 ta'wīḍ 3 isti'āda	١ - **تغطية** ٢ - **تعويض** ٣ - **استعادة** (استرداد)
Recovery cost (or expenditure)	taklifa mustaradda	**التكلفة المستردة** [تكلفة الأصل مطروحا منها أى جزء مستهلك من التكلفة أو الذى اعتبر مصروفا أو خسارة]
Recovery of damages	taḥsil al-'uṭl wa'ḍ-ḍarar	**تحصيل العطل والضرر**
Recovery of debts	istirdād ad-duyūn	**استرداد الديون**
Recovery value	al-qīma 'l-mustaradda	**القيمة المستردة** [القيمة المتوقع تحصيلها نتيجة بيع الأصل كخردة]
Rectification	ta'dīl	**تعديل** (تصحيح ، تقويم) [تكلفة اعادة تشغيل المنتجات المعيبية حتى تقبل في الفحص النهائي]
Rectify	yuṣaḥḥiḥ	**يصحح** (يقوم)
Recur	yatakarrar	**يتكـــرر**
Red clause credit	i'timād ad-dafa'a 'l-muqaddama	**اعتماد الدفعة المقدمة** [يتضمن شرطا بالحبر الأحمر يسمح للمستفيد بقبض دفعة مقدما وقبل الشحن

		لتجهيز البضاعة]
Red herring prospectus	al-iʿlān ʿan waṣf al-iṣdār al-mutawaqqaʿ li's-sanadāt	الاعلان عن وصف الاصدار المتوقع لسندات
Red ink entry	1 qayd bi'l-lawn al-aḥmar	١ - قيد باللون الأحمر [الدلالة على طرح القيد من مجموع العمود الذى ظهر به ويشبه وضع اشارة طرح بجانب القيد أو وضع القيد بين قوسين]
	2 khasāra	٢ - خسـارة
Redeem	1 yuṭfiʾ daynan	١ - يطفيء ـ دينا
	2 yusaddid	٢ - يسـدد
	3 yastahlik	٣ - يستهلك
Redeem a debenture	yastaridd qīmat sanad	يسترد قيمة سند
Redeem a loan	yusaddid qarḍan	يسدد قرضا
Redeem a mortgage	yafukk rahnan	يفـك رهنـا
Redeemable	qābil li't-tasdīd	قابل للتسديد (للاستهلاك ، للاطفاء)
Redeemable debentures	sanadāt qābila li't-tasdīd	سندات قابلة للتسديد
Redemption	1 tasdīd	١ - تسـديـد [تسديد قيمة الأسهم والسندات من قبل المصدر]
	2 iʿādat shirāʾ	٢ - اعادة شراء
Redemption fund	ṣundūq al-istihlākāt	صندوق الاستهلاكات
Redemption loan	qarḍ istihlāk	قرض استهلاك
Redemption premium	1 ʿalāwat tasdīd	١ - علاوة تسديد [علاوة تدفع عند رد قيمة السندات]
	2 ʿalāwat shirāʾ ash-shayʾ al-mubāʿ	٢ - علاوة شراء الشيء المباع
Redemption table	jadwal al-istilāk	جدول الاستهلاك
Redemptional	musaddad	مسـدد (مستهلك)
Rediscount (n.; v.)	1 iʿādat al-khaṣm	١ - اعادة الخصم
	2 adāh tijāriyya mutadāwala	٢ - أداة تجارية متداولة [حاز عليها بنك بخصم وباعها الى بنك احتياط فدرالي]
Rediscountable	qābil li'l-ḥasm thāniyatan	قابل للحسم ثانية
Rediscounted bill	kumbiyāla muʿād khaṣmuhā	كمبيالة معاد خصمها
Redistributed cost	at-takilfa 'l-muʿād tawzīʿ uhā	التكلفة المعاد توزيعها
Reduce	yukhaffiḍ	يخفض (يقلل ، ينقص)
Reducing balance form	uslūb at-taqrīr	اسلوب التقرير [الاسلوب المستعمل في عرض بيان الأرباح والخسائر حيث تقرأ مادته من الأعلى للاسفل مبتدئا بالمبيعات ومنتهيا بالربح الصافى]
Reducing instalment method	tarīqat al-qisṭ al-mutanāqiṣ	طريقة القسط المتناقص
Reduction	takhfīḍ	تخفيض (تقليل ـ تنقيص)
Re-endorse	yuẓahhir thāniyatan	يظهّر ثانية (سندا الخ)
Re-enter	yuʿīd tasjīl	يعيد تسجيل ـ بند في حساب

Re-entry	i'ādat at-tasjīl	**اعادة التسجيل**
Refer	1 yushīr ilā	**١ - يشير إلى**
	2 yarfa' ilā	**٢ - يرفع إلى** (يميل إلى)
Reference (n.; v.)	1 marji'	**١ - مرجع**
	2 ishāra	**٢ - اشارة**
	3 yurāji'	**٣ - يراجع**
		[وقائع وأرقام مسودة تقرير أو رسالة مع مصادر نشوئها وربطها ببعضها]
Referencing	murāja'a	**مراجعة**
Refund (n.; v.)	1 mardūd	**١ - مردود** (مسترجع مما دفع)
	2 ḥasm	**٢ - حسم**
	3 yusaddid	**٣ - يسدد**
	4 yu'assis daynan jadīdan	**٤ - يؤسس دينا جديدا**
Refund a debit	yusaddid daynan	**يسدد دينا**
Refund a mortgage	yarudd rahnan	**يرد رهنا**
Refund the excess on a tax	yarudd al-fā'iḍ min aḍ-ḍarība	**يرد الفائض من الضريبة**
Refundable	mumkin radduh	**ممكن رده**
Refunding bond	sanad adā'	**سند اداء**
		[السند الذى يحل محل سند آخر ويسدد به سند مستحق الأداء]
Register (n.; v.)	sijill	**سجل ـ يسجل**
Register of deeds	sijill ṣukūk at-tamalluk	**سجل صكوك التملك**
Register of receipts and issues	sijill al-idkhālāt wa 'l-ikhrājāt	**سجل الادخالات والاخراجات**
Registered bond	sanad shakhṣī	**سند شخصي**
		[سند لا يدفع رأسماله وفائدته الا إلى الشخص المسجل اسمه في الدفاتر]
Registered capital	ra'smāl muktatab bihi	**الرأسمال المكتتب به**
Registered office (of a company)	markaz ash-sharika-'arrasmī	**مركز الشركة الرسمي**
Registered shareholder	ḥāmil as-hum shakhṣiyya	**حامل أسهم شخصية**
Registered warrant	sanad musajjal	**سند مسجل**
		[من قبل المسؤول عن الدفع لتسديده في المستقبل لعدم وجود أموال في الوقت الحاضر ويجرى تسديده حسب ترتيبه في التسجيل]
Registered with notice of receipt	sijill ma' ish'ār bi'l-wuṣūl	**سجل مع اشعار بالوصول**
Registrar	musajjil	**مسجل**
		[مسجل العقود أو مسجل اصدار اسهم الشركة]
Registration	tasjīl	**تسجيل** (تدوين)
Registration and transfer fees	rusūm at-tasjīl wa 'l-intiqāl	**رسوم التسجيل والانتقال**
Registration statement	bayān tasjīl	**بيان تسجيل**
		[بيان رسمى تقدمه الشركة للحكومة يبين المعلومات المالية المتعلقة بالشركة للاطلاع عليها من قبل مشترى المستندات]

Registry	sijill	سجـل (قيد)
Regressive tax	ḍarība tanāzuliyya	ضريبة تنازلية
Regular	niẓāmī	نظامي (عادى)
Regular account	ḥisāb muntaẓim	حساب منتظم
Regular endorsement	taẓhīr niẓāmī	تظهير نظامي
Regularity of cheque	aṣ-ṣigha 'n-niẓāmiyya li-shīk	الصيغة النظامية لشيك
Regulate	yunaẓẓim	ينظم (يسوى ، يرتب)
Regulation	tanẓīm	تنظيم ـ لائحة ، قاعدة
Rehabilitate a company financially	yarudd ila 'sh-sharika ''tibāraha māliyyan	يرد الى الشركة اعتبارها ماليا
Rehabilitation	radd al-i'thibār	رد الاعتبار (تصحيح)
Reimbursable	qābil li't-tasdīd	قابل للتسديد (او الاسترداد)
Reimbursable indebtedness	dayn yumkin tasdīduh	دين يمكن تسديده
Reimburse	yusaddid	يسـدد
Reimbursement	sadād	سـداد
Reinsurance	i'ādāt ta'mīn	اعادة تأمين
Reinsure	yu'ammin thāniyatan	يؤمن ثانية
Reintegrate	yu'īd damj	يعيد دمج
Reinvest	yuwaẓẓif al-māl thāniyatan	يوظف المال ثانية
Reinvestment	i'ādat al-istithmār	اعادة الاستثمار
Reissue	1 iṣdār thānī	١ - اصدار ثان
	2 tajdīd muhlat saftaja	٢ - تجديد مهلة سفتجة
Reject	yarfuḍ	يـرفض
Rejectable quality level	mustawa 'n-'n-naw' iyya 'l-marfūḍ	مستوى النوعية المرفوض
Related company; affiliated company	sharika tābi'a	شركة تابعة
Related cost	taklifa murtabiṭa	التكلفة المرتبطة
		١ - [التي تؤدى إلى عملية بيع أو ايراد آخر]
		٢ - [التكلفة التي تؤدى إلى تكلفة اخرى]
		٣ - [تكلفـة عامـة]
Relative	nisbī	نسبـي
Relative prices	as'ār nisbiyya	أسعار نسبية
Release (n.; v.)	1 tabri'at dhimma	١ - تبرئة ذمة (تحرير من قيد رهن)
	2 ṭarḥ li 'l-bay'	٢ - طـرح للبيع
	3 nashra	٣ - نشـرة (مستند)
Release of documents	taslīm al-mustanadāt	تسليم المستندات (الافراج عنها)
Release someone from an obligation	yuḥarrir fardan min iltizam	يحرر فردا من التزام
Reliability	mawthūqiyya	موثوقيـة
Reliable	mawthūq	موثوق (يعتمد عليه)
Relief fund	ṣundūq al-I'ānāt	صندوق الاعانات (المساعدات)
Relieve	yurīḥ	يريـح (يخلص)
		[يخلص من التزام أو عبء مالى]
Remain	yabqā	يبقـى

Remainder	raṣīd	رصيد (باقي)
Remainderman	ṣāḥib al-ḥaqq	صاحب الحق [فى ملكية عقار عند انتهاء ملكية سابقة]
Remission	1 iʻfā'	١ - اعفــاء [من ضريبة كليا أو جزئيا]
	2 ta'jīl	٢ - تأجيــل
Remit	1 yuʻfī	١ - يعفــي [من التزام أو ضريبة]
	2 yursil mālan	٢ - يرسل مالا
Remit a debt (v.)	yuʻfī min dayn	يعفى من دين (يتخلى عن دين)
Remit for collection (v.)	yuʻīd as-sanad li'l-jibāya	يعيد السند للجباية
Remit money	yursil nuqūdan	يرسل نقودا
Remittance	1 dafʻa māliyya	١ - دفعة مالية
	2 tasdīd sanad tijārī	٢ - تسديد سند تجارى
	3 ta'jīl	٣ - تأجيــل
Remittance advice	ishʻār taḥwīl	اشعار تحويل
Remittance in cash	ad-daf' naqdan	الدفع نقدا
Remittance slip	ishʻār dafʻ	اشعار دفع
Removable	1 qābil li'l-intiqāl	١ - قابل للانتقال
	2 qābil li'l-istirdād	٢ - قابل للاسترداد
Remunerate	yukāfi'	يكافــىء [يعطي بدلا من عمل]
Remuneration	1 mukāfa'a	١ - مكافــأة
	2 taʻwīḍ	٢ - تعويــض
	3 badal	٣ - بدل (علاوة)
Remunerative	murbiḥ	مربــح
Remunerative business	tijāra murbiḥa	تجارة مربحة
Render an account	yuqaddim ḥisāban	يقدم حسابا
Rendering	taqdīm	تقديــم
Renegotiation	iʻādat at-tafāwuḍ	اعادة التفاوض [الطريقة التي تتبعها الوكالات الحكومية والتي تؤدى الى تعديل قيمة العقد بعد التسليم وبعد تحديد الأرباح الناتجة عن العقد]
Renegotiation reserve	iḥtiyāṭi iʻādat at-tafāwuḍ	احتياطي اعادة التفاوض [مطلوب متداول مقدر على أنه المبلغ القابل للتسديد بموجب العقود الحكومية]
Renew	yujaddid	يجــدد
Renewable	qābil li't-tajdīd	قابل للتجديد
Renewal	tajdīd	تجــديد
Renewal (or replacement) fund	iʻtimādāt at-tajdīd	اعتمادات التجديد [النقد أو السندات المخصصة لتجديد المصنع والمعدات]

Renounce a claim	yatanāzal ʿan ḥaqq	يتنازل عن حق
Renouncement	tanāzul	تنــازل
Rent (n.; v.)	ījār	ايجــار
Rent roll	sijill al-ījār	سجل الايجار
Rental expenses	maṣārīf ījār	مصاريف ايجار
Rental value	al-qīma 't-ta'jīriyya	القيمة التأجيرية
Renter	musta'jir	المستأجــر
Reorganisation	iʿādat tashkīl	اعادة تشكيل
		[تغيير رئيسي في النظام المالي لشركة أو مجموعة شركات متحدة وينتج عنه تغييرات في حصص وحقوق المساهمين]
Reorganise	yuʿīd tashkīl	يعيد تشكيل
Repair (n.; v.)	iṣlāḥ	اصلاح (ترميم)
Repair reserve method	ṭarīqat iḥtiyāṭi 's-ṣiyāna	طريقة احتياطي الصيانة
Repairable	qābil li't-taṣlīh	قابل للتصليح
Repairs and renewals	taṣlīḥāt wa tajdīdāt	التصليحات والتجديدات
Repartition	1 tawzīʿ ḥiṣaṣ	١ - توزيع حصص
	2 taqsīm	٢ - تقســيم
Repay	yusaddid	يســدد
Repay a loan	yusaddid qarḍan	يسدد قرضا
Repayability	qābiliyyat at-tasdīd	قابلية التسديد (امكانية الدفع)
Repayable	qābil li't-tasdid	قابل للتسديد (قابل للدفع)
Repayment	dafʿ	دفع (تسديد)
Repeat	yukarrir	يكــرر
Repeating audit; periodic audit	murājaʿa fatriyya	مراجعة فترية
Repetition	tikrār	تكـرار (اعادة)
Replace	1 yastabdil	١ - يستبــدل
	2 yaḥill maḥall	٢ - يحل محل (ينوب عنه)
Replacement	1 istibdāl	١ - استبدال (احلال)
	2 ināba	٢ - انابة ـ قانونية
	3 taʿwīḍ	٣ - تعويــض
		[قيمة أشياء مؤمن عليها]
Replacement cost (value)	siʿr al-iḥlāl	سعر الاحلال
Replacement method	ṭariqat al-iḥlāl	طريقة الاحلال
		[طريقة تقدير كلفة استبدال الاصول ذات الحياة المحدودة والمستعملة حاليا]
Replacement order	amr istibdāl	أمر استبدال
Replacement price	siʿr al-iḥlāl	سعر الاحلال
Replacement table	jadwal al-iḥlāl	جدول الاحلال
Replacement unit	wiḥdat al-iḥlal	وحدة الاحلال
		[الاصل أو جزء الأصل الذى حل محل وحدة مستبدلة]
Report (n.; v.)	1 bayān	١ - بيــان

	2 taqrīr	٢ - تقريـــر
	3 yarfa' taqrīran	٣ - يرفع تقريرا
Report form	uslūb at-taqrīr	اسلوب التقرير [الاسلوب المتبع عادة عند تقديم بيان الأرباح والخسائر حيث يقرأ الموضوع من الأعلى إلى الأسفل ابتداء بالمبيعات وانتهاء بالدخل الصافي]
Report of auditors	taqrīr mudaqqiqi 'l-ḥisābāt	تقرير مدققي الحسابات
Reporting	i'dād at-taqārīr	اعداد التقارير
Reporting standards	qawā'id i'dād at-taqāqārīr	قواعد اعداد التقارير
Represent	yumathil	يمثل (ينوب عنه)
Representation	tamthīl	تمثيل (نيابة)
Representation letter	kitāb at-tamthīl	كتاب التمثيل [بيان حقائق عن المؤسسة تعده الادارة خطيا وتسلمه إلى مدقق الحسابات]
Representative	mumathil	ممثل (وكيل ، مندوب)
Representative paper money	nuqūd waraqiyya kāmilat ar-raṣīd	نقود ورقية كاملة الرصيد
Representative sample	'ayyina 'ashwā'iyya	عينة عشوائية
Reprieve	yumhil	يمهـــل
Reproduce	yu'īd al-intāj	يعيد الانتاج
Reproduction	i'ādat intāj	اعادة الانتاج
Reproduction cost	takālīf i'ādat al-intāj	تكاليف اعادة الانتاج [اصطلاح مستعمل في تقييم الموجودات الثابتة]
Repudiate	1 yunkir	١ - ينكر ـ دينا
	2 yarfuḍ	٢ - يرفض ـ عقدا
Repurchase price	si'r i'ādat ash-shirā'	سعر اعادة الشراء (سعر الاسترداد)
Repurchased stock	ra'smāl mu'ād shirā'uh	الرأسمال المعاد شراؤه
Requisition	ṭalab rasmī	طلب رسمي
Resale (n.; v.)	i'ādat al-bay'	اعادة البيع
Rescind	yulghī	يلغي (يبطل ، ينقص ، يفسخ)
Rescission	ilghā'	الغاء (ابطال ، نقص ، فسخ)
Research cost	taklifat al-abḥāth	تكلفة الابحاث
Reservation	taḥaffuẓ	تحفـــظ
Reserve (n.; v.)	iḥtiyāttī	احتياطـــي
Reserve account	ḥisāb al-iḥtiyāṭī	حساب الاحتياطي
Reserve adequacy	kifāyat al-iḥtiyāṭī	كفاية الاحتياطي
Reserve capital	ra'smāl ihtiyāṭī	رأسمال احتياطي
Reserve for accidents	iḥtiyāṭi 'l-ḥawādith aṭ-ṭāri'a	احتياطي الحوادث الطارئة
Reserve for amortisation	iḥtiyaṭ 'l-iṭfā'	احتياطي الاطفاء
Reserve for depreciation of fixed assets	iḥtiyaṭi 'stihlāk mawjūdāt thābita	احتياطي استهلاك موجودات ثابتة
Reserve for discounts	iḥtiyāṭi 'l-khuṣūmāt an-naqdiyya	احتياطي الخصومات النقدية

		[حساب تقييم يبين مدى انخفاض اجمالي الذمم المدينة لدى منح خصومات نقدية للزبائن لتشجيعهم على التسديد]
Reserve for doubtful debts	iḥtiyāṭi 'd-duyān al-mashkūk fī taḥṣīliha	احتياطي الديون المشكوك في تحصيلها
Reserve for encumbrances	iḥtiyāṭi 'l-iltizāmāt ghayr al-muṣaffāh	احتياطي الالتزامات غير المصفاة
Reserve for leave indemnities	iḥtiyāṭī ta'wīḍāt al-ijāzāt	احتياطي تعويضات الاجازات
Reserve for overhead	iḥtiyāṭi 'l-maṣārif ar-ra'siyya	احتياطي المصاريف الرأسية
Reserve for renewals & replacements	iḥtiyāṭi 't-tajdīd wa 'l-istibdāl	احتياطي التجديد والاستبدال
Reserve for repairs	iḥtiyāṭi 't-taṣliḥāt	احتياطي التصليحات
Reserve for staff leaving indemnities	iḥtiyāṭi 'ṣ-ṣarf min al-khidma	احتياطي الصرف من الخدمة
Reserve for wear, tear, obsolescence, or inadequacy; reserve for depreciation	iḥtiyāṭi 'l-istihlāk	احتياطي الاستهلاك
Reserve fund	ṣundūq iḥtiyāṭī	صندوق احتياطي
Reserve, contingency	iḥtiyāṭi 'ṭ-ṭawāri'	احتياطي الطوارىء
Reserve, excess	iḥtiyāṭi zā'id	احتياطي زائد (تغطيات زائدة)
Residual cost (or value)	al-qīma 'l-mutabaqqiya	القيمة المتبقية [تكلفة الأصل ناقصا الجزء المطفأ منها أو المعتبر كمصروف أو خسارة]
Residual net income (or profit)	ad-dakhl aṣ-ṣāfī	الدخل الصافي (الربح المتبقي)
Residuary outlay	an-nafaqa 'l-mutabaqqiya	النفقة المتبقية
Resolution	qarār	قـــرار
Resources	1 al-maṣādir 'l-māliyya	١ - المصادر المالية
	2 maṣādir	٢ - مصادر (موارد)
Response (U.S.)	1 istijāba	١ - استجابة
	2 radd	٢ - رد
Responsibility	mas'ūliyya	مسؤولية (تبعة)
Responsibility costing	taklifat at-tabi'a	تكلفة التبعة [توزيع التكلفة على الاشخاص المسؤولين عن مراقبتها بدلا من توزيعها على المنتوجات أو المهمات]
Responsible	mas'ūl	مسؤول (ملتزم ، مكلف)
Restore	1 yu'īd	١ - يعيـــد
	2 yuṣliḥ	٢ - يصلح (يرمم)
Re-store	yu'īd takhzīn	يعيد تخزين
Restrict	yuqayyid	يقيد (يحصر ، يحدد)
Restricted cash	naqd muqayyad	نقد مقيد [رصيد نقدى لا يمكن سحبه أو سحب جزء منه الا بشروط خاصة]
Restricted fund	ṣundūq muqayyad	صندوق مقيد

		[يشرف على رأسماله أو ايراده الممول أو فرد خارجي]
Restricted random sampling	ikhtibār 'afwī muqayyad	**الاختبار العفوى المقيد**
		[أخذ العينات للاختبار بطريقة عفوية مقيدة بنظام]
Restricted receipts	maqbūḍāt muqayyada	**مقبوضات مقيدة**
		[مخصصة لأغراض معينة]
Restricted stock option	khayār shirā' al-as-hum al-mashrūṭ	**خيار شراء الأسهم المشروط**
		[الامتياز الذى تمنحه المؤسسة لموظفيها لشراء أسهمها]
Restriction	taqyīd	**تقييد** (تحديد ، تضييق)
Result (n.; v.)	1 natīja	١ - **نتيجة** (حاصل)
	2 yanjum 'an	٢ - **ينجم عن**
Result from operation	dakhl al-tashgheel	دخل التشغيل
Resume	1 yasta'īd	١ - **يستعيد ـ ملكية أو حق التمتع بملكية**
	2 yujaddid	٢ - **يجدد ـ ايجار الخ**
	3 yasta'nif	٣ - **يستأنـــف**
Resumption	1 istirdād	١ - **استرداد** (استرجاع)
	2 isti'nāf	٢ - **استئنـــاف**
Retail	al-mufarraq	**المفـــرق**
Retail accounting	muḥāsabat al-bay' bi'l-mufarraq	**محاسبة البيع بالمفرق**
Retail cost	taklifat al-mufarraq	**تكلفة المفرق**
		[طريقة الجرد الدفترى فى تقدير تكلفة المبيعات أو البضاعة]
Retail method	ṭarīqat al-jard ad-daftarī	**طريقة الجرد الدفترى**
Retail outlet	sūq at-taṣrīf li'l-mufarraq	**سوق التصريف للمفرق**
Retail prices	as'ār al-mufarraq	**أسعار المفرق**
Retailer	bā'i' al-mufarraq	**بائع المفرق**
Retain	yastabqī	**يستبقـــي**
Retained earnings	al-īrādāt al-muḥtafaẓa	**الايرادات المحتفظة**
Retained profits	al-arbāḥ al-muḥtafaẓa	**الارباح المحتفظة**
Retained surplus	al-fā'iḍ al-muḥtafaẓ	**الفائض المحتفظ**
Retention	iqtiṭā'	**اقتطـــاع**
Retire	1 yas-hab min at-tadāwul	١ - **يسحب من التداول**
	2 yataqā'ad	٢ - **يتقـــاعد**
	3 yastahlik	٣ - **يستهلك ـ دينا**
Retirement	1 taqā'ud	١ - **تقاعد** (ترك الخدمة)
	2 saḥb	٢ - **سحب ـ الأصل من الخدمة**
Retirement allowance	ta'wīḍ taqā'ud	**تعويض تقاعد**
Retirement curve	munḥana 'imtidād al-ḥayāh al-fi'lī	**منحني امتداد الحياة الفعلي**
Retirement pay	rātib at-taqā'ud	**راتب التقاعد**
Retirement plan	mashrū' at-taqā'ud	**مشروع التقاعد**
Retirement table	qā'imat tawaqqu'āt al-ḥayāh	**قائمة توقعات الحياة**

Retreat	yasḥab ʿarḍahu	يسحب عرضه ـ بورصة
Retroactive law	qānūn bi-mafʿūl rajʿī	قانون بمفعول رجعي
Retrospective rating	taʿdīl rajʿī	تعديل رجعي [طريقة لتسوية قسط التأمين مع الخسارة الفعلية خلال مدة الحماية]
Return	1 ʿāʾdāt	١ - عائدات (واردات)
	2 mardūd	٢ - مردود (مرتجع)
	3 bayān rasmī	٣ - بيان رسمي
Return of capital	tasdīd raʾsmāl	تسديد رأسمال
Return of income	bayān ad-dakhl	بيان الدخل
Return on capital	mardūd ar-raʾsmāl	مردود الرأسمال
Return on investment	ʿāʾidāt al-istithmār	عائدات الاستثمار
Returns inward	mardūdāt dākhila	مردودات داخلة
Returns outward	mardūdāt khārija	مردودات خارجة
Reuse price	siʿr iʿādat al-istikhdām	سعر اعادة الاستخدام
Revalorisation	istiʿādat al-qīma	استعادة القيمة [استعادة النقد قيمته السابقة أو العادية]
Revaluation	rafʿ siʿr al-ʿumla	رفع سعر العملة
Revaluation method	ṭarīqat iʿādat at-taqdīr	طريقة اعادة التقدير
Revaluation reserve (or excess or surplus)	iḥtiyāṭī iʿādat at-taqdīr	احتياطي اعادة التقدير
Revalue	yuʿīd at-taqdīr	يعيد التقدير
Revenue	dakhl	دخل (عائدات)
Revenue act	qānūn ad-dakhl	قانون الدخل
Revenue bond	sanad ʿāʾidāt	سند عائدات [سند دين تصدره الحكومة لتمويل بعض المشاريع ويسدد من دخل أو أرباح المشروع]
Revenue deduction	ḥasm ʿāʾidāt	حسم عائدات
Revenue expenditure	maṣrufāt īrādiyya	مصروفات ايرادية
Revenue expense	nafaqa īrādiyya	نفقة ايرادية
Revenue receipts	maqbūḍāt īrādiyya	مقبوضات ايرادية [مقبوضات نقدية خلال فترة معينة]
Revenue reserves	iḥtiyāti ʾl-īrād	احتياطي الايراد [ذلك الجزء من حقوق الشركاء الذى يمثل الدخل المحفوظ والذى يمكن سحبه من قبل مالكى المؤسسة]
Reverse	1 yulghī	١ - يلغي (يبطل ، يعكس)
	2 yuṣaḥḥiḥ	٢ - يصحح ـ قرارا
Reverse an entry	yaʾkis qaydan	يعكس قيدا
Reverse split-up	istidʿāʾ as-hum	استدعاء أسهم [الغاء أسهم أو اصدار أسهم اقل عددا]
Reversing entry	qayd ʿaksī	قيد عكسي

Reversion	ḥaqq istirjāʿ māl	**حق استرجاع مال** (حق استرداد ملك)
Review	murājaʿa	**مراجعة** (فحص)
Revise	yurājiʿ	**يراجع** (ينقح ، يعيد النظر)
Revision	murājaʿa	**مراجعة** (تعديل ، تنقيح)
Revision variance	muʿāmil at-taʿdīl	**معامل التعديل**
		[الاختلاف بين التكلفة المعيارية الأساسية والتكلفة المعيارية المعدلة]
Revocable credit	iʿtimād qābil li'n-naqḍ	**اعتماد قابل للنقض**
Revocable trust	waṣiyya qābila li'l-ilghā'	**وصية قابلة للالغاء**
		[من قبل الموصي]
Revoke	yulghī	**يلغـي** (يفسخ)
Revolving credit	iʿtimād mutajaddid	**اعتماد متجدد**
Revolving fund	ṣundūq mutajaddid	**صندوق متجدد**
Reward (n.; v.)	mukāfa'a	**مكافـأة**
Rider	mulḥaq īḍāḥī	**ملحق ايضاحي** (شرط اضافي)
Rig (n.; v.)	muḍāraba	**مضاربـة**
Rig the market (v.)	yuḥarrik as-sūq	**يحرك السوق** (يتلاعب بأوراق البورصة)
Right	1 ḥaqq	**١ - حـق**
	2 imtiyāz	**٢ - امتيـاز**
Right of choice	ḥaqq al-ikhtiyār	**حق الاختيار**
Right of communication	ḥaqq al-iṭṭilāʿ	**حق الاطلاع**
Right of set-off	ḥaqq al-muqāṣṣa	**حق المقاصة**
Right of way	ḥaqq al-istiʿmāl	**حق الاستعمال**
Right, acquired	haqq muktasab	**حق مكتسب**
Rights market	sūq imtiyāzāt al-iktitāb	**سوق امتيازات الاكتتاب ـ بورصة**
Rise (n.; v.)	ziyāda	**زيادة** (ارتفاع)
Risk	mujāzafa	**مجازفة** (مخاطرة ، مغامرة)
Risk capital	rasmāl dhū akhṭār	**رأسمال ذو اخطار**
Risk premium	qisṭ at-ta'mīn ḍed al-akhtar	**قسط التأمين ضد الأخطار**
Roll-back (U.S.)	inkhifaḍ al-asʿār al-mafrūḍa	**انخفاض الأسعار المفروضة**
Roll-forward	ziyādat al-asʿār ar-rasmiyya	**زيادة الأسعار الرسمية**
Rough draft	muswadda	**مسـودة**
		[مسودة مشروع كتاب أو رسالة الخ]
Round off	tadwīr	**تدوير ـ أرقام**
Round sum	raqm mudawwar	**رقم مدور**
Routine	watīrī	**وتيرى** (نمطي)
Routinise	yunammiṭ	**ينمـط**
		[يجعل الشيء وتيريا]
Royalty	atāwa	**اتـاوه**
		[ريع حق الامتياز]
Royalty interest	fā'idat al-milkiyya	**فائدة الملكية**
Rubber cheque	shīk dūna raṣīd	**شيك دون رصيد**
Rule	qāʿida	**قاعدة** (قانون ، قرار)

Rule off	yuqfil ḥisāban	**يقفل حساب**
Run a business	yudīr ʿamalan	**يدير عملا**
Running expenses	maṣārīf jāriya	**مصاريف جارية**
Running form; report form	uslūb at-taqrīr	**اسلوب التقرير** [الاسلوب المتبع عند تقديم بيان الأرباح والخسائر حيث يقرأ الموضوع من الأعلى إلى الاسفل ابتداء بالمبيعات وانتهاء بالدخل الصافي]
Rush orders	ṭalabat mustaʿjala	**الطلبات المستعجلة**
Sacrifice (n.; v.)	1 khasāra	**١ - خســارة**
	2 yabīʿ bi-khasāra	**٢ - يبيع بخسارة**
Sacrifice prices	asʿār khāsira	**أسعار خاسرة**
Safe	ṣundūq ḥadīdī	**صندوق حديدى**
Safe deposit box	ṣundūq ḥadīdī li'l-wadā'iʿ	**صندوق حديدى للودائع**
Safeguard (n.; v.)	1 ḥimāya	**١ - حماية** (وقاية ، ضمان)
	2 yaḥmī	**٢ - يحمي** (يحافظ على
Safety	amān	**أمان** (ضمان)
Salary	murattab	**مرتـب** (معاش)
Salary range	sullam al-ujūr	**سلم الاجور**
Salary roll	jadwal ar-rawātib	**جدول الرواتب**
Sale	1 bayʿ	**١ - بيــع**
	2 mazād	**٢ - مــزاد**
Sale by instalment	bayʿ bi't-taqsīṭ	**بيع بالتقسيط**
Sale by tender	bayʿ bi'l-munāqaṣa	**بيع بالمناقصة** [بموجب رسو المزايدة]
Sale value	qīmat al-bay'	**قيمة البيع**
Sales	mabīʿāt	**مبيعــات**
Sales allowance variance	inḥirāf khaṣm al-mabīʿāt	**انحراف خصم المبيعات**
Sales allowances	khuṣūmāt mabīʿāt	**خصومات مبيعات**
Sales commitment	iltizām al-bayʿ	**التزام البيع**
Sales cut-off	qaṭʿ al-mabīʿāt	**قطع المبيعات** [المبيعات لفترة سابقة ولاحقة لتاريخ معين]
Sales discount	khaṣm al-mabī'āt	**خصم المبيعات**
Sales invoice	fātūrat al-mabīʿāt	**فاتورة المبيعات**
Sales journal	yawmiyyat al-mabīʿāt	**يومية المبيعات**
Sales manager	mudīr al-mabīʿāt	**مدير المبيعات**
Sales mixture variance	inḥirāf mazj ʿal-mabīʿāt	**انحراف مزج** (تشكيلة ، تكوين) **المبيعات**
Sales operations	ʿamaliyyāt al-bay'	**عمليات البيع**
Sales order	ṭalab mabīʿāt	**طلب مبيعات**
Sales order department	dā'irat ṭalabāt al-mabīʿāt	**دائرة طلبات المبيعات**
Sales price variance	inḥirāf siʿr al-bayʿ	**انحراف سعر البيع**

Sales promotion	tarwīj al-mabī'āt	ترويج المبيعات
Sales record	sijill al-mabī'āt	سجل المبيعات
Sales register (S.R.)	sijill al-mabī'āt	سجل المبيعات
Sales returns	mardūdāt al-mabī'āt	مردودات المبيعات
Sales revenue	dakhl al-mabī'āt	دخل المبيعات
Sales tax	ḍarībat al-mabī'āt	ضريبة المبيعات
Sales territories	manāṭiq al-bay'	مناطق البيع
Sales value variance	al-inḥirāf al-kullī li'l-mabī'āt	الانحراف الكلي للمبيعات
Salesman	bā'i'	بائع
Salvage	1 qīmat al-mawādd al-munqadha	١ - قيمة المواد المنقذة ـ من الغرق أو الحريق
	2 qīmat al-khurda	٢ - قيمة الخردة
Salvage value; scrap value	qīmat al-khurda	قيمة الخردة
Sample (n.; v.)	1 'ayyina	١ - عينــة
	2 ya'khudh 'ayyina	٢ - يأخذ عينة
Sample size	ḥajm al-'ayyina	حجم العينة
Sampling	akhdh 'ayyināt	أخذ عينات
Sampling distribution	at-tawzī' al-'ayyinī	التوزيع العيني [توزيع نتيجة الاختبار العيني على شكل رسم بياني أو حسابي]
Sampling error	al-khaṭa' al-'ayyinī	الخطأ العيني [الخطأ المعيارى للاختبار العيني]
Sampling inspection	faḥṣ al-'ayyināt	فحص العينات [استعمال العينات لتحديد قابلية البضاعة المعروضة]
Satisfaction	1 daf' dayn	١ - دفع دين
	2 kifāya	٢ - كفايــة
Save	yaddakhir	يدخر (يوفر ، يقتصد)
Saving	iddikhār	ادخار
Saving bonds	sanadāt iddikhār	سندات ادخار
Saving clause	1 sharṭ al-ḥimāya	١ - شرط الحماية ـ تأمين
	2 sharṭ taḥaffuẓī	٢ - شرط تحفظي ـ في اتفاقية
Savings bank	maṣrif al-iddikhār	مصرف الادخار
Savings bank book	daftar ṣundūq at-tawfīr	دفتر صندوق التوفير
Savings fund	ṣundūq iddikhār	صندوق ادخار
Savings, domestic	al-muddakharāt al-waṭaniyya	المدخرات الوطنية
Scalp (U.S.) (n.; v.)	muḍāraba	مضاربــة [بيع بأدني من السعر العادى أو الرسمى يضارب بالانخفاض ـ بورصة]
Scan	yatafaḥḥaṣ	يتفحص ـ قيودا بصورة عامة وسريعة
Scarcity	nudra	ندرة (قلة وجود ، نقص)
Schedule	1 jadwal	١ - جدول
	2 khuṭṭat 'amal	٢ - خطة عمل

	3 mulḥaq mīzāniyya	٣ - ملحق ميزانية
Schedule cost; standard cost	at-taklifa 'l-mi'yāriyya	التكلفة المعيارية
Schedule of depreciation	jadwal istihlāk	جدول استهلاك
Scheme	mashrū'	مشروع (خطة)
Scope	madā	مدى (مجال ، نطاق)
Scope of audit	mada 't-tadqīq	مدى التدقيق
Scrap	mukhallafāt	مخلفات (نفاية)
Scrap (U.S.)	yastaghnī 'an	يستغنى عن (يصرف النظر عن ، يهمل ، يلغي)
Scrap value	qīmat al-khurda	قيم الخردة
Screen	yakhtār	يختار (يغربل)
Screening	gharbala	غربلـــة [تفتيش دقيق أثناء مراقبة الانتاج]
Scrip	ṣakk	صك (شهادة ، تعهد) ١ - [شهادة أسهم مؤقتة] ٢ - [تعهد بأرباح أسهم] ٣ - [أوراق « نقدية » تصدرها الشركات لدفع الاجور وتقبلها مخازن الشركة]
Scrip dividend	arbāḥ as-hum	أرباح أسهم [تدفع على شكل كمبيالات]
Season	faṣl	فصل (موسم)
Seasonal	faṣlī	فصلي (موسمي)
Seasonal variation	taghayyurāt mawsimiyya	تغيرات موسمية
Seasoning	fatrat istiqrār	فترات استقرار [الفترة المطلوبة لاستقرار سعر السندات المالية]
Second debentures	sanadāt daraja thāniya	سندات درجة ثانية
Second endorser	al-muẓahhir ath-thānī	المظهّر الثاني
Second mortgage	ar-rahn ath-thānī	الرهن الثاني
Secondary	thānawī	ثانـــوى
Secondary liability	iltizām thānī	التـــزام ثان [التزام طرف بدفع قيمة سند في حالة اخفاق الطرف الاول في تسديد قيمته]
Secret reserve	iḥtiyātī sirrī	احتياطي سرى
Secretary	amīn sirr	أمين سر (سكرتير)
Section	1 far'	١ - فـــرع (قسم)
	2 juz'	٢ - جزء (مادة) من فصل
Sectional balancing	at-tarṣīd al-juz'ī	الترصيد الجزئي
Secular	mustamirr	مستمـــر [مستمر على مدى طويل]
Secular price	al-si'r al-mustamirr	السعر المستمر [السعر الناتج من تفاعل العوامل الاقتصادية على مدى زمنى طويل]

Secular trend	al-ittijāh al-mustamirr	الاتجاه المستمر
Secure (adj.; v.)	1 maḍmūn	١ - مضمـــون
	2 yaḥṣul ʿalā	٢ - يحصل على
Secure investments	istithmārāt maḍmūna	استثمارات مضمونة
Secured account	ḥisāb maḍmūn	حساب مضمون (مكفول)
Secured bonds	sanadāt maḍmūna	سندات مضمونة
Secured creditor	dā'in mumtāz	دائن ممتاز
Secured liability	iltizām maḍmūn	التزام مضمون
Secured loan	qarḍ maḍmūn	قرض مضمون
Securities	sanadāt	سندات (أوراق مالية ، أسهم)
Securities trust	sharkit tawẓīfāt māliyya	شركة توظيفات مالية
Securities, bearer	sanadāt li-ḥāmilihā	سندات لحاملها
Securities, forward	sanadāt li-ajal	سندات لأجل
Securities, gilt edged	sanadāt maḍmūna	سندات مضمونة
Securities, government	sanadāt ḥukūmiyya	سندات حكومية [سندات دين عام]
Security	1 sanadāt maliyya	١ - سندات مالية
	2 ḍamān	٢ - ضمـــان [كفالة مالية كافية لتغطية دين]
Security deposit	wadīʿat kafāla	وديعة كفالة
Security income and expense	dakhl wa nafaqāt as-sanadāt	دخل ونفقات السندات
Security in kind	ta'mīn ʿaynī	تأمين عيني
Security, advance against	taslīf ʿalā kafāla	تسليف على كفالة
Security, collateral	kafāla maḍmūna	كفالة مضمونة
Security, joint	kafāla taḍāmuniyya	كفالة تضامنية
Seize	yaḥjiz	يحجز (يقبض على)
Seize up	1 yatajammad as-siʿr	١ - يتجمد السعر
	2 taqif dawrat al-muḍāraba	٢ - تقف دورة المضاربة
Seizure	ḥajz	حجـــز
Seizure of immovable property	ḥajz al-amwāl ghayr al-manqūla	حجز الأموال غير المنقولة
Seizure of movable property	ḥajz amwāl manqūla	حجز أموال منقولة
Self-balancing	dhāti 'l-ittizān	ذاتي الاتزان
Self-employment income	īrād dhawi 'l-mihan al-ḥurra	ايراد ذوى المهن الحرة
Self-sufficiency	iktifā' dhātī	الاكتفاء الذاتي
Sell	1 yabīʿ	١ - يبيـــع
	2 yurawwij	٢ - يـــروج
Sell and lease agreement	ittifāqiyyat bayʿ wa ījār	اتفاقية بيع وايجار
Sell off	bayʿ li't-taṣfiya	يبيع للتصفية
Sell on (U.S.)	yuqniʿ	يقنـــع [كان يقنع شخصا برأى أو بحجة]
Sell out	1 yabīʿ milkan	١ - يبيع ملكا
	2 yaḥsim sanadan	٢ - يحسم سندا
	3 yabīʿ thāniyatan	٣ - يبيع ثانية ـ بورصة

	4 yuṣaffī a'māl	٤ - يصفي أعمال (تجارة)
Seller's market	sūq al-bā'a	سوق الباعة
		[السوق التي يتحكم فيها الباعة بالمشترين نظرا لندرة البضاعة]
Seller of a call option	1 bā'i' sharṭī	١ - بائع شرطي
		[مع طلب حق الاختيار]
	2 bā'i' bi-si'r mubashir	٢ - بائع بسعر مباشر
Seller of a put option	1 mushatarī	١ - مشتر - عرض حق الاختيار
	2 bā'i' al-'arḍ ghayr al-mubāshir	٢ - بائع العرض غير المباشر
Seller's option	ḥaqq ikhtiyār al-bā'i'	حق اختيار البائع
		[في البيع خلال أجل]
Sellers over	as'ār al-bā'i'īn al-mukhaffaḍa	اسعار البائعين المخفضة
Seller, bear	bā'i' 'ala 'l-makshūf	بائع على المكشوف (بائع دون ضمان)
Selling	bay'	بيــع
Selling and administrative expenses	masarīf al-bay' wa 't-tawzī'	مصاريف البيع والتوزيع
Selling cost	taklifat al-bay'	تكلفة (مصروفات) البيع
Selling expenses	maṣārīf al-bay'	مصاريف البيع
Selling price	si'r al-bay'	سعر البيع
Semestrial	niṣf sanawī	نصف سنوى
Semi-contract	shibh 'aqd	شبه عقــد
Semi-fixed cost	taklifa shibh thābita	تكلفة شبه ثابتة
Semi-variable cost	taklifa shibh mutaghayyira	تكلفة شبه متغيرة
Senior	1 dhū afḍaliyya	١ - ذو افضلية (امتياز)
	2 aqdam	٢ - أقدم (أعلى مرتبة)
Senior accountant	muḥāsib ra'īsī	محاسب رئيسي
Senior shares	as-hum mumtāza	اسهم ممتازة
Separable cost	taklifa qābila li'l-faṣl	التكلفة القابلة للفصل
		[تكلفة مخصصة لمنتوج معين]
Separation of proprietorship	faṣl al-milkiyya	فصل الملكية
Sequence	tasalsul	تسلســل
Sequential	mutasalsil	متسلسل (مستمر ، متصل ، غير منقطع)
Sequential analysis	taḥlīl tatābu'ī	تحليل تتابعي
		[اخذ عينات عديدة في عملية مراقبة الانتاج]
Sequester	yaḥjiz	يحجز (يصادر)
Sequestered account	ḥisāb maḥjūz	حساب محجوز
		[بسبب دعوى قضائية]
Sequestered property	milkiyya maḥjūza	ملكية محجوزة
Sequestration	ḥajz	حجــز
		[حجز أموال المفلس وتوزيعها على الدائنين]
Sequestrator	ḥāris qaḍā'ī	حارس قضائي
Serial	mutasalsil	متسلسل (متتابع)

Serial bonds	sanadāt bi't-taqsīṭ	**سندات بالتقسيط** [اصدار السندات يجرى تسديد قيمتها على أقساط]
Serial numbers	arqām mutasalsila	**أرقام متسلسلة**
Series	silsila	**سلسلة** (سياق ، تتابع)
Service (adj.; n.)	1 nāfi'	١ - **نافــع**
	2 khidma	٢ - **خدمــة**
Service bureau	maktab khadamāt	**مكتب خدمات**
Service capacity	ṭāqat al-khidma	**طاقة الخدمة**
Service charge	nafaqāt al-khidma	**نفقات الخدمة**
Service cost centres	marākiz khadamāt intājiyya	**مراكز خدمات انتاجية**
Service costs	1 takālif al-khadamāt	١ - **تكاليف الخدمات**
	2 at-taklifa 'l-muṭfa'a	٢ - **التكلفة المطفأة** [أي تكلفة الاصل مطروحا منها المبلغ المتوقع استرداده نتيجة بيعه كخردة]
	3 at-taklifa 't-tashghīliyya li-dā'irat al-khadamāt	٣ - **التكلفة التشغيلية لدائرة الخدمات**
Service department	dā'irat khadamāt	**دائرة خدمات**
Service life	ḥayāt al-aṣl an-nāfi'a	**حياة الأصل النافعة**
Service unit	wiḥdat khadamāt	**وحدة خدمة**
Service yield basis	aṭ-tarīqa 'l-intājiyya li'l-istihlāk	**الطريقة الانتاجية للاستهلاك** [طريقة احتساب وتسجيل الاستهلاك حيث توزع التكلفة على مدة الانتفاع بصورة تتناسب مع وحدات الخدمة المستهلكة]
Servient tenement	amwāl khāḍi'a li-ḍarība	**أموال خاضعة ـ لضريبة**
Session	1 jalsa	١ - **جلســة**
	2 dawrat in'iqād	٢ - **دورة انعقاد**
Set	majmū'a	**مجموعة** (طقم)
Set aside	1 yaddakhir	١ - **يدخر** (يخصص)
	2 yaṭraḥ	٢ - **يطرح** (ينبذ)
Set back	1 tarāju'	١ - **تراجع ـ بورصة**
	2 takaddus	٢ - **تكــدس**
Set off accounts	at-taqāṣṣ bayn al-arṣida	**التقاص بين الأرصدة**
Setting up cost	taklifat at-tajhīz li'l-intāj	**تكلفة التجهيز للانتاج**
Settlement	1 taswiya	١ - **تسوية** (تصفية)
	2 tasdīd	٢ - **تسديــد**
Settlement account	ḥisāb taṣfiya	**حساب تصفية**
Settlement bargain	ṣafqa li-ajal	**صفقة لاجل ـ بورصة**
Settlement day	yawm at-taṣfiya	**يوم التصفية ـ بورصة**
Settlement price	1 si'r al-ilghā'	١ - **سعر الالغاء ـ بورصة**
	2 as-si'r li-ajal	٢ - **السعر لاجل**
Settlement warrant	wathīqat tafwīḍ taswiya	**وثيقة تفويض تسوية**

Set-up time	zaman at-taḥwīl	زمن التحويل
		[الوقت اللازم لتحويل ماكينة أو اسلوب انتاج من طريقة انتاج إلى اخرى]
Severance	1 tawaqquf istimrāriyyat ʿaqd	١ - توقف استمرارية عقد
	2 qaṭʿ	٢ - قطع (فصل)
Severance pay	taʿwīḍ at-tawqīf	تعويض التوقيف
		[التعويض الذى يدفع لقاء توقيف نفاذ عقد]
Sham dividend	arbāḥ ṣūriyya	أرباح صورية
Shape	shakl	شكـــل
Share	sahm	سهم (حصة)
Share bonus	as-hum minha	أسهم منحة
Share capital	ra'smāl as-hum	رأسمال أسهم
Share in kind	sahm ʿaynī	سهم عيني
Share premium	ʿalāwat iṣdār	علاوة اصدار
Share qualification	kafāla sahmiyya	كفالة سهمية
Share reinsurance	iʿādat ta'mīn nisbiyya	اعادة تأمين نسبية
		[تمييزا عن اعادة التأمين الكامل]
Share split	tajzi'at as-hum	تجزئة أسهم ـ كل سهم بسهمين مثلاً
Share warrant	hagy shira	حق شراء سهم بسعر معين
Share, cumulative preference	sahm mumtāz tarākumi 'l-arbāḥ	سهم ممتاز تراكمي الارباح
Shareholder	musāhim	مساهـــم
Shares, deferred	as-hum mu'ajjalat al-fawā'id	أسهم مؤجلة
Shares, founders'	as-hum al-mu'assisīn	أسهم المؤسسين
Shares, no-par-value	as-hum bilā qīma 'smiyya	أسهم بلا قيمة اسمية
Shares, nominative	as-hum ismiyya	أسهم اسمية
Shares, non-cumulative preference	as-hum mumtāza ghayr tarākumiyyat al-arbaḥ	أسهم ممتازة غير تراكمية الارباح
Shares, ordinary	as-hum ʿādiyya	أسهم عادية
Shares, paper	as-hum thiqa	أسهم ثقة
Shares, preferred	as-hum mumtāza	أسهم ممتازة
Shares, registered	as-hum ismiyya	أسهم اسمية
Shift	1 taghyīr	١ - تغييــر
		[الاسعار في البورصة]
	2 munawaba	٢ - مناوبة (دور)
Shipment	shaḥna	شحنة ـ بالسفن
Shipping company	sharikat milāḥa	شركة ملاحة
Shipping department	dā'irat ash-shaḥn	دائرة الشحن
Shop	1 maḥall tijārī	١ - محل تجارى
	2 mashghal	٢ - مشغـــل
Shop shares	as-hum fi'ṭ-ṭalīʿa	أسهم في الطليعة ـ بورصة
Short	1 ʿajz	١ - عجـــز
	2 bayʿ makshūf	٢ - بيع مكشوف
		[الاسهم التي لا يملكها البائع في البورصة]

	3 mablagh juz'ī	٣ - مبلغ جزئي
	4 qaṣīr	٤ - قصير (مختصر)
Short covering	taghtiyat al-bay' al-makshūf	**تغطية البيع المكشوف** [اعادة الشراء لتغطية ما بيع ـ بورصة]
Short rate	mu'addal mukhtaṣar	**المعدل المختصر** [معدل التأمين لفترة أقل من سنة وهو أعلى نسبيا من المعدل السنوى]
Short sale	bay' makshūf	**بيع مكشوف** [بيع مكشوف بدون ضمان لعدم حيازة البائع لما باعه]
Shortage	naqṣ	**نقص** (افتقار ، عدم كفاية)
Short-form procedure	ijrā' mukhtaṣar	**اجراء مختصر**
Short-form report	taqrīr al-mudaqqiq al-mukhtaṣar	**تقرير المدقق المختصر** [رأيه عن البيانات الحسابية المالية]
Short-term	qaṣīr al-ajal	**قصيـر الأجـل**
Short-term credit	i'timād qaṣīr al-ajal	**اعتماد قصير الأجل**
Short-term liabilities	iltizāmāt qaṣīrat al-ajal	**التزامات قصيرة الأجل**
Shrink	yatarāja'	**يتراجع** (يهبط ، ينكمش)
Shutdown (U.S.)	ighlāq	**اغلاق** (تجميد)
Side total	majmū' jānibī	**مجموع جانبي**
Sidehead	al-'unwān al-ufuqī	**العنوان الافقي**
Sight bill of exchange	kumbiyālat al-iṭṭilā'	**كمبيالة الاطلاع**
Sight credit	i'timād iṭṭilā'	**اعتماد اطلاع**
Sight deposits	wadā'i' ghibb aṭ-ṭalab	**ودائع غب الطلب**
Sight draft	saḥb bi'l-iṭṭilā'	**سحب بالاطلاع**
Sight rate	si'r aṣ-ṣarf lada 'ṭṭalab	**سعر الصرف لدى الطلب**
Sight, at	ghibb al-iṭṭilā'	**غب الاطلاع** (عند الطلب)
Significant	hāmm	**هام** (ذو شأن)
Significant amount	mablagh hāmm	**المبلغ الهام** [العدد المدور إلى أقرب رقم فمثلا ٤٣٩٥٦٧١/٣١٤ دك قد يدور إلى ٤,٤ مليون دك وهذا الاخير هو المبلغ الهام]
Significant units	wiḥdāt mumayyaza	**وحدات مميزة**
Silent partner	sharīk muwaṣṣī	**شريك موصي**
Silver standard	'iyār al-fiḍḍa	**عيار الفضة**
Simple	basīṭ	**بسيط** (عادى ، غير رسمي)
Simple average	al-mu'addal al-ḥisābī	**المعدل الحسابي** (المعدل البسيط)
Simple contract	'aqd ghayr rasmī	**عقد غير رسمي**
Simple debenture	sanad ghayr muwaththaq	**سند غير موثق**
Simple interest	fā'ida basīṭa	**فائدة بسيطة**
Simple trust	'i'timān basīṭ	**ائتمان بسيط** (شركة بسيطة) [الائتمان الذى يوزع أرباحا عموميا دون المساس بقيمة الائتمان الذى لا يوزع الا عند نهاية مدته]

Sine die	ilā ajal ghayr maʿlūm	إلى أجل غير معلوم
Single bill	kumbiyāla mufrada	كمبيالة مفردة
Single entry bookkeeping	aṭ-ṭarīqa ’l-mufrada fī mask ad-dafātir	الطريقة المفردة في مسك الدفاتر
Single rate of depreciation	al-muʿaddal al-fardī li’l-istihlāk	المعدل الفردى للاستهلاك
Single step income statement	bayān ad-dakhl dhu ’l-khuṭwa ’l-mufrada	بيان الدخل ذو الخطوة المفردة [وهو البيان الذى يظهر جميع عناصر المصاريف في قسم واحد وبذلك تحذف الأرصدة الوسيطة كاجمالي الربح وربح التشغيل الخ]
Sink	1 yastahlik	١ - يستهلك (يسدد ، يطفىء)
	2 yuwaẓẓif amwālan bi-khasāra	٢ - يوظف أموال بخسارة
	3 yaghraq	٣ - يغـــرق
Sinking fund account	ḥisāb al-iṭfā’ al-mustathmar	حساب الاطفاء المستثمر [حفظ النقد أو أية موجودات أخرى وفوائدها لغرض تسديد دين]
Sinking fund bond	sanad dhū iṭfā’ mustathmar	سند ذو اطفاء مسستثمر [اصدار سندات مع رصد مبالغ تكفي لتسديد قيمتها]
Sinking fund debenture	sanad dhū iṭfā’ mustathmar	سند ذو اطفاء مستثمر
Sinking fund method	ṭarīqat al-iṭfā’ al-mustathmar	طريقة الاطفاء المستثمر [حساب قسط الاطفاء على دفعات دورية متساوية بحيث اذا استثمرت هذه النفقات بفائدة مركبة بمعدل منتظم معلوم نحصل في نهاية المدة على مبلغ يعادل القيمة المهلكة للأصل]
Sinking fund reserve	iḥtyāṭī iṭfā’ as-sanadāt al-muṣaddara	احتياطي اطفاء السندات المصدرة
Site audit	tadqīq fi ’l-maqarr	تدقيق في المقر [تدقيق حسابات مؤسسة يتم في مقرها ومكاتبها وهو استعمال قديم في حسابات الحكومة]
Slack market	sūq kāsida	سوق كاسدة
Slash price	siʿr khāsir	سعر خاسر
Sleeping partner	sharīk mūṣī	شريك موص
Sliding scale	miʿyār mutaḥarrik	معيار متحرك
Slip	qasīma	قسيمة (بطاقة)
Slip back	yatarājaʿ	يتراجع (ينزلق)
Slip, deposit	qasīmat īdāʿ	قسيمة ايداع
Slow moving and obsolete stock	biḍāʿa kāsida baṭal istiʿmāluhā	بضاعة كاسدة بطل استعمالها
Sluggishness	rukūd	ركود ـ في البورصة
Slump	1 tadahwur	١ - تدهور ـ بأسعار البورصة
	2 azma qtiṣādiyya	٢ - أزمة اقتصادية

Smuggle	yuharrib	يهـرب
Social accounting	al-muḥāsaba 'l-ijtimā'iyya	المحاسبة الاجتماعية [للتحليل الاجتماعي الاقتصادى]
Social economics	al-iqtiṣād al-ijtimā'ī	الاقتصاد الاجتماعي
Social insurance	at-ta'mīn al-ijtimā'ī	التأمين الاجتماعي
Social security	aḍ-ḍamān al-ijtimā'ī	الضمان الاجتماعي
Society	jam'iyya	جمعيـــة
Soft currency	naqd ḍa'īf	نقـــد ضعيف [في قوته الشرائية]
Sold	mubā'	مبـــاع
Sold ledger	ustādh al-mabī'āt	استاذ المبيعات
Sole proprietorship	mu'assasa fardiyya	مؤسسة فردية
Solve	yaḥill	يحـــل
Solvency	yusr	يسر (ملاءة ، اقتدار) [قدرة على ايفاء الديون]
Solvent	mūṣir	موسر (ملىء ـ مقتدر)
Sort	ṣinf	صنف (نوع)
Sound	salīm	سليم (متين)
Sound currency	naqd salīm	نقد سليم
Sound value	al-qima al-ḥāliyya li'l-aṣl	القيمة الحالية للأصل
Source	mawrid	مورد (مصدر)
Source and disposition (or source and uses) statement	bayān maṣādir wa 'sti'mālāt al-amwāl	بيان مصادر واستعمالات الاموال
Source of income	maṣdar īrād	مصدر ايراد
Spare capital	māl jāhiz	مال جاهز
Spare parts	qiṭa' ghayār	قطع غيار
Special	khāṣṣ	خاص (خصوصي)
Special assessment	sharafiyya	شرفية [رسم حكومي علي المنتفع بالتحسينات أو الخدمات]
Special assessment bonds	sanadāt taḥsīnāt 'amma	سندات تحسينات عامة
Special assessment fund	ṣundūq taḥsīnāt 'amma	صندوق تحسينات عامة
Special audit	tadqīq khāṣṣ	تدقيق خاص [مداه محدد ومعين]
Special contingency reserve	iḥtiyāṭī khāṣṣ li'ṭ-ṭawāri'	احتياطي خاص للطوارىء
Special crossing	tasṭīr khāṣṣ	تسطير خاص [بالنسبة للشيك]
Special drawing rights (S.D.R.s)	ḥuqūq as-saḥb al-khāṣṣa	حقوق السحب الخاصة [ويطلق عليها ايضا اسم الذهب الورقي وهي نوع من السيولة الدولية ينشئها صندوق النقد الدولى ويوزعها على الدول الاعضاء المشتركة بنسبة حصصها في الصندوق]

Special endorsement	taẓhīr tāmm	**تظهير تام** [يذكر فيه اسم الشخص الذى يدفع له السند أو الشيك]
Special fund	ṣundūq khāṣṣ	**صندوق خاص** [يستخدم وفق قيود ادارية وقانونية معينة]
Special partnership	sharikat muḥaṣṣa	**شركة محاصة**
Special purpose financial statement	bayān mālī li-gharaḍ muḥaddad	**بيان مالي لغرض محدد**
Special revenue fund	ṣundūq ʿā'idāt khāṣṣ	صندوق عائدات خاص لتمويل نشاطات [لتمويل نشاطات معينة]
Specialisation	ikhtiṣāṣ	**اختصاص** (تخصص)
Specialised capital goods	al-muʿaddāt ar-ra'smāliyya 'l-mutakhaṣṣiṣa	**المعدات الرأسمالية المتخصصة**
Specialised equipment	muʿaddāt mutakkhaṣṣiṣa	**معدات متخصصة**
Specialist	ikhiṣṣā'ī	**اخصائـــي**
Specie	maskūkāt naqdiyya	**مسكوكات نقدية**
Specific	muḥaddad	**محـدد** (معين)
Specific cost rate	muʿaddal at-taklifa	**معدل التكلفة** [الموزعة على انتاج أو خدمة معينة على أساس كل وحدة حساب تكلفة]
Specific duties	rusūm muḥaddada	**الرسوم المحددة** [خلافا لرسم القيمة في الجمارك]
Specific invoice	fātūra muḥaddada	**فاتورة محددة**
Specific order cost system	niẓām taklifat aṭ-ṭalabiyya 'l-muḥaddada	**نظام تكلفة الطلبية المحددة** [احدى طرق محاسبة التكاليف المستعملة في تحديد تكلفة الشغلة الواحدة وذلك بتجميع عناصر التكلفة أثناء عملية الانتاج]
Specification list	qā'imat al-muwāṣafāt	**قائمة المواصفات**
Specifications	1 muwāṣafāt	**١ - مواصفـــات**
	2 daftar ash-shurūṭ	**٢ - دفتر الشروط**
Specify	yuʿayyin	**يعين** (يحدد)
Specimen of signatures card	biṭāqat namūdhaj at-tawqīʿ	**بطاقة نموذج التوقيع**
Speculate	yuḍārib	**يضـــارب**
Speculate for (on) a fall	yuḍārib bi'l-inkhifāḍ	**يضارب بالانخفاض**
Speculation	muḍāraba	**مضاربـــة**
Speculation for a rise	muḍāraba bi'l-irtifāʿ	**مضاربة بالارتفاع**
Speculation in differences	muḍāraba fi 'l-furūq	**مضاربة في الفروق**
Speculation, land	muḍāraba fi 'l-arāḍī	**مضاربة في الأراضي**
Speculation, stock	muḍāraba fi 'l-as-hum	**مضاربة في الأسهم**
Speculative	muḍārabī	**مضاربـــي** [له طابع المضاربة]
Spend	yunfiq	**ينفق** (يصرف)
Spending	infāq	**انفاق** (صرف)
Spending capacity	al-quwwa 'sh-shirā'iyya	**القوة الشرائية**

Spending estimate	taqdīr an-nafaqāt	**تقدير النفقات**
Spending, compensatory	al-infāq at-ta'wīḍī	**الانفاق التعويضي**
Spending, consumption	nafaqāt al-istihlāk	**نفقات الاستهلاك**
Spending, deficit	'ajz fi 'l-mizāniyya	**عجز في الميزانية**
Spending, government	nafaqāt ḥukūmiyya	**نفقات حكومية**
Spending, investment	nafaqāt istithmār	**نفقات استثمار** (توظيف)
Spin-off	taḥwīl al-mawjūdāt	**تحويل الموجودات** (تدوير الاصول) [تحويل بعض اصول شركة إلى شركة مؤسسة حديثا مقابل أسهم في الشركة الاخيرة]
Split off	muqāyaḍa	**مقايضـــة** [تحويل اسهم المساهمين في الشركة الأم لشركة فرعية مقابل التنازل عن جزء من اسهمهم في الشركة الأم]
Split up	iṣdār ashum iḍāfiyya	**اصدار أسهم اضافية** [إلى المساهمين الحاليين دون تغيير قيمة الرأسمال المدفوع]
Split-off point	al-ḥadd al-fāṣil	**الحد الفاصل** [بين التكاليف المشتركة لمنتوجين أو أكثر وبين التكاليف التي يمكن تحديدها لكل منتج]
Spot balance	raṣīd jāhiz	**رصيد جاهز**
Spot cash	naqd jāhiz	**نقد جاهز**
Spot check	taftīsh fujā'ī	**تفتيش فجائي**
Spot delivery	taslim mubāshir	**تسليم مباشر**
Spot exchange rate	si'r aṣ-ṣarf al-ānī	**سعر الصرف الآني**
Spot market	sūq al-biḍā'a 'l-ḥāḍira	**سوق البضاعة الحاضرة**
Spot price	si'r al-biḍā'a 'l-jāhiza	**سعر البضاعة الجاهزة**
Spot sale	bay' fawrī	**البيع الفورى** [البيع على أساس التسليم الفورى وغالبا ما يكون نقدا]
Spot transactions	ṣafaqāt fawriyya	**صفقات فورية**
Spread (n.; v.)	1 yuwazzi'	**١ - يوزع** (ينشر) [توزيع تكلفة مشتركة على مجموعة من الحسابات]
	2 farq	**٢ - فــرق** [الفرق بين السعر المعروض والسعر المدفوع] [الفرق بين سعر البيع والتكلفة المباشرة أى ربح البيع]
	3 'umūlat aḍ-ḍāmin	**٣ - عمولة الضامن**
Spread sheet	waraqat 'amal mufaṣṣala	**ورقة عمل مفصلة** [ورقة عمل لتحليل تكاليف أو معلومات محاسبية ذات بعدين]

Squander	yubaddid	يبدد (يسرف ، يبذر)
Square	yurṣid	يرصد (يسدد) حسابا
Square root	jadhr tarbīʿī	جذر تربيعي
Stabilisation	tathbīt	تثبيت (ترسيخ)
Stabilisation of money	tathbīt an-nuqūd	تثبيت النقود
Stability	istiqrār	استقرار (ثبات ، رسوخ)
Stable currency	ʿumla mustaqirra	عملة مستقرة
Staff	hay'at al-muwaẓẓafīn	هيئة الموظفين
Staff auditor	mudaqqiq	مدقق [مدقق يعمل لدى محاسب عام]
Staff provident fund	ṣundūq ṭawāri' al-muwaẓẓafīn	صندوق طوارىء الموظفين
Staffing	tawẓīf	تـوظيــــف [تكوين وتنمية الهيئة الادارية]
Stag (n.; v.)	maktab muḍārib	مكتتب مضارب [من يكتتب في أسهم جديدة بهدف بيعها بسعر يفوق سعر الاصدار]
Stage	marḥala	مرحلة (طور)
Stagnant	kāsid	كاسد (راكد ، ساكن)
Stagnation	kasād	كساد (ركود)
Stake	muqāmara	مقامرة (رهان) [حصة رأس مال في مقامرة]
Stale cheque	shīk mutaqādim	شيك متقادم
Stamp duty	rusūm damgha	رسوم دمغة
Stamp tax	ḍarībat al-khatm	ضريبة الختم
Stamp, inland revenue	ṭābaʿ mālī	طابع مالي
Stamp, receipt	ṭābāʿ mubarri' adh-dhimma	طابع مبرىء الذمة
Stand	1 yudrij 2 yasrī	١ - يـــدرج ٢ - يسرى [يبقى شرعيا أو صحيحا]
Stand over	yabqā muʿallaqan	يبقي معلقا
Standard	1 namūdhaj 2 mi'yār 3 miqyās at-taklifa	١ - نموذج ٢ - معيار ٣ - مقياس التكلفة
Standard allowance	samāh miʿyārī	سماح معيارى [قيمة النفقات التي يجب أن تحدث خلال فترة محددة في مستوى معين من النشاط الفعلى]
Standard cost	at-taklifa 'l-miʿyāriyya	التكلفة المعيارية
Standard cost rate	muʿaddal taklifa miʿyārī	معدل تكلفة معيارى
Standard cost system	niẓām at-takālīf al-miʿyāriyya	نظام التكاليف المعيارية
Standard labour time	zaman al-'āmil al-miʿyārī	زمن العامل المعيارى [لانتاج سلعة أو اتمام خدمة]
Standard machine time	zaman al-āla 'l-miʿyārī	زمن الآلة المعيارى [لانتاج سلعة معينة]

Standard margin	hāmish ar-ribḥ al-mi'yārī	**هامش الربح المعيارى**
Standard material	al-mawādd an-namūdhajiyya	**المواد النموذجية**
		[حسب المواصفات الموضوعة]
Standard method	aṭ-ṭarīqa 'l-qiyāsiyya	**الطريقة القياسية**
Standard of living	mustawa 'l-ma'īsha	**مستوى المعيشة**
Standard of value	miqyās al-qīma	**مقياس القيمـــة**
		[أساس القيمة في النظام النقدى]
Standard output	al-mardūd al-qiyāsī	**المردود القياسي**
		[كمية الانتاج المثالية]
Standard preparation hours	sā'at at-taḥḍīr al-mi'yāriyya	**ساعات التحضير المعيارية**
		[عدد الساعات المعيارية الضرورية للتحضير للعمل]
Standard price	si'r niẓāmī	**سعر نظامي** (ثابت)
Standard product	sil'a niẓāmiyya	**سلعة نظامية**
Standard profit	ribḥ niẓāmī	**ربح نظامي**
Standard purchase price	si'r ash-shirā' an-niẓāmī	**سعر الشراء النظامي**
Standard run quantity; economic lot size	al-hajm al-iqttiṣādī	**الحجم الاقتصادى**
		[عدد الوحدات المطلوبة في عملية شراء واحدة أو التي يتم انتاجها في دورة واحدة قبل تحويل الآلات إلى انتاج صنف آخر بحيث تحمل أقل نفقات ممكنة أو تتحقق اقصى الفوائد]
Standard, gold	qā'idat adh-dhahab	**قاعدة الذهب**
Standard, gold exchange	miqyās at-tabādul adh-dhahabī	**مقياس التبادل الذهبي**
Standard, gold specie	qā'idat al-masbūkāt adh-dhahabiyya	**قاعدة المسبوكات الذهبية**
Standard, monetary	al-qā'ida 'n-naqdiyya	القاعدة النقدية
Standardisation	tawḥīd	**توحيـــــد**
		[توحيد المقاييس أو النمط]
Standardise	yuwaḥḥid	**يوحـــد**
		[القياس أو النمط]
Standby	iḥtiyāṭī	**احتياطـــي**
Standby cost; fixed cost	at-taklifa 'th-thābita	**التكلفة الثابتـة**
Standby credit	i'timād da'm	**اعتماد دعـم**
Standby equipment	mu'addāt iḥtiyāṭiyya	**معدات احتياطية**
Standby underwriting	kafāla 'ḥtiyāṭiyya	**كفالة احتياطية**
		[اتفاقية لشراء ما تبقى من أصدار سندات بعد أن مارس جزء من المساهمين حق الشفعة باستبدال أسهمهم القديمة بجديدة]
Standing	1 dā'im	١ - **دائـم** (قائم ، سار)
	2 thābit	٢ - **ثابت** (محدد ، مستقر)
Standing body	hay'a dā'ima	**هيئة دائمة**
Standing cost (charge, or expenses)	nafaqāt 'āmma dā'ima	**نفقات عامة دائمة**

Standing order	amr dā'im	أمـــر دائـــم
Standing over accounts	ḥisābāt bāqiya makshūfa	حسابات باقية مكشوفة
Standing price	si'r thābit	سعر ثابت
Standstill	tawaqquf	توقف (سكون ، ركود)
Standstill, wage	tajmīd al-ujūr	تجميد الاجور
Staple	1 ra'īsī	١ - رئيسي (أساسي)
	2 mādda khāmm	٢ - مـادة خـام
Staple commodity	sil'a ra'īsiyya	سلعة رئيسية
Staple products	muntajāt al-istihlāk ar-ra'īsiyya	منتجات الاستهلاك الرئيسية
Starting load cost	taklifat at-tahayyu' li'l-'amal	تكلفة التهيؤ للعمل
Starvation wages	ujūr taḥt al-ḥadd al-adnā	أجور تحت الحد الأدنى
State bank	maṣrif ad-dawla	مصرف الدولة
Stated capital	1 ar-ra'smāl al-madfū'	١ - الرأسمال المدفوع
	2 ar-ra'smāl al-qānūnī	٢ - الرأسمال القانوني
Stated liabilities	al-iltizāmāt al-muṣarraḥ 'anhā	الالتزامات المصرح عنها [كما تظهر في دفاتر الحسابات أو في بيان مالي]
Stated value	qīmat as-sahm al-madfū'a	قيمة السهم المدفوعة
Statement	bayān	بيان (كشف)
Statement analysis	bayān taḥlīlī	بيان تحليلي
Statement form; report form	uslūb at-taqrīr	اسلوب التقرير
Statement heading	'unwān al-bayān	عنوان البيان
Statement of account	kashf al-ḥisāb	كشف الحساب
Statement of affairs	1 bayān al-awḍā' al-māliyya	١ - بيان الأوضاع المالية
	2 mīzāniyyat at-taṣfiya	٢ - ميزانية التصفية
Statement of assets and liabilities (or condition, financial condition or financial position)	1 mīzāniyya 'umūmiyya	١ - ميزانية عمومية
	2 bayān al-wad' al-mālī	٢ - بيان الوضع المالي [لمؤسسة لا تحتفظ بدفاتر قيد]
Statement of earned surplus	bayān al-arbāḥ al-muḥtafaẓa	بيان الأرباح المحتفظة
Statement of income	bayān ad-dakhl	بيان الدخـــل
Statement of loss and gain (or profit and loss)	bayān al-arbāḥ wa 'l-khasā'ir	بيان الأرباح والخسائر
Statement of realisation and liquidation	bayān at-taḥṣīl wa 't-taṣfiya	بيان التحصيل والتصفية [في حالة توقف شركة عن العمل]
Statement of receipts and disbursements	bayān al-maqbūḍāt wa 'l-madfū'āt	بيان المقبوضات والمدفوعات [بيان بالنقد الداخل والخارج خلال أية فترة محدودة]
Statement of resources and their application; statement of sources and application of funds	bayān maṣādir wa's-tikhdāmāt al-amwāl	بيان مصادر واستخدامات الأموال
Statement of revenues and expenditures	bayān al-īrādāt wa 'l-maṣrūfāt	بيان الايرادات والمصروفات

Statement of stockholders equity (or investment or net worth)	bayān ḥuqūq al-musāhimīn	**بيان حقوق المساهمين** [بيان يبين قيمة الرأسمال المدفوع والأرباح الصافية والتغيرات التي طرأت عليها منذ آخر تقرير]
Statement, cash	kashf aṣ-ṣundūq	**كشف الصندوق**
Statement, financial	kashf al bayānāt al māliyya	**البيانات المالية**
Statement, operating	kashf at-tashghīl	**كشف التشغيل** (بيان)
Stationery	qirṭāsiyya	**قرطاسيــــة**
Statistic	qīma iḥṣā'iyya	**قيمة احصائية**
Statistical	iḥṣā'ī	**احصـائـــــي**
Statistical control	ḍabṭ iḥṣā'ī	**الضبط الاحصائي**
Statistical distribution	tawzī' iḥṣā'ī	**التوزيع الاحصائي**
Statistical profit	ribḥ iḥṣā'ī	**ربح احصائي**
Statistical quality control	ar-riqāba 'n-naw'iyya 'l-iḥṣā'iyya	**الرقابة النوعية الاحصائية**
Statistical series	silsila iḥṣā'iyya	**سلسلة احصائية**
Statistics	1 'ilm al-iḥṣā'	**١ - علم الاحصاء**
	2 iḥṣā'iyyāt	**٢ - احصائيات**
Status, financial	al-waḍ' al-mālī	**الوضع المالي**
Statutory auditor	murāqib ḥisābāt qānūnī	**مراقب حسابات قانوني** [يعين من قبل المساهمين وفقا لنظام الشركة]
Statutory reserve	iḥtiyāṭī qānūnī	**احتياطي قانوني**
Steady price	si'r thābit	**سعر ثابت**
Steering committee	lajnat at-tawjīh	**لجنة التوجيه**
Stenography	ikhtizāl	**الاختـــزال**
Step up	yazīd as-si'r	**يزيد السعر**
Sterling area	mantiqat al-istirlīnī	**منطقة الاسترليني**
Sterling exchange standard	qā'idat aṣ-ṣarf bi'l-junayh al-istirlīnī	**قاعدة الصرف بالجنيه الاسترليني**
Stiff market	sūq mutamassika	**سوق متمسكة**
Stiff price	si'r fāḥsh	**سعــر فاحـش**
Stipend	rātib	**راتب** (معاش)
Stipendiary	dhū rātib mu'ayyan	**ذو راتب معين**
Stipulated damages; liquidated damages	aḍrār muttafaq 'ala mabālighihā	**أضرار متفق على مبالغها**
Stock	1 as-hum	**١ - أســـهم** [الرأسمال القانوني الموزع على أسهم]
	2 shahādat as-hum	**٢ - شهادة أسهم**
	3 al-biḍā'a	**٣ - البضاعة** [المخزون من السلع]
Stock adjustment	taswiyat al-makhāzin	**تسوية المخازن**
Stock allotment; bonds allotment	takhṣīṣ al-as-hum/as-sanadāt	**تخصيص الأسهم** (السندات) [تخصيص أنصبة المكتتبين في الأسهم أو السندات]
Stock arbitrage	taslīf 'alā as-hum	**تسليف على أسهم**

Stock book	daftar al-makhāzin	دفتر المخازن
Stock cards	biṭāqat al-makhāzin	بطاقات المخازن
Stock certificate	shahādat al-as-hum	شهادة الاسهم
Stock company	sharika musāhama	شركة مساهمة
Stock discount	khaṣm ʿala ʾs-sahm	خصم على السهم
		[زيادة القيمة الاسمية على الرأسمال المدفوع]
Stock dividend	sahm minḥa	سـهم منحـة
		[أرباح على شكل أسهم]
Stock exchange	sūq al-awrāq al-māliyya	سوق الاوراق المالية (بورصة)
Stock exchange list	lāʾiḥat asʿār al-burṣa	لائحة أسعار البورصة
Stock exchange operator	mudārib fi ʾl-burṣa	مضارب في البورصة
Stock exchange quotation	tasʿīrat al-burṣa	تسعيرة البورصة
Stock in trade	al-baḍāʾiʿ as-sāʾira	البضائع السا ئرة
		[البضائع المعدة للبيع ضمن نطاق العمل الاعتيادى]
Stock ledger	ustādh al-baḍāʾiʿ al-jāhiza	استاذ البضاعة الجاهزة
Stock market	sūq al-awrāq al-māliyya	سوق الاوراق المالية
Stock on hand	biḍāʿa fi ʾl-mutanāwal	بضاعة في المتناول
		[مخزون المواد الخام والبضائع وما شابه ذلك]
Stock option	khiyār al-as-hum	خيـار الأسـهم
		[الحق في شراء أسهم شركة تحت ظروف معينة تتعلق بالوقت والثمن والمبلغ]
Stock owner	mālik as-hum	مالـك أسـهم
Stock purchase warrant	imtiyāz shirāʾ as-hum	امتياز شراء أسهم
		[شهادة تمنح حاملها الحق في شراء عدد معين من الأسهم بسعر محدد وخلال فترة محددة]
Stock record card	biṭāqat al-makhzūn	بطاقة المخزون
Stock register	sijill al-as-hum	سجل الأسهم
Stock retirement	istirdād al-as-hum	استرداد الأسهم
Stock right	ḥaqq al-musāhimīn	حق المساهمين
		[في شراء الاسهم الجديدة]
Stock sheet	kashf jard	كشف جرد
Stock split	tajziʾat as-hum	تجزئة أسهم
Stock taking	jard al-makhāzin	جرد المخازن
Stock taking sale	bayʿ bi-sabab al-jard	بيع بسبب الجرد
Stock taking value	qīmat al-jard	قيمة الجرد
Stock taking (physical)	jard fiʿlī	جـرد فعلـي
Stock transfer book	sijill taḥwīl al-ashum	سجل تحويل الأسهم
Stock, capital	raʾsmāl ash-sharika	رأسمال الشركة
Stock, closing	biḍāʿat ākhir al-mudda	بضاعة آخر المدة
Stock, fixed	al-makhzūn ath-thābit	المخزون الثابت
Stock, fully paid-up	as-hum madfūʿat al-qiyam	أسهم مدفوعة القيم

Stock, gilt-edged	sanadāt maḍmūna	سندات مضمونة
Stock, glamour (U.S.)	al-as-hum aṭ-ṭalīʿiyya	الأسهم الطليعية [الأسهم الموجهة أو القدوة نظرا لشهرتها]
Stock, good delivery	sanadāt at-taslīm al-kāmil	سندات التسليم الكامل
Stock, government	sanadāt ḥukūmiyya	سندات حكومية (عامة)
Stock, joint	ra'smāl mushtarak	رأسمال مشترك
Stock, negotiable	sahm qābil li't-tadāwul	سهم قابل للتداول
Stock, operating	biḍāʿat awwal al-mudda	بضاعة أول المدة
Stock, registered	as-hum ismiyya	أسهم اسمية
Stock, stagnant	silaʿ kāsida	سلع كاسدة
Stockbroker	simsār al-as-hum	سمسار الاسهم
Stockholder	musāhim	مساهم
Stockholder's equity; net worth	ḥuqūq al-musāhimīn	حقوق المساهمين
Stockholder's tax	ḍarība ʿalā ʿā'idāt al-ashum	ضريبة على عائدات الأسهم
Stop payment	īqāf ad-dafʿ	ايقاف الدفع [التوقف عن صرف قيمة شيك بناء على طلب العميل]
Storage	khazn	خزن (تخزين)
Storage facilities	tashīlāt al-khazn	تسهيلات الخزن (وسائل الحفظ) تخزين
Store(n.; v.)	makhzan	مخزن ـ يخزن
Store accounting	muḥāsabat al-makhāzin	محاسبة المخازن
Stores	1 makhāzin 2 mawādd awwaliyya wa tajhizāt	١ - مخازن ٢ - مواد اولية وتجهيزات
Straight-line depreciation method	ṭarīqat al-qisṭ ath-thābit fī ḥisāb al-istihlāk	طريقة القسط الثابت في حساب الاستهلاك
Strike (n.; v.)	iḍrāb	اضراب ـ يضرب عن العمل
Strike a balance (v.)	yuthbit ar-raṣīd	يثبت الرصيد
Stringency	ʿusr	عسر [صعوبة الحصول على المال]
Strongroom; vault	ghurfa muḥaṣṣana	الغرفة المحصنة [غرفة كبيرة محصنة تكون عادة تحت الأرض توضع فيها أموال المصرف]
Stub	arūma	أرومة
Stumer cheque	shīk bi-dūn raṣīd	شيك بدون رصيد
Subcontract	ʿaqd farʿī	عقد فرعي
Subcontractor	muqawil min al-baṭin	مقاول من الباطن
Subdivide	yujazzi' al-ajzā'	يجزىء الأجزاء
Subject of the contract	mawḍū' al-'aqd	موضوع العقد
Subjective value	qīma dhātiyya	قيمة ذاتية [القيمة المخصصة لأصل من قبل الادارة دون الرجوع إلى سعر السوق]
Subjoin	yuḍīf	يضيف (يرفق بـ ، يضم)
Sublease	ījār thānawī	ايجار ثانوى

Sublet	yu'ajjir min al-bāṭin	يؤجر من الباطن
Submit	yuqaddim	يقــدم (يرفع إلــى)
Submit quotations	yuqaddim al-as'ār	يقدم الأســعار
Subordinate	mar'ūs	مرؤوس (تابع ، ثانوى)
Subordinate managers	mudīrūn far'iyyūn	المديرون الفرعيون
Subordinate principles	mabādi' far'iyya	مبادىء فرعية
Subordinated debt	dayn thānawī	ديـن ثانــوى [دين يأتي ترتيبه بعد المبالغ المستحقة للدائنين العموميين]
Subrogate	1 yunīb 2 yastabdil	١ - ينيب (يوكل) ٢ - يستبدل
Subrogation	1 ināba 2 iḥlāl	١ - انابة قانونية ٢ - احــــلال [حلول الشركة المؤمنة محل المؤمن في الحقوق والمطالبات]
Subscribe	yaktatib	يكتتب (يشترك في)
Subscribed capital stock	ra'smāl muktatab bihi	رأسمال مكتتب به
Subscriber	muktatab	مكتتب (مشترك)
Subscription	iktitāb	اكتتاب (اشتراك)
Subscription certificates	shahādāt iktitāb	شهادة اكتتاب
Subscription rental	dhimmat al-ishtirāk	ذمة الاشتراك
Subscription right (or warrant)	ḥaqq al-iktitāb	حــق الاكتتاب [صك بحق اكتتاب المساهم في أسهم جديدة]
Subsequent	lāḥiq	لاحــق (تـال)
Subsequent events	aḥdāth lāḥiqa	الأحداث اللاحقــة
Subsequent payments	madfū'āt lāḥiqa	مدفوعات لاحقة
Subsequent transactions	ṣafaqāt lāḥiqa	صفقات لاحقــة
Subsidiary	far'ī	فرعــي (اضافــي)
Subsidiary accounts	ḥisābāt thānawiyya	حسابات ثانوية
Subsidiary bank	maṣrif tābi'	المصـرف التابع
Subsidiary book	daftar musā'id	دفتـر مساعــد
Subsidiary company	sharika tābi'a	شركة تابعة (شركة فرعية)
Subsidiary company accounting	muḥāsabat ash-sharika 'l-far'iyya	محاسبة الشركة الفرعية [الطريقة التي تتبعها الشركة الفرعية في تسجيل العمليات التجارية مع الشركة الأم]
Subsidiary ledger	ustādh musā'id	استاذ مساعد
Subsidiary store	makhzan far'ī	مخزن فرعي
Subsidise	yu'īn māliyyan	يعين ماليا (يقدم اعانة مالية)
Subsidy	i'āna māliyya	اعانة مالية
Subsistence allowance	mukhaṣṣaṣāt al-i'āsha	مخصصات الاعاشة
Subsistence in kind	i'āsha 'ayniyya	اعاشة عينية
Substandard	dūn al-mustawā	دون المستــوى

Substantial	ḍarūrī	**ضروري** (جوهري ، أساسي ، لا يستهان به)
Substitute (n.; v.)	badīl	**بـديل ـ يبـدل**
Substitute materials	mawādd badīla	**مـواد بديلـة**
Substitution	istibdāl	**استبدال** (تبديل)
Subtenant	mu'ajjar min al-bāṭin	**مؤجر من الباطن**
Sub title	'unwān far'ī	**عنوان فرعي**
Subtotal	majmū' far'ī	**مجموع فرعي**
Subtract	yaṭraḥ	**يطـــــرح**
Subtraction	ṭarh	**طـــــرح**
Subvention	1 minḥa māliyya	**١ - منحة مالية** [من مؤسسة لفرد أو لمؤسسة]
	2 i'āna māliyya	**٢ - اعانة ماليـــة**
Succession tax	ḍarībat al-mīrāth	**ضريبة الميراث**
Sufficient	kāfī	**كـاف** (واف)
Sufficient condition	sharṭ kāfī	**شـرط كـاف**
Sum	1 mablagh	**١ - مبلـــغ**
	2 majmū'	**٢ - مجمـــوع**
Sum of the years (digits) method	ṭarīqat majmū' as-sanawāt	**طريقة مجموع السنوات** [هي طريقة حسابية للوصول إلى نسبة الاستهلاك فان كان عمر الأصل ٥ سنوات تكون النسبة الأولى ٥/١٥ (١٥ هي مجموع السنوات ٥ + ٤ + ٣ + ٢ + ١) والنسبة في آخر سنة هي ١/١٥]
Sum, exempted	al-mablagh al-mu'fā	**المبلغ المعفي**
Sum, lump	mablagh ijmālī	**مبلـغ اجمالـــي**
Summary	khulāṣa	**خـلاصـــة**
Summary of work done	khulāṣat al-'amal al-munjaz	**خلاصة العمل المنجز**
Sundries account	ḥisāb al-bunud al-mutanawwi'a	**حساب البنود المتنوعة**
Sundry	mutanawwi'	**متنوع** (متعدد)
Sundry expenses	maṣrūfāt mutanawwi'a	**مصروفات متنوعة** (نثرية)
Sunk cost	taklifa hālika	**تكلفة هالكـــة** [تكلفة ماضية ناتجة عن قرار لا يمكن تعديله حاليا]
Superannuation	al-iḥāla ila 'l-ma'āsh	**الاحالة إلى المعاش**
Supertax	ḍarība iḍāfiyya	**ضريبة اضافيـــة**
Supervise	yushrif 'alā	**يشرف على** (يراقب)
Supervision	ishrāf	**اشراف** (مراقبة ، ملاحظة)
Supervisor	mushrif	**مشرف** (مراقب)
Supplement (n.; v.)	takmila	**تكملة ـ يكمل**
Supplemental appropriation	i'timādāt iḍāfiyya	**اعتمادات اضافية**
Supplementary	takmīlī	**تكميلي** (اضافي ، ملحق)
Supplementary budget	mīzāniyya tikmīliyya	**ميزانية تكميلية**
Supplementary cost	taklifa iḍāfiyya	**تكلفة اضافية**

Supplier	muwarrid	مـــــورد (ممون)
Supplier's invoice	fātūrat muwarrid	فاتورة مورد
Supplies	tamwīnāt	تموينات (امدادات)
Supply	yumawwin	يمـــون (يجهز)
Supply and demand	al-ʿarḍ wa'ṭ-ṭalab	العرض والطلب
Supply curve	munḥana 'l-ʿarḍ	منحني العرض
Supply price	siʿr al-ʿarḍ	سعر العرض [السعر الواجب دفعه من أجل الحصول ضمن فترة محددة من الزمن وفي مكان محدد كمية من السلع]
Support (n.; v.)	daʿm	دعم (اعالة) - يدعم (يعيل)
Support price by buying	yudaʿim al-asʿār bi'ash-shirā'	يدعم الأسعار بالشراء
Suppporting record	sijillāt musāʿida	سجلات مساعدة [مجموعة من البطاقات أو الأوراق السائبة التي تساعد في المحافظة على دقة حساب الاستاذ]
Surcharge (n.; v.)	1 ḍarība iḍāfiyya 2 yazīd as-siʿr	١ - ضريبة إضافية ٢ - يزيد السعر
Surety	1 kafāla 2 kafīl	١ - كفالة (ضمانة) ٢ - كفيل (ضامن)
Surety bond	sanad kafāla	سند كفالـــة
Surety of a bill	ḍāmin as-sanad	ضامن السند
Surplus	fā'iḍ	فائض (زائد)
Surplus analysis	taḥlīl al-fā'iḍ	تحليل الفائض
Surplus at date of acquisition; acquired surplus	fā'iḍ muktasab	الفائض المكتسب
Surplus capacity	ṭāqa intājiyya fā'iḍa	طاقة انتاجية فائضة
Surplus charge	nafaqa fā'iḍa	نفقة فائضة [أية نفقة أو خسارة أو تكلفة تقيد مباشرة على حساب الفائض بدلا من قيدها من خلال بيان الايرادات والمصروفات]
Surplus dividend	ribḥ iḍāfī	ربح اضافـي [يوزع على المساهمين بالاضافة إلى الربح الأول]
Surplus from consolidation	fa'iḍ at-tawḥīd	فائض التوحيد [زيادة القيمة الدفترية في تاريخ الاقتناء على تكلفة اقتناء اسهم الشركات التابعة منقوصا منها العلاوات على شراء الأسهم الأخرى المقتناة]
Surplus from revaluation of fixed assets	fā'iḍ iʿādat taqyīm al-mawjūdat ath-thābita	فائض اعادة تقييم الموجودات الثابتة
Surplus profit	ribḥ fā'iḍ	ربح فائض
Surplus reserve	iḥtiyāṭī iḍāfī	احتياطي اضافي

Surplus value	fā'iḍ al-qīma	فائض القيمة (القيمة الزائدة)
Surprise audit	tadqīq mufāji'	تدقيق مفاجىء
Surprise count	ti'dād mufāji'	تعداد مفاجىء
Surprise test check	faḥṣ ikhtibārī mufāji'	الفحص الاختباری المفاجیء
Surrender value (of an insurance)	al-qīma 'l-mustaradda	القيمة المستردة [قيمة استرداد بوليصة تأمين لدى الغائها]
Surtax	ḍarība iḍāfiyya	ضريبة اضافية
Survey (n.; v.)	mu'āyana	معاينة (دراسة) - يستعرض
Survey report	taqrīr mu'āyana	تقرير معاينة
Survivor life curve	munḥana 'l-ḥayāh	منحني الحياة [المقدرة الحقيقية لمجموعة أفراد]
Suspend	yūqif	يوقف (يعلق)
Suspended action	da'wā mawqūfa	دعوى موقوفة
Suspended debts	dhimam mawqūfa	ذمم موقوفة
Suspense account	ḥisāb mu'allaq	حساب معلق
Suspension of payment	tawaqquf 'an ad-daf'	توقف عن الدفع
Suspension, complete	tawqīf kullī	توقيف كلي
Suspension, partial	tawqīf juz'ī	توقيف جزئي
Sustain	1 yataḥammal 2 yad'am	١ - يتحمل (يعاني) ٢ - يدعم
Swap (n.; v.)	mubādala	مبادلة (مقايضة) ـ يبادل (يقايض)
Swindle	yaghish	يغش (يحتال)
Swings	taqallubāt al-as'ār	تقلبات الأسعار
Swings, cyclical	taqallubāt dawriyya	التقلبات الدورية
Syndical	niqābī	نقابي
Syndicate	niqāba	نقابة
System	niẓām	نظام
System of accounts	niẓām muḥāsabī	نظام محاسبي
Systematic	niẓāmī	نظامي (منهجي)
Systematic error	khaṭa' muntaẓim	خطأ منتظم
Systematic sampling	mu'āyana muntaẓima	معاينة منتظمة [أخذ عينات بصورة منتظمة]
T-account	ḥisāb 'alā shakl T	حساب على شكل T [يستعمل لبيان تأثير عملية أو سلسلة عمليات لحل بعض الصعوبات المحاسبية]
Table	jadwal	جدول
Table of allowances	jadwal 'alāwāt	جدول علاوات (جدول مخصصات)
Table of contents	al-muḥtawayāt	المحتويات
Table of par values	jadwal al-qiyam al-mutakafi'a	جدول القيم المتكافئة
Tabular	mujadwal	مجدول
Tabulate	1 yujadwil	١ - يجدول

	2 yuṣannif	٢ - يصنـــف
Tabulating machine	ālat jadwala	آلة جدولــة
Tabulator	1 wāḍiʻ al-jadāwil	١ - واضع الجداول
	2 adāt rasm al-jadāwil	٢ - أداة رسم الجداول
Tacit renewal	tajdīd ḍimnī	تجديد ضمـني
Tag	biṭāqa	بطاقـــة [عادة صغيرة لاظهار السعر أو العنوان الخ]
Take issue	yuʻāriḍ	يعارض (يختلف مع ، يناقش)
Take off	yukhaffiḍ ath-thaman	يخفض الثمن (يطرح ، يحذف)
Take on	1 yataʻahhad bi	١ - يتعهد بـ
	2 yastakhdim	٢ - يستخدم ـ عمالا
Take out	1 yasḥab	١ - يسحـــب
	2 yatasallam	٢ - يتسلم (يحصل)
Take over an issue (v.)	yamtaṣ	يمتص (يستغرق اصدارا)
Take possession of	yaḍaʻ al-yad ʻalā	يضع اليد على
Take stock	yajrud	يجـــرد
Take up a bill (v.)	yadfaʻ qīmat kumbiyāla	يدفع قيمة كمبيالة
Take up shares (v.)	yaktatib fī as-hum	يكتتب في أسهم
Takeover	istīlā’	استيـــلاء [شركة على أخرى]
Tally sheet	ṣafḥat al-muṭābaqa	صفحة المطابقة
Tangible asset	aṣl ḥaqīqī	أصل حقيقي
Tangible value	qīmat al-aṣl al-haqīqī	قيمة الأصل الحقيقي
Tap a new market (v.)	yaftaḥ sūqan jadīda	يفتح سوقا جديدة
Tare	wazn al-fārigh	وزن الفـارغ
Target cost; standard cost	taklifa mi’yāriyya	تكلفة معيارية
Target date	tārīkh muḥaddad	تاريخ محدد
Tariff	rasm	رســـم (تعرفة)
Tariff insurance	taʻrifat at-ta’mīn	تعرفة التأمين
Tariff walls (or barriers)	al-ḥawājiz al-jumrukiyya	الحواجز الجمركية
Tariff, decreasing	at-ta’rifa’ t-tanāquṣiyya	التعرفة التناقصية
Tariff, fixed	taʻrifa maḥdūda	تعرفة محددة
Tariff, obligatory	taʻrifa jabriyya	تعرفة جبرية
Tariff, preferential	taʻrifa tafḍīliyya	تعرفة تفضيلية
Tariffication	ikhḍāʻ li-taʻrifa	اخضاع لتعرفة
Tax	ḍarība	ضريبـــة
Tax administration	maṣlaḥat aḍ-ḍarā’ib	مصلحة الضرائب
Tax anticipation note (or warrant)	ish‘ār jibāyat aḍ-ḍarā’ib	اشعار جباية الضرائب
Tax arrears	al-bāqī min aḍ-ḍarā’ib	الباقي من الضرائب
Tax assessment	taqdīr aḍ-ḍarība	تقدير الضريبة
Tax base	qāʻidat farḍ aḍ-ḍarā’ib	قاعدة فرض الضرائب

Tax benefit rule	qā'idat al-istifāda 'd-ḍarībiyya	قاعدة الاستفادة الضريبية [جواز حذف بنود من الدخل الاجمالى كاسترداد دين ميت إن كان الخصم الخاص بهذا الدين في سنة سابقة لم يؤثر في تخفيض ضريبة الدخل المدفوعة في تلك السنة]
Tax certificate	shahādat daf' aḍ-ḍarā'ib	شهادة دفع الضرائب
Tax dodging (U.S.)	taharrub min daf' aḍ-ḍarā'ib	تهرب من دفع الضرائب
Tax exemption	i'fā' min aḍ-ḍarā'ib	اعفاء من الضرائب
Tax free	mu'fā min aḍ-ḍarība	معفي من الضريبة
Tax lien	ḥajz ḍarā'ibī	حجز ضرائبي [حجز ممتلكات لحين دفع الضريبة]
Tax limit	al-ḥadd al-aqṣā li'd-ḍarība	الحد الأقصى للضريبة
Tax load (U.S.)	mablagh aḍ-ḍarība	مبلغ الضريبة
Tax payer	dāfi' aḍ-ḍarība	دافع الضريبة (مكلف)
Tax rate	mu'addal aḍ-ḍarība	معدل الضريبة
Tax relief	takhfīḍ aḍ-ḍarība	تخفيض الضريبة
Tax roll	jadwal at-taḥqquq aḍ-ḍarībī	جدول التحقق الضريبي
Tax table	jadwal ḍarā'ib	جدول ضرائب
Tax write-off (U.S.)	takhfīḍ min bayān aḍ-ḍarība	تخفيض من بيان الضريبة
Tax, gradual	ḍarība tadrījiyya	ضريبة تدريجية
Tax, progressive	ḍarība taṣā'idiyya	ضريبة تصاعدية
Tax, single-system	niẓām aḍ-ḍarība 'l-wāḥida	نظام الضريبة الواحدة
Tax, turnover	ḍarība 'alā raqm al-a'māl	ضريبة على رقم الاعمال
Tax, value added (V.A.T. –U.K.)	ḍarība iḍāfiyya 'ala 'l-qīma	ضريبة اضافية على القيمة
Taxable income	ad-dakhl al-khāḍi' li'd-ḍarība	الدخل الخاضع للضريبة
Taxable profits	arbāḥ khāḍi'a li'd-ḍarība	أرباح خاضعة للضريبة
Taxable year	sana ḍarībiyya	السنة الضريبية [السنة المالية التي تخضع حساباتها للضريبة]
Taxation	farḍ ḍarība	فرض ضريبة (تكليف بضريبة)
Taxation, double	izdiwāj aḍ-ḍarība	ازدواج الضريبة
Taxation, incentive	ḍarība ḥāfiza	الضريبة الحافزة
Taxes receivable	raṣīd ad-darā'ib ghayr al-muḥaṣṣala	رصيد الضرائب غير المحصلة
Taxes, delinquent	ḍarā'ib muta'akhkhira	ضرائب متأخرة [لم تدفع في موعدها]
Team work	'amal jamā'ī	عمل جماعي (مشترك)
Temporary admission	idkhāl mu'aqqat	ادخال مؤقت
Temporary disablement	'ajz mu'aqqat	عجز مؤقت ـ في عقود التأمين
Temporary investment	istithmār mu'aqqat	استثمار مؤقت
Temporary precautions	tadābīr mu'aqqata	تدابير مؤقتة
Temporary procedure	ijrā' mu'aqqat	اجراء مؤقت
Tenancy	1 Ījār 2 muddat al-isti'jar	١ - إيجـار ٢ - مدة الاستئجار

Tenancy in common	ījār mushtarak	إيجار مشترك
Tenant	musta'jir	مستأجــر
Tenant's (third party) risks	akhṭār nājima 'an at-ta'jīr	الأخطار الناجمة عن التأجير
Tender (n.; v.)	munāqaṣa	مناقصة (عطاء) ـ يقدم عرضا
Tender deposits	ta'mīnāt al-'aṭā'āt	تأمينات العطاءات
Tender, invitation for	ṭarḥ bi'l-munāqaṣa	طرح بالمناقصة (طلب عروض)
Tender, legal	si'r rasmī	سعـر رسمــي
Tender, sale by	bay' bi'l-munāqaṣa	بيع بالمناقصة
Tentative	tajrībī	تجريبي (اختباري ، تمهيدى)
Tentative balance sheet	mīzāniyya tamhīdiyya	ميزانية تمهيدية [ليست نهائية ومعدة للبحث وامكانية التعديل]
Tentative draft (U.S.)	mushrū' tamhīdī	مشروع تمهيدى
Term	1 mudda	١ - مدة (أجل)
	2 sharṭ	٢ - شــرط
	3 iṣṭilāḥ	٣ - اصطـلاح
Term bonds	sanadāt mawqūta	سندات موقوتة [تستحق في نفس التاريخ]
Term days	tawārīkh istiḥqāq al-ījārāt	تواريخ استحقاق الايجارات
Term insurance	ta'mīn mawqut	تأمين موقوت [التأمين على الحياة لتاريخ معين]
Term loan	qarḍ maḥdūd al-ajal	قرض محدود الأجل
Term of credit	muddat istiḥqāq	مدة استحقاق
Term of limitation	muddat at-taqādum	مدة التقادم
Term, initial	mudda aṣliyya	المدة الأصلية (الفترة الأولى)
Terms and conditions of account	shurūt al-ḥisāb	شروط الحساب
Terms of a ratio	ḥadd an-nisba	حــد النسبة
Terms of payment	shuruṭ ad-daf'	شــروط لدفع
Terminable	qābil li'l-faskh	قابل للفسخ (قابل للانتهاء)
Terminable annuity	daf'a sanawiyya	دفعة سنوية لأجل محدد [تدفع نظير مبلغ يدفع لشركة التأمين مقدما]
Terminal account	ḥisāb nihā'ī	حساب نهائي
Terminal cost	takālīf nihā'iyya	تكاليف نهائية
Terminal price	si'r at-taslīm	سعر التسليم (بورصة)
Terminate	yunhī	ينهى (يبطل ، يفسخ)
Termination	inhā'	انهــــاء
Territorial manager	mudīr iqlīmī	مدير اقليمي
Test (n.; v.)	ikhtibār	اختبار ـ يختبر
Test basis	asās ikhtibārī	أساس اختبارى
Test check	tadqīq	تدقيق (معاينة ، فحص)
Test count	ti'dād ikhtibārī	تعداد اختبارى
Testamentary trust	wadī'a mukawwana bi-waṣiyya	وديعة مكونة بوصية
Testator	al-mūṣī	الموصــي

Testing	ikhtibār	**اختبار** (امتحان ، تجربة)
Theft	sariqa	**سرقة** (اختلاس)
Theoretical inventory	al-jard an-naẓarī	**الجرد النظرى**
Theory of comparative costs	naẓariyyat an-nafaqāt an-nisbiyya	**نظرية النفقات النسبية**
Theory, double entry	naẓariyyat al-qayd al-muzdawij	**نظرية القيد المزدوج**
Third party	ṭaraf thālith	**طرف ثالث**
Third party insurance	ta'mīn ḍidd al-ghayr	**تأمين ضد الغير**
Third party liability	iltizāmāt al-ghayr	**التزامات الغير**
Through freight	ujrat shaḥn shāmila	**اجرة شحن شاملة**
Tickler	munabbih	**المنبـــــه** [كسجل الالتزامات المستحقة أو أية أمور هامة يجب الانتباه إليها في حينها]
Tie-in (U.S.)	sharṭī	**شرطـــــي**
Tie-in sale	bay' sharṭī	**بيع شرطي**
Tie up	yujammid	**يجمد** (يثبت)
Tied loan	qarḍ sharṭi	**قرض شرطي**
Tight money policy	siyāsat al-taḍyīq an-naqdī	**سياسة التضييق النقدى**
Till	ṣundūq nuqūd	**صندوق نقود**
Time bargain	'amaliyya ājila	**عملية آجلة ـ في بورصة الأوراق المالية**
Time bill	sanad li-ajal	**سند لأجــل**
Time cost; period cost	taklifa fatriyya	**تكلفة** (نفقات) **فترية**
Time deposit	wadī'a li-ajal	**وديعة لأجل**
Time draft	sanad li-ajal	**سند لأجــل**
Time sales (U.S.)	bay'bi't-taqsīṭ	**بيع بالتقسيط**
Time series analysis	dirāsat as-silsila 'z-zamaniyya	**دراسة السلسلة الزمنية** [دراسة نشاط التجارة والاقتصاد وأى حركة متعلقة بها لاسيا فيا يتعلق بهبوط الأسعار أو إنخفاض الانتاج في أوقات مختلفة]
Times interest ratio	nisbat ṣāfi 'd-dakhl ila 'l-fā'ida	**نسبة صافي الدخل إلى الفائدة**
Title	1 ḥujjat al-milkiyya	**١ - حجة الملكية**
	2 'unwān	**٢ - عنـــوان**
Title deed	sanad milkiyya	**سند ملكية**
Title insurance	ḍamān ḥujjat at-tamlīk	**ضمان حجة التمليك**
Token money	nuqūd ramziyya	**نقود رمزية**
Toll	maks	**مكس** (رسم ، ضريبة)
Toll charge	ḍarībat 'urbūr	**ضريبة عبور**
Tone	ittijāh 'āmm	**إتجاه عام**
Tools	'adad	**عــــدد** (أدوات)
Top executive	mudīr 'āmm	**مديــر عام**
Top management	al-idāra 'l-'ulyā	**الادارة العليا**
Top price	a'lā si'r	**أعلى سعر ـ بورصة**
Top up	yuḍīf	**يضيف** (يجمع)
Top-heavy price (U.S.)	sir fāḥish jiddan	**سعر فاحش جدا**

Total	majmūʿ	مجموع (جملة ، حاصل ، نتيجة)
Total accounts	ḥisābāt ijmāliyya	حسابات اجمالية
Total cost	taklifa ijmāliyya	تكلفة اجمالية
Total equity	ḥuqūq al-musāhimīn	حقوق المساهمين
Total income	dakhl ijmālī	دخل اجمالي
Total utility	manfaʿa kulliyya	المنفعة الكلية
Traceable cost; direct cost	taklifa mubāshira	التكلفة المباشرة
Trade (n.; v.)	1 tijāra	١ - تجارة ـ يتاجر
	2 ʿamal tijārī	٢ - عمل تجارى
Trade acceptance	qabul tijarī	قبول تجارى
Trade account payable	dhimma tijāriyya dā'ina	ذمة تجارية دائنة
Trade account receivable	dhimma tijāriyya madīna	ذمة تجارية مدينة
Trade association	niqāba ḥirafiyya	نقابة حرفية
Trade bills	sanadāt tijāriyya	سندات تجارية
Trade cycle	dawra tijāriyya	دورة تجارية
Trade discount	khaṣm tijārī	خصم تجارى
Trade in (U.S.) (n.; v.)	muqāyaḍa	مقايضة ـ يقايض
Trade liability	iltizām tijārī	التزام تجارى
Trade mark	ʿalāma tijāriyya	علامة تجارية
Trade name	ism tijārī	اسم تجارى
Trade note receivable	kumbiyāla tijāriyya	كمبيالة تجارية
Trade price	siʿr al-bā'iʿ	سعر البائع
Trade union	niqābat ʿummāl	نقابة عمال
Trading account	ḥisāb al-mutājara	حساب المتاجرة
Trading on the equity	ar-ribḥ al-majnī min al-qarḍ	الربح المجني من القرض [الفرق بين الربح الناتج من استثمار مبلغ مقترض وبين الفائدة المدفوعة على ذلك المبلغ]
Trading profit	1 ribḥ ijmālī	١ - الربح الاجمالي
	2 ribḥ al-muḍāraba	٢ - ربح المضاربة
Traffic	al-ḥaraka 't-tijāriyya	الحركة التجارية
Trainee	mutadarrib	متـــدرب
Transactions	ʿamaliyyāt tijāriyya	عمليات تجارية (صفقات)
Transfer	ḥawāla	حوالـــة
Transfer agent	wakīl taḥwīl	وكيل تحويل [تعينه الشركة ليقوم بتحويل أسهمها المتداولة]
Transfer of business	tanāzul ʿan munsha'a	تنازل عن منشأة
Transfer of proprietorship	intiqāl milkiyya	انتقال ملكية
Transfer of the debt	taḥwīl ad-dayn	تحويل الدين
Transfer tax	ḍarībat bayʿ ashum	ضريبة بيع أسهم
Transferable (or assignable) letter of credit	iʿtimād qābil li't-taḥwīl	الاعتماد القابل للتحويل [يمكن تحويل حق الاستفادة منه لشخص أو

		أشخاص آخرين يحددهم فاتح الاعتماد ولا يجوز تحويل الاعتماد إلا إذا ذكر المصرف صراحة أنه قابل للتحويل]
Transit	biḍā'a 'ābira	**البضاعة العابرة** (ترانزيت)
Transport (n.; v.)	naql	**نقل** (ينقل)
Transport charges	nafaqāt naql	**نفقات نقل**
Transportation cost	taklifat an-naql	**تكلفة النقل**
Travelling allowance	ta'wīḍāt safar	**تعويضات سفر**
Travelling auditor	mudaqqiq al-furū'	**مدقق الفروع**
Travelling expenses	nafaqāt safar	**نفقات سفر**
Treasurer	amīn al-khazīna	**أمين الخزينة**
Treasury	al-khazīna 'l-'āmma	**الخزينة العامة** (المالية)
Treasury bills	sanadāt 'ala 'l-khazīna	**سندات على الخزينة**
Treasury bond	sanadāt 'ala 'l-khazīna	**سندات على الخزينة**
Treasury stock	as-hum mustaradda	**أسهم مستردة** [أسهم رأسمال مسددة كليا ومستردة من قبل الشركة المصدرة اما كهدية أو عن طريق شرائها]
Treasury warrant	kafāla māliyya	**كفالة مالية**
Trend	ittijāh	**اتجــاه**
Trend analysis	taḥlīl al-ittijāh	**تحليل الاتجاه**
Trial	tajriba	**تجربة** (اختبار)
Trial balance	mīzan taḥaqquq	**ميزان تحقق ـ ميزان مراجعة**
True copy	ṣūra ṭibq al-aṣl	**صورة طبق الاصل**
True reserve	iḥtiyāṭī fā'iḍ	**احتياطي فائض**
Trust	1 wadī'a	١ - **وديعــة**
	2 wiṣāya	٢ - **وصايــة**
Trust company (U.S.)	sharikat idāra	**شركة ادارة ـ لمجموعة شركات**
Trust fund	amwāl taḥt al-wiṣāya	**أموال تحت الوصاية**
Trust indenture	shahādat amāna	**شهادة أمانة**
Trustee	waṣī	**وصي** (أمين ، وكيل)
Trusteeship	wiṣāya	**وصاية** (أمانة ، وكالة)
Turnover	1 mu'addal dawarān	١ - **معدل دوران**
	2 mabī'āt	٢ - **مبيعات** (استعمال بريطاني)
Type	namūdhaj	**نمــوذج**
Ultra vires	mutajāwiz li's-sulṭa	**متجاوز للسلطة** (مخالف للنظام)
Unacceptable	ghayr maqbūl	**غير مقبول**
Unaccounted	ghayr musajjal	**غير مسجل**
Unaccredited	ghayr mu'tamad	**غير معتمد**
Unadmitted assets	aṣl bi-qīma tadhkīriyya	**أصل بقيمة تذكيرية**
Unadulterated	ghayr muzawwar	**غير مزور**

Unallotted appropriation	mukhaṣṣaṣāt lam tuwazzaʿ	مخصصات لم توزع
Unamortised debt (or bond) discount	khaṣm ad-dayn	خصم الدين [الباقي للتوزيع على فترات في المستقبل]
Unapplied cash	naqd ghayr mukhaṣṣas	نقد غير مخصص
Unappropriated	ghayr muwazzaʿ	غير موزع
Unappropriated budget surplus	fā'iḍ al-muwāzana ghayr al-muwazzaʿ	فائض الموازنة غير الموزع
Unappropriated earned surplus; retained income	al-arbāḥ al-muḥtafaẓ bihā ghayr al-muwazzaʿ	الارباح المحتفظ بها غير الموزعة [الجزء الباقي من الأرباح المتراكمة دون توزيع]
Unappropriated income	ḥisāb ḍabṭ al-muwāzana	حساب ضبط الموازنة [يسجل له زيادة الدخل المقدرة على المصاريف المقدرة كما ورد في الميزانية المقرة]
Unassessed	1 ghayr muqaddar 2 ghayr mukallaf bi-ḍarība	١ - غير مقدر ٢ - غير مكلف بضريبة
Unassignable	ghayr qābil li'l-intiqāl	غير قابل للانتقال
Unavoidable cost	taklifa thābita	تكلفة ثابتة [لا يمكن تفاديها]
Unbalanced addition	iḍāfa ghayr mutawāzina	اضافة غير متوازنة [اقتناء آلة انتاجية تمثل جزءا من وحدة انتاج كاملة]
Uncertain	1 ghayr mu'akkad 2 ghayr muḥtamal	١ - غير مؤكد ٢ - غير محتمل
Unclaimed balances	arṣida ghayr muṭālab bihā	أرصدة غير مطالب بها
Unclaimed cheque	shīk ghayr muṭālab bihi	شيك غير مطالب به
Unclaimed dividends	arbāḥ ghayr muṭālab bihā	أرباح غير مطالب بها
Unclaimed wages	ujūr ghayr muṭālab bihā	أجور غير مطالب بها
Uncollected	ghayr muḥaṣṣal	غير محصل
Uncompleted contracts	maqāwalāt ghayr muntahiya	مقاولات غير منتهية
Unconfirmed	ghayr muthbat	غير مثبت (غير مؤكد)
Unconfirmed credit	iʿtimād ghayr muʿazzaz	اعتماد غير معزز (غير مثبت)
Unconvertible	ghayr qābil li't-taḥwīl	غير قابل للتحويل
Uncrossed	ghayr musaṭṭar	غير مسطر ـ شيك
Undeposited receipts	maqbūḍāt ghayr mūdaʿa	مقبوضات غير مودعة
Under-collection funds	amwāl bi-rasm at-taḥṣīl	أموال برسم التحصيل
Underlying company; subsidiary company	sharika tābiʿa	شركة تابعة
Underlying security	sanad li-sharika tābiʿa	سند لشركة تابعة
Underwrite	1 yu'ammin ʿalā 2 yataʿahhad 3 yaktatib	١ - يؤمن على ٢ - يتعهد (يضمن) ٣ - يكتتب
Underwriter	1 mutaʿahhid bi-taghṭiyat iṣdār 2 mu'ammin	١ - متعهد بتغطية اصدار ٢ - مؤمن (شركة تأمين)

	3 muktatib	٣- مكتتـــب
Underwriting contract	ʿaqd ḍamān taghṭiyat ashum	عقد ضمان تغطية أسهم
Underwriting syndicate	niqābat ḍāminī taghṭiyat al-ashum	نقابة ضامني تغطية الأسهم
Undistributed profit	ribḥ ghayr muwazzaʿ	ربح غير موزع
Undivided profit	ribḥ ghayr mutaṣarraf bihi	ربح غير متصرف به
		[ربح غير موزع وغير محول إلى حسابات الأرباح المتراكمة]
Undue	1 ghayr mustaḥaqq	١ - غير مستحق
	2 ghayr qānūnī	٢ - غير قانوني
Unearned increment	ziyāda ʿaradiyya	زيادة عرضية
		[زيادة في قيمة الممتلكات تعود إلى ظروف خارجة عن ارادة صاحبها]
Unearned revenue (or income)	1 īrādāt mu'ajjala	١ - ايرادات مؤجلة
		[ايرادات مقبوضة قبل اكتسابها]
	2 īrād min maṣādir ghayr al-khadāmat ash-shakhṣiyya	٢ - ايراد من مصادر غير الخدمات الشخصية ـ في الضرائب
Unemployment	baṭāla	بطالــة
Unencumbered	muḥarrar	محـــرر
		[خال من الموانع والمحظورات]
Unencumbered allotment	ḥiṣṣa muḥarrara	الحصة المحررة
		[حصة المال التي لم تصرف ولم تعتبر دينا]
Unencumbered appropriation	mukhaṣṣaṣāt muḥarrara	مخصصات المحررة
		[جزء من الأموال الخصصة لم يصرف ولم يعتبر دينا]
Unencumbered balance	raṣīd muḥarrar	رصيد محرر
		[ذلك الجزء من الأموال المخصصة الذى لم يصرف ولم يعتبر دينا]
Unexpended appropriation	mukhaṣṣaṣāt lam tuṣraf	مخصصات لم تصرف
		[مع احتمال اعتبار دينا كليا أو جزئيا]
Unexpended balance	raṣīd lam yuṣraf	رصيد لم يصرف
		[مع احتمال اعتباره دينا كليا أو جزئيا]
Unfair competition	munāfasa ghayr sharīfa	منافسة غير شريفة
Unfavourable exchange	ṣarf ghayr mulā'im	صرف غير ملائم (صرف فوق التعادل)
Uniform	muwaḥḥad	موحد (منسق ، على نمط واحد ، منتظم)
Uniform accounting system	niẓām muḥāsabī muwaḥḥad	نظام محاسبي موحد
Uniform costs	takālif muwaḥḥada	تكاليف موحدة
Union	ittiḥād	اتحاد (نقابة)
Unissued	ghayr muṣdar	غير مصدر
Unissued capital stock	ashum ar-ra'smāl ghayr al-muṣdara	أسهم الرأسمال غير المصدرة
Unit	wiḥda	وحـــدة
Unit cost	kulfat al-wiḥda	كلفة الوحدة
Unlimited liability	mas'ūliyya ghayr muḥaddada	مسؤولية غير محددة
Unliquidated encumbrance	dayn ghayr musaddad	دين غير مسدد

Unpaid dividend	arbāḥ ashum lam tudfaʿ	أرباح أسهم لم تدفع
Unpatentable	lā yumkin iṣdār bara'at ikhtirāʿ lahu	لا يمكن اصدار براءة اختراع له
Unproductive wages	ujūr ghayr muntija	أجور غير منتجة (غير مباشر)
Unprofitable	ghayr murbiḥ	غير مربح
Unrealised revenue	īrād ghayr muḥaqqaq	ايراد غير محقق [ايراد يعزى إلى عملية تجارية متممة وتقترن باستلام أصل غير متداول]
Unrecorded liabilities	maṭlūbāt ghayr musajjala	مطلوبات غير مسجلة
Unredeemable	ghayr qābil li't-tasdīd	غير قابل للتسديد
Unrestricted random sampling	akhdh ʿayyināt ʿashwā'iyyan bi-dūn qayd	أخذ عينات عشوائيا بدون قيد
Unsecured account	ḥisāb ghayr maḍmūn	حساب غير مضمون
Unsecured liability	iltizām ghayr maḍmūn	التزام غير مضمون
Upset price	as-siʿr al-adnā	السعر الادنى [الذى يرضى به البائع او المحدد قبل افتتاح المـزاد]
Urgent	muliḥḥ	ملـح (مستعجل ، ضروری)
Use and occupancy insurance	ta'mīn li-daf 'al-maṣārīf ad-da'ima	تأمين لدفع المصاريف الدائمة [في حالة توقف أعمال المؤسسة]
Useful	nāfiʿ	نافـع (مفيـد)
Useful life	ʿumr intājī	عمر انتاجي [المدة التي تستخدم خلالها الآلة أوأى أصل ثابـت]
Usury	ribā fāḥish	ربـا فاحـش
Utilisable	mumkin istiʿmāluh	ممكن استعماله
Utilisation of credit	istiʿmāl al-iʿtimād	استعمال الاعتماد
Utilities (U.S.)	marāfiq ʿāmma	مرافق عامـة
Utility	1 manfaʿa	١ - منفعـة (فائدة)
	2 khadamāt ʿāmma	٢ - خدمات عامة
Valid	1 ṣaḥīḥ	١ - صحيح (دقيق ، موثوق)
	2 qānūnī	٢ - قانونـي (شرعي)
Validate	1 yuṣādiq rasmiyyan	١ - يصادق رسميا
	2 yuthbit sharʿiyyan	٢ - يثبت شرعيا
Validation	ithbāt	اثبـات (تصديق)
Validity	1 ṣiḥḥa	١ - صحـة (دقـة)
	2 sharʿiyya	٢ - شرعيـة (قانونية)
Validity of the credit	muddat sarayān al-iʿtimād	مدة سريان الاعتماد
Valorisation	1 taqyīm	١ - تقييـم
	2 tathbīt al-asʿār	٢ - تثبيت الاسعار
Valorise	1 yuqayyim	١ - يقيـم
	2 yuthabbit al-asʿār	٢ - يثبت الاسعار

Valuable	1 thamīn	١ - **ثميــن** (ذو قيمة)
	2 qābil li't-taqyīm	٢ - **قابل للتقييم**
Valuation	taqyīm	**تقييــم** (تثمين)
Valuation account (or reserve)	ḥisāb taqyīm	**حساب تقييم**
Value	qīma	**قيمــــة**
Value added	qīma muḍāfa	**القيمة المضافـة** [ذلك الجزء من الكلفة الذى يعزى إلى عمل اجرى على المواد الخام المكونة لاحد المنتجات]
Value in exchange	qīmat al-mubādala	**قيمة المبادلة**
Value judgement	ḥukm qīma	**حكم قيمــــة** [اختيار او تفصيل او موافقة مبنية على أكثر من غاية أو سياسة واحدة]
Value variance	farq al-qīma	**فرق القيمة**
Value, appraised	al-qīma 'l-muqaddara	**القيمة المقدرة**
Value, book	al-qīma 'd-daftariyya	**القيمة الدفترية**
Value, exchange	qīmat aṣ-ṣarf	**قيمة الصرف**
Value, face	al-qīma 'l-ismiyya	**القيمة الاسمية**
Value, invoice	qīmat al-fātūra	**قيمة الفاتورة**
Value, nominal	al-qīma 'l-ismiyya	**القيمة الاسمية** (سعر الاصدار)
Value, par	qīmat at-ta'ādul	**قيمة التعادل** [القيمة الرسمية لوحدة النقد فى بلد معين بالمقارنة مع القيمة المقدرة فى سوق النقد]
Value, redemption	qīmat at-tasdīd	**قيمة التسديد**
Valued policy	'aqd ta'mīn muqaddar al-qīma	**عقد تأمين مقدر القيمة**
Variable	mutaḥawwil	**متحــول**
Variable annuity	sanahiyya mutaḥawwila	**سناهية متحولة** [عقد شركة تأمين أو استثمار تدفع بموجبه الشركة إلى المستثمر دفعات متفاوتة القيمة حسب تغير أسعار السندات]
Variable budget	mizāniyya marina	**ميزانية مرنة** [ميزانية تخضع للتغير كلما تقدمت العمليات]
Variable cost (or expense)	at-taklifa 'l-mutaghayyira	**التكلفة المتغيرة** [بتغير حجم الانتاج أو المبيعات أو أى قياس آخر للنشاط كالمواد المستعملة والاجور المباشرة]
Variable cost ratio	nisbat at-taklifa 'l-mutaghayyira	**نسبة التكلفة المتغيرة** [النسبة بين المبيعات والتكلفة المتغيرة]
Variable expenses	maṣrūfāt mutaghayyira	**مصروفات متغيرة**
Variable overhead	maṣārīf ra'siyya mutaghayyira	**مصاريف رأسية متغيرة**
Variance	1 inḥrāf	١ - **انحــراف**
	2 ikhtilāf	٢ - **اختلاف** (فرق)
Variety	tanawwu'	**تنــوع**

V.A.T. (value added tax)	ḍarība iḍāfiyya ʿala ʾl-qīma	ضريبة اضافية على القيمة
Vault	ṣundūq fūladhī	صندوق فولاذى
Vault cash (U.S.)	iḥtiyāṭī min an-naqd	احتياطي من النقد
Vendor	bāʾiʿ	بائـــــع
Venture	mughāmara	مغامرة ـ في مشروع
Verification	taḥaqqaq	تحقق (اثبات ، استقصاء)
Verify	yataḥaqqaq min	يتحقق من (يستقصي)
Verify an account	yataḥaqqaq min ḥisāb	يتحقق من حساب
Viability	qābiliyyat al-ḥayaḥ	قابلية الحياة [المقدرة على الحياة والاستمرار]
Vice-president	nāʾib raʾīs	نائب رئـــيس
Vis-á-vis	biʾl-muqārana maʿ	بالمقارنة مع (وجها لوجه)
Void	lāghin	لاغ (باطل)
Voidable	qābil liʾl-ilghāʾ	قابل للالغاء (ممكن ابطاله)
Voidance	ilghāʾ	الغاء (إبطـــال)
Volume	ḥajm	حجم (كميـــة)
Volume cost	kulfat al-ḥajm	كلفة الحجم [الكلفة الادنى المتأثرة بحجم الانتاج]
Volume discount	khaṣm al-ḥajm	خصم الحجـم
Voluntary liquidation	taṣfiya ikhtīyāriyya	تصفية اختيارية
Vostro account	ḥisābukum	حسابـــكم [حساب المراسل طرف المصرف]
Vote (n.; v.)	ṣawt	صوت ـ يصوت
Voting share	sahm dhū ṣawt	سهم ذو صوت [سهم يحق لحامله أن يصوت]
Voting trust	ittiḥād al-muṣawwitīn	اتحاد المصوتين [اتحاد احتكار الاصوات في الشركات]
Voting trust certificate	shahādat iḥtikār al-aṣwāt	شهادة احتكار الأصوات
Vouch	1 yataḥaqqaq min ṣiḥḥat mustanad	١ - يتحقق من ـ صحة مستند
	2 yuṣādiq ʾalā	٢ - يصادق على ـ صحة مصروفات
Voucher	1 īṣāl	١ - ايصـــال
	2 sanad	٢ - سنـــد
Voucher audit	1 tadqīq mustandī	١ - تدقيق مستندى [التدقيق الاولى لمصروفات فردية يقوم بها امين الصندوق العام]
	2 tadqīq lāḥiq	٢ - تدقيق لاحق ـ في المحاسبة الحكومية
Voucher cheque	shīk mufaṣṣal al-bunūd	شيك مفصل البنود
Voucher index	fahris mustanadāt	فهرس مستندات [يبين ابجديا أسماء المدفوع لهم وعادة ما يكون متعلقا بسجل المستندات]
Voucher payable	mustanad liʾd-dafʿ	مستند للدفع
Voucher register	sijill mustanadāt	سجل مستندات

Voucher system	niẓām al-mustanadāt	**نظام المستندات**
Vouching	1 iʻdad al-mustanadāt	**١ - اعــداد المستندات**
		[من اجل القيد والتوزيع والدفع]
	2 al-murājaʻa ʼl-mustanadiyya	**٢ - المراجعة المستندية**
Wage	ajr	**اجــــر**
Wages	ujūr	**اجــــور**
Wages sheet	kashf al-ujūr	**كشف الاجور**
Waive	yatanāzal ʻan	**يتنازل عن** (يتخلى عن)
Warehouse	makhzan	**مخــزن** (مستودع)
Warehouse charges	nafaqāt takhzīn	**نفقات تخــزين**
Warehouse receipt	īṣāl takhzīn	**ايصال تخزين**
Warehouse to warehouse clause	sharṭ at-taʼmīn min al-makhzan ila ʼl-makhzan	**شرط التأمين من المخزن الى المخزن**
Warehousing entry	qayd takhzīn	**قيــد تخزين**
Warrant	1 ṣakk	**١ - صــك** (كفالة)
	2 idhn ṣarf	**٢ - اذن صـــرف**
	3 tafwīḍ	**٣ - تفـــويض**
Warranted	1 maḍmūn	**١ - مضمون** (مرخص به)
	2 mubarrar	**٢ - مـــــبرر**
Warrants payable	sanadāt dafʻ	**سندات دفــع**
		[مستحقة وغير مسددة]
Warranty	kafāla	**كفـــالة**
Wash transaction	ʻamaliyyat īhām	**عملية ايهـــام**
		[عملية تعكس أو تلغى بعد حدوثها بقصد اغراء المشترين بالشراء بالسعر السائد]
Wastage	ḍayāʻ	**ضياع** (تلف ، خسارة)
Waste (n.; v.)	1 ḍayāʻ	**١ - ضيـــــاع**
	2 yutlif	**٢ - يتـــــلف**
	3 yubadhdhir	**٣ - يبــــذر**
Wasting assets	1 mawjudāt thābita	**١ - موجودات ثابتة**
		[لها عمر انتاجي محدد وقابلة للاستهلاك]
	2 mawjūdāt hālika	**٢ - موجودات هالكة** (متناقصة)
		[كالمناجم والغابات]
Watered capital	raʼsmāl ḍaʻīf al-qīma	**رأسمال ضعيف القيمة** [غير مغطى]
Watered stock	ashum mumawwaha	**أسهم مموهــة**
		[تصدرها الشركة باعتبارها مستوفاة القيمة بينما لا تكون في الواقع كذلك]
Wealth	tharwa	**ثـــــــروة**
Wear and tear	ihtirāʼ	**اهــــتراء**
		[ناتج عن الاستعمال]

Weighted average	al-muʿaddal al-mawzūn	**المعدل الموزون**
		[معدل بسيط للبنود مردود إلى أساس مشترك]
Welfare	rafāhiya	**رفاهيــــــة**
White collar worker	muwaẓẓaf idārī	**موظف ادارى**
Wholesale	al-jumla	**الجملـــــة**
Wholesale enterprise	tijārat al-jumla	**تجارة الجملة**
Wholesale prices	asʿār al-jumla	**أسعار الجملة**
Wholly-owned subsidiary	sharīka tābiʿa mamlūka bi-kāmilihā	**شركة تابعة** (مملوكة بكاملها)
Will	waṣiyya	**وصـــــية**
Win	yarbaḥ	**يربح** (يكسب)
Windfall profit (U.S.)	ribḥ ghayr mutawāqqaʿ	**ربح غير متوقع**
Winding up	taṣfiya	**تصفيـــة** (الشركة)
Window dressing	tazyīf al-waḍʿ	**تزييف الوضع** (تزيين الواجهة)
		[محاولة عرض وضع مالي جيد بقصد التزييف أو الاحتيال]
Wipe off (out)	yamsaḥ	**يمسح** (يحذف ، يقفل ، يصفي)
		[يمسح الحسابات نهائيا]
Wiping off (out)	taṣfiyat dayn	**تصفية ديـن**
With particular average clause (W.P.A.)	sharṭ al-iltizām bi't-talaf al-juz'ī	**شرط الالتزام بالتلف الجزئي**
Withdraw	1 yasḥab	**١ - يسحـــب**
	2 yansaḥib	**٢ - ينسحـــب**
Withdraw securities	yasḥab sanadāt	**يسحب سندات ـ من الايداع**
Withdrawal	saḥb	**سحـــب**
		[أموال من الحسابات]
Withholding	iqtiṭāʿ	**اقتطـــاع**
		[ضريبـة الراتــب]
Withholding tax exemption	iʿfā' min aḍ-ḍarība 'l-muqtaṭaʿa	**الاعفاء من الضريبة المقتطعة**
Without protest	bidūn iḥtijāj	**بدون احتجاج** (بدون بروتستو)
Witness	shāhid	**شاهـــد**
Work in process (or in progress)	ʿamaliyyāt taḥsīn at-tashghīl	**عمليات تحت التشغيل**
Work orders	awāmir tashghīl	**أوامر التشغيـل**
Work programme	barnāmaj ʿamal	**برنامـــج عمـــل**
Work unit	wiḥdat ʿamal	**وحـــدة عمـــل**
Working asset	aṣl ʿāmil	**أصـــل عامـــل**
Working capital	ra'smāl ʿāmil	**رأسمال عامل**
Working capital fund	ṣundūq tamwīl al-ʿamaliyyāt	**صندوق تمويل العمليات**
Working capital ratio	nisbat ra'sil-māl al-ʿāmil	**نسبة رأس المال العامل**
		[نسبة الموجودات المتداولة إلى المطلوبات المتدالة]
Working conditions	dẓurūf al-ʿamal	**ظـروف العمـــل**
Working fund	sulfa li't-tashghīl	**سلفـة للتشغيل**
		[يجرى تعويضها حسب الحاجة]

Working hours method	ṭarīqat sāʿāt at-tashghīl	**طريقة ساعات التشغيل** [في احتساب الاستهلاك]
Working interest	ḥiṣṣat ṣāḥib al-arāḍī	**حصة صاحب الأرض** [حصة صاحب قسيمة الأرض من انتاج الزيت الخام والغاز]
Working papers	awrāq ʿamal	**أوراق عمـــل**
Working power	al-quwwa 'l-ʿāmila	**القوة العاملة**
Working trial balance	mīzān at-taḥaqquq al-ʿāmil	**ميزان التحقق العامـل**
Workman's accident insurance	ta'mīn ḥawādith al-ʿummāl	**تأمين حوادث العمال**
Workman's compensation insurance	ta'mīn taʿwīḍāt al-ʿummāl	**تأمين تعويضات العمال**
Workshop	warsha	**ورشـــة** (مشغل)
Worth	qīma	**قيمـــة**
Worthless	dūna qīma	**دون قيمـــة**
Write down	yukhaffiḍ	**يخفـــض** [بتحويل جزء من رصيد حساب أصل إلى حساب المصاريف أو إلى حساب الأرباح والخسائر]
Write off	1 yastahlīk daynan	**١ - يستهلك دينا**
	2 yuqfil	**٢ - يقفـــل** (يحـذف) [ينقل رصيد حساب كان معتبرا كأصل إلى حساب المصاريف أو إلى حساب الأرباح والخسائر]
Write up	1 yarfaʿ	**١ - يرفـــع** [يسجل زيادة في القيمة الدفترية لاصل من الاصول]
	2 yuḥarrir	**٢ - يحـــرر ـ وثيقة مـــا**
Written confirmation	tathbīt khaṭṭī	**تثبيت خطـــي**
Year	sana	**سنـــة** (عـــام)
Year of assessment	sanat at-taklīf aḍ-ḍarā'ibī	**سنة التكليف الضرائبي**
Year end	nihāyat as-sana	**نهاية السنة**
Year-end adjustment	taʿdīl nihāyat as-sana	**تعديل نهاية السنة**
Year-end dividend	arbāḥ ashum nihāyat as-sana	**أرباح أسهم نهاية السنة**
Year-end inventory	biḍāʿat ākhir as-sana	**بضاعة آخر السنة**
Yearly income	dakhl sanawī	**دخـــل سنوى**
Yearly premium	qisṭ sanawī	**قسط سنوى ـ تأمين**
Yield	al-mardūd al-fiʿlī	**المردود الفعلي ـ للاموال المستثمرة**
Yield of shares	mardūd al-as-hum	**مردود الأسهم**
Yield, average	al-mardūd al-mutawassiṭ	**المردود المتوسط**
Zero	ṣifr	**صفـــر**

Zero date	fatra mu'ayyana	**فترة معينة** [في الحسابات الجارية مع الفائدة]
Zone	manṭiqa	**منطقـــة**
Zone system (of pricing)	niẓām tas'īr al-manṭiqa	**نظام تسعير المنطقة** [تحديد سعر ثابت للبضاعة المسلمة لأى مشتر داخل منطقة معينة بغض النظر عن مصدر تلك البضاعة]
Zone, free	manṭiqa ḥurra	**المنطقة الحـــرة**
Zoom (U.S.)	yuṣa''id as-si'r	**يصعّـد السعـر**